ECONOMIC EVENTS, IDEAS, AND POLICIES

ECONOMIC EVENTS, IDEAS, AND POLICIES

THE 1960s AND AFTER

GEORGE L. PERRY

JAMES TOBIN

editors

BROOKINGS INSTITUTION PRESS

Washington, D.C.

Library of Congress Cataloging-in-Publication data

Economic events, ideas, and policies : the 1960s and after / George L. Perry
and James Tobin, editors.
   p.   cm.
Includes bibliographical references and index.
   ISBN 0-8157-7012-X (hc : acid-free)
   ISBN 0-8157-7011-1 (pb : acid-free)
1. United States—Economic policy—1961–1971. 2. United
States—Economic policy. 3. United States—Economic
conditions—1961–1971. 4. United States—Economic conditions.
I. Perry, George L., 1934– II. Tobin, James, 1918–
HC106.6 .E237 2000   00-009634
338.973′009′046–dc21   CIP

9 8 7 6 5 4 3 2 1

Typeset in Adobe Garamond

Composition by Circle Graphics
Columbia, Maryland

Printed by R. R. Donnelley and Sons
Harrisonburg, Virginia

ℬ THE BROOKINGS INSTITUTION

The Brookings Institution is an independent organization devoted to nonpartisan research, education, and publication in economics, government, foreign policy, and the social sciences generally. Its principal purposes are to aid in the development of sound public policies and to promote public understanding of issues of national importance.

The Institution was founded on December 8, 1927, to merge the activities of the Institute for Government Research, founded in 1916, the Institute of Economics, founded in 1922, and the Robert Brookings Graduate School of Economics and Government, founded in 1924.

The general administration of the Institution is the responsibility of a Board of Trustees charged with safeguarding the independence of the staff and fostering the most favorable conditions for scientific research and publication. The immediate direction of the policies, program, and staff is vested in the president, assisted by an advisory committee of the officers and staff.

In publishing a study, the Institution presents it as a competent treatment of a subject worthy of public consideration. The interpretations or conclusions in such publications are those of the author or authors and do not necessarily reflect the views of the other staff members, officers, or trustees of the Brookings Institution.

Foreword

It has been twenty years since Arthur Okun's untimely death at the age of fifty-one. For the previous decade, he had been a leader of the Brookings Economics Studies program. In the 1960s, he was with the Council of Economic Advisers, first as a senior staff member and then as a member of the council and finally as its chairman and chief economic adviser to President Johnson during the difficult last years of that decade. As he matured in these roles, Art Okun added political understanding and sophistication to his intellectual brilliance as an economist. He became one of those rare individuals who is respected both by men of affairs in government and the business community for his wise advice and by his peers for the insight and rigor of his professional work. Finally, and equally important, he is still missed and remembered as a dear and loyal friend by his former colleagues at Yale, the Council of Economic Advisers, and Brookings. The present volume is dedicated to Okun's memory, and its subject matter naturally relates to his many interests and concerns as an economist.

The 1960s were years of important transitions in the challenges that confronted U.S. policymakers and the initiatives that were undertaken to meet them. The economic doldrums at the start of the decade gave way to strong expansion and prosperity that ended, however, with excessive inflation. The years that followed were the most turbulent of the postwar period, with global shock waves from oil prices, deep recessions, and historic changes in the international financial system. Eventually this period led to the prolonged U.S. economic expansion that we still enjoy today. Both policymaking and economic thinking have evolved over this long period. The papers in the present volume examine the economics of the 1960s as the starting point in this evolution.

The Brookings Institution and Yale University are grateful to Charles Ellis for financing the conference for which these papers were prepared and the publication of the accompanying volume. The editors also would like to thank Nancy Morrison for editing the volume, Takako Tsuji for verifying it, Barbara Malczak for proofreading, Julia Petrakis for indexing the pages, and Peter Kimball and Kathey Bucholz for their help in organizing the conference.

MICHAEL H. ARMACOST
President

May 2000
Washington, D.C.

Contents

Preface

In November 1999 the Brookings Institution and Yale University jointly sponsored a conference to reconsider the national economic policies of the 1960s and the theories that influenced them in light of subsequent events in the economy and of developments in economic theory and research. This volume contains the papers and comments of the participants.

The beginning of the Kennedy presidency in 1961 was widely perceived to bring to Washington a "New Economics." John F. Kennedy, as senator and presidential candidate, had sought the advice of academic economists. As president, he appeared to be more interested in economic analysis and in the ideas of economists and their policy implications than had been his predecessor, Dwight Eisenhower. This interest was reflected in the appointment to his administration of a number of academic economists. Their work was at the forefront of current research, and their views were informed by Keynesian ideas, as modified and integrated with traditional theory after World War II. But what was truly new about the New Economics was that it became a strong intellectual force in government.

As Kennedy was being inaugurated, the economy was at the bottom of a recession, the third since 1953. The unemployment rate was 7 percent, compared to 3 percent at the end of the Korean War and 4 percent at the peak of the expansion in the mid-1950s. Improving the disappointing performance of the economy was the most urgent challenge to the new administration. Debate raged as to how much of the increase in unemployment was structural—that is, attributable to changes in demographics and labor market institutions—and how much was cyclical—that is, attributable to shortfalls of aggregate demand for goods and services. Had the unemployment rate at full employment risen, or was employment less than full? The distinction was more than academic. If unemployment was cyclical, it could be remedied by federal fiscal and monetary policies. If it was structural, then fiscal and monetary stimuli to demand would be inflationary. The Eisenhower administration and Federal Reserve Chairman William McChesney Martin held the structuralist view, while the Kennedy economists thought the unemployment problem was amenable to active fiscal and monetary policies designed to stabilize aggregate demand at full-employment levels. The expansionary policies of the first half of the decade reflected their analysis. So did the policies to restrict aggregate demand that were eventually undertaken by the Johnson administration and the Federal Reserve during the Vietnam War.

Some observers today credit the New Economics and its influence on the policies of the Kennedy-Johnson years for the sustained prosperity of the 1960s, and thus regard them as an example worth emulating. Others see the legacy of those policies in the 6 percent inflation rate at the end of the decade, when unemployment fell to 3.5 percent—a level too low for stability. That period was followed by the stagflation of the 1970s. In the economics profession, the idea that activist discretionary policies could produce and preserve stability came under attack. The natural rate of unemployment, rational expectations, the new classical economics, and real business cycle theory offered powerful theoretical arguments against the economics of the 1960s, which—rightly or wrongly—was charged with overstimulating demand under the mistaken expectation that lower unemployment could be sustained at an acceptable increase in inflation.

The attempt to stabilize the economy at high levels of employment was not the only hallmark of 1960s economics. Policymakers had to contend with the dollar's evolving role in the world and its eventual overvaluation, which marked the beginning of the end of the Bretton Woods system of international financial arrangements. Tax changes were aimed at encouraging investment for long-run economic growth. And significant initiatives were taken to strengthen the nation's social safety net, including the introduction of Medicare. Thus while stabilization issues most clearly defined the decade for economists and are the subject of some papers in this volume, other papers examine developments in these other spheres—international, fiscal, and social as viewed through the lens of economics.

The conference was also a tribute to the memory of Arthur Okun, a major figure in the economic policies throughout the Kennedy-Johnson era, in Yale economics, and at Brookings. The subject matter and scope of the conference reflect Okun's interests and contributions, cut short by his untimely death in 1980 at the age of 51. Okun's public service began early in 1961, when he was still at Yale. His colleague James Tobin had become a member of Kennedy's Council of Economic Advisers and stayed in close touch with Okun. This council was trying to convince the new president and his political team of the need for expansionary policies to bring unemployment down from 7 to 4 percent. The White House was not impressed by the gain in employment from 93 to 96 percent, which JFK likened to raising a college grade from A— to A. Was that achievement worth the political cost of risking a budget deficit? The council knew that the overall economic gains that would accompany the three-point decline in unemployment were much more important than the White House metaphor suggested. In making the point concretely, Art Okun produced what came to be known as Okun's Law. Time has proved it to be one of the most reliable and important empirical regularities in macroeconomics, a signal contribution to economic knowledge as well as to practical policy. JFK committed himself to a 4 percent unemployment target. Okun soon came to the council staff, where he worked together with the two chairmen of this conference. He later became, on leave from his professorship at Yale, a member of the Council of Economic Advisers under President Johnson and ultimately its chairman.

Then, in 1969, he came to Brookings where, with George Perry, he set up the Brookings Panel on Economic Activity and its journal, the *Brookings Papers on Economic Activity*, and where he resumed his research in economics—research that reflected his trademark devotion to both rigor and relevance. Two books he wrote during the 1970s are still widely cited. *Prices and Quantities* foreshadowed many current insights in macroeconomic theory, and *Equity and Efficiency* appears on many college reading lists as an accessible analysis of a basic tradeoff that confronts economic and social policies.

Several of the contributors to this volume were researchers who were involved in policymaking in the 1960s. Their papers provide firsthand insights to the analyses and political priorities of that period and a starting point for examining subsequent policies and economic ideas. Younger scholars represented in the volume, who know that period only as a part of history, bring a different perspective. All participants have been active in economic research since the 1960s and collectively represent a wide range of expertise in applied economic analysis.

Subject to writing within a broad area, each author was free to choose the particular subject of his paper. Four of the papers concern macro-economic stabilization and growth. William Baumol probes the heart of the capitalist growth process, modeling the relation between spillovers from innovation and income distribution and how these affect overall living standards and inequality. William Brainard and George Perry assess stabilization policies from the 1960s to the present using a model that challenges today's prevailing views of the options confronting policymakers. Paul Krugman explores why in recent years the economics profession has largely ignored the role of fiscal policy in stabilization. Robert Solow examines the model of economic growth that informed the Kennedy Council of Economic Advisers' analysis of the longer run and relates it to subsequent developments in growth theory. Richard Cooper and Barry Eichengreen each analyze U.S. foreign economic policy in the watershed period when the Bretton Woods system was coming under pressure, and relate those events to subsequent developments in the international monetary sphere. Robert Haveman analyzes the changing faces of poverty over the last four decades, and Alan Krueger examines the shifting emphasis in labor policy and labor research over that same period.

Together, these economists have provided a fitting tribute to Arthur Okun and his legacy.

PART I

Stabilization
and Growth

WILLIAM J. BAUMOL $\quad$ 1

Rapid Economic Growth, Equitable Income Distribution, and the Optimal Range of Innovation Spillovers

[If] everyone received the full measure of his marginal product and no joint inputs existed, the benefits generated by great entrepreneurs and inventors would accrue entirely to them. There would be no "trickle-down" of progress to the masses. . . . The trickle-down of benefits is a merit of capitalism in the real world, and it works insofar as the distribution of income departs from the strict standard of reward for personal contribution to production.

ARTHUR OKUN, *Equality and Efficiency: The Big Tradeoff*[1]

This paper deals with the heart of the capitalist growth process: the private payoff to innovation and the speed with which new technology and new products become available. The paper indicates that a very substantial proportion of the GDP is composed of innovation spillovers. Yet the paper shows that, despite their efficiency implications as disincentives

My debts here are great. I am particularly grateful to Ralph Gomory for graphic constructs that we originally designed to analyze another subject in our 1998 work, "A Country's Maximal Gains from Trade and Conflicting National Interests," and to Charles Wilson for saving me from a major error. I am deeply indebted to George Akerlof and Martin Baily, my discussants at the Brookings conference; to Professor Jean Gadrey of the University of Lille and his colleagues; and to Sue Anne Batey Blackman, Richard Nelson, and Edward Wolff for very helpful comments and suggestions. I must thank the Alfred P. Sloan Foundation, the Russell Sage Foundation, and the C.V. Starr Center for their generous support of this work.
    1. Okun (1975, pp. 46–47).

3

for innovation, these spillovers can reasonably be considered desirable on balance. For it is to them that we must ultimately look if poverty and inequality are to be dealt with effectively. It is the main purpose of the paper to go one step beyond showing the conflict that can arise between efficiency and distributive goals. It aims to show one way in which theoretical analysis can deal with the tradeoff and incorporate the issue into its more formal structure.[2]

This paper offers several interrelated conclusions:

—In the history of the industrial economies, the time trajectory of poverty and inequality is far more convoluted than is often recognized. Apparently, the market has no dependable and automatic mechanism that invariably moves these matters in a desirable direction. That obviously constitutes an opportunity for economic analysis in the design of appropriate and effective policy.

—Formal welfare economics has tended to evade issues of income distribution. Its excuse is a hypothetical process, the lump-sum transfer, taken as the theoretically ideal instrument of redistribution. I argue that lump-sum transfers are in reality often impossible to achieve.[3] In particular, I maintain that proposing to use them to undo the redistributive effects of eliminating an externality is self-contradictory.

—Because lump-sum transfers are often impossible, there is generally a tradeoff between distributive goals and the requirements of economic efficiency.[4] There are—perhaps frequently—what amount to Pareto-optimal outcomes that violate the efficiency conditions.

---

2. Regrettably, I cannot claim to have been a close friend of Arthur Okun. Still, we met quite often, and it was always stimulating and enjoyable because he was such a pleasant person, because his clear thinking had an aesthetic quality, and because we shared views on desirable goals for society and the appropriate role of government in pursuit of those goals. Though not quite on the topic I have been assigned, my contribution to this volume is, I hope, suitably related to it. More important, this paper is in a spirit Arthur himself embraced, as the quotation that opens this study indisputably confirms. I nevertheless apologize for the failure to carry out my original assignment because of incapacity, since I patently qualify neither as a macroeconomist nor as a practitioner of sophisticated empirical research.

3. I fully agree with George Akerlof's observation here: applied economists are well aware that, generally, lump-sum transfers are simply not possible. More than that, even most pure theorists must know this in their hearts. But this does not stop them in their formal writings from using this mythical device to focus exclusively on allocative efficiency, assuming away the implications for distribution.

4. Throughout this paper, I use the term "efficiency" in the standard sense, to exclude any consideration of distribution. Obviously, if an allocation has reprehensible distributive consequences but does meet standard efficiency requirements, my use of the term should not be taken to mean that I approve of the result.

—Finally, I illustrate these conclusions with an examination of the distributive implications of the spillovers of innovation. The significance of this example is underscored by my contention that a very substantial proportion of GDP is composed of innovation spillovers. Moreover, I show that these spillovers can be considered desirable on balance—despite their efficiency implications. For it is to these spillovers that we must ultimately look if we are to deal with poverty and inequality effectively.

The Convoluted Long-Term Path of Income Distribution

The recent history of income distribution, and the subjects associated with it, is well known. The early postwar period in the United States was characterized by declining dispersion of income in the population. During that period, poverty fell; the share of people living below the poverty line declined from over 25 percent in 1955 to about 11 percent in 1973. Since then inequality has grown significantly, and the proportion of the population that is impoverished has risen, though it has not returned to its earlier level. All this is associated with a sharp break in the historic trend of real wages, which generally had moved up markedly at least from the beginning of the century until the early 1970s.

There is some dispute as to whether real wages have actually declined since then. Those who argue that real wages have not declined claim that the rise in the deflator indices exaggerates the true rate of inflation and assert that real compensation—that is, wages plus fringe benefits—has not been falling.[5] What seems indisputable is that there has been a sharp departure from the historical upward trend. Though wages have recently begun to improve, a return to the old path seems far away.

There is a general impression that the break in trends that occurred around 1973 is unprecedented. Until then, it would seem, history was locked into an upward path in real workers' earnings and a decline in inequality. This apparently came to an abrupt end in the mid-1970s, changing to directions that had never been taken before. But that is

5. There exists an extensive and valuable literature on income distribution, for example, Williamson and Lindert (1988), Goldin and Katz (1999), and Margo (1999). Care must be taken here because the rise in expenditure on fringe benefits is to a substantial degree attributable to the sharply rising cost of services such as health care and education. The rise in these costs has persistently and significantly exceeded the overall rate of inflation. Hence the growth in spending on fringe benefits—even if deflated by the index used to calculate real wages—probably considerably exaggerates the rise in the real value of the benefits.

emphatically not so. One may understandably reject as irrelevant ancient history the apparently substantial fall in English real wages from the mid-fifteenth century until the time of Shakespeare, some 150 years later.[6] But developments since the Industrial Revolution seem more pertinent. And the evidence since that time indicates neither that real wages are always fated to rise nor inequality to fall.

The story on real wages includes long periods of decline in the United Kingdom, notably throughout the second half of the eighteenth century.[7] In the United States, wages—at least agricultural wages—followed a most unsteady path in the nineteenth century, according to estimates provided by Stanley Lebergott and the Census Bureau (see figure 1-1).[8] There certainly is suggestive evidence indicating that the real U.S. standard of living fell through much of the first half of the nineteenth century as the work force moved from farms to urban factories. Between about 1750 and 1825, the average life expectancy at age 10 of native-born males fell nearly 8 percent, while between 1825 and 1875 their average height at maturity declined nearly 3 percent, according to Robert Fogel's estimates.[9]

The dispersion of real income also has a basically nonlinear history. On the trajectory of the range of U.S. inequality, Lebergott reports, "Unfortunately, the existing studies are not comparable enough to tell us much [about trends in concentration of wealth before 1860. They] imply an unreasonably great increase in concentration by 1870, and, therefore, a great decrease thereafter."[10] Though firm data are lacking, there are solid grounds for the conclusion that the period (say, the half-century) just preceding and the period just following the Industrial Revolution were characterized by a pronounced increase in inequality in living standards, following a marked earlier decrease. Then, in the mid-nineteenth century it was the turn of the lower- and middle-income groups to move toward catching up with the wealthy, a trend that continued into the beginning of the 1970s.

The earlier era was characterized by miserable living conditions even for the wealthy and powerful, up until the middle or even the end of the eighteenth century. Not that their wealth failed to give them ostentatious clothing, exotic foods, and armies of servants. But the problem for them

---

6. Phelps Brown and Hopkins (1956).
7. Phelps Brown and Hopkins (1956).
8. Lebergott (1984); U.S. Bureau of the Census (1975).
9. Fogel (1986, p. 511).
10. Lebergott (1984, p. 72 and footnote).

Figure 1-1. *Real Monthly Earnings of Farm Laborers, 1800–1948*

Monthly earnings (1967 dollars)

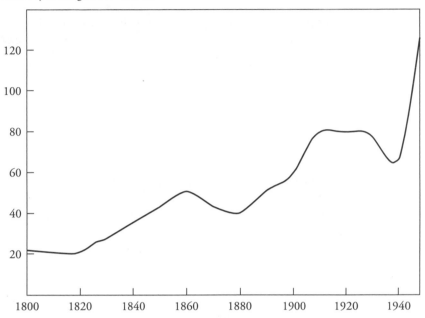

Source: CPI and earnings, 1818–1948: U.S. Bureau of the Census (1975). Earnings, 1800: extrapolated from Lebergott (1984).

was that little of the technology of human comfort had yet been invented. Two examples will illustrate my point. One is a description of the 1732 journey of the pregnant Wilhelmina, favorite sister of Frederick the Great, between Berlin and Bayreuth:[11]

> Ten strenuous, abnormally frigid days were spent upon roads, bad enough in summer, now deep with snow. On the second day out the carriage in which Wilhelmina was riding turned over. She was buried under an avalanche of luggage . . . Everyone expected a miscarriage and wanted Wilhelmina to rest in bed for several days. . . . Mountains appeared after Leipzig had been passed . . .Wilhelmina was frightened by the steepness of the roads and preferred to get out and walk

11. Wright (1965, p. 142).

to being whacked about as the carriages jolted down from boulder to boulder.

A second illustration of the standards of discomfort for the rich and powerful before the Industrial Revolution is the oft-cited report by the Princess Palatine, German sister-in-law of Louis XIV, that in the winter of 1695 in the Hall of Mirrors at Versailles, at the king's table, the wine froze in the glasses![12]

Statistics and other pieces of evidence tell a story consistent with such anecdotes. Using genealogical records, Fogel estimates that between 1550 and 1700 the life expectancy at birth of members of the British nobility, male and female, was virtually the same as that of the population as a whole.[13] Indeed, the average longevity for the general male and female population slightly exceeded that for members of the peerage for a substantial part of this period. Soon after that, however, things began to change. The life expectancy of peers leaped upward and ahead of the rest of the British population. Early in the eighteenth century, indoor heating was revolutionized by inventions such as the Franklin stove. At the beginning of the nineteenth century, railroads were born, and through these and other advances, the upper classes in Victorian society soon enjoyed historically unprecedented levels of comfort.

But after that point the less affluent began to catch up. As Nathan Rosenberg and L. E. Birdzell Jr. note, "Western economic growth . . . benefited the life-style of the very rich much less than it benefited the life-style of the less well-off. . . . The very rich were as well-housed, clothed and adorned in 1885 as in 1985. . . . In fact, the innovations of positive value to the rich are relatively few: advances in medical care, air conditioning, and improvements in transportation and preservation of food."[14] In contrast, the lower classes still had very far to go, as is described further below. For now I merely recall that regular famines, at least once per decade on average, with starvation widespread, had begun to disappear in the nineteenth century. Still, famines continued occasionally well into the nineteenth, and not only in Ireland. Thus, in relatively wealthy Belgium, "[d]uring the great crisis of 1846, the newspapers would tell daily of cases of death from starvation. . . . At Wynghene, cases became so frequent that

---

12. Braudel (1979, p. 299).
13. Fogel (1986, p. 511).
14. Rosenberg and Birdzell (1986, pp. 26–27).

the local policeman was given the job of calling at all houses each day to see if the inhabitants were still alive."[15]

The description of the horrors of the existence of the lower-income classes at that time can go on and on, but the point is clear. It is they who had the furthest to go. And improve their circumstances they did. There is no better way to demonstrate these advances than to report some figures on how much the purchasing power of an "average worker's" hour of labor has increased over the course of the twentieth century. The Federal Reserve Bank of Dallas reports that "earning our daily bread" literally takes less than one-third the time it did early in this century. In 1919 the average worker labored 13 minutes in order to earn enough to buy a pound of bread, compared to just 4 minutes in 1997. The work time required to buy a three-pound chicken in 1919—more than 21/2 hours—had fallen to just 14 minutes in 1997. In 1910, 345 hours of work time bought a kitchen range and 553 hours of work time bought a clothes washer; those numbers had dropped to 22 hours and 26 hours by 1997. There are many other eye-opening comparisons. The purchase of a calculating device in 1916 required 494 hours of labor-time but only 46 minutes in 1996; a 1954 color television required 562 hours of work but 23 hours in 1997; and the purchase of a 1908 Model T automobile necessitated 4,696 hours of labor as against 1,365 hours for a 1997 Ford Taurus.[16]

My argument so far has two main goals. The first, as already noted, is to make clear that the historic course of reduction in income dispersion and reduction of poverty has hardly been undeviating. Rather, its direction has swung violently several times, meaning that the change that occurred in the 1970s was hardly unique. The implication is that there may be no mechanism that automatically keeps the trajectory of wealth and income distribution from meandering substantially—and perhaps even unpredictably.

That brings me to my second point, and the central subject of this paper. If there is nothing automatic in the progress toward equality and the elimination of poverty, we must give serious consideration to intervention designed to promote this goal. But it seems to me that welfare economics—the theory of economic policy—has sedulously avoided this burden. And it has excused itself from this task by repeatedly leaning on a fairy tale: the legend that one can somehow aim for efficiency in resource allocation and then rectify any resulting damage to desirable distribution of

15. de Meeüs (1962, p. 305).
16. Federal Reserve Bank of Dallas (1997, pp. 5–17).

wealth and income through lump-sum redistribution of income and wealth. I will argue next that, at least for applied analysis, this is emphatically unacceptable.

On the Limited Applicability of Lump-Sum Redistributions

Fairy tales indisputably have their value, but there are times when it is appropriate to go beyond them. The concept of lump-sum transfers, as a mode of redistribution that can preserve economic efficiency unscathed, is such a legend. Here I will show why in certain significant circumstances such tranfers cannot occur, and illustrate what can be learned if one is willing, at least sometimes, to abandon the premise. This is not just another tedious and counterproductive plea for greater realism in economic models, as an end in itself. For I hope to show that much of substance and importance can be learned by dropping the assumption. Once it is recognized that a desired distribution cannot be achieved without some sacrifice in economic efficiency, one is led to study the nature of the tradeoff and the means to minimize its cost to society.

Moreover, if society is divided into any different groups, it can be expected that one group will prefer an efficiency-distribution combination different from that preferred by another. To simplify, let Y be some index of total net output of the community and E be an index of degree of equality of distribution (as measured, perhaps, by the reciprocal of variance) and assume that there are incentive compatibility constraints making Y decrease monotonically as E increases. Suppose that the maximum amount of Y the economy can produce, consistent with incentive compatibility constraints, is $Y = e$. Let society be divided into two groups: Group I most prefers the combination (Y_1, E_1), while Group II's optimum is (Y_2, E_2). Then, if each group's valuation of an outcome decreases steadily as its distance from its preferred (Y, E) increases, every intermediate (Y, E) combination *must* be Pareto optimal, though for many such combinations $Y < e$. That is, from any such point in (Y, E) space, it will be impossible to make one group better off without harming the other. To emphasize that these are *constrained* Pareto optima, I will refer to any such outcome as "*NLS Pareto optimal*"; that is, optimal so long as *no lump-sum transfers* are possible, at least if they are attempted pervasively and repeatedly.

To illustrate the significance of these observations, let me apply them to the economy's investment in innovation and examine the effects of the difference between its social and private benefits. It is generally concluded that these spillovers tend to reduce the amount of innovative activity considerably below the level that would be efficient if distribution were no concern or lump-sum transfers of any magnitude and duration could be carried out without any real cost. But I argue that the bulk of these spillovers are constituted by the dramatic rise in living standards since the Industrial Revolution. This rise in living standards must surely be considered a very desirable development—not a regrettable loss to society. So the spillovers from innovation, far from constituting a pure social loss, have provided a valuable tradeoff; and their magnitude may have even been within the NLS Pareto-optimal range.

On the Impossibility of Repeated and Pervasive Lump-Sum Transfers

It is, of course, sometimes analytically convenient and even, occasionally, basically harmless to assume that lump-sum transfers are possible and that they can be carried out systematically. But as has just been indicated, there are issues whose analysis is substantially distorted by such a premise—if it is in fact untrue. And it is easy to argue that the assumption is, in reality, often false.

By a lump-sum transfer is meant an income or wealth transfer *with absolutely no efficiency-damaging incentive effects*. That is, those persons from whom the transfers are derived must not wish to or must not be able to do anything that damages the economy's efficiency in order to reduce the magnitudes of their losses. Similarly, the recipients of the transfers must not be led by their windfall to change their behavior in a manner that impedes efficiency. But even a once-and-for-all transfer cannot plausibly be expected to be free of any distortion in incentives if one supposes that it depends on any aspect or consequence of market activity.

The likelihood of distortion is far greater if the ostensibly lump-sum transfers are to be adopted as a long-lived corrective of any objectionable distribution consequences resulting from the choice of the pattern of resource allocation required for allocative efficiency. Then, simply by definition of a correction of an undesired distributive effect, those whose activities are deemed to have contributed to their excessive income or wealth must become the providers of the resources to be transferred, and those considered inadequately endowed with income and wealth must become the recipients. In such a repeated game, members of each group will soon learn that their economic activities—those that contributed to their pre-transfer wealth or income levels—also condemn them to the role of transfer payer or recipient. Clearly, this is an incentive to the payers to cut back on the activities that force them into that position, and an incentive for the recipients to do the reverse.[17]

But it is important to recognize that such a transfer can nevertheless be lump-sum if the effects of the transfer include no externalities or deviations from perfect competition. The Arrow-Debreu theorems state that if the economy is perfectly competitive and there are no externalities, then a change in the distribution of wealth will simply lead to a new equilibrium that can also be Pareto optimal. Prices and the allocation of resources can all be changed in a manner compatible with the new Pareto optimum.

So much for the theory, but reality is generally different. There is no need to remind the reader that real markets are not perfectly competitive, and externalities in the real world are arguably far from zero (see below). More important for the discussion of this paper is the fact that the very act of reducing an externality, whether marginal, average, or total, is tantamount to a redistribution of real income between the recipients of those benefits and the agents whose activities generate them. For an externality, by definition, is simply a matter of the distribution of the costs or benefits of an activity between those directly involved in the activity and those who are not. Consequently, if a decrease in externalities is necessary for an increase in efficiency, then there clearly must be a redistributive effect. And any measure that undoes that distributive effect must automatically recre-

---

17. Even a transfer unconnected with wealth or income cannot easily be made lump-sum. A clearly silly example will bring out the point. Suppose a fixed and substantial tax payment were imposed upon the birth of a child to a family whose surname begins with a letter in the first half of the alphabet. The tax payment would be transferred upon each birth to families with names later in the alphabet (with name changes prohibited by law). This would surely entail an incentive affecting family sizes in the two groups. More important, such a scheme could not be used to correct what was deemed to be a maldistribution of income resulting from the requirements of economic efficiency or from the behavior of the market. It could not be used for that purpose precisely because it would be designed to have no connection with any choices of economic behavior. There is no reason for the members of the lexicographically disadvantaged group to be the same as those who have acquired what is deemed to be excessive wealth.

ate the externality. Such offsetting changes in distribution must patently affect efficiency and so, by definition, they cannot be lump-sum.

The difficulty, in short, is this: Suppose one starts with an acceptable distribution accompanied by externalities that prevent efficiency. One then undertakes a two-stage approach toward optimality, first eliminating the externalities and then correcting any undesired redistribution effects. The very act of distributive modification recreates the externalities indirectly, because at the end, those who were better off as a result of the externalities still end up with benefits for which they made no contribution.[18] And those who initially were deprived by the externalities of part of the benefits generated by their activities still suffer the same damage as before. Thus the externality is simply reconstituted by the redistribution, this time via a two-stage process rather than a direct one. One just cannot eliminate the distributive consequences of prevention of the externalities without restoring the unearned rewards and burdens initially stemming from the activities that generated the externalities. They are inseparable Siamese twins. Thus elimination of externalities, and restoration of the initial distribution by means of lump-sum transfers, is inherently a self-contradictory notion. This problem for the lump-sum transfer scenario will be brought out concretely by my later application of the analysis to the enormous (and arguably beneficial) spillovers of the innovation process.

The Range of Non-Lump-Sum Pareto Optima

I turn now to a graph to describe the locus of NLS Pareto optima that emerge in a world in which lump-sum distributions are ruled out. The vertical axis in figure 1-2 indicates some scalar measure of the total welfare benefits, Y, that are currently attainable by the two-group economy.[19] Y can be thought of as total output in a one-good economy, and the two groups

18. The concept is unfamiliar, so an example may be needed to bring out the point. Let individual A be the generator of, say, a beneficial externality worth D dollars to both parties in question. Assume that B receives the externality. Suppose the resulting distribution of benefits is desirable, but the efficiency effects are not. Accordingly, we take Step 1 and eliminate the externality. In Step 2, we use a tax to get back to the previous distribution. Step 2 requires taxing A the amount D dollars and giving the D dollars to B. If A and B recognize what has happened and why, are we not back at the previous inefficiency incentives?

19. In effect, this assumes that utility is transferable so that efficient behavior is independent of the distribution of benefits. This is a heroic assumption, to be sure, but one that does no real damage in this context. I adopt it only to facilitate a simple graphical exposition.

Figure 1-2. *Locus of Non-Lump-Sum Pareto Optima*

Total welfare

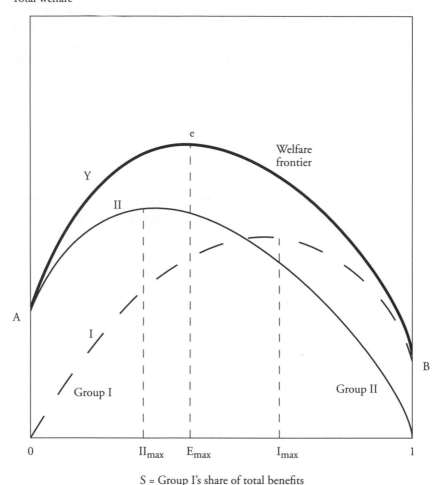

S = Group I's share of total benefits

as producers and nonproducers. The horizontal axis measures (from left to right) S, the share of the total benefits that accrues to Group I. The share of the benefits to Group II, $(1 - S)$, is measured from right to left along the same axis. In the absence of lump-sum transfers, suppose that incentive compatibility constraints on individual behavior imply that the maximum Y depends on S. For instance, there may be no feasible contract that is able to separate the incentive to work from the level of compensation. Let point e denote the (S, Y) combination at which Y is maximized. At this efficient point OE_{max} is the share of the benefits that happens to accrue to Group I, so that $1 - E_{max}$ is the share of Group II. In the absence of lump-sum transfers, any other distribution—that is, any other value of S—must reduce Y because of the decline in allocative efficiency, ignoring the incentive compatibility constraints. For simplicity, I assume that the remaining distribution share values, S, yield values of Y that are bounded from above by a smooth, hill-shaped welfare frontier, the heavy solid curve $AYeB$, which, for brevity, will be called curve Y.

Next, it is easy to derive from the overall benefit-distribution frontier Y the two corresponding upper frontiers for Groups I and II. These obviously are given by the expressions SY and $(1 - S)Y$, for Groups I and II, respectively, and immediately yield the corresponding two curves labeled I and II. For example, curve I must start off at zero at the left end of the graph where $S = 0$, and then asymptotically approach Y as one moves toward the extreme right where $S = 1$. The same procedure, but this time moving from right to left, yields curve II. These curves will be concave at least at maximum Y (at $S = E_{max}$) and to its right (left) in the case of Group I (Group II), so long as Y is concave.[20] So it can be assumed that each curve will also have a single maximum. They have their maxima at share levels $S = I_{max}$ and $S = II_{max}$, respectively.

It also follows that $I_{max} > E_{max} > II_{max}$; that is, Group I's maximum must lie to the right of Group II's. To see this, note that at E_{max}, where $Y' = 0$, $(SY)' = Y > 0$ and $[(1 - S)Y]' = -Y < 0$, so that Group I's benefits increase as one moves to the right of E and Group II's benefits increase as one moves to its left. It follows that at each of the maxima for the individual groups there must be some loss of overall efficiency, because Y must be below its maximum, e. That will also be true throughout the range between the two group maxima, with the exception of the single point at $S = E_{max}$. Thus there will indeed be a tradeoff between efficiency and virtually any desired distribution of the benefits.

The range between the maxima for the two groups clearly is also a region in which it is impossible (along the efficient frontier) to benefit

---

20. If the functions are twice differentiable, the situation is straightforward. For example, the Group I curve, SY, has the first derivative $SY' + Y$, which is positive at $Y' = 0$. SY has the second derivative $SY'' + 2Y'$ which is certainly negative anywhere in the region $Y' \leq 0$ if $Y'' < 0$.

either group without harming the other. In other words, the frontier points within this range are all, indisputably, NLS Pareto optima. Such a range must always exist where the efficient point, e, is an interior maximum of Y, the measure of social welfare, and where the Y frontier is hill-shaped. For then, any change in distribution must favor some group(s) of individuals at the expense of others, since the change must also decrease Y, the total size of the pie available for distribution.

Application: NLS Pareto-Optimal Levels of Innovation Externalities

Let us now turn to an important application of the preceding observations: to the NLS Pareto optimality of nonzero spillovers (externalities) from *innovation*, with the conjecture that the plausible range of optimality may include spillovers that are very large. This is, of course, in direct conflict with the view that only zero externalities are consistent with an optimal allocation of investment to innovation activity. As William Nordhaus put this conclusion, "External economies are an important aspect of the production of knowledge. The greater the externality, the more inefficient is the final equilibrium."[21]

The reason why a zero spillover level in innovation is not optimal is the tradeoff between increased flow of invention and the distribution of benefits to others—the resulting rise in overall living standards. Moreover, it will be shown that there is no single level of spillovers that is unambiguously optimal. Instead, there is a range of values of what will be called the *spillover ratio*, that is, the share of the benefits of innovation that goes to persons other than the investors, within which all values of the ratio are NLS Pareto-optimal. Thus they are all what may be considered second-best Pareto optima, subject to a constraint that rules out hypothetical but totally infeasible redistributive arrangements.

My analysis takes off from a pathbreaking paper by Paul Romer that introduces a more profound view of the spillovers generated in the innovation process.[22] It observes that general gains in real wages that result from innovation must constitute spillovers, since they are social benefits that are not private benefits to the innovator. Along with this, it can be argued that the bulk of the unprecedented rise in the developed world's living standards

21. Nordhaus (1969, p. 39).
22. Romer (1994).

since the Industrial Revolution could not have occurred without the revolution's innovations.[23] Consequently, a very substantial share of the benefits of innovation must have gone to persons other than the innovators in the form of spillovers.[24]

Romer studies the role of these differences between private and social benefits—the spillovers of innovation—as an impediment to innovative activity, discussing the difficulty innovators face in covering their sunk costs and the resulting reduction in innovative activity and output. That is part of the story that I will retell in this paper. However, I will also emphasize another side of the matter, to which Romer alludes only in passing: the inevitable tradeoff between the number of innovations actually produced and the standard of living of the majority of the population. In this scenario, as overall GDP is raised by innovation, any increase in workers' standards of living constitutes a rise in the spillovers from innovation that depresses the flow of further innovation. Thus the more the general public benefits from such growth in GDP, the slower that growth must be.

This is more than just an embellishment of the old story of the tradeoff between output and distributive equality. The mechanism under discussion here is very different and does not involve the disincentive to work that results from a reduction of the marginal return to worker effort. Rather, I am concerned here with the heart of the capitalist growth process: the private payoff to innovation and the speed with which new technology and new products become available.

Our scenario is by far the more dramatic. Romer notes in passing that, if the innovators had not lost *any* of the benefits they generated—if spillovers had been zero—then real wages would hardly have risen from their levels before the Industrial Revolution![25] It is almost impossible to

23. Many observers have emphasized the leading role of innovation in the growth process. In addition to Romer, there are, of course, Solow (1956), Nordhaus (1969), and Nelson (1996), among others.

24. Some writers on innovation use the term "spillovers" in a more restricted sense to refer, for example, to direct gains of knowledge by customers of the industry that supplies the R&D in question (see Grilliches, 1979). Such use of the term is, of course, entirely legitimate. However, here, the term is taken as synonymous with *total* external effects. It represents *all* the social benefits of innovation that do not accrue as private benefits to the inventor or to those who invested in or otherwise contributed to it. This connotation is clearly required by the issue under discussion—the disincentive to innovation activity resulting from the difference between its social and private rewards.

25. A reader of this paper has argued that this conclusion is unrealistic because innovations *do* benefit workers. That is, of course, correct. However, by definition, zero externalities mean that no such benefits go to the workers. This implies that zero externalities cannot occur in the world of reality—that it is an unattainable goal. The question that remains is whether that imaginary goal, if it could somehow be achieved, could be accepted as optimal. The answer of this paper, emphatically, is that it

imagine how great a difference that would have made. What are probably the best available estimates put U.S. per capita GDP in 1820 at less than one-seventeenth of what it is today, and even as late as 1870 real per capita GDP is estimated to have been less than one-ninth its current level.[26] If one assumes the most extreme case—that the spillovers from innovation could somehow have been reduced to (anywhere near) zero—the living standards of the vast majority of the citizens of today's rich countries would have stalled at pre-Industrial Revolution levels. One can hardly accept the notion that it would be socially preferable to achieve a total GDP far higher than today's through maximal incentives for innovation while, simultaneously, condemning most of the population to near-medieval living standards. But that is the world that a zero-spillovers premise depicts.

Marginal Cost, Total Cost, and Adoption of Socially Beneficial Innovations

Before constructing a more formal model of the socially optimal level of spillovers from innovation, I must briefly review an important issue for the analysis that, as Romer notes, goes back to Jules Dupuit. This is the role of *total cost* relative to that of *marginal cost* in "lumpy" decisions, such as the decision to build a bridge or to launch an innovation process. Where such an activity has substantial fixed and sunk costs or where scale economies make small-scale entry infeasible, one cannot rely on marginal analysis because marginal data relate only to small adjustments.[27]

This means that, when deciding whether to build a bridge or to launch a large-scale research project, the pertinent criterion is whether the *total yield* will exceed the *total cost*. A profit-seeking firm will not undertake an

---

would not be optimal, contrary to what might be inferred from the literature. Though it would increase the number of beneficial innovations, it would, tautologically, preclude any of the benefits from going to persons other than the innovators. Romer puts the matter very clearly: "This pattern of industrialization without wage gains is what it would take to ensure that the industrialist captures all of the benefits he creates when he introduces machinery. . . . [This] cannot be a historically accurate description of the process of development in industrial countries, for if it were, unskilled labor would still earn what it earned prior to the Industrial Revolution" (Romer, 1994, p. 29).

26. Maddison (1995, pp. 196–97).

27. That is not to deny the important role of marginal considerations in the theory of innovation. For example, in deciding how much to increase or decrease the budget for R&D on improvement of a particular invention, or how much longer to work on it before releasing it to the market, the usual sorts of marginal calculation apply, as I, among many others, have shown elsewhere (see Baumol, 1993).

innovation unless the total revenue is expected to be greater than the total cost, and society should not undertake it unless its total benefits are expected to exceed total costs.

The very legitimate argument conventionally linking this to the spillovers of innovation, then, is straightforward. It suggests that there are many prospective innovations that promise total net social benefits but will nevertheless not be carried out by private enterprise, even if *marginal* spillovers, at whatever margin is relevant, are all zero. This is because there are many potential innovations whose prospective total benefits (including their contributions to consumers' surpluses) are greater than their total costs; however, no one will find it profitable to carry them out because a considerable proportion of the total benefits would go to persons other than the innovator (in the form of spillovers). In this paper, I will carry on with the story from this point and provide a somewhat different ending.

A Model and Graphic Analysis of Optimal Spillovers

Next, I turn to a formal analysis of the relation between the spillover ratio and optimality. I will adopt two premises to facilitate the discussion. First, production uses only two inputs, labor and innovation, so that income earners are divided into innovators and (non-innovating) workers. Second, with a given labor force, the production frontier can be shifted outward only by innovation.

Let S represent the spillover ratio—the share of the benefits of innovation that does not accrue to the innovator, relative to the total benefit contributed by innovation. Consider two scenarios. In the first, the value of S is assumed to be fixed exogenously. In the other scenario, it is treated as a modifiable parameter.

The model follows Romer in recognizing that there is a vast set of potential innovations and that they offer society different amounts of total net benefit, over and above their sunk costs. Each such innovation, I, also requires a sunk expenditure, $C(i)$, where i is the index assigned to invention I, as described below. Assume that both benefits and costs can be translated into money terms and that the total gross benefit, $B(i)$ (before deduction of sunk cost), is given by the discounted present value of the stream of the benefits and other costs expected from invention I from now to eternity.

Then, clearly, maximization of the direct benefits from innovation requires that at any given time the economy carry out every recognized prospective innovation, I, for which $B(i) - C(i) > 0$. However, given the spillover ratio, private enterprise will undertake only those innovations for which $B(i)(1 - S) - C(i) > 0$. This means that the beneficial innovations, J, for which $C(j)/(1 - S) > B(j) > C(j)$, will be lost to society. That is, roughly speaking, where the story stands in much of the literature.

To take it further, I will utilize a few simple graphs. Figure 1-3 is a standard depiction of the relationship between the benefits from innovation and the share of innovations that are actually carried out from among those currently considered possible by prospective innovators. It shows how spillovers limit the number of prospectively useful innovations that are actually undertaken. In this graph it is assumed that the spillovers are a fixed percentage (for example, $S = 0.75$) of the total future benefits of an innovation. The potential innovations currently recognized as possibly worth carrying out are taken to be a continuum (or, one can assume that they can be approximated by one). It is also assumed that the sunk investment required to carry out a single innovation is fixed at the level C.[28] The horizontal axis, which extends from zero to unity, represents the share of currently recognized innovation possibilities that is actually carried out. Innovations are indexed *in descending order* of incremental gross benefit, B. Here, gross benefit is defined as the discounted present value of all current and future gains an innovation provides, minus the discounted value of all current and future costs other than the sunk costs needed to carry it out. The descending order of benefits, then, means that $B(i) > B(j)$ if $i < j$. For simplicity of presentation, the gross benefits curve, B, is taken to be linear. It must have a negative slope throughout by construction—because of the way in which the potential innovations are ordered.

Then, with S a given constant, one can easily also draw in the innovator's gross-benefits curve, the lower straight line $(1 - S)B$. Point N, where the B and C lines intersect, represents the exhaustion of all recognized innovations that currently promise a net gain to the economy. That is, at N the economy has adopted every recognized innovation that offers benefits that exceed its sunk costs.[29] However, private enterprise will be unable

28. Jean Gadrey has noted that C is unlikely to be horizontal in reality, with more beneficial innovations apt to incur a higher sunk cost, so that the line (curve) may well have a negative slope. It is easy to see that this change leads to no fundamental modification of the analysis.

29. The association of point N with optimality in the set of innovations that are carried out forces me to use the very broad definition of spillovers employed in this paper, rather than a more restricted concept, such as one including only unpaid-for benefits obtained by an innovator's competitors. Clearly, in itself, an innovation is beneficial to society if its costs are exceeded by the sum of the bene-

Figure 1-3. *Spillover Ratio, Optimality, and Equilibrium*

Total gross benefits

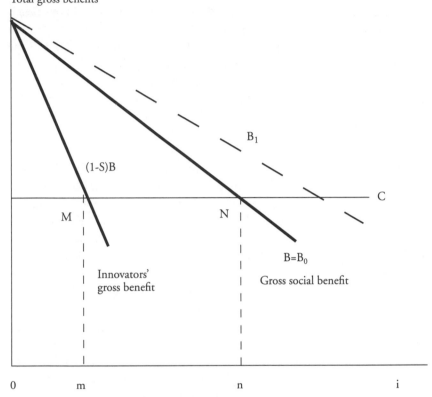

Proportion of potential innovations actually carried out

to go beyond point *M*, with its much lower output of innovation because spillovers, *SB*, will prevent it from covering the sunk costs of any additional innovations.[30] The implication is that the level of innovation can be much below the socially efficient level, *n*.

It should be noted, incidentally, that this is not a problem of private enterprise alone. The public sector can fare no better without financing the

fits to *anyone*, including consumers in other countries, unrelated producers, and members of future generations.

30. More generally, it is easy to prove that so long as there is no shift in *B*, $di/dS < 0$ at the least remunerative invention *I* whose production causes no loss at the given *S* value. For zero profit requires $(1 - S)B(i) - C = 0$, so that $(1 - S)B'di = BdS$, or, since $B' = dB/di < 0$ by construction, $di/dS = B/(1 - S)B' < 0$.

shortfall out of the gain that would otherwise accrue to the labor force. Of course, private innovators can do just as well if at the margin they can be subsidized or use some other source of revenue to offset the share of total benefit that escapes them as spillovers.

Next, consider what happens in figure 1-3 when there is a change in the spillover ratio. Obviously, if the B line remains fixed in its initial position, B_0, as S increases, the line $(1 - S)B_0$ will simply move steadily lower and become steadily steeper, with the curve rotating clockwise. However, this overlooks the possibility that, at least up to a point, the spillovers themselves will contribute to productivity and innovation and, hence, to the total benefits the economy derives from innovation.

In reality, there are at least two ways in which this can occur. First, the spillovers from innovation facilitate further innovation. They do so by cutting down the need for and the expenses involved in the design of duplicative technology by competing firms. Moreover, to the extent that technical advance is cumulative, with one step facilitating the next, as is certainly true in many fields, today's technological advance by one firm lays the groundwork for tomorrow's advance by different firms or by others. In addition, spillovers increase the number of inventors who can work effectively from the base provided by the new technology.[31]

Second, zero spillovers, as the term is interpreted here, means that the labor force is condemned to the nutrition and educational levels that prevailed before the Industrial Revolution. The evidence indicates, however, that the transfer to workers of some of the benefits of innovation in the form of improved nutrition and education can contribute materially to labor productivity. Consequently, as S increases above zero, say to S_1, at least initially line B can be expected to shift upward or rotate counterclockwise, sufficiently to yield a social benefit line B_1 that lies above B (see figure 1-3). However, when S becomes sufficiently large, further increases in S will indeed lower and steepen the line $(1 - S)B$ monotonically.

The relationships and their implications yield more interesting insights with the aid of figure 1-4, which focuses on the effects of changes *in the spillover ratio*. In figure 1-4, the horizontal axis represents S, the size of the spillover ratio. Like the i on the horizontal axis of figure 1-3, it ranges between $S = 0$ and $S = 1$. The upper curve, B^*, is the integral of $[B(i) - C]$ from $i = 0$ to the profit-maximizing value of i in figure 1-3, where $(1 - S)B(i) = C$. In the

31. I owe the observations in this paragraph to Richard Nelson. Indeed, most of the paragraph is a lightly edited quotation from a letter he sent to me (June 10, 1998).

Figure 1-4. *Benefits as a Function of Spillover Ratio*

Discounted benefits

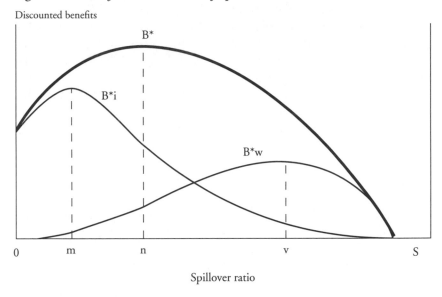

Spillover ratio

region to the right of n in the graph the slope of the B^* curve must be negative since by construction $dB^*/di = B - C > 0$ and from footnote 30, $di/dS = B/B'(1 - S) < 0$, so

(1) $\qquad dB^*/dS = (dB^*/di)(di/dS) = (B - C)B/(1 - S)B'.$

It is also easy to verify by taking the second derivative that in this region the B^* curve is normally concave, as drawn.[32]

The negative slope would persist throughout the graph if innovation were the only direct input to productivity growth or if innovation were not facilitated by spillovers from other innovations. However, as has been noted, in reality productivity growth *is* enhanced, up to a point, by better nutrition and education of the labor force, which are severely reduced as the value of S approaches zero, and by the spillovers from innovation that facilitate and stimulate further innovation. Thus, since the left-hand end of the graph represents a state of affairs with workers ill-fed and ill-educated,

32. Continuing to assume $B'' = 0$ for simplicity, and writing $b = dB^*/di = B - C$, so $b' < 0$, equation (1) indicates that $d^2B^*/dS^2 = [(b'B + bB')(1 - S)B'di/dS - bBB']/K^2 = (2bBB' + b'B^2)/K^2 < 0$, where K is the denominator of dB^*/dS and, as shown in footnote 30, $di/dS = B/(1 - S)B'$. However, to the right of $S = 1 - C/B(0)$ at which *any* investment becomes unprofitable there will be no investment, no costs and no benefits, so that the B^* curve will follow the horizontal axis.

and with innovation benefiting very little from other innovations, the B^* curve begins by rising initially as S begins to rise above zero. That is, toward the left $dB^*/dS > 0$; this portion of the B^* curve has a positive slope. All of this together yields the shape of the B^* curve depicted in the graph. It has a unique maximum at $S = n$. Here, current investment in innovation maximizes the net total gain to society.

However, the rest of the story differs for the two classes into which society is divided—the innovators and the workers. It is the same story that was told above in the section on the range of NLS Pareto optima. For example, the benefits added by innovation going to the workers are shown by the B^*w curve given by the expression SB^*; that is, the workers' benefit equals the total social benefit, B^*, multiplied by the share, S, that goes to these noninnovators. This lower curve must start off at zero at its left-hand end, where $S = 0$, and it must approach steadily closer to the B^* curve as S increases toward unity, with the two curves meeting at or before the extreme right, where S equals or is close to unity (see note 32). B^*w has the derivative

$$(2) \qquad\qquad dSB^*/dS = B^* + SB^{*\prime},$$

which is positive at the maximum, n, of the upper curve, B^*, where $B^{*\prime} = 0$. This means that v, the maximum of B^*w, must occur *to the right* of n, the maximum of B^*. The reason is that slightly to the right of the maximum of B^*, though the total size of the social output pie is decreasing, the workers' share of that shrinking pie increases sufficiently to make them better off, on balance. Eventually, though, the size of the social output gain shrinks so much that further increases in S are damaging even to workers. The workers' benefit maximum requires $B^* = -SB^{*\prime}$, which has a straightforward intuitive interpretation in terms of the total benefit pie and the size of the workers' slice. B^* is the workers' gain from a unit increase in their *share* of the pie, while $SB^{*\prime}$ is the loss to them from the accompanying decrease in *total size* of the pie, $B^{*\prime}$, and maximization requires this marginal loss to equal the marginal gain.

Similarly, the graph depicts an innovators' benefits curve, B^*i. Its equation is $B^*i = (1 - S)B^*$. Its relation to the B^* curve is perfectly analogous to that of the workers, except that the innovators' curve's behavior going from right to left (as $1 - S$ increases) corresponds exactly to that of the workers' curve going from left to right (as S increases). Thus $S = m$, the maximum[33] of B^*i, must always lie *to the left* of n, the maximum of the social gain curve B^*.

33. This can conceivably be a corner maximum at $S = 0$. That will occur if at this point $B^* > B^{*\prime} > 0$, so that at $S = 0$ the slope of the innovators' benefit curve, $(1 - S)B^{*\prime} - B^*$, is negative.

Several substantive conclusions follow from this discussion. First, it is clear that innovators do not obtain their maximum reward if they receive *all* of the benefits their innovations can yield—that is, if spillovers are zero. Rather, their gain is maximized at $S = m > 0$. Their preferred value of S may even be higher than this if, for example, they derive some utility from altruistic egalitarianism, or if higher wages reduce crime and thereby increase the safety of the innovators.

For the same reason, the welfare of workers will be reduced if *all* of the benefits of innovation go to them in the form of spillovers because then, of course, there will be no innovation and no benefits to accrue to them. They will be better off if $S = v$, corresponding to the maximum point on their benefits curve. They may derive indirect gains from a value of S somewhat lower than v if greater innovator wealth leads to such outcomes as increased donations to hospitals, from which workers benefit.

Thus point n (at which productive efficiency is maximized) is *not* preferred by either party, and while n is a possible compromise between the two groups, it is hardly the only available compromise position. Every point in the entire range $m \leq S \leq v$ is a possible solution since any change from a point within that range must harm one of the groups while benefiting the other. That is, the corresponding range of a utilities-possibility frontier, which can easily be derived from our model, must have a negative slope throughout. So there is a range of S values, all of which are (NLS) Pareto optimal, rather than a unique and clearly definable global optimum.[34]

Pigouvian Subsidies, Consumers' Surplus, and Lump-Sum Transfers

The preceding analysis naturally prompts the question whether, at least in theory, one cannot have it both ways, somehow providing the incentive for the socially optimal amount of innovation, with a subsequent redistribution of the resulting gains, thereby making all parties better off. But even if all socially beneficial innovations could somehow be obtained through

---

34. The issue here and my conclusion have close analogies in the literature on optimal patent life, notably in the work of William Nordhaus (1969) and Frederic Scherer (1965). There the issue is the tradeoff between reward to the inventor (before the time of patent expiration) and the transfer of subsequent benefits to the general public.

the market, the lump-sum transfers needed to distribute the benefits to the general population without distorting the equilibrium would remain a figment of the theorist's imagination. I have already argued why, *in general,* there can be no such thing as a lump-sum transfer in the real world. In the particular case of innovation, the unreality of the proposal is far more striking. If, as the next section argues, spillover ratios probably exceed 0.75, their elimination would give innovators a huge addition to their current earnings. If the remainder of the population were subsequently to be compensated by ostensibly lump-sum transfers, the resources could not conceivably come from anyone except the super-rich innovators who would be the recipients of the bulk of the economy's GDP. They could hardly avoid noticing that most of their innovation payoff was being taxed away. Surely, this would affect the amounts of the resources and effort they were willing to invest in the innovation process. The idea that lump-sum transfers are pertinent to the problem, even in theory, is tantamount to assuming the problem away.

Another attribute that makes innovation spillovers different from other beneficial externalities, as Romer rightly emphasizes, stems from the heavy sunk costs of the innovation process. These mean that even if the prices of the products of innovation are adjusted to cover the marginal costs of supplying them, the sunk costs will generally not be covered. Thus, even if Pigouvian subsidies are added to those prices so that they cover all of the pertinent *marginal* costs, private enterprise will not be willing to invest in every socially beneficial innovation. Here, the obvious test of social desirability is whether the total benefits of the innovation, *including consumers' surpluses now and in the future,* can be expected to cover the *total* costs, both those that are sunk and those that are not.

It is tempting to argue that one can in theory induce the market to provide all innovations that are expected to be beneficial *ex ante* by means of a patent system that perfectly protects intellectual property rights and enables innovators to acquire all consumers' surpluses by perfect price discrimination. Romer emphasizes how difficult (if not impossible) such price discrimination is to carry out in practice.

The bottom line, simply, is this: there is no way *in reality* to escape the tradeoff between the incentives required to elicit the "optimal" level of investment in innovation and the desire for the resulting rise in real productivity to benefit everyone, and not just the innovators.

How Large Are the Spillovers?

As already indicated, the total size of the spillovers from innovation is hardly negligible. If one provisionally accepts the conclusion that the bulk of the rise in per capita GDP and the rise in productivity since the Industrial Revolution *ultimately* could not have occurred without innovation, it is possible to arrive at a very crudely estimated lower bound for the spillover ratio. For this purpose, it may be noted that per capita GDP has increased almost ninefold in the United States since 1870, according to estimates by Angus Maddison.[35] Such a rise in GDP per person implies that fully eight-ninths, or nearly 90 percent, of current GDP was contributed by innovation carried out since 1870.[36] The total contribution of innovation is certainly even greater than that, since pre-1870 innovations, such as the steam engine, the railroad, and many other inventions of an earlier era, still add to today's GDP. Moreover, the difference between the increase in productivity (estimated by Maddison to have risen thirteen-fold since 1870) and the increase in GDP is attributable in good part to enhanced leisure, surely a benefit over and above reported GDP, and a benefit also made possible largely by innovation.[37]

At the same time, the share of total investment income in GDP during this period was certainly less than 30 percent. But investment in innova-

---

35. Maddison (1995).

36. The discussion of the amount that innovation has added to growth may seem to argue that contributions to economic growth from all other sources must have been negligible. No such assumption, however, is intended (nor is this or any related premise critical for my main argument). It is clear that enormous contributions have been made by education and other forms of investment in human capital, by investment in plant and equipment, and by other stimuli. Still, the enormous expansion of outlays on education and physical productive capacity in the world's industrialized countries themselves would not have been possible without the resources provided by innovation in the course of the Industrial Revolution. In this sense, a burst of innovation constituted a necessary condition for the economic expansion that has occurred since the eighteenth century. If new technology in agriculture, mining, and manufacturing had not appeared with the Industrial Revolution and the centuries that preceded it, it is arguable that miserably low per capita income levels would have prevented any substantial savings. Therefore no significant increase in investment in plant, equipment, education, or health of the labor force would have been possible. If so, innovation must be considered the ultimate source of most of the investment in human and physical capital that, along with the innovation itself, is surely responsible for most of the growth in production, production per capita, and productivity that followed the Industrial Revolution.

Moreover, the cross partial derivatives of national output growth among the input variables are undoubtedly substantial. For example, innovation surely stimulates educational expenditure both by providing the necessary resources and increasing the returns to education. But education, in turn, clearly facilitates innovation.

37. Maddison (1995, p. 249).

tion is only a part of total investment. In 1996 R&D expenditures made up only 15 percent of total investment in the United States.[38] Thus, if the return on innovation investment were the same (after adjustment for risk) as the return to investment of other types, the return to innovation would have been less than $(30)(0.15) = 4.5$ percent of GDP. This makes it implausible that returns to innovators can have been much more than 10 percent of GDP. It follows that S, the spillover ratio, may well have been as high as 0.8. That is, some 80 percent of the benefits may plausibly have gone to persons who made no direct contribution to innovation. The rather startling implication of all this is that *the spillovers of innovation, direct and indirect, can be estimated to constitute well over half of current GDP*—and it can even be argued that this is a very conservative figure.

The very crude estimates offered here are not out of line with the available estimates of private and social returns to innovation.[39] Edward Wolff, for instance, estimates the social rate of return to be 53 percent (in line with previous work on the subject) and the private rate of return to be between 10.1 and 12.6 percent or less (a figure slightly below earlier estimates).[40] These yield a spillover ratio of about 80 percent. For our story, the precise figure does not matter. What is noteworthy is that the spillover ratio seems clearly to be surprisingly large.

Relevance of the Analysis for Reality

At first glance the optimality arguments of this paper may appear far-fetched and remote from the real world. However, a little reflection will suggest that this is not true. I have never come across a discussion of the consequences of the Industrial Revolution that did not stress that its main social benefit was its ultimate contribution to the living standards of the population as a whole—fostering improvements in health, longevity, education, reduction of poverty, and so on. But these *are* the main spillovers from innovation and the focus of this paper. One can only begin to suggest the shocking levels of poverty to which a world without the spillovers from innovation would condemn the labor force. Histories of Europe confirm that for many centuries before the Industrial Revolution the vast majority

38. U.S. Bureau of the Census (1997).
39. See, for example, Nadiri (1991), Mohnen (1992), and Wolff (1997).
40. Wolff (1997, p. 16).

of the population struggled simply to exist. Most families spent nearly half their food budgets on "breadstuffs." As late as 1790 in France, according to Robert Palmer, "The price of bread, even in normal times, in the amount needed for a man with a wife and three children, was half as much as the daily wage of common labor."[41] Still more commonly, the breadstuff took the form of gruel (in good years) consumed in life-sustaining quantities. But there were many years when even gruel was unavailable. Devastating famines threatened Europe as late as the beginning of the nineteenth century, and earlier they had been a fact of life. Fernand Braudel's remarkable history of Europe documents the depths of human misery before the Industrial Revolution:

A few overfed rich do not alter the rule. . . . Cereal yields were poor; two consecutive bad harvests spelt disaster. . . . Any national calculation shows a sad story. France, by any standards a privileged country, is reckoned to have experienced 10 *general* famines during the tenth century; 26 in the eleventh; 2 in the twelfth; 4 in the fourteenth; 7 in the fifteenth; 13 in the sixteenth; 11 in the seventeenth; and 16 in the eighteenth. . . . The same could be said of any country in Europe. In Germany, famine was a persistent visitor to the towns and flatlands. Even when the easier times came, in the eighteenth and nineteenth centuries, catastrophes could still happen. . . .

The poor in the towns and countryside . . . lived in a state of almost complete deprivation. Their furniture consisted of next to nothing, at least before the eighteenth century, when a rudimentary luxury began to spread. . . . Inventories made after death, which are reliable documents, testify almost invariably to the general destitution. . . a few old clothes, a stool, a table, a bench, the planks of a bed, sacks filled with straw. Official reports for Burgundy between the sixteenth and the eighteenth centuries are full of references to people [sleeping] on straw . . . with no bed or furniture, who were only separated from the pigs by a screen. . . .

Paradoxically the countryside sometimes experienced far greater suffering [from famines than the townspeople]. The peasants . . . had scarcely any reserves of their own. They had no solution in case of

41. Palmer (1964, p. 49).

famine except to turn to the town where they crowded together, begging in the streets and often dying in public squares. . . .[42]

Surely, few of us would be prepared to argue that it would be optimal to multiply the wealth of the world's richest innovators far above their current levels while condemning the rest of the population to the miserable living standards of the bulk of the seventeenth century population. But that is just what zero spillovers would mean.

Concluding Comment

This view of the matter also suggests an alternative and, perhaps, more acceptable interpretation of my basic conclusion. The range of choices for society under discussion here can be thought of as possible movements along an *efficiency-distribution frontier*, rather than as a choice among alternative and second-best Pareto optima. The issue is a matter of determining an optimal tradeoff between economic efficiency and the variance of income, subject to the constraint that the only feasible way to achieve substantial transfers is by means of spillovers.

Most of us *do* recognize the beneficial spillovers that innovation, seems to have contributed, and, more than that, we all seem to agree that this enhancement of living standards is a very desirable outcome. In other words, perhaps without realizing that we were discussing the *spillovers* of innovation, we have concluded that they are a very good thing. It follows immediately that even if zero spillovers had increased innovation, they would certainly have been far from optimal. Here, the standard reaction of economists—that disinterested academicians cannot defensibly take a stand on income distribution—just will not do. Virtually no one aspires to a world in which innovators receive incomes in the trillions of dollars (putting Bill Gates's income into the shade), while the remainder of the community languishes in seventeenth-century poverty. Of course, there is a value judgment involved, but only cowardice will induce us to reject it. (My own value judgment on this issue is summed up in the G.B.S. dictum that there is no crime greater than poverty.) Once something like this value judgment is accepted, then we must also go on to reject the conclusion that spillovers are incompatible with optimality in the growth process. And

42. Braudel (1979, vol. 1, pp. 73–75 and 283).

once the last conclusion is recognized, what remains is a matter of haggling about degree of deviation from zero. I myself believe that the most desirable value of S is *very* much larger than zero—perhaps not far from its current value.

Of course, those innovations that have never been launched do constitute a loss to society. But the point here is that there is an inescapable tradeoff between two desirable phenomena: further increases in innovative activity versus diversion of the benefits to bring society out of medieval poverty, to spread education and health care, and to finance the better life not just for the fortunate few, but for the population as a whole.

If there is such a tradeoff, and I do not see how that can be denied, we are back in the realm in which economists are most comfortable; following Lionel Robbins, we are back at the allocation of scarce resources among competing (and desirable) ends. The analysis of such tradeoffs is the meat and potatoes of economists' professional activity. This paper has sought to provide a possible step toward a formal theory of income distribution policy, by presenting an introduction to the analysis of the choice between low and high spillover ratios. And it has argued that progress in that arena requires us to abandon the issue-dodging assumption that distributive shortcomings can be cured by lump-sum transfers.

COMMENT BY
George Akerlof

William Baumol has written a very interesting paper. It is full of insight and wisdom. It meets the criterion for a fine economics paper; it forces the reader to see the world differently.

However, I should also say that I disagree wholeheartedly with at least two of the basic premises of the paper—although I do not disagree with its conclusion that the government should correct unwanted long-term swings in the distribution of income.

The first premise of this paper with which I disagree is that economists believe in the "fairy tale" of lump-sum distributions. This belief, Baumol argues, has caused economists to urge economic policies in favor of economic efficiency at the expense of redistribution and give the wrong-minded advice that such redistributions are cheap and easy to obtain.

My own reading of the economics literature is that economists are well aware of the difficulties of redistributive policies—indeed, so aware of the difficulties that they have shied away from income distribution. Consider the work of Martin Feldstein. Most sensible people think that taxing capital gains would be a good idea. Most wealth is held by the wealthy. The assets held by most of the not so wealthy tend to be in the form of pension funds and housing, which are not subject to capital gains taxation. So why not tax capital gains? Not so, says Feldstein. Taxing returns to capital deprives people of the opportunity to save their money at the rate of interest corresponding to the marginal efficiency of capital, which he claims has been historically high. There are massive deadweight losses from taking away this opportunity.[43]

Well, if capital gains taxation does not work, we might look elsewhere for other redistributive policies. For example, we might give some poor kids a chance to go to college, on a scholarship. You had better think twice about that, say Feldstein and also my Berkeley colleague Aaron Edlin. If you make that college scholarship asset-based, parents will have incentives to spend their money rather than to save it, thereby preserving for their kiddies the possibility of getting cushy college scholarships.

Maybe we would like to give some money to the poor. Maybe we want to have a negative income tax. That poses huge problems, as we unfortunately learned in the early 1970s when it was proposed by Richard Nixon as the Family Assistance Plan and by George McGovern as the negative income tax.

The problem is implicit in a formula first discovered by James Tobin.[44] With all tax revenues from a linear income tax, the marginal rate of taxation will be the sum of the demogrant given to those with zero income as a fraction of average income plus the share of government in income. A reasonable demogrant—say one-third—plus the government share of national income of another third, yields a very high marginal rate of taxation: two-thirds. This is such a high marginal rate of taxation that even liberals like me—from Berkeley, Yale, and the Brookings Institution—worry about the deadweight losses.

More complicated systems than negative income taxation attempt to give special tax schedules, or special benefits, to those in need by "tagging" those people, such as the old, through Social Security, or single mothers with children, or the working poor. With the exception of the old, this system has the problem of very bad incentives. The current welfare system is the result of those problems. The old system has been changed because the

43. Feldstein (1978).
44. Tobin (1970).

public felt that there were too many welfare cheats. The system was unfair to the working poor relative to the nonworking poor. So it was deemed that single mothers would in due course have to find jobs. This may restore equity to the working poor, but it places massive burdens on poor single mothers. When Jimmy Carter was asked whether he thought there were welfare cheats, he gave the correct answer: Yes, he said, there are welfare cheats, but there are also many on welfare who need it—desperately.

A quite successful measure to re-create equity between the working poor and the nonworking poor has been the earned income tax credit. The earned income tax credit is an attempt to give special aid to those in special need of it—to tag people. It gives special aid to parents with low earnings. But any such system to tag people almost invariably creates some disincentives. In the case of the earned income tax credit, there may be an annual penalty of as much as $6,000 for a family of four that earns $25,000 per year.

I believe economists are now aware of these difficulties in making income redistributions. Theoretically, the costs and the benefits of income distribution by taxation have been spelled out most cogently by Ray Fair and James Mirrlees, both writing on the tradeoff between efficiency and equity in optimal income taxation.[45]

In contrast to Professor Baumol's paper, this previous work, theoretical and empirical, has rested on static models. It is in the dynamic context that Professor Baumol makes his contribution. He poses the question as to whether we should make redistributions in dynamic models—that is, in dynamic models in which there is endogenous invention—so that technology changes because of the effort of individual entrepreneurs and inventors.

Baumol has a very original and intriguing way of looking at this problem. He looks back over history, over long periods of time, at the change in total factor productivity. He uses the famous result of Robert Solow that almost all of our growth in per capita income is due to the growth in total factor productivity.[46] Most growth is due to invention and technical change. Baumol then asserts that if the people responsible for this change in total productivity received their rightful due—the changes in output for which they were responsible—then the lion's share of GDP would go to them. Indeed, if all changes in output due to invention since 1750 went to

45. Fair (1971); Mirrlees (1971).
46. Solow (1957).

the inventors, rather than spilled over to the public at large, then the large-scale famines and dire poverty that characterized the eighteenth century would still be common. The prosperity that is widespread today is due to the appropriation of the returns that have accrued from the work of generations of innovators, who have changed western technology for centuries, one step at a time. Since society has made such a large redistribution in favor of the general public and against those who have introduced the new technology—which is the foundation of our current prosperity—we should not be afraid of other large-scale income distributions, including one to undo the growing income inequality that has occurred in the last twenty or thirty years. I consider this an interesting way to look at the problem of income redistribution and a real contribution.

Despite the fact that I have learned a great deal from this line of thinking, I still disagree with another one of the author's basic premises. Baumol defines the efficient distribution as one in which the inventors receive the additional product created from their ideas. But perhaps Professor Baumol is prepared to pay them too much. I would not take this as the baseline for payments in the efficient society.

Let me abstract, as has Professor Baumol, from the truly messy problem that in the case of invention, it is unclear even with complete information how to decide who has made what contribution. For example, how much of the value of computer technology is due to Alan Turing, to John von Neumann, to Norbert Weiner, or even to Bill Gates? It would be hard to devise a system that would parse out the rewards in any way that would be fair.

But let us forget that all but insurmountable problem; let us assume that we *could* identify who contributed what and pay them accordingly. Why should we pay them *their contribution?* Why should we not pay such people a much lower sum, which is their opportunity cost for turning out the ideas that have made society a happier and more prosperous place? In this case, if this is the system of payment, the rest of society will get the invention, the inventors will engage in their process of invention, and technological change will proceed apace. In my view this is an approximate description of the income distribution that now prevails, in which inventors do get some reward from the general public. Some such distribution does occur in favor of inventors, as governments tax the public and subsidize research in industry, government labs, and universities. To attract inventors and those with other ideas into this sector, research workers and thinkers must be paid at least as much as they would earn elsewhere. The magnitude of this important activity, however, is fairly small relative to GDP. R&D expenditures in the United States are about 2.7 percent of GDP; the costs of basic and applied research are one-third of that cost. The difference between Professor Baumol and myself in this regard is that he sees the redistribution that occurs as *the contribution* of those who have contributed to the new technologies. I see no reason ever to pay the inventors more than their own opportunity cost, which is likely to be an order of magnitude less.

That opportunity cost may even be zero. If Albert Einstein invents the theory of relativity while he travels the streetcar between home and the patent office, simply as his way of avoiding boredom on the tram, there is no need to pay him even a single dime for that activity. As indicated by the history of the Horndal iron works, which had no capital improvements yet increased its productivity year after year, changes in productivity may occur where the opportunity cost of the time used for invention is absolutely zero.

In addition, there are two currencies other than money that induce people to develop new ideas, thus obviating the need for large sums to go to inventors to promote economic efficiency. From others, inventors sometimes get fame; they may obtain the respect of their peers. But perhaps most important of all, from themselves, they obtain self-respect—since the greatest pleasure of having a new idea is the pleasure of having invented it oneself.

In closing, I should say that while I disagree with some of the premises of this paper, it is extraordinarily original and points out something truly important. Whatever we would have had to pay inventors to obtain the ideas that they have passed on to us, the gains have accrued mainly to us, and not to them. In a selfish world, where people claim that the government should not take away what they consider the fruits of their labor or of their saving to redistribute money to the needy, Professor Baumol has shown us that the fruits of that current labor or that current savings are due almost entirely to the cumulative process of learning that has taken us from stone age poverty to twenty-first century affluence. I agree wholeheartedly.

There is no inherent reason not to try to counteract major adverse swings in the income distribution by changing tax policies. I also agree with Professor Baumol: our marginal products are not ours alone. We also owe our current standard of living to the inventor of the fishhook, the discoverer of fire, the first cultivator of the peach, the first trainer of the dog, and an unknowably long list of later inventors, who have given us our current standard of living.

COMMENT BY
Martin Neil Baily

I have followed George Akerlof as a discussant before, so I know he is a hard act to follow. I agree with most of what George said. In particular, I agree that economists have not generally asserted that lump-sum transfers are easy to make and avoid efficiency losses. Certainly Art Okun was well aware of the enormous tradeoff between equality and efficiency. With his typical gift for language, he described the task of transferring resources from rich to poor in terms of using a leaky bucket. Moving water in a leaky bucket inevitably involves some loss of the water along the way, just as transferring funds involves a loss of economic efficiency.

There is much discussion in Art's book, *Equality and Efficiency: The Big Tradeoff,* about how much of a leak society should tolerate while still being willing to make transfers. He poses that issue as a question to the reader: Should society tolerate a 10 percent leak, a 50 percent leak, or a 99 percent leak? [47] As he points out, the John Rawls view is that as long as any water remains in the bucket, one should keep transferring to the worst off in society. Milton Friedman, on the other hand, probably would not want to transfer anything in the bucket because any leak would be too much. Art ventured that he himself would be willing to make transfers, up to the point that there was a leak in income of 60 percent. [48]

The context of Will Baumol's paper is somewhat different, with its focus on technology and spillovers. He points to the substantial variability in wage increases over time and concludes that growth sometimes does and sometimes does not increase wages. That is indeed so. In the agricultural sector, for example, technical progress, combined with demand conditions, has resulted in a dramatic decline in the demand for labor in this industry, thereby holding down the wages of agricultural workers. More recently, there has been a concern about skill-biased technical change that may have reduced the relative wages, and possibly the absolute wages, of low-skilled workers.

Baumol argues that the vast increase in living standards of the broad population that has occurred in the past hundred years or more could not have happened in the absence of technology spillovers. Such spillovers, he argues, are central to the pattern of economic development that has taken

---

47. Okun (1975, pp. 91–92).
48. Okun (1975, p. 94).

place. I am puzzled by that argument because in principle, I can imagine an economy without spillovers where wages keep rising. Suppose there are separate firms and each one makes private decisions to increase its knowledge capital and physical capital. Nobody is looking over the fence at anybody else's activities; nevertheless, the increase in capital would increase the marginal product of labor and the wage. Of course, in order for this process to continue without driving down the return to capital, there would have to be increasing returns. And increasing returns create the same market failure problems that spillovers create. So for Baumol's argument, the distinction perhaps does not matter. Still conceptually, there is a difference between increasing returns and spillovers that is worth making.

My main issue with the paper is to think about the right model of innovation to incorporate in growth models. In the original model by Robert Solow, knowledge capital increases over time exogenously, like manna from heaven.[49] There was no private activity identified in the model that increased the flow of knowledge. Bob Solow attended this conference and can speak for himself, but I always understood the model not to state that technology literally comes out of the sky. Rather, the assumption of exogenous technological change is not only convenient, but also leads to theoretical and empirical results that fit the actual path of economic growth in the United States and other industrial countries quite well. At the outset, the model was consistent with the famous stylized facts of growth. My reading of subsequent literature is that, for advanced countries, it is hard to refute the model; it is hard to find one that works better. In particular, there is mixed evidence on the link between the rate of growth of total factor productivity over time or cross-sectionally and observable measures of innovative activity—at least at the aggregate level.

The simple Solow model does not work to explain why some countries have converged toward U.S. levels of productivity and others have not, and this has been suggested as a fatal objection to it. But whatever weakness or incompleteness of the growth model is revealed by the multicountry studies, it is hard to rectify this with changes in the assumptions about innovation. Institutional and legal framework differences among countries are much more important.

One reason it is hard to link innovative activity and growth is described by Nathan Rosenberg.[50] Reading his work, I am not impressed with the

49. Solow (1956).
50. See, for example, Rosenberg's pieces in Landau and Rosenberg (1986).

idea that there is a direct connection between the amount of innovative activity and the actual flow of major innovations. He describes the innovation process as serendipitous, and he points out that a lot of innovations initially have little economic value. It is only when other innovations have taken place that economic value is revealed. Lasers are an example. Computers, initially, were thought to have a very minor consequence on the economy. One recalls the famous estimate by Thomas Watson, IBM's original head, of how few computers would be needed in the U.S. economy.

The most frequently used measure of innovative effort is R&D, but most of what is done under this heading is development. The innovating company knows pretty much what is going to come out of the process, and it is a matter of taking existing knowledge and putting it into a form that will generate a return in the market. While there are spillovers from R&D, any company that wanted to copy or imitate the resulting new products or processes would have to go through the same development and testing process as the original innovator. In the development of new drugs, for example, any new chemical must go through clinical trials, where much of the development expense occurs.

Another reason it is difficult to link innovative activity to growth is that it is hard to identify and measure innovative activity. A lot of innovation is not technological in nature at all. It can be described as soft innovation: business system redesign, development of new lines of business, or development of new formats within an existing industry. Soft innovation is often linked to hard innovation—for example, the application of IT—but it does not follow automatically from it. When productivity levels across countries are compared, the big differences in performance rarely reflect differential access to hard technology. Instead, they reflect differences in industry structure, workplace organization, and the way hard technology is used.

George Akerlof made a point about the Baumol paper that I would like to amplify. Does the existence of spillovers mean that there is more or less innovation than would occur if there were no spillovers? Suppose the big disincentive to innovation is that other companies will copy one's ideas. If that were the case, I would expect innovation to take place in isolated locations, away from prying eyes. An ambitious young academic, according to this argument, would locate at Walden Pond or some place away from potential idea-thieves. In practice this is not what happens. People choose to agglomerate with other people making innovations. Even though they are contributing their own externalities to the people around them, they are also the recipients of externalities from others. The most attractive places to locate R&D or a start-up company are in spots like Silicon Valley or Austin, Texas, or New York City, for those in the financial industry.

Given the difficulties in determining the right innovation model, what is the right technology policy? In the areas where the spillover is greatest and there is very little private return, direct support for science and pre-commercial technology is warranted. That is something that the United States has done for a long time, and it seems entirely correct. The private sector does get some technology free; it comes from universities and sponsored research. How much money to give to these activities is always a lively part of the budget debate. I have always favored increases in the science budget. However, for the reasons given earlier, one cannot do marginal analysis and find a real optimum.

To address the spillover from commercial R&D, a tax credit can be used. In addition, R&D receives favorable tax treatment because it is expensed. The empirical evidence of spillovers in this area is very strong, and I also support these tax incentives.

The issue Will Baumol raises about the tradeoff between technology and wages is a very timely one. The distribution of wages and family incomes started to widen in the 1970s and widened dramatically during the 1980s. This widening has been associated with several factors, but the most important, as I noted earlier, is said to be skill-biased technical change. Over this period, there was an odd combination of very slow total factor productivity growth, presumably slow technical change, and yet dramatic shifts in the distribution of income as a result. The distributional issue raised by Baumol is starkly posed in this situation. When technical change was apparently generating rather little productivity growth to begin with, should there be a major effort at redistribution that would potentially worsen the already-weak productivity performance?

The lesson of the 1990s is much more encouraging. First, efforts to help workers at the bottom have made a difference, particularly the earned income tax credit (EITC), which has not only helped on the distributional side, but has also encouraged people to work. Increases in the minimum wage are often not economists' favorite policy, but they do seem to have positive distributional effects and they certainly do not seem to have discouraged employment growth in this decade.

Most important, though, is that since 1995 there has been an acceleration of productivity growth that has allowed the United States to operate a high-pressure economy. Openness to trade and investment has also helped hold down inflation. And in a high-pressure economy workers at the bottom of the skill ladder are able to move up. Since 1994 there has been a very different distributional pattern, with low-wage workers receiving wage increases comparable to those of high-wage workers. Household income growth also looks much more even, with comparable increases for all quintiles.

It is dangerous to extrapolate too far from a short span of data in the 1990s, but adding the experience of the 1990s to that of the 1950s and 1960s, one can make the case that rapid technical change and productivity growth in an economy with low average unemployment does not cause adverse distributional effects. When Baumol assesses the tradeoff between technology and spillovers, it is important to remember that rapid technical change also facilitates a high-pressure economy.

The wage and income numbers I just described do not include the impact of the large increases in the stock market. This economy is generating huge wealth for a small group of successful technology entrepreneurs. Is this inequality something to accept as part of the package of efficiency and technology gains in a dynamic economy?

High returns are necessary to encourage risk-taking. I have little patience with those who want to penalize success just for the sake of it. On the other hand, there are proposals around to eliminate the capital gains tax or to repeal the estate tax or to reduce sharply the top marginal tax brackets. Given the explosion of innovation and risk-taking occurring in the United States today, and the crazy hours being worked by very talented individuals, it is hard to see that these taxes are currently discouraging innovation and work effort.

References

Baumol, William J. 1993. *Entrepreneurship, Management and the Structure of Payoffs.* MIT Press.

Braudel, Fernand. 1979. *Civilization and Capitalism, 15th to 18th Century,* vol. 1. Harper and Row.

de Meeüs, Adrien. 1962. *History of the Belgians.* Praeger.

Fair, Ray. 1971. "The Optimal Distribution of Income." *Quarterly Journal of Economics* 85 (November): 557–79.

Feldstein, Martin S. 1978. "The Welfare Cost of Capital Gains Taxation." *Journal of Political Economy* 86 (April, part 2): S29–S51.

Federal Reserve Bank of Dallas. 1997. *1997 Annual Report. Time Well Spent: The Declining Real Cost of Living in America.* Dallas, Tex.

Fogel, Robert W. 1986. "Nutrition and the Decline of Mortality since 1700: Some Preliminary Findings." In *Long-Term Factors in American Economic Growth,* edited by Stanley L. Engerman and Robert E. Gallman. University of Chicago Press.

Goldin, Claudia, and Lawrence F. Katz. 1999. "The Returns to Skill in the United States across the Twentieth Century." Working Paper 7126. Cambridge, Mass.: National Bureau of Economic Research (May).

Gomory, Ralph E., and William J. Baumol. 1998. "A Country's Maximal Gains from Trade and Conflicting National Interests." C. V. Starr Center for Applied Economics, Research Report 98–22, New York University (June).

Grilliches, Zvi. 1979. "Issues in Assessing the Contribution of Research and Development to Productivity Growth." *Bell Journal of Economics* 10 (Spring): 92–116.

Landau, Ralph, and Nathan Rosenberg, eds. 1986. *The Positive Sum Strategy: Harnessing Technology for Economic Growth.* Washington: National Academy Press.

Lebergott, Stanley. 1984. *The Americans: An Economic Record.* W. W. Norton and Company.

Maddison, Angus. 1995. *Monitoring the World Economy, 1820–1992.* Paris: Organization for Economic Cooperation and Development.

Margo, Robert A. 1999. "The History of Wage Inequality in America 1820 to 1970." Working Paper 286. Annandale-on-Hudson, N.Y.: Jerome Levy Economics Institute of Bard College (August).

Mirrlees, James A. 1971. "An Exploration in the Theory of Optimum Income." *Review of Economic Studies* 38 (April): 175–208.

Mohnen, Pierre. 1992. *The Relationship between R&D and Productivity Growth in Canada and Other Industrialized Countries.* Ottawa: Canada Communications Group.

Nadiri, M. Ishaq. 1991. "Innovations and Technological Spillovers." New York University.

National Science Board. 1996. *Science and Engineering Indicators, 1996.* U.S. Government Printing Office.

Nelson, Richard R. 1996. *The Sources of Economic Growth.* Harvard University Press.

Nordhaus, William D. 1969. *Invention, Growth and Welfare: A Theoretical Treatment of Technological Change.* MIT Press.

Okun, Arthur M. 1975. *Equality and Efficiency: The Big Tradeoff.* Brookings.

Palmer, Robert R. 1964. *The Age of Democratic Revolution: A Political History of Europe and America, 1760–1800*, vol. 2. Princeton University Press.

Phelps Brown, E. H., and Sheila V. Hopkins. 1956. "Seven Centuries of the Prices of Consumables, Compared with Builders' Wage-Rates." *Economica* 23 (November): 296–314.

Romer, Paul. 1994. "New Goods, Old Theory and the Welfare Costs of Trade Restrictions." *Journal of Development Economics* 43 (February): 5–38.

Rosenberg, Nathan, and L. E Birdzell Jr. 1986. *How the West Grew Rich: The Economic Transformation of the Industrial World.* Basic Books.

Scherer, Frederic M. 1965. "Firm Size, Market Structure, Opportunity and the Output of Patented Inventions." *American Economic Review* 55 (December): 1097–125.

Solow, Robert M. 1956. "A Contribution to the Theory of Economic Growth." *Quarterly Journal of Economics* 70 (February): 65–94.

———. 1957. "Technical Change and the Aggregate Production Function." *Review of Economics and Statistics* 39 (August): 312–20.

Tobin, James. 1970. "On Limiting the Domain of Inequality." *Journal of Law and Economics* 13 (October): 263–77.

U.S. Bureau of the Census. 1975. *Historical Statistics of the United States, Colonial Times to 1970*, Part I. Government Printing Office.

———. 1997. *Statistical Abstract of the United States, 1997*, 117th ed. Government Printing Office.

Williamson, Jeffrey G., and Peter H. Lindert. 1980. *American Inequality: A Macroeconomic History.* Academic Press.

Wolff, Edward N. 1997. "Spillovers, Linkages and Technical Change." *Economic Systems Research* 9 (March): 9–23.

Wright, Constance. 1965. *A Royal Affinity.* Charles Scribner's Sons.

WILLIAM C. BRAINARD
GEORGE L. PERRY

2

Making Policy in a Changing World

The era that is the subject of this conference begins and ends with decades of outstanding U.S. economic performance. In both the 1960s and 1990s, the economy surpassed what seemed achievable in light of what had come before. The long expansion of the 1960s was preceded by an era of frequent recessions and, before that, the Great Depression that ended only with World War II. It ended with a rise in inflation that accompanied the Vietnam War. That inflation was exacerbated by the supply shocks of the 1970s and was finally subdued by historically high interest rates and the massive recessions that they brought on at the start of the 1980s. The subsequent recovery and expansion lasted seven years, but business capital formation and productivity growth remained slow by historical standards and estimates of attainable unemployment rates drifted higher. The expansion of the 1990s thus began with inflation under control but with disappointing prospects for how fast the economy could grow and how far unemployment could be reduced.

The widely varying performance of the economy during different periods over the the past fifty years reflects a combination of special shocks, possible changes in macroeconomic relations confronting policymakers, and differing policy reactions. However, many econometricians have char-

We are grateful to Kathey Bucholz and Peter Kimball for their assistance in the preparation of this paper.

acterized the entire period as one in which stable parameters relate the twin policy concerns of inflation and unemployment. In this paper, we describe why conventional analysis overstates the stability of this relation and identify ways in which it has changed. We attempt to characterize those changes, examine how policymakers were reacting, and provide some general observations on making policy when key relations vary.

An Episodic Overview

The combination of growth, unemployment, and price stability achieved in the closing years of the century has been remarkable. Beginning from what was widely judged to be a mature stage of recovery from the early 1990s recession, the economy re-accelerated after mid-1995 and expanded at a 4 percent annual rate over the rest of the decade. This strong growth in output reduced unemployment to 4 percent and was accompanied by sustained low rates of core inflation. However one explains this economic performance, the willingness of the Federal Reserve, under the leadership of Alan Greenspan, to let the unemployment rate decline below 6 percent—which many observers had regarded as the lowest rate that would not lead to accelerating inflation—was critical to its achievement. The performance of the past few years has forced a reevaluation of the macroeconomic model that led to these predictions. It has required a reestimation of its parameters and has renewed doubts about the model as a description of the inflationary process.

This is hardly the first reevaluation driven by events. The unemployment rate had last gotten down to 4 percent during the 1960s, the decade that most closely rivals the 1990s for sustained economic growth and widespread prosperity. At that time, based on Arthur Okun's analysis of the postwar economy, an unemployment rate of roughly 4 percent had been estimated as the full employment target for policymakers.[1] The postwar period had been marked by frequent recessions, and avoiding them through active stabilization policy that targeted full employment was a principal goal of the incoming Kennedy administration. When, in the last years of that decade, the Vietnam War took precedence over stabilization policy, unemployment was pushed well below that target and inflation

---

1. See, for example, Arthur Okun's introduction to Okun (1972).

gradually rose. Furthermore, analysis of the changing demographics of the U.S. labor market showed that the full-employment unemployment rate had risen by the end of the decade and would rise further in the 1970s.[2]

With that amendment, the developments of the 1960s were roughly consistent with the predictions of the cyclical Phillips curve that had been estimated from postwar experience. Nonetheless, the resurgence in the classical concept of a natural unemployment rate that came from the Friedman and Phelps models and the emergence of the theory of rational expectations in the inflationary 1970s led to substantial changes in empirical modeling and in the focus of policymakers.[3] Franco Modigliani and Lucas Papademos introduced the concept of the nonaccelerating inflation rate of unemployment, or NAIRU, which used adaptive expectations to modify the short-run Phillips curve in a way that gave it some features of the natural rate model.[4] Robert Gordon and others have elaborated on this concept and provided estimates showing a relatively constant NAIRU throughout most of the postwar period.[5]

Skeptics have come from many quarters. Ray Fair and others disputed the accelerationist specification, finding the key elasticity between current and past inflation was less than one.[6] Others questioned the validity of modeling expectations as adaptive. Many noted that the failure to observe ever-faster deflation when unemployment was persistently high cast doubt on both the theoretical natural rate models and the empirical NAIRU model, as has the evidence that wages rarely decline.[7] And some objected to the idea of modeling inflation with a modified Phillips curve framework at all, stressing the fact that it is not a structural relationship but a relationship among endogenous variables, with a host of difficulties of identification and interpretation.

Despite these misgivings, the NAIRU model has continued to play a central role in policy discussions. Unemployment and inflation are central concerns of stabilization policy, and few deny that upward pressures on wages and prices are likely to occur as the economy approaches the limits of capacity. Policy discussions need a simple organizing framework incor-

---

2. See Perry (1970).
3. Friedman (1968); Phelps (1968).
4. Modigliani and Papademos (1975).
5. See, for example, Gordon (1998).
6. See, for example, Fair (2000).
7. See, for example, Akerlof, Dickens, and Perry (1996).

porating that idea, and the NAIRU model has filled that need. And until the last few years, such a model could explain U.S. experience starting with the 1970s reasonably well, once it allowed for exogenous price shocks and for some limited variation in the NAIRU.

In this paper, we examine the conduct of policy over the past four decades in light of what was known at the time about the inflation-unemployment relation and without assuming the confines of a NAIRU framework. We also provide empirical evidence of important changes in that relation and discuss how policymakers can best respond to the uncertainty inherent in such changes. Our evidence indicates that, during periods of low inflation, conventional estimates using the NAIRU framework do not provide reliable guidance for policymakers about how low an unemployment rate is sustainable.

Data and Decisionmaking

Policymakers and econometricians must always grapple with how much weight to attach to recent developments relative to historical regularities. It is our casual observation that good policymakers implicitly give more weight to recent developments than do most econometricians, though that assessment may be unduly influenced by the Federal Reserve's recent success. Statistical theory provides precise answers about confidence intervals, but only under strong assumptions about underlying processes. The believers in a model that has fit historically are likely to stick to their beliefs until the data speak clearly. Economists trained in classical statistics are accustomed to requiring odds of twenty to one against before rejecting their null hypothesis. In practice, the ruling paradigm itself becomes the null, and it is common to accept the parameters of a model as constant until a change in a parameter is statistically significant, with a t-statistic of two. But twenty to one are long odds for a policymaker, for whom the costs of following the model when it is wrong can be significant.

A formal Bayesian decision theoretic approach would avoid this difficulty by treating the parameters of the model as stochastic and using a loss function in the estimation process. In our analysis we do not model formal Bayesian decisionmaking, but we do explicitly allow for stochastic drift in crucial parameters. This allows us to illustrate the role that parameter uncertainty can play in both model-based and judgmental policymaking.

What We Knew and When

To illustrate the uncertainties that confront the policymaker, we examine the inflation-unemployment relation over the past forty years. Although focusing on this simple model is open to many objections, we believe it is a good framework within which to explore the central problem confronting policymakers. We want to allow for the possibility that this relation has changed over time and that policymakers have had to contend with signs of such change. We report three sets of estimates for the central parameters of price and wage equations. The first set is simply the time series of estimates from recursive least squares. While these estimates change as the sample of observations grows, by hypothesis the true parameters are constant—the same over all samples of different lengths. In practice, when the residuals become large or the coefficient estimates change markedly over a sample, it is common to test for a structural break. The implicit assumption built into this type of structural test is that change takes place at specific points in time rather than gradually. While this assumption may be appropriate for such events as changes in exchange rate regimes or dramatic monetary reforms, it seems quite implausible to us that changes in the wage and price processes and in their relationship to the labor market and unemployment shift in such a discontinuous and infrequent way. Rather, it seems more likely that changes would be spread over time and, within the framework of our model, better represented as stochastic drifts in the coefficients.

This leads us to estimate the wage and price relationships with a time-varying parameters model, making use of Kalman filters. Specifically we allow the intercept, the coefficient on current unemployment, and the sum of coefficients on past inflation (and, in the price equation, the coefficient on productivity) to vary over time. Each is allowed to follow a random walk, with a variance chosen to minimize forecast error in a manner described below. Allowing for time variation in this set of parameters is likely to change the estimates of other parameters in the model as well, even though these other parameters are assumed to be constant. While the assumption of a random walk cannot be literally true over long periods, we want to avoid the assumption that the parameters tend to return to some constant mean that would be implicit in assuming a stationary autoregressive process for the parameters. As will be seen, relatively small amounts of period-by-period variation in the coefficients are all that is needed to produce substantial movements in point estimates over five- or ten-year intervals.

The Kalman filter methodology provides two sets of estimates for the time-varying relationship. The first, which we call the contemporary filter estimates, are parameter estimates for each date that use only data available up to that date, just as the recursive least squares estimates do. Since we start the recursive least squares and time-varying estimates with the same initial values, these two sets of estimates are quite similar for a number of periods, diverging only after several years. By the end of the entire sample, however, they can be quite different. Recursive least squares and contemporary filter estimates are both available in real time to a policymaker.

The second set of time-varying parameter estimates, which we call backward estimates, take a historical view, using all of the data available up to the present. With the hindsight provided by the backward filter estimates, it is possible in some cases to see why the policymaker, not having the historian's advantage, may have gone wrong.

Estimating with Filters

For the reader unfamiliar with Kalman filters, it may be useful to give an informal explanation of how they work in our setting. In the contemporary estimation, the filter calculates the forecast error for the current period making use of the estimate of the coefficients from the previous period along with the current value of exogenous variables. By assumption, this forecast error is the sum of two errors: the "measurement" error in the equation relating the dependent variable—in our case, wages or prices—to the exogenous variables; and the error implied by using last period's estimates rather than the true coefficients for this period. In contemporary filter estimation, as in recursive least squares, there is estimation error in last period's estimates of last period's true coefficients. With time-varying coefficients there is an additional error arising from the innovations in the coefficients themselves. The contribution of these coefficient errors to the forecast error depends on the values of the corresponding exogenous variable. If the variable is "large," it contributes more to the forecast error than if it is small.[8] The optimal allocation of the observed forecast error

8. This statement assumes that the covariances of coefficients across variables is zero. In general, the contribution depends on the entire variance-covariance matrix and the values of the other variables.

between measurement error and revised coefficient estimates depends on the relative variances and covariances of the coefficients, the values of the variables, and the variance of the measurement error. The filter does this optimization, updating the estimates of the coefficients and of the variances themselves. If the variances are normal, the updating is maximum likelihood. In our estimation we assume that the measurement error and innovations to the coefficients are independent.

At the end of the sample period, the contemporary estimates have utilized all of the information in the observed data, but the parameter estimates for earlier periods can be improved by utilizing the information that arrived later in the sample. The backward filter revises the contemporary estimates, starting at the end of the period and working backward. For each time period, t, the backward estimates are calculated by adjusting the contemporary estimates for t by a fraction of the difference between those estimates and the backward estimates for $t + 1$, both of which give unbiased estimates of the true parameters at time t. The weights depend on the relative variances of these two. Backward estimates are sometimes called "smoothed" estimates since, in the scalar case, fluctuations in the contemporary estimates will be dampened by this procedure.

Starting the Kaman filter requires initial estimates of the coefficients, the covariances of the coefficients, the covariances of the parameter innovations, and the measurement variance. If one is following a Bayesian approach, these are simply the priors one brings to the data. In practice, a variety of methods are used to choose these priors. In our case, we used the variance-covariance matrix from a least squares regression for the period 1948:1 to 1959:4 to provide the initial values for the coefficients' covariances. However, we used the point estimates from equations with fewer lags, setting the priors at zero for the omitted variables. Rather than specify a priori the magnitude of the variances of the innovations to the coefficients, we used a search procedure to find the magnitudes that minimized the mean squared forecast error over the entire sample, under the assumption that coefficient innovations are independent. The search procedure always started with zero values for the innovation variances, which would make the estimates the same as the recursive estimates. While choosing innovation variances by looking at the likelihood of the entire sample is appropriate for the historian, the use of these estimates in the contemporary filtering incorporates more information than would be available to a policymaker in real time.

Estimating the Productivity Trend

The trend rate of productivity change is potentially an important variable both for explaining price and wage developments and for informing policy deliberations. A faster rising productivity trend would permit faster real growth in the longer run and would make any target rate of price inflation consistent with faster wage growth. However, inferring the trend from actual productivity data is tricky. Quarterly changes in productivity are subject both to considerable measurement error and to systematic variation associated with cyclical and shorter-term fluctuations in the rate of economic expansion. Most attempts to estimate the trend in productivity from these data have fit trends across cyclical peaks, or regressed quarterly changes on cyclical variables and dummy variables to allow for changes in the trend where the data seemed to call for it. But the productivity trend is more likely to change gradually as innovations diffuse over different firms and parts of the economy.

To address this problem, we apply our time-varying methodology. We take as our estimate of the time-varying productivity trend the backward filter estimates from an equation explaining the quarterly change in the log of productivity with a time-varying constant and the change in the unemployment rate in the current and seven lagged quarters.

$$(1) \qquad \Delta \ln(PR_t) = A_t + \Sigma a_i \Delta U_{it} + u_t,$$

where $A_t = A_{t-1} + e_t$, and u_t and e_t are i.i.d.

The productivity data are for the private nonfarm economy. For the period since the end of 1995, we adjusted these data to eliminate the part of the productivity change that came from changes in the measurement of prices.[9]

Figure 2-1 compares the changing trend from contemporary and backward filter estimates of equation 1 and the trends recently estimated by Gordon.[10] The recursive trends become less meaningful in the last half of the period since, by then, the slowdown in productivity growth was widely recognized and nobody would have run a regression that assumed a constant trend. But little variation was apparent before that. In 1960, with the short postwar data period then available, Okun had treated trend productivity as a constant when he estimated Okun's law and the economy's potential growth path. A roughly constant trend was still generally

9. As in Gordon (1999).
10. Gordon (1999).

accepted through the mid-1970s. Recursive regressions, not shown in the figure, reveal that except for a few quarters, the constant trend that would have been estimated at any time between 1962 and 1977 from an ordinary least squares regression would have ranged only between 2.65 and 2.75 percent a year.

Our point here is that standard research techniques were slow to detect the change in the trend. This reflected researchers' knowledge of two things: First, a constant trend had been a good approximation for a long time, making it a natural prior that would require strong evidence to reject. Second, observed productivity varies substantially around the trend, and allowing for this makes it difficult to detect whether the trend has changed, especially around a recession.[11]

Our backward Kalman filter (BKF) regression allows for cyclical departures of productivity from its trend but looks for drift in the trend at all times. BKF estimates in figure 2-1 show the trend ranging even more widely than Gordon's latest estimates using discrete trend breaks. More important, it shows a gradual and persistent slowdown in productivity growth between the mid-1960s and 1980. And it shows the trend during 1998, the last period in the estimation sample, rising 0.4 percentage point faster than Gordon's estimates. We make use of this productivity series in the inflation-unemployment model that we turn to next. To relate this series to currently published data, some adjustments are needed. First, adding back the effect of changes in price measurement that were introduced over the past several years would add 0.4 percentage point to 1998 trend productivity growth. Second, the revisions to the GDP accounts announced in late October 1999 add 0.5 percentage point to productivity growth during 1998, and some of this would have been added to a trend estimated with the new data. Finally, productivity growth continued to accelerate during 1999 and would lead to a higher estimate of the trend if that year were now included in estimation.

The Inflation Model and Data

We specify empirical models for wage change and price change to encompass in a parsimonious way the empirical work used by many policymak-

11. One of the present authors, writing in early 1977, found evidence of a productivity slowdown ambiguous even at that late date. If he could expunge one of his professional papers from the record, it would be this one. See Perry (1977).

Figure 2-1. *Three Estimates of the Productivity Trend, 1960–98*[a]

Percent

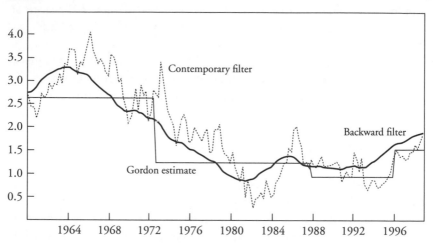

Source: Authors' estimates as described in text and Gordon (1999).
a. The authors' two filter series use sigma = 0.006.

ers and analysts since the 1960s. A highly elaborated model could fit the data somewhat better but is unlikely to affect our main points. Although current models frequently explain price rather than wage change, a wage equation would have been typical in the 1960s and we show both. Wage change can be connected to price inflation through the usual expedient of relating prices and trend unit labor costs. Our price and wage equations have the form

$$(2)\ \Delta\ln(X_t) = B_t + \Sigma b_{1it}1/U_{it} + \Sigma b_{2it}\Delta\ln(P_{it}) + b_{3t}\Delta\ln(PR_t) + \text{dummies} + u_t,$$

where now the time-varying coefficients are each of the form $Z_t = Z_{t-1} + e_t$, where u_t and e_t are i.i.d, as in equation (1). X is either wages (defined below) or the consumer price index (CPI). We allow time variation in the intercept in the coefficient on current unemployment, and in the sum of coefficients in past inflation (and, in the price equations, in the coefficient on productivity). We also tried the CPI less food and fuel as a left-hand variable, but the results were much the same as with the CPI and are not shown. U is the unemployment rate for males aged 25 to 54 (to avoid effects of demographic changes); P is the CPI; and PR, which does not appear in the wage equation, is the trend in labor productivity in the nonfarm business sector. Although it has become popular to use the change in trend unit labor costs—change in wages less the productivity trend—as the left-hand variable in a wage equation, in our estimation the productivity trend as an explanatory variable was insignificant. Dummy variables are used for the period of Korean War controls, the years when wage and price guideposts were actively used in the 1960s, and the years in the 1970s when Nixon price controls were put on and taken off. The CPI term has eight lags, starting with $(t - 1)$ and the unemployment term uses the current and three lagged quarters. No continuous series for hourly wage costs is available, so we spliced three series that were: from 1980 to the present, the Employment Cost Index for wages and salaries; from 1961 to 1980, straight time hourly earnings for the private non-farm economy; and from 1948 to 1961, the hourly earnings index for manufacturing. For this early period, we do not know how similar the quarterly patterns were for manufacturing and the broader economy, but their total increases over the fourteen-year period were nearly the same: 91 percent and 89 percent, respectively.

Tables 2-1 and 2-2 summarize the parameters for the wage and price equations, in each case estimated with our three alternative techniques. The summary statistics in the tables show the considerable improvements in fit as we move across estimates. For wages, going from recursive to BKF estimation improves the root mean-squared error (RMSE) from 1.06 to 0.76, while the Durbin-Watson (DW) proxy statistic goes from 1.07 to 1.88. For the CPI, the corresponding forecast errors go from 1.53 to 1.23 and the DWs go from 1.81 to 2.12. It should be noted that these DW proxies are calculated for the forecast errors and so are not the same as usually reported for least squares regressions. Estimates for the key parameters are shown at five-year intervals starting in 1965.

Figures 2-2 and 2-3 plot the parameters continuously. The period from 1948 through 1959 was used to provide startup values for the Kalman filter regressions, and estimates for the years immediately following this period were highly volatile in both the wage and price equations, with large and offsetting variations in some parameters. Because the general story that emerges is much the same looking at either wages or prices, we will concentrate our discussion on the CPI equation.

Up until the late 1970s, the recursive and contemporary Kalman filter (CKF) estimates for all the parameters track each other pretty closely, with both sets of estimates varying markedly over time. Both estimates would have looked very different in 1975 than they had in 1965. After 1975 the

Table 2-1. *Characteristics of Wage Equations, 1965–98*

Regression type and date[a]	Coefficient			U rate for low inflation[b]
	Lagged prices	Unemployment	Intercept	
Recursive				
1965	0.45	10.53	0.00	2.5
1970	0.44	6.25	1.14	2.7
1975	0.53	5.74	1.19	4.0
1980	0.60	4.84	1.38	13.3
1985	0.57	5.00	1.40	6.1
1990	0.58	5.71	1.05	6.2
1995	0.59	6.64	0.63	4.0
1998	0.60	6.76	0.55	3.2
Summary statistic[c]				
RMSE 1.057[d]				
DW proxy 1.069[d]				
Contemporary filters				
1965	0.39	10.45	0.01	2.4
1970	0.22	8.66	0.41	2.5
1975	0.51	6.41	0.88	3.7
1980	0.58	5.68	1.17	9.2
1985	0.52	5.52	1.32	5.6
1990	0.40	5.53	1.15	4.7
1995	0.29	5.69	0.99	3.0
1998	0.32	5.84	1.06	2.7
Summary statistic				
RMSE 0.941				
DW proxy 1.479				
Backward filters				
1965	0.37	5.84	1.02	1.7
1970	0.49	5.83	1.06	2.5
1975	0.54	5.84	1.10	4.0
1980	0.57	5.84	1.12	8.5
1985	0.50	5.84	1.10	4.6
1990	0.37	5.83	1.06	4.3
1995	0.29	5.83	1.04	3.2
1998	0.32	5.84	1.06	2.7
Summary statistic				
RMSE 0.763				
DW proxy 1.881				

Source: Equations for 1960–98 as described in text.

a. First quarter of year shown, except 1998 is fourth quarter.

b. Unemployment rate for males aged 25–54 associated with 2 percent inflation rate.

c. RMSE is the root mean-squared error. DW is the Durbin-Watson statistic.

d. For recursive regressions, these are for the 1960–98 estimation period.

Table 2-2. *Characteristics of Price Equations, 1965–98*[a]

Regression type and date[a]	Coefficient			
	Lagged prices	Unemployment	Productivity	Intercept
Recursive				
1965	0.52	6.77	–0.10	–1.04
1970	0.55	5.71	–0.32	–0.24
1975	0.75	4.12	–0.54	0.57
1980	0.77	3.12	–1.22	2.60
1985	0.72	3.94	–1.11	2.17
1990	0.75	4.17	–0.96	1.63
1995	0.77	4.39	–0.84	1.18
1998	0.79	4.31	–0.79	1.00
Summary statistic[b]				
RMSE 1.526[c]				
DW proxy 1.808[c]				
Contemporary filters				
1965	0.48	6.89	–0.05	–1.22
1970	0.56	5.93	–0.25	–0.46
1975	0.73	4.76	–0.42	0.32
1980	0.94	4.26	–0.71	1.34
1985	0.60	4.29	–0.94	2.05
1990	0.55	4.34	–1.01	2.19
1995	0.46	4.50	–1.02	2.10
1998	0.41	4.26	–1.11	2.16
Summary statistic				
RMSE 1.470				
DW proxy 2.060				
Backward filters				
1965	0.58	4.28	–1.05	2.20
1970	0.67	4.27	–1.08	2.19
1975	0.71	4.27	–1.07	2.20
1980	0.80	4.28	–1.03	2.23
1985	0.55	4.28	–1.05	2.21
1990	0.52	4.27	–1.06	2.20
1995	0.44	4.27	–1.09	2.18
1998	0.41	4.26	–1.11	2.16
Summary statistic				
RMSE 1.228				
DW proxy 2.115				

Source: Equations for 1960–98 as described in text.

a. First quarter of year shown, except 1998 is fourth quarter.

b. RMSE is the root mean-squared error. DW is the Durbin-Watson statistic.

c. For recursive regressions, these are for the 1960–98 estimation period.

Figure 2-2. *Wage Equation Parameters from Recursive and Time-varying Filter Estimates, 1960–98*

Intercept

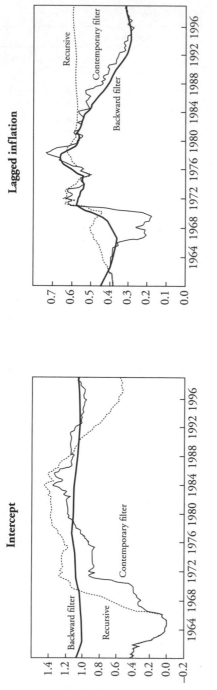

Lagged inflation

Inverse unemployment

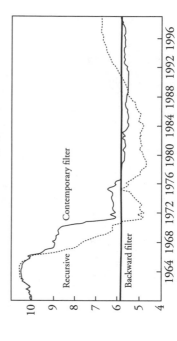

Source: Authors' calculations from regressions in table 2-1.

Figure 2-3. *CPI Equation Parameters from Recursive and Time-varying Filter Estimates, 1960–98*

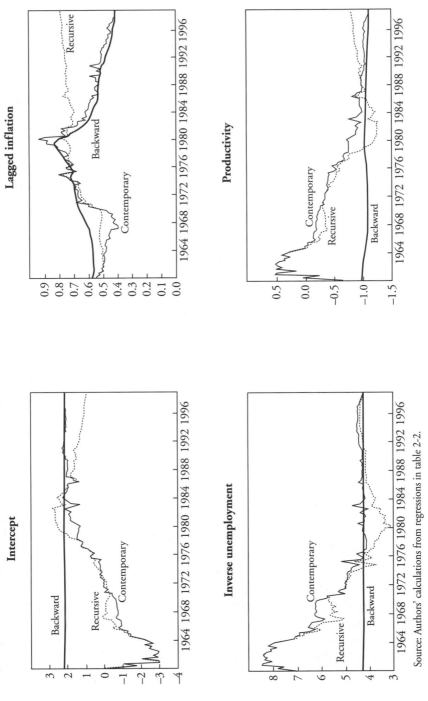

Source: Authors' calculations from regressions in table 2-2.

two estimators diverge noticeably, particularly in estimating the effect of lagged inflation. Recursive estimates of lagged price effects rise slowly right up to the present, while CKF estimates peak in the late 1970s and then decline to near their lowest level at present. Only the recursive estimates come close to satisfying the NAIRU assumption of this key parameter, and those estimates seem to be dominated in the data by the high inflation years of the 1970s.

The BKF regressions provide our best estimates of the relation at all past dates from the vantage point of 1999, and the results are striking. Almost no time variation is allocated to coefficients other than lagged inflation. The estimates for the parameters other than lagged inflation are, perhaps surprisingly, stable throughout the past forty years. By contrast, the effect of lagged inflation is moderate at the start, rises even above the OLS estimate by 1980, and then declines to its lowest level at present. According to these estimates, there is little inflation persistence today, and there was only moderate persistence in the early 1960s. But there was great inflation persistence by the end of the high inflation decade of the 1970s. At that time, the relation was nearly accelerationist, approximating the NAIRU model.

The characterization of parameter changes in the early part of the sample is broadly the same if we stop the analysis a decade or two sooner. Figure 2-4 compares the BKF estimates from the wage regression, which ran through 1998, with estimates running through 1990 and 1980. The parameters are multiplied by the respective variable means to make their impact on inflation comparable. The great variability in the role of lagged inflation and the relative constancy of the other three parameters is apparent in all three.

What Does it Mean?

The BKF results support both the strategy of focusing on the unemployment-inflation relation and the importance of parameter instability. The near constant estimates for the unemployment and productivity parameters and the intercept suggest that labor market tightness or ease and the notion of a full employment range are useful concepts, reasonably proxied by a broad measure of unemployment clean of demographic distortions. A nonlinear relation between unemployment and cyclical inflation identifies a region of resource utilization where additional tightening

Figure 2-4. *Backward Filter Estimates of Wage Equation Parameters, Alternative Estimation Endpoints, Calibrated for Impact on Wage Inflation, 1960–98*[a]

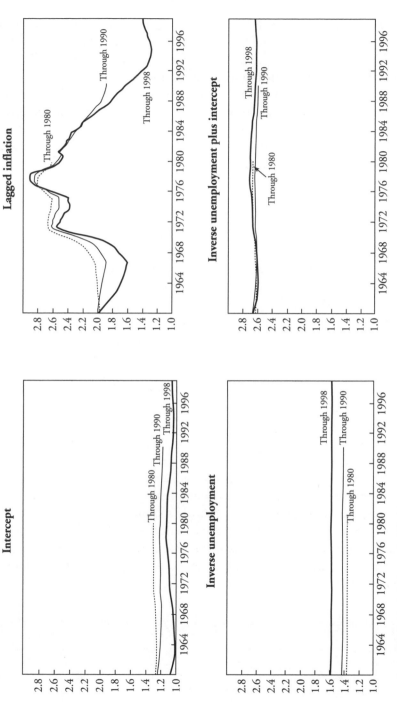

Intercept

Lagged inflation

Inverse unemployment

Inverse unemployment plus intercept

Source: Authors' calculations as described in text.
a. Calibrated by multiplying variable means by their time-varying parameter from backward filter estimates.

is accompanied by increases in inflation rates. In both the beginning and the end of the period, when inflation rates were low, the feedback of past inflation on wages and prices seems far from complete. This much resembles the macroeconomic modeling of the 1960s.

The full dynamic of the inflationary process is not so well established. As characterized by the sum of the coefficients on lagged inflation, it has varied markedly during the four decades we analyze. It appears that as experienced inflation rose in the late 1960s and then continued high, so did the impact of past inflation on present inflation. This is consistent with the view that expectations and institutions adapt to the actual inflation experienced. It is plausible that with sustained high rates of inflation the feedback of inflation to wages would be complete and the estimated sum of coefficients would equal one. It is also plausible that in a regime of low inflation, even if it were sustained, the feedback would not be complete. Such a pattern could be an endogenous response of wage and price setters to inflation itself that would be consistent with Alan Greenspan's identification of low inflation as a period in which people do not think about inflation.[12] However, there is only one episode on which to observe this parameter shifting and so little basis to confirm any particular mechanisms at work. Furthermore, as Thomas Sargent has emphasized, rational expectations does not imply that the sum of estimated coefficients on lagged inflation need be one.[13] For example, in rational expectations models, if agents expect the Federal Reserve to reduce inflation, the sum would be less than 1.0, and if they expect inflation to accelerate, it would exceed 1.0. In a forthcoming paper, George Akerlof, William Dickens, and George Perry examine the kind of endogenous response of price and wage setting we have sketched out here and address the Sargent critique by using data on price expectations to complement their results with lagged inflation.[14]

Our estimates approximate a NAIRU specification only during the most inflationary part of the four-decade period we examined. However, the unemployment rates associated with maintaining low inflation can be calculated for any point in time. These are shown in the last column of table 1. (We provide these estimates only for the wage equation since the

---

12. In his statement of January 24, 1989, before the House Committee on Banking, Finance, and Urban Affairs, Greenspan stated that the Fed's strategy was to reach "price levels sufficiently stable so that expectations of change do not become major factors in key economic decisions." See Greenspan (1989, p. 141).

13. Sargent (1971).

14. See Akerlof, Dickens, and Perry (forthcoming).

point estimates from the price equation were extremely high and volatile in the 1970s.) These estimates do not describe what would have happened if outcomes had differed from the historical ones because we suspect that parameter changes reflect in some complicated way experienced inflation. Nor do they describe what unemployment rates would have been required indefinitely to maintain low inflation, since the parameters would have been expected to change under those circumstances—as, in fact, they did. The estimates are a simple way to characterize the changing situation that policymakers confronted—a situation that is not easily inferred from individual parameters. For both wage and price regressions they show the much greater sensitivity to inflation that developed in the 1970s. Figure 2-5 plots the continuous estimates of the low inflation unemployment rate from the backward filter along with actual unemployment rates. The figure uses the familiar total unemployment rate by converting the estimates based on the 25- to 54-year-old male rate that were used in the regressions. For comparison, the figure also plots the NAIRUs estimated by the Congressional Budget Office (CBO), which correspond closely to estimates by Gordon and others.[15]

Armed with these estimates and insights from the time-varying regressions, we now take a closer look at economic performance over the past forty years and assess how the challenges to policymaking were met.

The 1960s

During the first fifteen years following World War II, the U.S. economy suffered four recessions, starting in 1949, 1953, 1957, and 1960. The incoming Kennedy economic team emphasized the need to avoid the frequent recessions of the past, to sustain the nascent recovery of 1961, and to encourage investment for long-run growth. Though these goals could have been the homilies of any new administration, in this instance they were supported by original diagnoses by the Council of Economic Advisers and accompanied by important policy initiatives. Inflation was seen as a problem confounding stabilization goals because it picked up moderately before full employment had been achieved. Okun's estimates of full employment and potential growth were translated into estimates of the full employment budget surplus as an indicator of the thrust of fiscal policy.

---

15. See Congressional Budget Office (2000).

Figure 2-5. *Actual and Low Inflation Total Unemployment Rates and the NAIRU, 1960–98*[a]

Percent

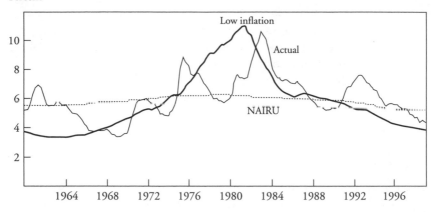

Source: Authors' calculations from coefficients in BKF wage regressions and trend productivity, Congressional Budget Office (2000), and data from the Bureau of Labor Statistics.

a. The male unemployment rates calculated from the wage regressions were converted to corresponding total unemployment rates in each quarter using a regression of log(total U rate) on log(male 25–54 U rate) and t, t^2, and t^3 (where t = time). The NAIRU is CBO's estimate.

With that indicator, the most recent recession was attributed to an unwarranted tightening of fiscal policy by about 2 percent of GDP in FY1960.

On the policy front, the Kennedy administration pursued a more expansionary budget, initially through higher defense spending and before long through tax reductions. Depreciation rules were made more generous, business equipment spending received a tax credit, and income tax rates were reduced, with the top marginal rate cut from 91 percent to 70 percent. By 1965, the structural surplus had been reduced by about 0.7 percent of GDP from its level five years earlier. In response to the idea that inflation quickened before full employment was reached, the 1962 *Economic Report of the President* first introduced the idea of guideposts for wages and prices. While never having the force of law, these guideposts became a conspicuous and active initiative of administration policy, especially in 1964–65 under Lyndon Johnson, and they cast a shadow that extended throughout the 1970s when the Council on Wage and Price Stability operated in the executive branch.

Though the guideposts policy was always controversial, the view of inflation that motivated it had ample empirical support. The Phillips curve had emerged as a characterization of the cyclical behavior of the macroeconomy, although both what microeconomic behavior generated it and how the cyclical behavior might play out in the longer run were unsettled questions. In their paper to the December 1959 meeting of the American Economic Association, Paul Samuelson and Robert Solow display their awareness of the range of possible answers to these questions, many of which have reemerged in the years since. In particular, they anticipate the idea that the short-run Phillips curve may change under experienced inflation, but are open about how far such a change will go:

[A] period of high demand and rising prices molds attitudes, expectations, even institutions in such a way as to bias the future in favor of further inflation. Unlike some other economists, we do not draw the firm conclusion that unless a firm stop is put, the rate of price increase must accelerate. We leave it as an open question: It may be that creeping inflation leads only to creeping inflation.[16]

In interpreting the period, we should emphasize that this and other informed discussions of the time had nothing to do with desiring inflation as a way to promote employment, or with tolerance for the inflationary consequences of pushing unemployment below the full employment range. Keeping inflation low was a goal of policy then as now, and full employment and potential output were concepts of what was achievable with existing resources and under normal circumstances. One key contrast to the NAIRU models that emerged in subsequent decades was that a modest cyclical rise in inflation was not considered a sign that employment had exceeded sustainable levels.

For the years through 1970, our recursive estimates are not far from a least squares regression fit at the start of the 1960s. Forecasts from this regression are quite good for the rest of the decade. The econometrician who kept extending the sample would have found little reason to suspect instability in the relation in 1965 or even in 1970. By the late 1960s, he would have concluded that the economy had passed beyond the full employment region, that aggregate demand was excessive, and that the rise in inflation that was observed was about what was expected.

It is well documented that policymakers had been concerned about excess demand in the economy ever since the mid-1960s when the original full employment goal was reached and the Vietnam War began raising

---

16. Samuelson and Solow (1960, p. 185).

defense spending. The contemporary Kalman filter results would have added little additional information, but none was needed. Nonetheless, little was done to slow the expansion. Monetary policy was not then the aggressive instrument of policy that it later became, and Lyndon Johnson believed his social agenda would be sidetracked if he called for a tax increase to finance the war. In the three years after FY 1965, the structural surplus declined by 2.9 percent of GDP, leaving it in large deficit. The investment credit for business equipment was temporarily suspended in late 1966. But the temporary suspension had such a sharp effect that it threatened to cause a recession and the credit was reinstated only months later. An income tax increase was finally passed, effective in 1969, by which time unemployment was down to 3.5 percent and inflation had risen to 5.4 percent.

The paralysis of fiscal policy as a stabilization tool in this period was a problem recognized at the time as well as today. Why monetary policy did not react more forcefully is a question we cannot answer convincingly here. But recall that the Fed had been constrained by Treasury's financing needs during World War II, freeing itself only in the early 1950s. It is easy to imagine that the legendary persuasive powers of Lyndon Johnson and the pressure to cooperate with the nation again at war would have made it difficult for any Fed chairman to tighten decisively. In any event, as figure 2-6 shows, the real federal funds rate was lower in early 1969 than it had been four years earlier.

What policy reactions would have been implied by present day NAIRU models? According to the Congressional Budget Office, the economy was at its NAIRU of 5.5 percent as early as 1962 and had clearly shot past it in 1965. These models would have led policymakers to reject the initial fiscal stimulus of the early 1960s, including the tax cuts that were passed, and to call for tighter monetary policy to slow the expansion that ensued in those years. Yet the years between 1962 and 1966 were the best of the decade and widely applauded by contemporary accounts. In contrast to NAIRU models, the BKF model summarized in figure 2-5 gives a picture consistent with the contemporary account. It shows a considerable excess of unemployment in 1962–64 and would have supported the Kennedy fiscal stimulus and monetary policies of that period.

The OPEC Years

The turbulent 1970s challenged policymakers at the time and have challenged econometricians ever since. While widely remembered as the decade

Figure 2-6. *Real and Nominal Federal Funds Rates, 1957–98*

Percent

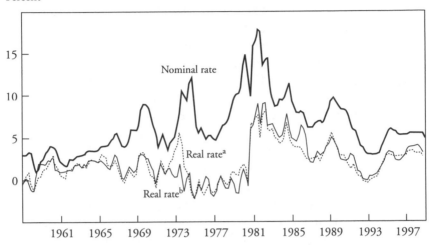

Source: Authors' calculations using data from *International Financial Statistics CD-ROM*, 1999.

a. Federal funds rate minus the three-quarter centered average of the one-quarter change in the logarithm of CPI-U (a.r.).

b. Federal funds rate minus the three-quarter centered average of the one-quarter change in the logarithm of CPI-U less food and energy (a.r.).

of two explosions in world oil prices, other shocks were just as important and as difficult to model with confidence. At the start of the decade, wages in the then-important union sector, most of which were negotiated on a three-year cycle, accelerated in the midst of recession, masking the slowdown that occurred in other wages. In mid-1971, the Nixon administration imposed wage and price controls. During 1973, a major run-up in consumer food prices, which had been decontrolled, added 5 percentage points to the PPI and 3 percentage points to the CPI for the year. The first OPEC price shock hit at the end of 1973, and soon thereafter all wage and price controls were lifted in this environment of already rapid inflation. Finally, recall from figure 2-1 that the productivity trend slowed sharply over the course of the decade.

Except for the productivity slowdown, the special nature of these shocks was recognized both by policymakers at the time and by most econometricians since then. But then as now, there was no way to model their ultimate impact on the economy with confidence. Did controls simply store up wage and price increases? The data seem to say yes, but this can hardly be a prediction good for all times and circumstances. The controls during the Korean War abruptly slowed inflation, but their removal produced no inflationary surge like that in 1974. Did the wage accelerations that accompanied the price shocks demonstrate the NAIRU assumption that the price-to-wage elasticity is one? The recursive regressions in tables 2-1 and 2-2 show how the observations from the early 1970s dominate least squares estimates of lagged price effects from then on. However, our filter estimates indicate that the least squares results are misleading. They reveal that the relatively high estimates for the 1970s are outliers relative to the estimates for periods both before and after.

Both the CKF and recursive regressions show a more inflationary relation emerging in the 1970s. However, it would have been hard to detect in the presence of the shocks in that period and, as we noted earlier, the productivity slowdown was not detected until late in the decade. Following the deep and prolonged recession that followed the first oil price shock, it was appropriate for policy to be expansionary. But by 1978, policymakers had ample warning that inflation was quickening and might have detected that the relation itself was worsening. NAIRU estimates for those years would not have flashed a warning, showing unemployment well above the NAIRU in 1977 and about at the NAIRU in 1978. However, our time-varying estimates show the low inflation unemployment rate was rising sharply. In any case, monetary policy remained expansionary. The real federal funds rate, shown in figure 2-6, remained negative throughout most of this period.

The Volcker Era

When the second OPEC shock added to an already troublesome inflation, President Carter appointed Paul Volcker to head the Federal Reserve. With a clear mandate to control inflation, the Volcker Fed produced the massive recessions of 1980 and 1981–82. The federal funds rate averaged 16.4 percent in 1981, double the rate of three years earlier. The unemployment rate rose to over 10 percent in 1982, easily the highest rate since the Great Depression. And as figure 2-4 shows, the parameters shifted dramatically in a less inflationary direction following these policies and the unemployment they produced.

Then as now there was disagreement about whether a more gradual disinflation back then would have been less costly, and it is difficult to imagine tests that would answer that question objectively. The credibility of monetary policy was being modeled as a key determinant of policy effectiveness and the Fed's Draconian monetary policy should be viewed in that context. But in 1984, five years after the Volcker tightening began, inflation had been down to 4 percent for two years, yet the yield on 30-year government bonds was still over 12 percent. We can infer either that credibility about fighting inflation was still not established or that financial markets expected that historically high real interest rates would persist for a very long time. The latter view received support from the fiscal policies of the time. Under the Reagan combination of tax cuts and defense buildup, the structural surplus declined by 3 percent of GDP between 1980 and 1986, reaching a deficit of 5 percent of GDP in FY1986. By then the pure fiscal explanation for high long-term rates works less well since the long bond rate fell below 8 percent that year.

The 1990s

We have already described the remarkable performance of the economy in the last half of this decade. And it is in this period that our estimates provide the most dramatically different view of policy choices from those suggested by traditional analysis. Figure 2-5 again summarizes the changing relation that policymakers confronted. By the mid-1990s, when NAIRU models were warning that unemployment should not decline further, our estimates show the relation between inflation and the unemployment rate improving steadily. If we associate good policymaking with the judgmental equivalent of being alert to changing parameter values, the willingness of the Greenspan Fed to allow rapid expansion to continue after 1995 gets very high marks. The civilian unemployment rate averaged 5.6 percent in 1995, already below contemporary estimates of NAIRU, and is today near 4 percent. The economy's potential growth rate was estimated to be around 2.5 percent in 1995. Yet real GDP has risen by 4 percent a year since then. Policymakers could not have fully anticipated this performance of the economy in this period. But by 1995, the contemporary filter estimates summarized in table 2-1 would already have alerted them that a substantially lower unemployment rate was consistent with low inflation.

Some Lessons for the Conduct of Policy

Our simplified price and wage equations are not much different than the equations used by a variety of authors to examine optimal policy. If we combined our equations relating unemployment and output with a relation to monetary policy and specified a loss function in inflation and output or employment, we could formally investigate how the performance of various policy rules would be affected by allowing for time variation in parameters. Such an analysis is beyond the scope of this paper. However, we venture a few thoughts about the lessons that would likely emerge.

If structural change is important and continuous, conventional estimation procedures can be misleading. Sticking with prior estimates, unless recent observations fall outside of conventional confidence intervals, will be a mistake. Compared with conventional policy analysis, policymaking that is alert to parameter drift will respond less to the prescription from conventional econometric estimates and more to recent shocks. The policymaking episodes that we discussed earlier demonstrate the potency of this problem. The failure in the 1970s to detect the change to a more inflationary relation was a costly mistake, and the Fed's reluctance in recent years to observe the prescription of NAIRU models permitted the lower unemployment and faster growth that the U.S. economy has enjoyed.

On a related issue, we know that uncertainty about the response to policy actions calls for deviation from certainty-equivalent behavior.[17] Several authors, finding small standard errors in their estimates of response, have suggested that uncertainty is small so that the appropriate behavior is approximately certainty-equivalent. However, their confidence is misplaced if parameters in fact time vary. If they do, allowing for time variation not only will improve the estimate of the parameter at any point in time, but may also enlarge estimated standard errors. Moreover, in light of the uncertainties of specification and the profession's collective mining of available data, we believe the true uncertainty about policy response is greater than even our time-varying model reveals. For all these reasons, certainty-equivalent behavior is likely to be far from optimal.

Our results indicate that a full employment range is reasonably well defined and that concern over rising inflation is well placed. They also cast doubt on NAIRU models as adequate descriptions of the economy's behavior. Although we did not formally test a NAIRU form of the inflation

17. See Brainard (1967).

equations, the unconstrained estimates provided no support for the NAIRU formulation. Our results also indicate that conventional estimates from a NAIRU model do not identify the full employment range with a degree of accuracy that is useful to policymaking.

Finally, our findings on time-varying parameters bring some new evidence to bear on the choice between simple policy rules and policy discretion. Rules have been framed in terms of departures of actual performance from fixed target values for unemployment and inflation rates. Such rules would lead to policy mistakes with the kind of time-varying parameters that we estimate. Other simple rules, such as fixing the nominal growth rate of the economy, will be inappropriate if the productivity trend is time-varying, as it has been over the postwar period. Our general conclusion that policy should be framed with continuing attention to changing parameters strengthens the argument that policymakers need to be constantly alert to unexpected developments, both shocks and changes to the economic structure.

COMMENT BY
Ray C. Fair

Bill Brainard and George Perry take exception to the view that coefficients of price and wage equations have remained stable over time. They postulate that the coefficients follow a random walk, and they estimate their price and wage equations using the Kalman filter. Can we trust their results as showing that the coefficients have changed? There are at least four reasons to be cautious.

First, the use of the CPI as the price variable is problematic. The CPI is not a good measure of the prices set by U.S. firms because it includes import prices and indirect business taxes. A much better measure is the business nonfarm price deflator. Let YY be nominal business nonfarm output, let IBT be total indirect business taxes, and let Y be business nonfarm output in 1992 dollars.[18] Then a measure of the business nonfarm deflator is simply $(YY-IBT)/Y$. This deflator is net of indirect business taxes, farm output, government output, and imports. In a recent study, I found that

---

18. These data are from the Bureau of Economic Analysis, National Income and Product Accounts (NIPA). Nominal business nonfarm output is from NIPA table 1.7, line 3. Total indirect business taxes are from NIPA table 3.1, line 4. Business nonfarm output is from NIPA table 1.8, line 3.

the results of testing the dynamics of price equations are somewhat sensitive to the use of the CPI rather than the business nonfarm deflator.[19]

Second, the theory behind the price and wage equations is unclear. If one has a set of structural equations in mind, where price inflation depends on wage inflation and some variables Z, and wage inflation depends on price inflation and some variables Q, then the reduced form equations for both price inflation and wage inflation depend on Z and Q. Yet Brainard and Perry exclude the productivity variable from their wage equation. Also, it is not clear what identifies the structural price and wage equations. What is in Z that is not in Q, and what is in Q that is not in Z? One possibility is that lagged values of wage inflation appear in the structural wage equation but not in the structural price equation. If this is true, then the lagged values of wage inflation should appear in both reduced form equations; however, they appear in neither.

Third, a key explanatory variable that is missing is some measure of cost shocks, which I will take here as being measured by the import price deflator, denoted PM. Figure 2-7 below plots log PF and log PM for the 1954:1–1999:4 period. PF is similar to the business nonfarm price deflator discussed above. It is the main price variable I use in my U.S. model. It seems clear from the figure that PM affects PF. When I use log PM in my equation explaining log PF, I get a t-statistic of around 20! Not including any variables like PM in a price equation is likely to have a serious effect on the results. This is not likely to be a minor specification error.

Fourth, ten years (forty quarters) can be a small sample using macroeconomic time-series data. There are not that many cycles. For example, figure 2-8 plots the inflation rate for the 1954:1–1999:4 period (using PF as the price variable), and it is clear that all the large inflation rates were in the 1970s. If the 1970s are excluded from the estimation period, a lot of information is lost.

The Kalman filter forgets past observations at a certain rate per coefficient, and it is probably the case that observations more than ten years back get almost no weight for any coefficient. It is thus not surprising that as one moves away from the 1970s the estimates change, and this could simply be a small sample problem. For purposes of this comment, I did rolling regressions using my structural price equation with a window of seventy-six quarters, and I got noticeable changes in some of the coefficients. If instead I fixed the beginning quarter at 1954:1 and did recursive

19. Fair (2000).

Figure 2-7. *Business Nonfarm Price Deflator and Import Price Deflator*[a]

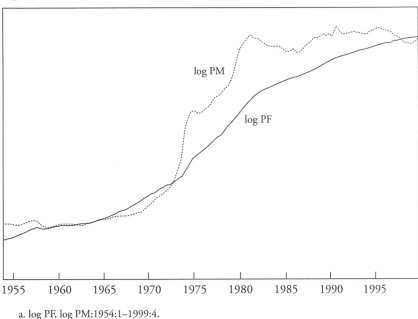

log PM

log PF

1955 1960 1965 1970 1975 1980 1985 1990 1995

a. log PF, log PM;1954:1–1999:4.

regressions, the coefficients settle down by the mid-1970s. I need the early 1970s to tie down the coefficient of log *PM* in the equation because, as can be seen in figure 2-7, before about 1970 there was almost no variation in *PM*. After the mid-1970s, however, the recursive coefficient estimates change very little.

Thus there may be a small sample problem using the Kalman filter, and so the analysis cries out for some tests. Are the coefficient changes that Brainard and Perry estimate significant? The obvious hypothesis to test is that the variances of the error terms in the random walk equations are zero. James Stock and Mark Watson test this hypothesis (and many others) for seventy-six variables.[20] The specific test for this hypothesis is due to Jukka Nyblom.[21] The Nyblom test rejects stability at the 5 percent significance level 17.1 percent of the time in the Stock and Watson study (thirteen variables out of seventy-six).[22] It is interesting that the stability hypothesis is

20. Stock and Watson (1996).
21. Nyblom (1989)
22. Stock and Watson (1996, p. 15).

Figure 2-8. *Inflation Rate*[a]

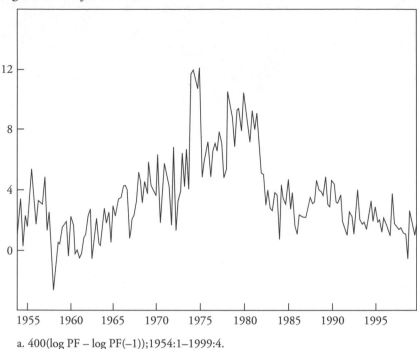

a. 400(log PF – log PF(–1));1954:1–1999:4.

rejected for the CPI but not the consumer expenditure deflator. This again shows that results can be sensitive to the price variable used. (Stock and Watson do not consider the business nonfarm price deflator.)

To conclude, before this study can convince anyone to give up the working hypothesis of stability, a better measure of the price level should be used, the theory should be made clearer and the specification improved, and tests need to be done. Many of the somewhat sweeping statements in the paper are simply not justified by the current results.

COMMENT BY

John B. Taylor

I enjoyed reading the paper by Bill Brainard and George Perry. Continuing in the tradition of Arthur Okun, it provides quantitative measures of key policy parameters. I have long admired Okun's ability to translate complex macroeconomic ideas into simple, quantitative, and highly useful constructs, such as potential GNP and Okun's law. One of the reasons that I first got interested in macroeconomics was a fascination with how such quantitative methods were being used to help formulate policy in Washington in the 1960s. My undergraduate thesis project was on monetary and fiscal policy rules, which I viewed as part of the same quantitative approach that Arthur Okun and others were using at the Council of Economic Advisers (CEA). I think the approach taken to quantitative formulation of policy at the CEA in the 1960s still has a significant influence on normative policy evaluation. For example, potential GDP (though now defined as a level of real GDP around which actual real GDP fluctuates, rather than an upper bound) and the deviations from potential GDP figure prominently in current monetary policy research.[23] Potential GDP is a factor in the simple monetary policy rule I suggested in the early 1990s.[24]

The Brainard-Perry paper is a highly original endeavor to measure the uncertainty faced by policymakers from the 1960s through the present. I found the "backward" filter calculations of productivity growth and the wage-price equations to be fascinating, and potentially important for interpreting history. One important application, which I think should be pursued further, is the problem of estimating changes in potential GDP growth. For example, some argue that policymakers were too slow to react to the slowdown in productivity growth in the 1970s.[25] This may have been one reason why the Federal Reserve was too easy in certain periods in the 1970s. Athanasios Orphanides uses contemporary estimates of potential GDP from the CEA as evidence.[26] An alternative estimate would be based on the backward filters of productivity in figure 2-1 of the Brainard-Perry paper. The backward filter estimates in figure 2-1 show that the slowdown was occurring as soon as the late 1960s. To get another measure of how things may have looked, one could start the backward filter in the mid 1970s rather than in the late 1990s, as Brainard and Perry have done. Even if one questioned such a calculation as a descriptive device of how policymakers viewed the world back then, it might give an indication of how such methods would work today, say for estimating the size of the potential GDP growth pick-up.

23. See Orphanides and others (1999), for example.
24. Taylor (1993).
25. See Orphanides (1998).
26. Orphanides (1998).

Rather than focus my comments solely on the econometric methodology, I will spend most of my time on Brainard and Perry's interpretations of the results. In doing so I will be meeting the discussant's responsibility of concentrating on the parts of the paper with which I disagree. My comments can be divided into three parts. First, I want to comment on their interpretation of the results as implying that there is no NAIRU or, equivalently, that there is a long-run Phillips curve tradeoff. Second, I want to comment on their historical review of economic performance, in which they argue that the 1960s were good, the 1970s and 1980s were bad, and the 1990s were good again. Third, I want to comment on their conclusion that their results add weight to the discretion side of the "rules versus discretion" debate.

Bringing Endogenous Expectations Back into the Analysis

Brainard and Perry conclude that there is no NAIRU in their model: "Although we did not formally test a NAIRU form of the inflation equations, the unconstrained estimates provided no support for the NAIRU formulation." In other words, they find that there is a long-run tradeoff between the inflation rate and the unemployment rate; higher inflation would imply lower unemployment. This view is implicit in their calculation of specific unemployment rates corresponding to a 2 percent inflation rate in the paper. I know that they are guarded in drawing policy implications from this interpretation, but I worry that their interpretation gives a misleading view of the macroeconomic history and could therefore be misleading in the future.

Let me start by stating how a simple look at the facts of U.S. inflation and unemployment over the last fifty years shows a near-zero correlation between inflation and unemployment over the long run, thereby indicating that there is no long-run tradeoff between inflation and unemployment. It is best to take averages over long periods of time—decades, to yield a measure of the long run. In the 1950s and early 1960s, inflation was low; in the late 1960s and 1970s, it was high; and in the late 1980s and 1990s, it was low again. But the average unemployment rate in all these periods was roughly the same: around 5 or 6 percent. If anything, unemployment was higher during the high inflation periods than in the low inflation periods, indicating a slight positive correlation between inflation and unemployment. In any case, one cannot see any long-run negative tradeoff in the post–World War II inflation and unemployment data using these simple averages.

However, this is not what the estimated equations of Brainard and Perry show. The sum of the coefficients on lagged inflation in their wage and price equations never gets as high as one. Thus their estimates can be interpreted as stating that there is a permanent long-run tradeoff between inflation and unemployment; higher inflation will result in lower unemployment.

However, they do find that their estimated long-run tradeoff shifts by a large amount. These shifts are illustrated in figure 2-9 below. Brainard and Perry find that the unemployment rate associated with 2 percent inflation is around 2 percent in the 1960s, around 9 percent in the late 1970s and early 1980s, and around 3 percent in the 1990s (these estimates use the "prime age" male unemployment measures and are drawn from the contemporary filters section of their table 2-1). I show these three unemployment rate estimates in figure 2-9, where I have sketched three long-run Phillips curves. The three levels of unemployment—corresponding to the 1960s (shown as 1965), the late 1970s and early 1980s (shown as 1980), and the 1990s (shown as 1995)—are found at the intersection of three long-run Phillips curve tradeoffs. Thus the long-run Phillips curves that I have sketched in figure 2-9 correspond to the long-run tradeoffs implicit in the Brainard-Perry wage equations for those three years.

These shifts show how Brainard and Perry's equations (which have a long-run tradeoff) fit the data (which show no long-run tradeoff). From 1965 to 1980, the curve shifts to the right; then, from 1980 to 1995, the curve shifts back to the left. The period of high inflation and roughly average unemployment in the late 1970s and early 1980s (before the disinflation) can be placed on the upper part of the 1980 curve. Thus these high inflation and average unemployment years are explained by a shift in the curve to the right (compared with the positions of the 1960s and 1990s), along with a movement to a higher inflation point on the 1980 curve.

The problem I have with their interpretation is that these shifts are portrayed as exogenous to policy, while in fact I think they are very much endogenous to policy. Note that the sum of the coefficients on lagged inflation in the wage inflation equations rises and falls as historical inflation rates rise and fall; see table 2-1 of their paper. This is one reason why the unemployment rate associated with 2 percent inflation moves higher and then lower. Thus one can interpret the rightward and leftward shifts of the

Figure 2-9. *Long-Run Phillips Curves Corresponding to Three Unemployment Rates Associated with 2 Percent Inflation, 1965, 1980, and 1995*[a]

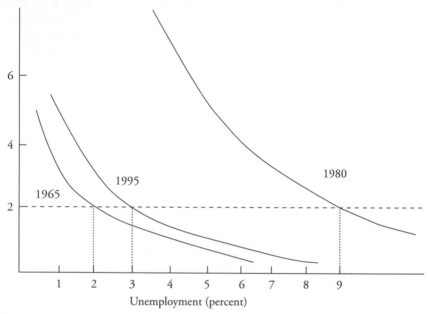

Inflation (percent)

Unemployment (percent)

a. The unemployment rates are rounded versions of those reported in the middle panel of table 2-1 of the Brainard-Perry paper and the curves are sketched to pass through those points.

curves in figure 2-9 as shifts up and down due mainly to changes in expectations of inflation. In my view, the reason the curves shifted from the 1960s to the 1970s was that policy led to higher inflation, which shifted up inflationary expectations.

This higher inflation, along with higher expectations of inflation, required a difficult period of disinflation in the early 1980s. Policymakers should be concerned about having to go through such a painful process in the future, and they therefore should guard against it. Expectations of inflation and the Phillips curve may indeed appear to be exogenous to policy; however, as one tries to use policy to move systematically along the curve, expectations of inflation will rise, and the curve will begin to shift up. This rise in inflation will eventually require a painful policy to bring it back down. To help avoid such an event, I think it is important to incorporate endogenous expectations (perhaps even rational expectations as an approximation) into the analysis. At the least, one needs to emphasize that the changing parameters (the coefficients on the lagged inflation rates) are endogenous to policy.

Defining Episodes of Macroeconomic Stability and Policy Regimes

Bill Brainard and George Perry's characterization of economic performance in the 1960s and 1990s as outstanding in comparison with "what had come before" in the 1950s and 1980s is misleading. In my view, there are alternative historical break-points that can be better delineated by statistical analysis and that also can be related to specific documented changes in economic policy.

The alternative characterization of episodes does not start or end with any particular decade, and it overlaps different policymakers. It defines a watershed in the early 1980s, around the time of the end of the disinflation. Macroeconomic stability—as measured by the fluctuations of real output and prices, by the length of expansions, by the frequency of recessions, or by the softness of slowdowns—has been much better since this watershed of the early 1980s than during any period of similar length before it.

Consider the volatility of real output—either deviations of real GDP from potential GDP or the size of the fluctuations in the growth rate of real GDP. Figure 2-10 shows the GDP gap since 1959 using a Hodrick-Prescott trend as a measure of potential GDP. This trend captures the productivity slowdown of the early 1970s. Better estimates of potential GDP that formally take productivity and labor force growth into account would provide a similar picture. The volatility of real output seems much smaller in the later periods than in earlier periods, even than in the shorter period of the 1960s. The two horizontal lines at the maximum and minimum deviations since the early 1980s are meant to help visualize the reduced volatility. Figure 2-11 shows the same reduced volatility using the quarterly growth rates of real GDP rather than the GDP gap.

The following table summarizes the visual evidence in the pictures showing the standard deviation of the GDP gap (σ_{gap}) or the real GDP growth rate (σ_{growth}) using the data in figures 2-9 and 2-10:

Figure 2-10. *Percentage Deviations of Real GDP from Trend, 1960–99*[a]

Percent

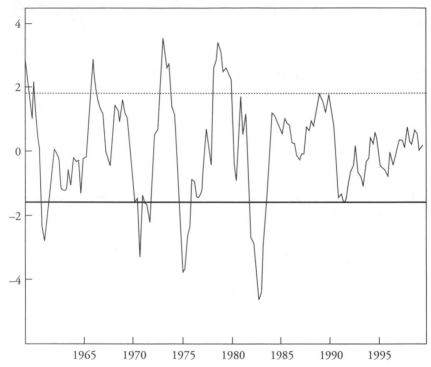

Source: Bureau of Economic Analysis (www.bea.doc.gov [November 3, 1999]).
a. The plotted series is (log (real GDP) − HPTrend) * 100, where HP trend is the Hodrick-Prescott filter of log (real GDP).

Period	σ_{gap}	σ_{growth}
1959.2–1999.3	1.6	3.6
1959.2–1982.4	1.8	4.3
1982.4–1999.3	1.1	2.3
1960.1–1969.4	1.3	3.5

The period since the early 1980s (the fourth quarter of 1982, to be exact) has the greatest macroeconomic stability of the periods shown, confirming the visual evidence in figures 2-9 and 2-10 of these comments.

One can also make a comparison based on the length of expansions or the frequency of recessions. The period of the 1980s and 1990s contains

Figure 2-11. *Quarterly Growth Rate of Real GDP, 1960–99*

Percent

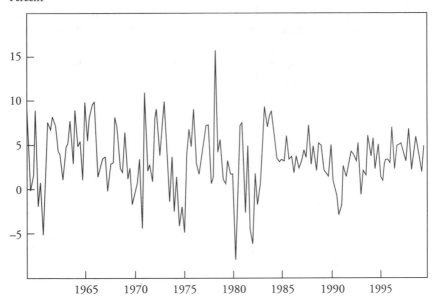

Source: Bureau of Economic Analysis (www.bea.doc.gov [November 3, 1999]).

the first and second longest peacetime expansions in U.S. history, back-to-back and separated by a relatively short recession. If one does not restrict oneself to peacetime, it contains two of the three longest expansions in U.S. history, again back-to-back. Such a long period of stability is unprecedented. The longest expansion occurred in the 1960s, but that long expansion was preceded and followed by short expansions.

There is another reason to choose the early 1980s as the watershed. There was a big shift in U.S. monetary policy toward price stability at that time. I am not referring solely to the disinflation—although that was a necessary part of the transition toward a policy of price stability. I am referring to the difference in the way policy has been conducted since the disinflation. This difference is evident in terms of a policy rule that describes action by the Federal Reserve. The response of the Fed to inflation has been larger in the more recent period; the response of the federal funds rate to an increase in inflation has doubled, and the reaction of the federal funds rate to real output is also larger.[27]

27. See Taylor (1999) for a review of the estimated responses.

It is not surprising that price stability increased as a result of a policy that has focused more on price stability. What may appear more surprising is that output stability increased, too. I think the reason is that a monetary policy that has focused more on price stability has prevented the large run-ups of inflation that have preceded previous recessions; in other words, the problem of the boom-bust cycle had diminished. There are, of course, other explanations for the improved output stability during the two long expansions of the 1980s and 1990s, including smaller shocks, but in my view the change in monetary policy is the major factor.[28]

Implications of Uncertainty for Rules versus Discretion

Finally, I would like to focus on the implications of the paper for the use of policy rules. Brainard and Perry suggest that their results about uncertainty indicate the need for more discretion in policymaking. In practice, of course, policy rules are used as guidelines from which policymakers must deviate in special cases.[29] But I see the Brainard-Perry results as showing the potential for using less, not more, discretion.

First, parameter uncertainty makes life difficult for policymakers whether they are trying to use rules to guide policy or not. For example, not knowing potential GDP growth, or the natural rate of unemployment, will make it difficult to decide whether to raise or lower interest rates, whether or not one is using a policy rule as a guideline.

Second, in my view, it is easier to take account of the uncertainty, which Brainard and Perry document quantitatively, through a policy rule approach than through a discretion-oriented approach. Stochastic optimization methods that underlie research on policy rules take account of the uncertainty explicitly. How does one take account of such research findings about uncertainty otherwise? For example, how does one take account of a finding that the coefficient on the unemployment rate follows a random walk with a standard deviation of 1.4 if one is using discretion? In fact, seminal research by Bill Brainard on optimal control with parameter uncertainty showed the benefits of a formal policy approach a long time ago.[30] And George Perry's research on demographic adjustments to the unem-

28. See Taylor (1998) for a review of other factors and an explanation of the role of monetary policy.
29. See Taylor (1993) for further discussion.
30. Brainard (1967).

ployment rate has provided a procedure that can be used with policy rules that react to the gap between the unemployment rate and the natural unemployment rate, or other measures of capacity utilization.[31] The newer work in the Brainard-Perry paper can also be helpful in improving policy rules: most likely one will find that policy should down-weight the coefficients in policy rules because of the parameter uncertainty à la Brainard, but in complex dynamic models the adjustment could be up rather than down.

There are many reasons why a monetary policy that is built on a rules-based, systematic, transparent framework works well. Brainard and Perry have provided the kind of research in this paper that can make such an approach work even better in the future. In sum, my view is that the Brainard-Perry research on quantifying uncertainty enables policy to be more rule-like, and in this sense strengthens the arguments for rules rather than for discretion.

References

Akerlof, George A., William T. Dickens, and George L. Perry. 1996. "The Macroeconomics of Low Inflation." *Brookings Papers on Economic Activity, 1:1996*, 1–59.

———. Forthcoming. "Near-Rational Wage and Price Setting and the Optimal Rates of Inflation and Unemployment." *Brookings Papers on Economic Activity, 1:2000*.

Brainard, William C. 1967. "Uncertainty and the Effectiveness of Policy." *American Economic Review* 57(2): 411–25

Congressional Budget Office. 2000. *The Budget and Economic Outlook: Fiscal Years 2001–2010*.

Fair, Ray C. 2000. "Testing the NAIRU Model for the United States." *Review of Economics and Statistics* 82 (February): 64–71.

Friedman, Milton. 1968. "The Role of Monetary Policy." *American Economic Review* 58 (March): 1–17.

Gordon, Robert J. 1998. "Foundations of the Goldilocks Economy: Supply Shocks and the Time-Varying NAIRU." *Brookings Papers on Economic Activity, 2:1998*, 297–333.

———. 1999. "Has the 'New Economy' Rendered the Productivity Slowdown Obsolete?" Paper prepared for the CBO Panel of Economic Advisers meeting, June 2.

Greenspan, Alan. 1989. "Statement before the Committee on Banking, Finance and Urban Affairs, U.S. House of Representatives." *Federal Reserve Board Bulletin* 75(3): 139–42 (March).

Modigliani, Franco, and Lucas Papademos. 1975. "Targets for Monetary Policy in the Coming Year." *Brookings Papers on Economic Activity, 1:1975*, 141–63.

Nyblom, Jukka. 1989. "Testing for the Constancy of Parameters over Time." *Journal of the American Statistical Association* 84 (March): 223–30.

31. Perry (1970).

Okun, Arthur M. 1972. *The Battle against Unemployment*. Norton.

Orphanides, Athanasios. 1998. "Monetary Policy Rules Based on Real-Time Data." Finance and Economics Discussion Series, Working Paper 1998-03. Board of Governors of the Federal Reserve System.

Orphanides, Athanasios, and others. 1999. "Errors in the Measurement of the Output Gap and the Design of Monetary Policy." Finance and Economics Discussion Series, Working Paper 1999-45. Board of Governors of the Federal Reserve System.

Perry, George L. 1970. "Changing Labor Markets and Inflation." *Brookings Papers on Economic Activity*, 3:1970, 411–48.

———. 1977. "Potential Output and Productivity." *Brookings Papers on Economic Activity*, 1:1977, 11–47.

Phelps, Edmund S. 1968. "Money-Wage Dynamics and Labor-Market Equilibrium." *Journal of Political Economy* 76 (July/August, Part 2): 678–711.

Samuelson, Paul A., and Robert M. Solow. 1960. "Analytical Aspects of Anti-Inflation Policy." *American Economic Review, Papers and Proceedings* 50(2): 177–94 (May).

Sargent, Thomas J. 1971. "A Note on the 'Accelerationist' Controversy." *Journal of Money, Credit, and Banking* 3(3): 721–25.

Stock, James H., and Mark W. Watson. 1996. "Evidence on Structural Instability in Macroeconomic Time Series Relations." *Journal of Business and Economic Statistics* 14 (January): 11–30.

Taylor, John B. 1993. "Discretion versus Policy Rules in Practice." *Carnegie Rochester Conference Series on Public Policy* (December): 195–214.

———. 1998. "Monetary Policy and the Long Boom." *Review*, Federal Reserve Bank of St. Louis (November–December): 3–11.

———. 1999. "A Historical Analysis of Monetary Policy Rules." In *Monetary Policy Rules*, edited by John B. Taylor, 319–41. University of Chicago Press.

PAUL KRUGMAN ***3***

The End of
Stabilization Policy?

Just before the first draft of this paper was written, Fernando de la Rua
was elected president of Argentina. While a perception of widespread
corruption among the ruling Peronists contributed to his victory, the crucial factor was an economic slump, with a 4.9 percent fall in real GDP in
the year ending in the second quarter of 1999. The causes of the slump
were fairly clear: it was pretty obviously a demand-driven recession,
brought on by the devaluation in neighboring Brazil, general investor ner-
vousness about emerging markets, and a decline in consumer confidence.

A mainstream economist from the 1960s would not have hesitated to
prescribe the general shape of a recovery strategy in such a case. Unless an
economy is threatened with inflation—and consumer prices in Argentina
fell 1.9 percent in the year ending in August 1999—a recession should be
fought with measures to pump up demand. These could include reducing
interest rates, devaluing the currency, cutting taxes, increasing government
spending, or all of the above. Indeed, since the 1940s it has been a working assumption of most applied economists that such measures would
routinely be taken in the face of demand-side slump. It is the presumption
that policy will take care of the demand side, rather than faith in the long-
run automatic tendency toward full employment, that really justifies our
willingness to assume full employment when analyzing microeconomic
issues.

But while de la Rua's winning Alliance coalition did promise to deliver recovery, it did not propose to do so through monetary or fiscal stimulus. Devaluation was firmly ruled out (although the Peronists tried to claim otherwise with the taunting slogan "de la Rua devalua"). On the contrary, Argentina's "convertibility" law, which pegged the peso to the U.S. dollar through a currency board, was treated by all parties as sacrosanct. The currency board system, of course, implied a passive monetary policy. And while de la Rua did propose changes in fiscal policy, they were *contractionary:* austerity measures intended to reduce the budget deficit, about 2 percent of GDP in 1999. The hope was that a lower deficit would improve confidence, and thus indirectly prove expansionary—a line of argument that would have sounded completely familiar to European financial officials circa, say, 1930.

And that, of course, is the point of this story. The language of policy discussion in Argentina at the end of the twentieth century is essentially pre-Keynesian: recessions are acts of God, at best; punishment for the economy's sins, at worst; and cannot be actively fought. The government's role is limited to providing sound money and a sound budget, with recovery left up to the spontaneous workings of the market. The idea of an active stabilization policy that uses fiscal and monetary tools to increase demand when it is inadequate has been abandoned.

There would be little reason for the rest of us to cry for Argentina if this retreat from stabilization policy were unique—but it is not. Argentina's currency board is still unusual, but many countries have come, rightly or wrongly, to the conclusion that currency depreciation is either unacceptable or counterproductive, and have therefore in effect dedicated monetary policy to the stabilization of the currency rather than the real economy. And while the blunt claim that fiscal contraction is expansionary is not that common, in practice many countries have become sufficiently concerned about the fiscal balance that they do respond to recession not with spending programs and tax cuts, but with austerity.

In short, the applied Keynesianism that seemed to have triumphed in the 1960s is in retreat. It has by no means vanished from the world: Anglo-Saxon central banks continue to act as if they believed in something like the IS-LM model, and the Japanese government obviously thinks that budget deficits are expansionary rather than contractionary. But something has convinced much of the rest of the world to revert to a pre-Keynesian passivity with respect to the business cycle.

The purpose of this paper is to inquire into the sources of this new passivity. It asks in particular whether the change is in the world or in our heads: that is, whether active stabilization policy has actually become less possible, or whether it has simply become unfashionable.

The Puzzle of Policy Diffidence

How much of the world has given up on stabilization policy? In mid-1998 the apparent answer was all emerging markets except China, plus euroland (the European nations that had agreed to join the monetary union at the beginning of 1999). In the face of the financial crisis, just about every emerging market economy both raised interest rates and adopted some fiscal austerity; and European nations both abandoned independent monetary policies and placed themselves under binding fiscal constraints, first under the rules of the Maastricht treaty, then under the post–European Monetary Union stability pact.

Since then a bit of Keynesianism has returned to the developing world: the original Asian crisis countries have turned to fiscal stimulus and have taken advantage of returning confidence to lower interest rates. So one could argue that active stabilization policy has staged a comeback. But anti-Keynesian policies are still being followed to a considerable extent. Argentina of course provides the clearest example, but one can also point to Brazil, which pursued tight monetary and fiscal policies in defense of the *real,* and has continued to pursue fiscal austerity and be cautious on the monetary side even though that defense has been abandoned. Within Europe, the adoption of a common currency has of course eliminated the option of monetary expansion for economies that seem to suffer from excess supply; and concerns over meeting budgetary targets have not only precluded fiscal expansion in Germany and Italy, they have led the government of the former to propose large spending cuts, and that of the latter to at least suggest that budget cuts may be necessary if growth remains disappointing.

Beyond the actual practice of policy, what is striking if hard to document is the change in attitude on the part of policymakers. Thirty years ago the debate was between optimists who thought that activist demand management could "fine tune" the economy, and skeptics who thought that only a cruder, less ambitious form of stabilization was possible; but it was taken for granted that governments could and would move decisively to end drastic recessions. Today one finds governments of nations that are clearly operating far below capacity, basically hoping that private demand will pick up, rather than being determined to provide the demand the economy needs. And one even sees a reappearance of the old idea that economic slumps are somehow healthy and necessary, providing a necessary purge of previous excesses, and that it would be wrong to try to shield the economy from this cleansing process.

Why have policymakers retreated from stabilization policy, both in theory and in practice? In general, there are three possible stories.

The first story—the one that finds favor, for example, with the *Wall Street Journal* editorial page—is that Keynesianism was always a snare and a delusion. According to this view, the whole idea that monetary and fiscal policy could be used to fight recessions, perhaps even the idea that demand had anything to do with the business cycle, was an appealing story that turns out to be nonsense—something like Freudian psychology or Lamarckian biology. And governments, having finally figured this out, have returned to the wisdom of their grandfathers.

The second story says that Keynesianism used to be valid, perhaps still is valid for some economies, but that for other economies the environment has changed in ways that make monetary and fiscal policy unusable, ineffective, or counterproductive. The most prominent candidate for that change in the environment is globalization, especially of the capital markets; thus large countries like the United States may retain some ability to pursue independent monetary and fiscal policies, but smaller nations do not.

The third story is the obverse of the first: it says that more or less Keynesian policies still work, that the option of active stabilization policy remains available, but that a combination of ideology and misinterpretation of the evidence has led countries to the false belief that they cannot or should not fight recessions. In this case what we see is a true retrogression: policymakers have returned not to the wisdom but the errors of their grandfathers.

Let me not be too coy about where this paper is going. I believe that the true explanation of macroeconomic policy diffidence is a combination of the second and third stories. To some extent, and in some cases, globalization and other changes in the environment have restricted the ability of nations to pursue independent monetary and fiscal policies. But in most of the world such policies remain available, and do work when tried. The conviction of many policymakers that there is nothing they can do to stabilize the economy is based on misinterpretation of the evidence at best, simple prejudice at worst.

But where might this conviction have come from?

The Legacy of Stagflation

The 1970s was a pivotal decade for macroeconomics. Before that decade macroeconomists and policymakers clearly had far too much faith in their understanding of and power over the business cycle. One can argue that the experience of the 1970s should not have been taken too hard: after all, the natural-rate hypothesis had been propounded and widely accepted even before stagflation became a familiar reality, and one should not have been surprised to see models that had not allowed for oil shocks go off track when those shocks materialized. Nonetheless, in practice the experience of stagflation had the effect of undermining belief in the practicality or desirability of stabilization policy. Consider three consequences of the experience of the 1970s (and to some extent of the 1980s as well).

First, the triumph of the Friedman-Phelps natural-rate hypothesis, which seemed validated by the experience of stagflation, vastly enhanced the credibility of the idea that a proper business-cycle theory should do away with the assumption of money illusion. Hence equilibrium business-cycle theory à la Robert Lucas was taken much more seriously than otherwise might have been the case. And that theory seemed to imply that activist policy could never be stabilizing: since only unanticipated money could matter, active monetary policy could at best add noise to output movements.[1] Lucas was then followed by real business-cycle theory, which denied any real effects of demand policy at all. Policymakers may not have taken any of this literally, but they surely imbibed a sense that serious academic research had become skeptical of the possibility not only of fine tuning but of useful demand-side management at all. This surely helped encourage a reversion to old-fashioned notions of policy prudence. (The sense of academic macroeconomics in disarray also helped make the entry of outsider doctrines like supply-side economics considerably easier.)

Second, the stress placed by the natural-rate hypothesis on expectations made credibility a central policy issue; central bankers and finance ministers could justify inaction in the face of recession by arguing that any action would undermine long-run inflation-fighting credibility. More generally,

1. Lucas (1981).

the classic argument of those who preach austerity in slumps is that the adverse effects of countercyclical policies on confidence will outweigh any direct positives. The new emphasis on expectations at least made that sort of argument more plausible.

Finally, what happened in the 1970s and 1980s was not just a fairly convincing demonstration that policy can do no more than stabilize unemployment around the natural rate; there was also, in many countries (especially in Europe), a strong upward trend in the natural rate. This upward trend often had the effect of making even short-run stabilization policy look ineffective. Consider, for example, the repeated attempts of European nations during the 1970s and early 1980s (British prime minister Edward Heath's "dash for growth," French President François Mitterand's initial expansionary program) to drive unemployment down toward 1960s levels. The inflationary consequences of these attempts might be explained by orthodox economists as the result of overambitious unemployment targets; but it was all too natural for policymakers to reach the simpler conclusion that expansionary monetary policy always leads to inflation rather than growth—period.

It might, incidentally, be worth mentioning a related problem: in an economy where the natural rate of unemployment shifts over time, how does one even know whether there is economic slack, or how big that slack actually is? Official estimates of output gaps now typically rely on some kind of smoothing procedure, like the Hodrick-Prescott filter. In effect, they estimate the economy's potential growth from a weighted average of past growth rates, and also assume that over the sample period, the average output gap has been zero. As a number of people have pointed out, this sort of procedure automatically interprets any sustained economic slump as structural; in a 1998 paper, following a suggestion by Robert Gordon, I applied Hodrick-Prescott to the Great Depression and discovered that the estimated U.S. output gap had been eliminated by 1935.[2] In other words, the effect of the uncertainty over where potential growth lies is to bias policymakers of depressed economies toward making low estimates of the amount of economic slack, suggesting that the payoff to Keynesian policies, even if successful, would be small.

The legacy of stagflation and its cousin Eurosclerosis, then, has been to instill skepticism among policymakers about the possibility of achieving much from stabilization policies. This skepticism has interacted with a new

2. Krugman (1998b).

set of reasons not to stabilize, arising from increasing integration of goods and especially capital markets.

The Incompatible Trinity

It was in the 1960s that Robert Mundell first gave the catchy title of "incompatible trinity" to the inconsistency that inevitably emerges among three seemingly plausible goals: independent monetary policy, stable exchange rates, and free movement of capital. Countries must choose two out of three: fixed rates plus capital mobility means loss of monetary policy, as in Argentina or the members of euroland; independent monetary policy plus capital mobility means a fluctuating exchange rate, as in Britain or Canada; a pegged exchange rate together with an autonomous monetary policy can only be sustained with capital controls, as in China. In the 1960s, however, few would have seen the first option—the abandonment of monetary policy—as a desirable prescription for any but the smallest countries. Capital controls, though much less effective since the establishment of current account convertibility, were still widespread and not viewed with the horror they inspire today. And while Bretton Woods was still being defended, many economists were sympathetic to the idea that floating rates would prove an attractive alternative.

Thirty years later, the landscape is transformed: currency union in Europe, currency boards (which had seemed a quaint colonial relic) established in several smaller nations, much talk of dollarization, and a general perception at least among smaller countries that the days of monetary independence are coming to an end. Why this change in views? Let us start with the good reasons, then turn to the bad ones.

First, while capital controls may not be as impractical or disastrous as current conventional wisdom has it—Malaysia's experience is open to interpretation, but it certainly has not had the dire consequences predicted by many—the case against such controls except as emergency measures is now overwhelming. Trade in goods and services has increased steadily as a share of GDP in most countries, and the advantages of such trade have become ever more apparent; yet controls on capital cannot be implemented without some form of monitoring on current transactions, and any such process threatens both to strangle legitimate transactions with red tape and to be a source of corruption. So most countries are very loath to reimpose the sort of sustained restrictions on capital movement that would allow them to choose the monetary-autonomy-with-stability-corner of the triangle.

Second, flexible exchange rates have turned out to be much more volatile than anyone in the 1960s expected. The main postwar experiment in floating rates before 1970 was that of the Canadian dollar from 1949 to 1962, an encouraging case: speculation was strongly stabilizing, and the exchange rate fluctuated only narrowly around parity. It turned out, however, that this was exceptional, perhaps because most people expected policy to ensure that a dollar was always worth more or less a dollar. In any case, since the breakup of fixed rates in 1973 exchange rates have turned out to be massively unstable, even when countries have similar inflation rates and no obvious major exogenous shocks. Anyone contemplating the gyrations of the yen-dollar rate since the early 1990s can remain an advocate of floating rates only by regarding them as the lesser of two evils.

Finally, the financial crises of the 1990s have highlighted the importance of an effect long stressed by practical men, but largely ignored in the traditional economic theory of devaluation: balance sheet implications of currency realignments. Many observers believe that the severe recessions that were instigated by the Asian currency crisis were largely a result of balance sheet effects: when highly leveraged firms with large debt denominated in dollars or yen were confronted with large depreciations of their national currency, they were forced to stop investing, and this contractionary impact at least initially outweighed the usual expansionary effect of increased net exports. Concern about balance sheet effects is a reason for countries to be hesitant about expansionary monetary policies that might depress the currency. It also suggests that countries can be subject to self-fulfilling loss of confidence, in which speculation leads to currency depreciation, depreciation leads to collapsing investment, and the collapse of investment ratifies the depreciation.[3] One answer to this risk is a credible commitment to a stable exchange rate, which again rules out monetary independence.

There are, then, some real reasons why some countries—especially emerging market economies—might feel themselves pushed into a regime that sacrifices monetary autonomy in favor of currency stability. In fairness to the Argentines, in particular, we might note that in addition to having a large dollar-denominated external debt, much of their economy's *internal* debt is also dollar-denominated. Perhaps they should consider how,

3. Krugman (1999). See also Aghion, Bacchetta, and Banerjee (1999).

over the longer term, to discourage this practice; in any event, there is a fairly compelling case against any consideration of peso devaluation anytime soon.

While there are very good reasons why capital controls should be avoided except in extreme cases, and fairly good reasons why countries might be skeptical about flexible exchange rates, there is another argument against exchange rate flexibility that seems to play a powerful role in actual policy, yet has been decisively refuted just about every time it has been tested by experience: the claim that currency depreciation is ineffective because it will quickly be dissipated in inflation.

It would be beyond the scope of this paper to try to document the rise of this belief, but I can report from personal experience and conversations that it was very widespread in Europe at the time of the 1992 currency crises, and in Brazil on the eve of the 1998–99 crisis—and that it remains a common assertion of policymakers in countries that have chosen to sacrifice monetary autonomy in defense of a fixed exchange rate.

In 1992 the typical assertion was that the United Kingdom, Sweden, and other depressed economies suffering recessions simply did not have the option of pursuing an expansionary monetary policy, even if they did drop out of the exchange rate mechanism (ERM), because any decline in their currencies against the Deutsche mark would quickly lead to an equal rise in domestic prices. What actually happened when some of the European economies nonetheless dropped out of the ERM was that they did in fact achieve real as well as nominal depreciations and, in the case of both the United Kingdom and Sweden, appear to have succeeded in getting a real payoff in terms of monetary autonomy. Indeed, the inflationary consequences of the 1992 devaluations were so mild that some economists came to believe that there had been a macroeconomic "free lunch," with not even the import price increases predicted by standard open economy–models. It was this extreme proposition, rather than the view that devaluations would be dissipated through inflation, that Robert Gordon felt it was necessary to test (and, as it happens, reject) in a forthcoming paper.[4]

Policymakers in developing countries have tended to argue that this benign experience carries few lessons for them; that countries with a severe history of inflation, in which the public has learned to think in foreign currency, will in fact find that their wages and prices are effectively indexed to the major currencies. However, two recent unintended tests of this

4. Gordon (forthcoming).

proposition have gone the other way. Israel's sudden depreciation in 1998 produced a one-time shock to prices but not an inflationary spiral; indeed, anecdotal evidence is that even contracts supposedly indexed to the dollar were in fact enforced at the old exchange rate: that is, in effect, turned out to be shekel-denominated. Most dramatically, Brazil—which had near-hyperinflation conditions as recently as 1995 and had defended the real at high cost in the belief that a devaluation would bring a quick inflationary surge—turns out to have experienced a 1992-style devaluation in which import prices rise but domestic wages and prices do not follow. (Unlike its neighbor, Brazil does not have large private-sector dollar-denominated debt, so none of the feared consequences of depreciation—except the invariable result, dismissal of the finance minister—have materialized.)

The puzzle is why, despite this experience, the belief that currency depreciation is quickly dissipated in inflation arose—and why it persists in the face of repeated favorable experiences.

A guess is that the conviction that depreciation leads quickly to inflation arose from misinterpretation of events that occurred in the 1970s and 1980s: that is, in a generally inflationary environment. A case in point is the way Swedish policymakers interpreted the results of the 1982 devaluation of the krona. During 1992 one heard this experience frequently cited as evidence that in Sweden devaluation was not a useful option; after all, the last one had led to an inflationary surge and eventually to a severe recession. In fact the inflation that followed the 1982 devaluation was not the result of any sort of implicit indexing of wages and prices: it built gradually over time as the result of an overheated domestic economy, itself the product of a loss of fiscal discipline and a runaway banking sector. So even in 1992 it should have been possible for Swedes to make an intellectual case for the efficacy of exchange rate adjustment in the face of a depressed economy. But this would have been a complicated story, and given the predisposition of officials at the time to place a priority on currency stability, it was perhaps natural simply to declare that the 1982 devaluation had failed, and so would any successor.

The persistence of this pessimism about depreciation in the face of the experience of the 1990s is a bit harder to explain. In the European case, one suspects that an important part of the answer lies in institutional and professional sunk costs. Can central bankers, finance ministry officials, and politicians who have spent most of the decade dedicating their careers to the proposition that monetary union was essential and inevitable really be expected to concede that Sweden-sized economies apparently can still do pretty well with their own currencies and monetary policies? And the success of the Europeans in getting to monetary union—whether it is a good idea or not—probably helps feed a broader perception that independent currencies for small countries are on the way out, even if the hard evidence that the economics of independent monetary policy has turned adverse is hard to find.

In short, a fair number of countries seem to be renouncing monetary policy as a tool of stabilization based on a belief that it is ineffective for open economies—a belief that is false. The experiences of Canada, Australia, Sweden, the United Kingdom, and others seem, if anything, to suggest that the late-1960s conventional wisdom about the usefulness of a floating rate system continues to be valid; but much of the world believes otherwise.

The Liquidity Trap

Most of this paper is concerned with cases where countries have renounced the use of stabilization policy; but one cannot avoid mentioning the case of the world's second largest economy, which has pushed conventional monetary policy to its limits and found it inadequate.

Exactly why Japan finds itself in a position in which even a zero interest rate is not enough to eliminate a large output gap is a matter of considerable dispute. Is it the result of balance-sheet problems in the private sector, the legacy of the 1980s bubble, or is it the result of deeper structural causes (declining work force, sluggish technical progress, high savings propensity)? But whatever the reasons, the reality of a liquidity trap in a major economy is deeply unsettling because it undermines one of the supposed certainties of stabilization policy.

Put it this way: a country that is willing to allow its currency to float can use monetary policy freely; and it has become almost universally accepted that monetary rather than fiscal policy should be the prime tool of stabilization, both for reasons of political economy (monetary policy is easier to change, and also easier to insulate from interest group politics) and because fiscal policy can be limited by the government's own actual or perceived budget constraints (see below). But now economists face the reality that in one important economy monetary policy cannot do the trick, and hence at least the possibility that the same problem can happen elsewhere.

What does one do in this case? The conventional Keynesian answer is to use fiscal policy instead, and that is what Japan has in fact done, with projected budget deficits of approximately 10 percent of GDP. Nor is there much question that fiscal policy works in the Keynesian direction in Japan. Whatever the arguments that fiscal austerity is good for confidence, Adam Simon Posen has pointed out that in the 1990s, fiscal expansion in Japan has invariably been followed by expansion, fiscal contraction by recession.[5]

At the same time, however, the experience of an actual liquidity trap has helped concentrate our minds about the difficulties of such a reliance on fiscal policy. Textbook expositions of fiscal policy in a liquidity trap—back when the textbooks still mentioned that possibility!—tended to be static, ignoring the long-run consequences for the government's budget. Underlying this short time horizon, one might suggest, was an implicit belief in a "pump-priming" or "jump-start" effect: for reasons not explicitly put into the formal model, fiscal stimulus would not have to be sustained for a long period of time. After all, the public works program known as World War II came to an end after four years, yet seemingly pushed the U.S. economy into a self-sustaining boom.

Once one confronts the reality of a stubbornly liquidity-trapped economy, however, it becomes necessary to think this through more carefully—at which point it becomes apparent that short-run effectiveness of fiscal expansion and the ability to jump-start an economy are by no means the same thing. If the jump-start idea means anything, it is that the stimulus need be only temporary—which in turn must involve some notion of multiple equilibria, so that a temporary stimulus can produce a permanently higher level of private spending. This could be true, but it is fairly exotic stuff on which to base economic policy. And for what it is worth, the current Japanese fiscal stimulus program seems at the time of writing to be producing only modest increases in private consumption, while private investment continues to decline. Unless the situation improves, this means that even to keep the output gap from rising will require massive deficit spending as far as the eye can see. Can the government afford this? I will turn to the constraints on fiscal policy below.

Is there an alternative? The idea that no monetary policy can effectively stimulate an economy with deficient demand is or should be deeply disturbing, not only on a practical but on a philosophical level. Surely it is a fundamental principle that doubling the money supply more or less

5. Posen (1998).

doubles the equilibrium price level, and therefore increases real demand if sticky prices are currently holding the price level above that equilibrium. My own take on this conundrum is that, properly speaking, the equilibrium price level will double only if the current money supply *and the expected future money supply* both double, so that the ineffectiveness of monetary policy is at base a credibility problem. If the public expected the central bank to sustain a current money increase, the liquidity trap would be avoided.[6] This is the route that leads to the conclusion that monetary policy would still be effective in a liquidity trap if there was a credible commitment to inflation—or, to quote the phrase that has caused much grief, if the central bank could "credibly promise to be irresponsible."[7]

The point for current purposes is that thus far the Bank of Japan has been unwilling to make that kind of promise; instead, it insists that it is doing all that can be done, and that if this is not enough to close the output gap, that is not the bank's problem. This abdication from stabilization policy is different in its causes from that of central bankers who declare that they cannot do anything in the face of their commitment to a fixed exchange rate; but the effect of a retreat from stabilization, in which one hopes that demand recovers rather than actively seeking to increase it, is the same.

Of course Japan retains the use of fiscal policy—as do even small economies with fixed exchange rates. But that then leads us to the limits of fiscal policy.

The Limits of Fiscal Policy

Here is some offbeat intellectual history. In 1962 Robert Mundell, drawing on his IS-LM–based models of open economies, suggested that countries that were unwilling to float their exchange rates but anxious to maintain full employment could achieve their short-run goals with a fiscal-monetary policy mix: tight money to attract capital inflows, deficit spending to pump up domestic demand.[8] This utterly Keynesian argument (actually, rather similar to arguments Keynes himself made in the 1920s) for a tight-money loose-fiscal mix is what, in later mythology, commentators like Paul Craig Roberts would cite as the key step in Mundell's supposed invention of supply-side economics. Oh well.

6. Krugman (1998b).
7. Krugman (1998a).
8. Mundell (1962).

But Mundell's original point still stands: even if one has a fixed exchange rate that one is unwilling to abandon, and hence must dedicate monetary policy to the maintenance of that rate, it is still possible to fight demand-side slumps with expansionary fiscal policy. Similarly, even if monetary policy has been rendered ineffectual by a liquidity trap, fiscal stimulus is still an effective policy tool. Or is it?

The current scene with regard to fiscal policy is somewhat confusing. In Asia at the time of writing, more-or-less Keynesian fiscal policy is in use, with considerable short-run success. In Japan, the fiscal packages have clearly rescued the economy from what last year looked like the imminent risk of a deflationary spiral. In the crisis countries, fiscal stimulus has been widely given credit for much of their bounceback. But in Japan, at least, there are growing worries about the sustainability of the current level of stimulus. And elsewhere in the world fiscal policy seems broadly to be operating in a pro- rather than countercyclical fashion, with austerity programs in depressed Latin American economies and the prospect of austerity in the less successful nations of the euro-zone as well.

There are at least three reasons why fiscal policy in much of the world is far less able to play a stabilizing role than economists in the 1960s might have imagined.

First is the role of international capital markets, especially for countries with substantial short-term debt. If one looks at the underlying fiscal numbers for Brazil, they do not seem particularly alarming: at this point the country has a small primary surplus, and its public debt burden is only about 50 percent of GDP. Given that the economy is currently depressed relative to potential, one might well argue that the country has good reason to be relaxed about its fiscal position, perhaps even that some temporary loosening might be in order. But in fact Brazil faces the urgent necessity of demonstrating fiscal discipline because much of its debt is short term—and the interest rates on that short-term debt tend to spike at even the hint of fiscal weakness. (At the time of writing the short-term interest rate is approximately 18 percent, in a country with low inflation and what is generally regarded as a quite competitive exchange rate; in 1998 interest rates were more than 40 percent.) The result is that despite the seemingly benign fundamentals, Brazil is extremely vulnerable to a sort of self-fulfilling process of fiscal collapse. Investors become dubious about the country's fiscal health, interest rates surge, the headline deficit number rises into double digits, and interest rates go still higher. The result is that the government must devote its fiscal efforts to confidence-building and is not free to regard fiscal policy as an instrument of demand management. And recessions, which worsen the primary surplus, generally must be met with austerity rather than expansion.

Brazil's case is rather extreme, but weaker forms of the same logic appear elsewhere; the effect is to take fiscal policy off the table, or even make it procyclical, in many countries.

A second reason for the paralysis of fiscal policy is the issue of long-run government solvency. This issue more or less crept up on advanced countries in the 1990s, mainly as a result of demography. Where it had previously seemed that deficits of a few percent of GDP could be carried indefinitely, the date at which it would become necessary to provide social insurance for a rapidly growing older population out of taxes on a shrinking working-age population moved from the distant to the not-so-distant future. Now it has become standard to add huge implicit liabilities to relatively moderate overall debt levels, and suggest that even countries with favorable-looking current budget numbers must worry about their longer-run positions. On a short-run macroeconomic basis, Germany looks like a candidate for fiscal stimulus; thanks to demography-driven long-run concerns, the Schröder government is instead trying to push through austerity. It is also worth noting that Japan's much-criticized 1997 tax increase, which has now been so massively reversed, was driven by concerns about the long-run solvency issue. That issue remains as pressing as ever—or rather, it is now two years and a number of trillion yen in Japanese government bonds more pressing than before—and poses the main problem for the continuation of the current policy of keeping the economy afloat through deficit spending. So it turns out that there is a qualification to Keynes's famous dictum: in the long run, unfortunately, many of us won't be dead, only retired, and that prospect makes it hard to base fiscal policy on short-run considerations.

Finally, in some cases fiscal policy has been ruled out by fiat. The initial International Monetary Fund (IMF) programs for Asia included fiscal austerity, contributing at least at the margin to the severity of the recessions. (The IMF did learn from experience and eventually became more Keynesian than the governments themselves.) In the advanced world, the new European monetary union will surely face temporary asymmetric shocks that produce booms in some regions, slumps in others. National fiscal policies might have been a partial answer to such instability. But in fact the countries are bound by a "stability pact" that sharply limits their ability to use fiscal policy as a demand-management tool. (The reasons for that pact remain somewhat unclear: the Federal Reserve does not police state budgets. One view is that there is a lingering fear that the European Central Bank will end up being forced to monetize national debts. If so, this is another case of the wrong lessons having been learned from the era of inflation.)

Again, fiscal policy has not been completely banished. It is being used to considerable effect in Asia, and presumably would be used should Anglo-Saxon nations find themselves in liquidity traps. But fiscal policy has turned out to be more subject to restrictions, and more constrained by the long run, than textbook economics had suggested, and therefore is a very imperfect substitute for the loss of monetary policy in a number of countries.

Stabilization Policy: Going or Coming Back?

The world economic crisis of 1997–? (it ain't over until the sumo wrestler sings) was not, as measured by its effect on gross world product, as severe as either the first or the second oil shock. What made it different was that it was more or less purely a demand-side event. In 1979–82, as the world economy suffered, advanced countries had very good reasons not simply to pump up demand with monetary and fiscal policy: they faced inflationary pressures and felt they needed to wring the inflationary expectations out of their economies before reflating. But in 1997–99, everyone agreed that the troubled economies needed more demand. And we were supposed to know how to create demand; indeed, for most of the postwar period the trouble has been that creating demand is not only easy but pleasant, tempting governments to overindulge. Yet in the late crisis governments were often unable or unwilling to ease monetary and fiscal policy, despite severe slumps.

Is this the beginning of a trend or the furthest swing of a pendulum? It depends on whom you ask. Roughly speaking, I would say that Washington—the IMF and the World Bank, the Treasury and the Fed—seems to have emerged from the crisis with a renewed respect for expansionary policies. The new Washington consensus urges countries to adopt floating exchange rates so that they retain monetary autonomy, has good things to say about deficit spending when it is in their judgment appropriate, and in general has become discreetly Keynesian. On the other hand,

New York—the people who move money and the people who disseminate business opinion about economics—continues to approve of the Victorian virtues, favoring currency boards and dollarization, fiscal austerity in recessions to gain confidence, and so on.

Which side is winning? Well, look at it from Mr. de la Rua's point of view. Argentina's deficit does not look all that bad as a share of GDP; but a lot of refinancing must take place next year, and that refinancing will take place in New York rather than Washington. And one way or another, one may guess that the retreat from stabilization policy will continue, at least for a while. This is not to deny the essential value of active policies to increase demand when it is inadequate, and the virtues of such things as independent currencies and discretionary fiscal policies. In the long run these virtues will again be widely appreciated, and nations will try to undo the structural features like foreign currency–denominated debt that have in some cases rendered stabilization policy ineffective. But in the long run. . . .

COMMENT BY
Stanley Fischer

It goes almost without saying that Paul Krugman has produced an interesting and well-written paper. It is eminently fair in its comments on the Asian IMF-supported programs, and on the fact that recent events have given many in Washington a renewed respect for the potential effects of expansionary fiscal policy.

Since I agree with most of the paper, and I have to comment, my main task is to find something to complain about. My main complaint is that the paper is mistitled. It should have been called "The Limits of Simple Keynesian Stabilization Policies," for the question it addresses is why monetary and fiscal policies are not in practice always driven by the implications of the textbook version of the closed economy ISLM model.

Paul gives three potential answers: Keynesianism was always a snare and a delusion; the world has changed—particularly for countries that have liberalized their capital accounts; and foolishness—that "policymakers have returned not to the wisdom but the errors of their grandfathers." He argues that the explanation lies in a mixture of the last two reasons.

Those surely are the two main reasons. Paul gives the impression that he believes foolishness is about 75 percent of the story, and changes in the environment about 25 percent. My guess is that the percentages should be reversed, and that the basic reason simple Keynesian stabilization policies are not used in some crises and recessions is that several factors omitted from the basic ISLM model, but embodied in more sophisticated versions of the model, are believed to and do matter in practice.

These include: open economy aspects that are not in the simplest model; inflation and the fear of inflation, something we should certainly emphasize on this occasion, for Art Okun stood out among Keynesians for his insistence that inflation was far more important politically than had been thought in the 1960s; expectations, particularly the recognition that the effects of a policy action sometimes depend on whether it is regarded as a one-time event or part of a continuing pattern; intertemporal budget constraints and debt dynamics—a factor that is recognized by Paul; and a concern about the long-run behavior of the economy—another factor referred to in the Krugman paper. Let me try to establish this by taking up three of the cases discussed by Paul: Argentina, Brazil, and euroland.

Argentina acquired its currency board after discretionary monetary policy had generated a hyperinflation. And for many years before that, Argentina had experienced very high inflations, followed by brief stabilizations, followed by high inflations.

The currency board has been in place for a decade, during which Argentina has experienced two very bad recessions. It seems obvious that Argentina must have made a mistake. But the last decade of the twentieth century was also the decade of highest growth in Argentina in the century, bar one. That suggests that the currency board straitjacket may have been less costly on average than implied in Paul's paper.

Further, the currency board arrangement commands wide assent. Paul's opening paragraph refers to the election of President de la Rua. He and his opponent were running neck and neck in the polls, until the latter started making suggestions that led the public to believe that he would give up the currency board, or as it is called in Argentina, convertibility. At that point the current president moved 15 percentage points ahead in the polls and did not look back.

The currency board is not something being palmed off on an unsuspecting public that does not understand the issue. The plain fact is nobody wants to go back to the good old days of high inflation, and they believe in the economics of the slippery slope. More formally, convertibility is a very effective commitment device.

Having watched Argentina stabilize three times and lose those stabilizations, I believe that they are right to stay with the currency board commitment. Not only has it brought monetary stability, it has also led Argentina to focus far more clearly than ever before on the serious structural obstacles to growth in that country. For instance, they have built a very strong banking system. At some point, when they regard stability as being assured, they could change the monetary arrangement, although I suspect that their next change might be to dollarize.

Why not go the Mundell-Fleming route and ease up on fiscal policy? The answer is very simple—and the same point will come up in the European context—because they did not make room earlier for an expansionary fiscal policy in bad times. Argentina has been running at the edge of what the markets will accept for several years. They were urged to tighten fiscal policy when the going was good, so that expansionary fiscal policy could be available in a crisis. But that was not done, and that is why expansionary fiscal policy was not available in 1999–2000—the intertemporal budget constraint exists.

Brazil ended its very high inflation in 1994 using an exchange rate peg. Among heterodox stabilizations, Brazil's is close to the most ingenious and the most well executed. The Brazilian policymakers decided that their inflation was a result of too much inertia in the system, and they got rid of the inertia by tying all contracts to the dollar and shortening them.

Once contracts had become very short and indexed to the dollar, they fixed the dollar exchange rate. Then they got rid of the dollar indexation. It was a brilliant exercise. It was also extremely popular, in part because it was followed by a remarkable improvement in the distribution of income. The poor appeared to be the main beneficiaries of stabilization. But the fiscal follow-through was unfortunately inadequate.

Now, why not use fiscal expansion following their January 1999 devaluation, especially given Brazil's high unemployment? It was because they were on the edge of a debt trap. The short-term real interest rate is about 12 percent. The debt is just below 50 percent of GDP, so the real interest bill is high. If Brazil was perceived not to be on a path on which the debt dynamics was favorable, the real rate would increase and debt dynamics would become more questionable.

So in Brazil, the fundamental problem is debt dynamics. This is nothing that Paul disagrees with, but it is something left out of the ISLM model and its open economy version: fiscal dynamics and the possibility of a debt trap kept Brazil from doing the obvious in a recession, easing fiscal policy.

Despite many criticisms about details, the monetary policy of the European Central Bank has generally been countercyclical, along the lines suggested by the IS-LM model. (Incidentally, I do not believe that the invention of the euro is based on a view that exchange rate devaluations are useless because they lead to inflation. Rather, Europeans moved toward a common currency in part—only in part—because they believed the opposite, namely, that nominal exchange rate changes led to real exchange rate changes, producing a competitive advantage for the devaluing country.)

Similarly, the design of the European fiscal framework permits the use of countercyclical fiscal policies, at least to the extent that automatic stabilizers should be allowed to operate. But the designers of the fiscal framework want countercyclical policy to operate around a position of long-run fiscal sustainability. One can always argue with the parameters, with a 60 percent debt to GDP ratio, and a roughly balanced budget. But the basic construct is fully consistent with the simple Keynesian idea that fiscal policy should retain the capacity to be expansionary, or at least run a larger deficit, in a recession.

The Europeans may well reject Keynesian rhetoric; they might even go to the stake proclaiming they are not Keynesians. But the principles on which the stability pact is based permit an active fiscal policy, while taking into account the possibilities of adverse debt dynamics, which are based in part on the very bad demographics that many of those countries face.

Let me turn now to a few other points. First, consider the desire for low inflation. Argentina and Brazil have voted for low inflation, which is politically very popular indeed. That puts constraints on policies. Whether those constraints are justified is a judgment that I trust more to those who have been through high inflations than to those who have not. But I have noticed a tendency for people, who in their own countries would certainly be unwilling to live with, for example, a 15 percent inflation rate, to say that moderate inflations are reasonable for other countries. Typically the citizens of those countries, given the opportunity, prefer to live with lower inflation. And that supports Art Okun's argument that the costs of inflation were generally underestimated in the 1960s and early 1970s.

Second, Paul focuses on the question of the circumstances under which nominal devaluations become real. It is true that nominal devaluations in the 1990s have almost all turned into real devaluations. But they have done that in contexts in which other policies or high unemployment helped ensure that outcome.

For instance, Paul comments on the Israeli devaluation (in the context of an exchange rate floating within a band) at the end of 1998. That became real (indeed the nominal devaluation was reversed to some extent) because the central bank raised interest rates sharply following the devaluation. Similarly, it was not an accident that Brazil's devaluation in 1999 became real. That happened in large part because of the contractionary fiscal policy and the tight monetary policy that followed the devaluation. It would have been easy to allow the shift to a flexible exchange rate to develop into an ongoing inflation. It was a policy decision not to.

Third, consider expansionary fiscal contractions. I believe that some of the changed views about fiscal policy were a result of too much generalization from a few cases of expansionary fiscal contractions. The famous paper by Francesco Giavazzi and Marco Pagano established that fiscal contractions in Denmark and Ireland in the early 1990s were expansionary.[9] The mechanism was that the removal of the fear of unstable debt dynamics led to both lower interest rates and more consumption—in other words, to the view that fiscal contraction would generate a confidence effect. The return of confidence could even lead to more capital inflows as a result of the contraction, despite lower interest rates. Similar arguments have been made in the case of Italy's fiscal contractions later in the decade.

Quite possibly those results influenced thinking about fiscal policy more than they should have. By putting the confidence effect center stage, they may have led to too much emphasis on the confidence-raising effects of fiscal contractions.

That emphasis began to change, at least in the IMF, as a result of Japan's experience in mid-1997. The Japanese, having had a couple of quarters of very rapid expansion, decided that it was time to attend to their long-run fiscal problems, which reflect their aging population. They increased taxes very significantly, by about 2 percent of GDP, in April 1997. Furthermore, they did so by increasing the consumption tax, with the result that intertemporal substitution led the authorities to believe the economy was much stronger before they raised taxes than it really was. Then the bottom fell out of the economy. That, plus the experience in Asia, had an effect that tended to restore some of the faith in expansionary fiscal policy.

Thus Paul is right that, on this issue, some in the policy community have in the last few years moved a little closer to the basic Keynesian model of thirty-five years ago. But to the extent that they have not, it is not so

9. Giavazzi and Pagano (1990).

much a reflection of ignorance, as a recognition that the world is a good deal more complicated than that of the 1960s textbook model.

COMMENT BY
Benjamin M. Friedman

Ours is an era of "can't" in macroeconomics policy. It is also an era of cant. Consider fiscal policy: In one country after another throughout the developing world that has faced the need to revive an economy floored by currency crisis, fiscal expansion has been missing in action—taken prisoner by the forces of a perceived need to preserve one or another form of "credibility." In Japan until just recently, calls for genuine fiscal expansion routinely evoked fears, based on the government's high gross (but not net) debt-to-income ratio, that the policy would prove unsustainable—even though the very notion of countercyclical fiscal policy in the first place *is* that such a policy is not supposed to be sustained, much less sustainable. In the meantime, the European countries have engaged in an intricately choreographed fiscal ballet, the climax of which consisted, in effect, of lacing up one another's straitjackets. In the United States—at the same time that our elected officials of both parties assess every issue relating to nontransfer federal spending in terms of the jobs to be created or lost, and the best way to ensure approval of any new weapons program is to arrange for at least some small piece of the hardware to be manufactured in each of 435 congressional districts—many economists regularly reject out of hand the possibility that fiscal actions have the ability to shape real economic outcomes.

Or consider monetary policy: Central bankers around the world now compete among themselves to see who can appear most macho in denying any policy objective whatever apart from stable prices. Europe's central bankers know that the gold standard is gone, presumably forever; but apparently recalling that the properties that gave gold its value stemmed from its being an inert metal, they urgently seek in their own behavior to imitate this characteristic. Even in the United States, where the governing legislation expressly directs the central bank to conduct monetary policy so as to promote "maximum employment" (among other objectives), it is possible for the Federal Reserve System's number-two ranking official to see his suitability for that position called into question for committing the unpardonable faux pas of admitting in public that he and his colleagues indeed comply with the law.

It was not always so, and the task Paul Krugman sets himself in this paper is to shed light on how we came to this sorry state of affairs. I agree with Krugman's assessment—including his description of currently fashionable thinking (and thus implicitly the change since a third of a century ago), as well as his account of how we got here from there. Rather than nitpick at second- or even third-order matters of interpretation, therefore, I shall devote my comments to filling in a few more pieces of the story, pieces that are in no way inconsistent with Krugman's sensible account. Because Krugman devotes so much of his paper to the situation in countries other than the United States, where international considerations (including in particular globalization of the financial markets) bulk large in these matters, I shall focus primarily on how these important changes in policy attitudes came about in the United States.

To begin, macroeconomics, as a would-be science lacking the ability to conduct controlled, replicable experiments, inevitably responds sharply to actual events. I think four events, two from the 1970s and two from the 1980s, have played especially important parts in bringing about the turn of fashion away from activist macroeconomic policy that Krugman describes.

First, as Krugman acknowledges, the failure of the Phillips curve to remain stable in the face of efforts to exploit it was a first-order disappointment. To be sure, it is easy to overstate this proposition, and many economists today often do just that. Arthur Okun and others on President Johnson's Council of Economic Advisers urged a tax increase much earlier on than actually occurred; had the president taken their advice, some part of the overutilization of resources that led to the subsequent inflation would no doubt have been avoided. It is one thing to argue that 1960s macroeconomics failed in its ambitions. It is unfair to point, as evidence of that failure, to ambitions that 1960s economics never had. But it is certainly true that some ambition to exploit a Phillips curve, on the hope that it would remain stable, was part of the economics of that time. In the end neither the ambition nor the hope was realized.

Second, not surprisingly, the two oil price increases imposed by the OPEC cartel undermined the 1960s policy strategy. To recall, the essence of that strategy was to anticipate disturbances to aggregate demand to whatever extent was possible, to recognize as quickly as possible those that did occur, and to use fiscal or monetary policy, or both, to offset anticipated or observed demand disturbances in whole or in part. But an oil price increase, to a country that is heavily dependent on foreign oil, is not just a demand disturbance. In retrospect, I am impressed by how *rapidly* the professional literature of the 1970s recognized these supply shocks for what they were, and even got right, analytically, many of their most salient macroeconomic implications. But it was true, and the profession recognized, that the problem the United States faced on this account was one that the conceptual framework of the 1960s was not prepared to encompass.

Third—and in this case ironically—the fact that the disinflation of the 1980s proved costly also undermined the 1960s approach to macroeconomic stabilization. One of the chief reasons for the appeal of the rational expectations construct of the 1970s was that this line of thinking held out the prospect that a disinflationary monetary policy might be significantly less costly, in terms of foregone output and employment, than conventional models of the day indicated. In the limit, the rational expectations model suggested that under the right conditions disinflation would be entirely costless. By contrast, a 1978 paper by Okun, based on his survey of pre-rational-expectations macroeconometric models, gave a median estimate that each 1 percentage point reduction in inflation would require 3.5 "point-years" of unemployment.[10] In fact, the unemployment produced over time in the course of the Volcker disinflation corresponded astonishingly closely to this estimate. Because of a shift in the "Okun's Law" relationship between unemployment and output, the output cost of the Volcker disinflation was about one-third less than Okun's median estimate had implied. Even so, on either measure the rational expectations prediction of costless disinflation had not just failed but failed spectacularly.

But—and here is the irony—instead of leading to renewed confidence in the 1960s approach underlying the models Okun had used, this dramatic demonstration of the costs of disinflation only made policymakers all the more determined to avoid getting into an inflation in the first place. For at least a decade afterward, appealing to metaphors of the "slippery slope" (in other words, a nonlinearity for which there was not, and is not, empirical evidence) somehow seemed adequate grounds for resisting any temptation to use macroeconomic policy to put unused resources back to work. Arthur Okun's economics had won a round, but in winning nonetheless had lost again.

Fourth, the large federal budget deficits of the 1980s and early 1990s placed a further barrier in the way of any talk of using fiscal policy to stimulate economic activity, should the need arise. Full-employment deficits

10. Okun (1978, p. 348).

averaging nearly 4 percent of GDP were unprecedented in the United States apart from major wars. Given conventional built-in fiscal responses, in the event of a serious recession, the actual deficit would go to 6 or even 7 percent of GDP. Short of an emergency like that of the 1930s, or a lingering stagnation like Japan's today, who would have been prepared to recommend pushing the deficit to 10 percent of GDP? Fortunately, this particular impediment to thinking in terms of what once was standard macroeconomic policy has now been removed. It is too soon to say whether, and if so how, policymakers' attitudes will change in response.

Macroeconomics responds so importantly to external events like these because it is not a laboratory science. But like any other science, it also has an internal dynamic driven by the interplay of ideas. I believe that the macroeconomic policy presumptions of the 1960s also fell victim, in part, to this kind of internal conceptual turmoil.

As is well known, macroeconomics has long suffered from the conceptual gulf separating what we think we know about the "short run" (think of this as a time horizon within which various forms of rigidities, imperfections in markets and in information, adjustment costs, coordination failures, and the like importantly shape the consequences of policy actions) and the "long run" (think of this as the time horizon within which such impediments to achieving classical equilibrium lose their force). How to make what we think we know at one horizon consistent with what we think we know at the other is perhaps the chief challenge confronting our subdiscipline. To our credit, we pursue that task in hopes of both simplicity of thought and precision of argument.

Ours is not the only discipline to face the challenge posed by such a dichotomy. As Oxford mathematician Roger Penrose has argued, modern physics now confronts the need to unify what it knows about phenomena that take place at large scale, mostly following Newtonian relationships, and what it knows at extremely small scale, heavily relying on quantum principles. But as Penrose has articulately explained, one solution that does not work is simply to take what physicists know at small scale and apply these ideas, unadulterated, to large-scale phenomena. Doing so yields absurdities—in Penrose's example, the conclusion that a baseball can be in two places at once.[11] The field must try harder than that if it is to make genuine progress in unifying its two currently dichotomous bodies of knowledge.

11. Claudia Dreifus, "A Mathematician at Play in the Fields of Space-Time," *New York Times,* January 19, 1999, p. F3.

I believe that part of the route from the macroeconomic policy presumptions of the 1960s to the contrary attitudes fashionable today also involved a detour in which economists tried—at the theoretical level—to bridge the gulf between what we know about the short run and what we know about the long run by assuming, in effect, that the two are the same. The result of doing so is not exactly analogous to finding that a baseball is in two places at once, but as the example of the costless disinflation proposition shows, it does lead readily to ideas that are false. Some of those false ideas, however, have played an important part in the evolution of thinking about macroeconomic policy.

Part of the problem here too, I think, is that our quest for simplicity and precision sometimes leads us in directions that conceal rather than illuminate aspects of how macroeconomic policies work. We must choose to use these policy tools, or forbear their use, in a world that is not populated by identical representative agents. Moreover, it is not necessarily true that the behavior of any of those nonidentical agents corresponds to maximization of a simple function of one or two standard variables, subject to the conventional textbook constraints. Alfred North Whitehead enjoined us to seek simplicity but distrust it. In macroeconomics we too often remember only half of this advice. Nor does the field have a satisfactory answer to Amartya Sen's question asking why we must reject the vaguely right in favor of being precisely wrong.

But let me conclude, as I think Art Okun would have done, on an optimistic note. Circumstances change, and in some ways that bear importantly on macroeconomic policy they are already doing so. The Reagan-Bush deficits are gone. Nobody any more says disinflation is costless. The claim that we will achieve price stability only by subjecting the central bank to some form of external constraint, because of the "time inconsistency" problem to which discretionary policymaking can be subject, looks increasingly pale in the glare of the near-stability of prices (actual stability on some measures) that the United States has achieved without any such change in institutional arrangements. The Europeans are a hardy people; having survived the Mongol invasions, the Black Death, and two world wars, they will no doubt survive the Maastricht agreements and the European Central Bank also.

Thomas Huxley wrote that most successful ideas in science begin as heresy, advance to orthodoxy, and eventually become dogma. Perhaps there is a little truth in this notion as applied to the macroeconomic policy ideas of the 1960s. No doubt there were some economists, and some policymakers too, who held elements of that thinking above the need for empirical verification and hence above the fray of potential empirical disconfirmation. It is now decades later, and they have been swept aside.

But the same path from heresy to orthodoxy to dogma seems all the more to describe important elements of the thinking of the 1970s and 1980s that proved so subversive of the policy attitudes of Arthur Okun's day. In time they too will be swept aside. The process has already begun.

References

Aghion, Philippe, Philippe Bacchetta, and Abhijit Banerjee. 1999. "A Simple Model of Monetary Policy and Currency Crises." University College London.

Giavazzi, Francesco, and Marco Pagano. 1990. "Can Severe Fiscal Contractions be Expansionary? Tales of Two Small European Countries." In *NBER Macroeconomics Annual 1990,* edited by Stanley Fischer, 75–111. MIT Press.

Gordon, Robert J. Forthcoming. "The Aftermath of the 1992 ERM Breakup: Was There a Macroeconomic Free Lunch?" In *Currency Crises,* edited by Paul Krugman. University of Chicago Press.

Krugman, Paul. 1998a. "Japan's Trap." (web.mit.edu/krugman/www/)

——. 1998b. "It's Baaack: Japan's Slump and the Return of the Liquidity Trap." *Brookings Papers on Economic Activity, 2:1998,* 137–206.

——. 1999. "Analytical Afterthoughts on the Asian Crisis." (web.mit.edu/krugman/www/MINICRIS.htm)

Lucas, Robert E. 1981. *Studies in Business-Cycle Theory.* MIT Press.

Mundell, Robert A. 1962. "The Appropriate Use of Monetary and Fiscal Policy for Internal and External Stability." *IMF Staff Papers* (March): 70–79.

Okun, Arthur M. 1978. "Efficient Disinflationary Policies." *American Economic Review* 68 (May): 348–52.

Posen, Adam Simon. 1998. *Restoring Japan's Economic Growth.* Institute for International Economics.

ROBERT M. SOLOW 4

The Kennedy Council and the Long Run

M ost of the discussion of macroeconomics in this book will be about day-to-day, quarter-to-quarter, short-run macroeconomics. There are two good reasons for this. The first is that short-run macroeconomics is what the Council of Economic Advisers actually *does* most of the time, when it is doing macroeconomics at all. Interpreting events for the president in real time is a preeminent demand, and the demand gets met.[1]

The second reason is that short-run macroeconomics is where the controversy is. In the 1960s, the macroeconomics deployed by the Council of Economic Advisers (CEA) was perhaps a little bit ahead of the macroeconomics of the intermediate textbooks of the time and not very different from the articles then appearing in learned journals. The novel element was that we took it seriously and used it in real-time policymaking.[2] Today, the journals have changed a lot. Textbook macroeconomics has also changed, but rather less. (Is that just a sign of cultural lag, or is it because a naive student cannot be expected to believe the things that an assistant professor can

---

1. I was a member of the Council staff, along with Arthur Okun, from January 1961 to February 1962. Then I went back to teaching at MIT and Art stayed on. During the next year or so, I spent a lot of time at the Council helping out, especially at report time. I can say that the hundreds of hours that the five of us—Walter Heller, Jim Tobin, Kermit Gordon, Art, and I—put into thinking about economic policy, deciding on our position, and figuring out how best to explain it, have ever since sustained my belief that economics is good stuff.

2. In what follows, I am going to talk a lot about what "we" thought. That usage is intended as a reminder that the Council and staff did a lot of talking and trying out ideas.

manage to accept?) The macroeconomics of the *Economic Report of the President* may have changed least of all. If so, that is certainly worth trying to understand and will no doubt be much discussed.

In turn, I have three reasons for devoting this paper to the Council's implicit model of the long run. The first is that it would be a pity to skip it. The Council had ideas about the theory and practice of economic growth, and they were somehow connected with its view of short-run macroeconomic theory and policy. The second reason is that it sticks in my mind. The senior staff at the CEA worked frenetically on the whole *Report*, but one of my own main assignments was to plan and coordinate chapter 2 of the 1962 *Report*. So naturally I want to go back to it and see how it looks from today's perspective.

Third, my hope is that this look back will illuminate some of the ways that economic thinking evolves out of the interplay between theoretical ideas and policy needs. The common understandings of the economics profession coalesce, and then eventually change, under the influence of internal logic and external events. Arthur Okun's thinking was an important foundation of our basic understanding of the link between short-run and long-run macroeconomics and has endured for nearly forty years.

In understanding where we economists were and how we have evolved, the intellectual context has to be kept in mind. In 1961, the basic articles on modern growth theory by James Tobin and me (and Trevor Swan) were only five years old.[3] They were the tools we had in mind when we thought about the macroeconomics of the long run. We really had them in mind: both Tobin and I wrote and published articles on growth theory while we were at the Council. They were suitable for the time, too. Tobin's was on "Economic Growth as an Objective of Government Policy."[4] Mine was on "Technical Progress, Capital Formation, and Economic Growth."[5] I'll discuss that subject below.

First, I want to make some connections between the macroeconomics of the long and the short run. We took it for granted that the main goal of short-run macroeconomics was to explain deviations from "full employment," and thus suggest policies and institutions to keep these deviations small. (There was nothing special about employment; "full utilization" would have done just as well.) What we took for granted many of today's

---

3. Tobin (1955); Swan (1956).
4. Tobin (1964).
5. Solow (1962).

protagonists of real-business-cycle theory would describe as fundamentally misconceived. In their way of thinking, whatever is *is* optimal adaptation; there is nothing practically relevant for it to be a deviation from. We thought there was, and Arthur Okun had a way of approximating it. His name for it was "potential output," and that concept has survived in applied macroeconomics.

The connection with long-term growth is this; we (or I, anyway) thought of growth theory as being the macroeconomics of a national economy that always—by hook or by crook—manages to keep its actual aggregate output very close to its potential output. To put it in a slightly different way, growth-oriented policy was policy aimed at increasing potential output. Note that this is not equivalent to defining growth-oriented policy as policy aimed at increasing the long-term growth rate—though it would include that possibility if we knew how to achieve it. The focus on the malleability of the long-term growth rate, now so commonplace, is a by-product—or perhaps the main product—of the "endogenous growth theory" that has dominated the literature since the mid-1980s.

The article on growth that I wrote at the Council (with assistance from Dick Attiyeh, Sidney Winter, and Roy Wehrle) was an attempt to build the Okun formulation into an estimate of the aggregate production function for potential output. I think that I had the ambition eventually to produce a model in which both actual and potential output figured explicitly. Such a model would be a step toward unifying short-run and long-run macroeconomics. The task still has not been accomplished, unless one accepts the postulate of real-business-cycle theory that they are one and the same. A bit later in this paper I will sketch out what such a model might look like—but it will be only a sketch, leaving the real work still to be done. The idea here simply is to convey the sort of model we had in mind when we thought out what we should say in the *Report*.

There was yet another matter that nagged at us on both sides of the short-run–long-run divide. It concerned one of the strong implications of any reasonably calibrated growth model of the standard sort. Even a large increase in the permanent saving-investment rate (meaning large enough that one could just barely imagine accomplishing it through acceptable policy tools) would have a disappointingly small effect on the level of the steady-state path of potential output. In other words: imagine a model economy with a constant ratio of investment to GDP equal to s, whose steady-state growth path can be described as $Y^* e^{gt}$. (Y^* will depend on the various parameters of the model and some of the initial conditions.) Then it is hard to escape the impression that the elasticity of Y with respect to s is fairly small.

That is a discouraging inference for anyone interested in promoting economic growth. Later, endogenous growth theory was able to find many apparently easy ways to increase the steady-state growth rate. Our theoretical framework could not even find an easy way to raise the level of the steady-state growth path. We thought quite a bit about possible improvements to the basic model that could plausibly produce more optimistic implications. Shortly before joining the Council staff, I had experimented with a model in which new technology could enter production only when it had been embodied in newly produced capital. That would certainly enhance the productivity-raising effect of additional gross investment. Tobin and I (and our collaborators Christian von Weizsäcker and Menahem Yaari) later worked out a model in which higher investment would imply quicker displacement of less productive capital equipment.[6] So we had some ideas; none of them was empirically solid enough to be the basis of quantitative thinking about growth policy, but they helped us to make a general case for growth-promoting investment.

Chapter 2 of the 1962 *Report* began with a brief argument that smaller amplitude of short-run fluctuations, as well as fuller utilization of the economy's potential, would favor long-run *growth* (that is, a higher path of potential output). The idea was simply that both would lead to a higher average level of investment—the second because profits would be higher, the first because cyclical risk would be less. For the same reasons, innovation would also be expected to increase.

There was probably a certain amount of walking on eggs going on here. We were very conscious of the standard neoclassical result that a higher maintained investment quota would have only a temporary effect on the growth rate of potential GDP, and no permanent effect on the steady-state growth rate. So we were very careful to include an explicit reference to the favorable effect of better day-to-day macroeconomic performance on the rate of innovation. There was no solid empirical basis for any quantitative inference about the rate of technological progress, but it seemed safe enough as a general qualitative proposition. We paid special attention to the determinants of innovation later in the chapter, as will be seen in due course.

---

6. Solow and others (1966).

A contemporary reader will realize immediately that the modern theory of endogenous growth would have endorsed a much stronger statement than the one we made. But that version of growth theory was still a quarter-century in the future—and I am not sure there is much empirical foundation even now for confident statements about the rate of innovation. I remember that we talked about this issue and worried about what we might legitimately write in the *Report,* but I cannot remember exactly what we said. I know what I would say now, and I suspect—perhaps wishfully—that something similar was in my mind in the old days. I think it is rash to claim much insight into the quantitative determination of the rate of innovation, or even of the *amount* of innovation. But nowadays I would not hesitate to define anything that merely permanently raises the *level* of the growth path as a contribution to "economic growth" even if it leaves the steady-state growth rate where it was. I hope that chapter 2 is consistent with that view; the many references to the rate of growth, inevitable in nontechnical writing, can be read in context as referring to annual growth rates rather than permanently sustainable steady-state growth rates. But we might have slipped up here or there.

There was another delicate matter that concerned us, and here I wonder if we were not worrying too much about nothing. The question was, should economic growth be an object of public policy at all? Our concern arose from two quite opposite sources. The first was the popular fear—maybe even more visible then than it is now—that technological progress leads to persistent technological unemployment and to socially destructive displacement of workers, as whole industries and occupations decay or disappear. Our answer was that generalized technological unemployment had never been a serious danger and could in any case be adequately met by proper attention to the volume of aggregate demand. The social cost of displacement, on the other hand, was quite real and serious; if growth is a proper object of public policy, then so are the adjustment, training, and infrastructure needs of those who are adversely affected by technological change. We made a point of saying this.

The second source of worry was the possible charge that "growth-oriented policy" was just a code word for "planning." With hindsight, I wonder if we were too apprehensive on this point. In any case we emphasized that realized economic growth is fundamentally an outcome of individual decisions by firms and households. Of course, in the fields of activity traditionally allocated to them, units of government can act in ways favorable to or inimical to rapid growth; there is no definable "neutral" stance. Elsewhere, public policy aims only at the incentives that affect firms and households. But we thought such policy should do so in ways generally favorable to growth (either level or rate, as mentioned earlier).

This is where Tobin's 1964 article comes in. It was published after he had left the Council, but it is a fair—and much more elegant—reflection of our thinking about growth-oriented policy. The paper has lost none of its force and grace after thirty-five years; I would endorse its argument today.

The relevant point here is Tobin's case that (faster or slower) growth is a legitimate object of public policy, and that faster growth was the proper goal in the conditions that then prevailed. (It is perfectly clear from the context that "growth" is meant to include *lifting* the growth path of consumption per head, even without *tilting* it.)

I will simply list the elements in Tobin's case. First, individuals' revealed preferences between current and future aggregate consumption are just as worthy of respect when they are expressed through the ballot box as when they are expressed in markets. Second, democratically determined actions of government are an important instrumentality for representing and ensuring the permanence and continuity of society, perhaps especially when they serve to permit a generation to protect the future against its own occasional shortsightedness. Third, commitment to public education, resource conservation, and the like are evidence of a felt obligation to future generations, so arguments about the desirability of more or less are clearly in order. In any event, there is no practical possibility of defining a "neutral" stance. Fourth, over and above these considerations, private capital markets fail to reflect social preferences accurately. There are several reasons for this, including the presence of monopoly elements. Perhaps the most important is the fact that many private risks—such as the chance that an investment will lose out to another firm—are not social risks, if only because society can pool investment risks so extensively. Another is the favorable externalities associated with R&D and very likely many other forms of investment. Finally, the best available estimates of the social, or even the private, rate of return to investment seem comfortably to exceed the rate of time preference (as measured by the interest rate that private savers are willing to accept).

So we had no inhibition about the importance of supply-side policies. We estimated that potential GNP (not GDP, which was not then much discussed) had grown at an annual rate of 4.4 percent from 1947 to 1954, but at only 3.5 percent between 1954 and 1960. The corresponding growth rates of labor productivity (potential GNP per hour worked) were 3.8 and 2.6 percent annually.[7] That was a substantial deceleration, and remember that the famous "productivity slowdown" that economists still talk about was way in the future.

The unavoidable question was, how much of that deceleration could be reversed with reasonable policy and average luck? We did not know, but we spent a lot of time putting together plausible scenarios. In the end we proposed what we called an "illustration" for 1970. It involved a growth of potential hours worked of 1.2 percent a year (up from 0.9 percent in 1954–60) and growth of potential productivity of 3 percent a year (up from the already mentioned 2.6 percent). So our illustrative scenario showed potential GNP growing at 4.3 percent a year between 1960 and 1970.[8] Combined with the closing of a 6 percent Okun gap between current GNP and potential GNP, that would allow actual GNP to grow at 4.9 percent a year to 1970. We thought the hypothetical productivity gain to be reasonable in the context of an investment-led prosperity that would also encourage expanded participation of labor.

As things turned out, we were substantially off the mark. Our "illustration" had potential GNP per hour growing at 3 percent per year between 1960 and 1970. A reasonable estimate of what potential GNP actually was in 1970 would yield a productivity growth rate of about 2.3 per year. We did not foresee the Vietnam War, obviously, or the roller-coaster ride it gave our economy. More important, we did not foresee the—still fairly mysterious—productivity slowdown, which is usually dated from about 1973, but was already partially visible in the late 1960s. A different sort of explanation is that investment incentives of the early 1960s, although they had some favorable effect on plant and equipment spending, had a smaller effect than we had expected. Despite these deficiencies, I read the outcome as suggesting, at a minimum, that such exercises are not mere fantasy.[9] It has to be said that no one is very good at forecasting productivity.

Note that we made no use of the concept of total factor productivity. We knew about it, of course; it was all of four years old. But in those days there were no adequate and up-to-date figures on the stock of plant and equipment, and certainly no official data, so we had to deal almost exclu-

7. Council of Economic Advisers (1962, p. 113).

8. Council of Economic Advisers (1962, p. 115).

9. For a more detailed post mortem on that exercise, see my contribution to a *Festschrift* for Walter W. Heller, "Where Have All the Flowers Gone: Economic Growth in the 1960s" (Solow, 1982).

sively in terms of labor productivity. Today this kind of scenario-building would routinely take explicit account of alternative projections of fixed capital investment. This would have fit very well with the Council's emphasis on investment in the broadest sense.

The rest of chapter 2 of the 1962 *Report* is given over to detailed commentary on the important components of a broadly based strategy of high investment that might realize the "illustrative" scenario for the decade of the 1960s. There was insistent emphasis on the complementarities among various forms of capital, including public infrastructure. But it is especially interesting that we gave pride of place to investment in human resources, considerably before human capital began to play such a conspicuous role in theories of endogenous growth. I do not remember if this was an explicit decision, but it surely reflected an intention to interpret the idea of investment as broadly as possible.

The content of the passage on "Investment in Human Resources" suggests rather strongly that we were also aiming at an extended definition of the notion of a "contribution to economic growth." As I mentioned earlier, it makes good intellectual sense to think of anything that permanently lifts the long-run path as a contribution to economic growth, even if the steady-state growth rate remains unchanged. The section in the *Report* on human resources begins with the desirability of increased investment in education, but it then continues by advocating the importance of better health and the elimination of racial discrimination as part of a portfolio of growth-oriented policies. It would be hard to argue that a healthier society, or one characterized by racial equity, would have, for those reasons, a higher steady-state growth rate than before. But it is more or less obvious that the achievement of a healthier labor force, or the elimination of the allocative inefficiencies induced by racial discrimination in the labor market, will *lift* the growth path forever. That should qualify as a contribution to economic growth. The fact that the Council classified it that way, as a matter of course, is an indication that it had thought the matter through. It is pretty clear that we were not adopting the much stronger assumptions that underlie modern endogenous growth theory.

The section on "Investment in Technological Progress" does not break new ground, but there are a couple of observations worth making. Roughly equal billing goes to research and development as a source of technological progress and an object of policy, and to "more effective use of existing technology" (or shortening the lag between invention and effective use of new technology). The second of these emphases is another example of a level-increasing rather than a rate-of-growth-increasing option for policy. On the side of R&D, the *Report* advocates a shift of resources toward basic research, for the standard reason that it is bound to carry more non-capturable advantages than applied research. There is a rather hesitant remark to the effect that some firms are too small to have an effective R&D program, while others just lack a research tradition. In both cases, as well as some in which the social return exceeds the private return substantially, the *Report* makes a low-key pitch for increased public expenditure to subsidize research. On the whole, the passage on technological change is very cautious, even about the connection between R&D and growth of productivity. With a look ahead at the popularity of endogenous growth theory, one could wonder if we were too cautious. Personally, I am not sure (said he, cautiously).

Eventually, the chapter gets around to "Investment in Plant and Equipment." Here the *Report* makes use of a data series on the stock of business capital (whose details are not specified). It could evidently not be matched with a series on potential output and hours worked, so the calculations are in terms of capital and output per worker. The crude correlations are obvious. Capital stock per worker was essentially unchanged between 1929 and 1947, so the relatively slow growth of output per worker—1.5 percent per year—is attributed to technical progress and improved quality of inputs. (For labor, that is straightforward; for capital there are complications.) In the postwar intervals from 1947 to 1954 and 1954 to 1960, capital stock per worker grew at 3.5 and 1.9 percent annually, and output per worker at 3.3 and 2.1 percent annually.[10] Today it would be second nature to subtract about one-third of the growth rate of capital per worker to yield total factor productivity growth of about 2 percent and 1.5 percent in the two subperiods.

The *Report* notices that faster growth of the capital-labor ratio is associated with faster growth of productivity; however, it avoids the explicit calculation of total factor productivity. I do not remember why. Maybe the reason is hinted at in the comment that follows the crude observation. "These (productivity) gains were not simply the result of the separate contributions of the advance of knowledge, the improved skills of the working population, and the rise in capital per worker, but came in large part from the interaction of all three. Investment in new equipment serves as a vehicle for technological improvements and is perhaps the most important way in

10. Council of Economic Advisers (1962, p. 129).

which laboratory discoveries become incorporated in the production process."[11]

As I mentioned earlier, we had the "embodiment effect" firmly (and hopefully) in mind and suspected that it could explain certain apparent paradoxes. But we had no basis for using it quantitatively. Looking back, I think it would have been better to have made the formal total factor productivity decomposition in as much detail as we could have managed. We could then have made more or less plausible guesses about the modifications to be expected from interactions such as the embodiment effect.

We then used these general observations as support for policy measures designed to stimulate investment in plant and equipment. Our main case was for the maintenance of adequate aggregate demand, with the important addition that it should be accomplished, when necessary, by the combination of relatively tight fiscal policy and relatively easy monetary policy. This was a hallmark of the Council's general position. It was never taken for granted that growth in potential would be quickly and automatically matched by growth in demand. The Council was optimistic enough to believe that the goal of a budget surplus at full employment was reachable, but not foolish enough to think it would just happen. Of course now, almost forty years later, it has happened (though not "just"). With all that in mind, in addition to the human capital and R&D measures already mentioned, we pushed for an investment tax credit and, with rather less enthusiasm, liberalized depreciation guidelines. (The feeling was that accelerated depreciation would be dissipated too much in windfalls for investments that would have been made anyway.)

It is at least mildly interesting that chapter 2 contained a brief section on natural resource scarcity as a possible drag on long-term economic growth. The main emphasis was on the long-run trend of the relative price of raw materials. Some resource products had risen in price since, say, 1925 to 1929, the sharpest increase having taken place in forest products. Metals prices had risen slightly since then, but were no higher than they had been at the turn of the century. Fuels were up slightly, but construction materials had fallen at a comparable rate. Our conclusion from this review was: "First, it is likely that increasing resource scarcity has had only a negligible retarding effect on economic growth during the present century. Rising real costs of obtaining some resources have been largely compensated by declining costs of obtaining others. Second, the historical record does not

---

11. Council of Economic Advisers (1962, p. 129).

indicate that more rapid economic growth will simply result in our 'running out of resources' more quickly. On the contrary, past investments have permitted resources to be extracted more efficiently and used more efficiently."[12] The subsequent thirty-eight years have offered no reason to change that judgment. But this is now: I wonder how many readers would accept that judgment for the next thirty-eight years. I think I would.

The striking omission in the chapter is the absence of any serious discussion of environmental resources. We did include a page on water supplies as the most likely immediate resource bottleneck. And there we did talk about water quality and pollution control. Both as to quality and quantity, we recommended the usual economists' case for reliance on pricing to achieve efficient allocation of scarce water and to help finance necessary investments. Today there would surely and properly be much more emphasis on the environment.

It would be fair to summarize the Council's position this way. The prime task of macroeconomic policy in 1962 was to close the "Okun gap" between current GNP and potential GNP. Beyond that, there was reason to believe that an economy like ours would be underinvesting even when it reached potential GNP. Once there, macroeconomic policy could validly aim at shifting the composition of output modestly from current consumption to broadly conceived current investment, and thus ultimately to future consumption, public and private. But then it would be desirable if the added aggregate demand needed to close the Okun gap were to be overweighted in the direction of extra investment. Chapter 2, as described, outlined a small bundle of proposals aimed in that direction, particularly to stimulate private and public spending on plant and equipment, but also to encourage the building of human capital (in the form of health and education and broader opportunities for minorities), to promote R&D (especially basic research), and to improve the protection of natural resources.

One might ask, so what else was new? There was in fact some theory behind this way of looking at macroeconomic policy. It was not very detailed or refined, but it may be useful to lay out in a bland way how we explained ourselves to ourselves. A shorthand way of putting it is that we were believers in what is usually called "the neoclassical synthesis." The phrase was Paul Samuelson's coinage. The idea was that a modern industrial market economy often responds very sluggishly to real (or nominal) shocks to aggregate demand that disturb it from full-employment equilib-

12. Council of Economic Advisers (1962, p. 135).

rium. It may tend to return to a new full-employment equilibrium too slowly for comfort. In extreme cases it may have only a very weak tendency to return to full employment at all. During those sojourns away from full equilibrium, especially when aggregate output is demand-limited, the usual rules of resource allocation and calculation of opportunity cost do not apply in the normal way (because some shadow prices are zero or nearly so). If, however, monetary-fiscal policy (or the well-known tendency of God to look after the United States of America) succeeds in balancing aggregate supply and aggregate demand, then the old marginalist rules come back into play.

To put it a bit more pungently, the Council was Keynesian in the short run and neoclassical in the long run. Short-run macroeconomic policy was mostly aimed at influencing aggregate demand; growth-oriented macro-economic policy was mostly aimed at influencing aggregate supply.

It is possible to be a little more formal than that. I do not remember ever writing down a model like the following one, but I think it is a fair translation of what was in our collective mind when we thought about an economy in recession.

Suppose current real output Y falls short of current potential output Y_p. Then Y is determined by something like a standard ISLM model. That is an oversimplification, but it will do just fine for my purposes. Imagine the ISLM model already solved for Y, the real net investment I, and the real interest rate r. Thus, if M/P is an indicator of the stance of monetary policy and F, an indicator of the stance of fiscal policy, one can say that

$$Y = y(M/P,F,Y_p).$$

(1) $$I = i(M/P,F,Y_p).$$

$$r = r(M/P,F,Y_p).$$

Y_p appears in these solutions because one has to expect the investment function in the underlying ISLM model to depend (negatively) on Y_p. Other things being equal, the larger the amount of spare capacity, the smaller the amount of investment elicited. Something similar might be true of the consumption function, but probably in the other direction if Y_p is an indicator of permanent income.

Potential output can be read off from the aggregate production function, so

(2) $$Y_p = F(K,L,A),$$

where K is the existing stock of capital, L is the available labor supply (with frictional unemployment already subtracted), and A is the usual index of the level of technology. One might choose the convenient labor-augmenting form $F(K,AL)$, but it hardly matters since I do not intend actually to *do* growth theory here.

Current output also depends on the production function but in a different way. Suppose that

(3) $$Y = F([1-v(u)]K,[1-u]L,A).$$

The idea is first that u is the unemployment rate, so $(1-u)L$ is current employment. The technical and institutional arrangements are such that when a fraction u of the labor force is unemployed, a fraction $v(u)$ of the capital stock is left idle. This is a fudge, of course; in principle $v(u)$ is a decision made by firms, so it should have an endogenous rationale. But as fudges go, this is not a very bad one. (Quite possibly the technology index A should also be modified as u varies, to allow for the influence of "normal" utilization rates. However, nothing turns on this in a mere exposition.)

Two comments are worth making. Notice first how the causality goes: Y comes from the ISLM model, and then this last equation translates Y into an unemployment rate. Further, in this set-up, the two production-function representations for Y_p and Y determine the form of Okun's Law, the relation between the gap and the unemployment rate. Just divide one by the other. In principle this relation depends on K and L (and A), but it would be easy to choose the details to reduce or eliminate this dependence; a Cobb-Douglas form for F leads to something that looks very like the original Okun's Law. This way of doing it draws attention to the importance of short-run variations in the utilization of capital and in the efficiency of production, things that Okun thought about, though they seem to have vanished from later discussion.

Finally, there are three more or less automatic equations:

$$dK/dt = I.$$

(4) $$L = L(t).$$

$$dA/dt = a(Y/Y_p,Z).$$

The first needs no comment. The second makes the labor force exogenous, as is usual in growth theory. It would not be hard to throw in some endogeneity, as Okun did. The third equation is meant to allow for the possibility that the size of the Okun gap could influence technological progress. Z is meant to stand for a bunch of exogenous variables, one of which might well be A itself. In fact, the standard Old Growth Theory equation would just say $dA/dt = aA$. We only knew about Old Growth Theory but, as I have documented earlier, we thought that the evolution of A was subject to influence from incentives for firms to do R&D, from the educational system, and perhaps from elsewhere. Nobody ever thought of A as "really" exogenous.

I do not intend to do anything concrete with this model. As it stands it has the price level fixed, like the ancient textbook ISLM stories. It would lead much too far afield to append some price dynamics, vintage 1962 or vintage 1999. But as it stands it does contain eight equations in the eight unknowns: L, K, I, r, A, Y, Y_P, and u. So, given M/P and F, one could in principle do something.

I would not claim that this bland construction solves the problem of knitting together short-run and long-run macroeconomics. At least it reminds us that investment and capital stock are an important part of the connection. All of the subtle questions are glossed over, and a different regime would have to be patched together for dealing with situations of excess demand. But even so simple a model serves the purpose of emphasizing the fundamental principle underlying the Kennedy Council's view of macroeconomic policy: aggregate output is sometimes limited by aggregate demand and sometimes limited by aggregate supply. The proper policy decisions depend crucially on which constraint is relevant at any particular time.

COMMENT BY
Robert E. Hall

Bob Solow's interesting and provocative paper disparages modern macroeconomics as irrelevant to policymaking. Rather, Solow believes, the type of macroeconomic theory that was new in the 1960s (and still inhabits textbooks) guided serious economic policy thought when he was the fourth member of the Council of Economic Advisers and still should guide macroeconomic policymaking. I would like to be able to take the opposite view—that today's consensus macroeconomic theory, founded in dynamic stochastic general equilibrium economics, actually should supplant the theory of the 1960s. But I cannot. I am a great believer in the intellectual value of the new research, but I do not recommend it for practical policymaking.

I agree with Bob that we do not have tools much beyond the ISLM model and the growth model to think about policy. Research since the 1960s— that is, during my career as a macroeconomist from its beginning in 1967 when Bob signed my Ph.D. thesis—has mainly made me more humble about our macroeconomic policy pronouncements.

Bob's paper is compelling evidence against the idea that a paradigm shift has occurred in macroeconomics. After a true paradigm shift, a good scientist like Bob would be telling us that the old ideas were about as useful as, say, phlogiston. Instead, he makes a strong case that the old ideas are still basically right.

Let me summarize what I believe are the central principles of practical, policymaking macroeconomics—and also, as Bob points out, the central principles of undergraduate textbooks in macroeconomics:

—A Solow growth model describes the long run. Its predicted level of output is a useful benchmark in the short run called potential output.

—Output and employment can deviate from potential in the short run. When actual is below potential, unemployment is high and utilization of capital is low. Unemployment fluctuates around a normal level.

—Prices and wages adjust slowly in the direction that restores output to potential.

Rather than either confirming these principles or replacing them with others, much of the research of the past three decades has pointed out puzzles. The behavior of output does not conform to the model of a smooth trend plus temporary cyclical movements. Rather, the trend is stochastic. The trend has random permanent jumps that Solow never told us about. The trend growth rate varies in a way that the growth model cannot explain. For example, growth was rapid in the 1950s and 1960s, slow in the 1970s and 1980s, and then rose again in the late 1990s. No factor considered in the growth model has helped explain these important fluctuations.

There is no practical way to separate the business cycle from other components of the movements of output. Current questions about the state of the economy illustrate this point. Real GDP has grown at rates over 4 percent per year for several years. Is this a cyclical boom or just a period of rapid growth? The question has first-order importance because a temporary boom would be followed by a return to normal levels; the economy would later have a period of below-normal growth. By contrast, a period of rapid growth would most likely be followed by a period of normal growth. Economists do not know the answer, though debate has been vigorous.

Moreover, there is little support in the data for the concept of a stable natural rate of unemployment. In fact, there is good evidence that a market economy can function without any unemployment, as Sweden and Israel did for many years and Minneapolis is close to doing now. Every time actual unemployment changes, economists update their ideas about the natural rate, hardly the sign of a stable feature of the economy. Today in an economy humming along at 4.1 percent unemployment, we are entertaining the hypothesis that would have been unthinkable just a few years ago: that the natural rate is in the range of 4 percent.

The textbook model explains that the economy would be at potential and unemployment at its natural rate at all times if prices and wages adjusted rapidly. But the idea that periods of high unemployment reflect sluggishness in the adjustment of prices and wages has remarkably little support, as well. Of course, it is true that prices move sluggishly, on the one hand, and that unemployment is sometimes persistently high, on the other hand. But there is no evidence capable of persuading a slightly skeptical neutral observer of a causal relationship. Data from the postwar United States are mildly supportive, but data from the early 1920s, the Great Depression in the 1930s, and from Europe at all times are quite unsupportive.

It is important to say that neither classical pre-Keynesian ideas nor the modern ideas Bob Solow distrusts are of much help in understanding these mysteries. A top priority in research is achieving a deep understanding of fluctuations in resource utilization, especially unemployment. Peter Diamond and Dale Mortensen have made some progress in this area, but we have a long way to go. Many scholars are working on this topic today with open minds. Solow's accusation that the younger generation believes that what is observed must be optimal is off the point, I think. The models I have seen contain externalities, and the resulting inefficiencies are plainly acknowledged by the models' creators.

Another top priority is to understand the strange stochastic nature of growth. Why did the growth rate fall discontinuously in 1970? Why did growth resume at high rates in the late 1990s? Why did the level of output fall in 1974 and apparently never recover the amount lost in the fall? I have no clue.

Despite the wide gap between the behavior of the aggregate economy and our understanding of the behavior, the ideas promoted in the Kennedy Council were surely good ones. There is no cause for apology from today's perspective. For example, one key idea, the investment tax credit, clearly lowered the tax bias against capital formation. Recent advances in public finance theory have shown this kind of tax change to be an unambiguous improvement.

The intellectual honesty of the Kennedy Council comes through strongly in Bob's paper. First, the council (taken to include Bob himself) felt seriously constrained by the Solow model's implication that the steady-state growth rate is exogenous. Bob characterizes endogenous growth theory as supporting the idea that policy can affect long-run growth rates, but I believe that few modern growth theorists hold that view today. Rather, all of the progress in growth theory in the past fifteen years has resulted primarily in added respect for the Solow model. One of the most famous papers in modern growth economics concludes that the Solow model can account for the important facts of growth across a large number of countries.[13]

The other area of remarkable honesty is the recognition that policies to raise the level of output make sense only if there are externalities inhibiting output. Most public discussions miss this point. For example, declarations that the U.S. savings rate is far too low rarely identify the externality under-lying that conclusion. The Kennedy Council properly stressed that the most important anti-investment externalities impeded human capital formation. This theme resonates today.

There is only one element of the paper that I disagree with sharply: the statement that the central principles of economics do not apply when the economy is in recession. Since economists do not understand the economics of recessions, I cannot say that this is wrong for sure. But I think a lot of mischief could flow from an endorsement of the view that resources are available to the government at low social opportunity costs when unemployment is above normal.

COMMENT BY

Charles L. Schultze

Many at this conference have emphasized, and rightly, Art Okun's lasting contributions to macroeconomic theory and policy analysis. Let me add that he was also a superb colleague with whom to work and from whom to seek counsel. He gave freely of his time and thought. His finely tuned eco-

13. Mankiw, Romer, and Weil (1992).

nomic instincts, solid common sense, and extraordinary ability to present complex ideas in an understandable way not only informed his own work, but were a resource that contributed importantly to the research and writing of those around him.

Bob Solow begins and ends his paper by emphasizing a proposition that underlay the Kennedy Council's macroeconomic thinking: namely, that national output is sometimes constrained by aggregate demand and sometimes by aggregate supply and that good macroeconomic decisions depend critically on distinguishing which limitation is the operative one in any given situation. Before getting to Bob's discussion of economic growth, I want to comment on that proposition.

As I remember it, in the world of the Kennedy Council the task of macroeconomic stabilization was essentially one of trying to raise and then keep an uncertain and prone-to-fluctuate aggregate demand close to a more easily identifiable, stable, and slowly growing potential GNP. With some dissents, there was pretty wide agreement that deviations from full employment principally arose from unwanted shortfalls and sometimes excesses of aggregate demand below and above a long-run aggregate supply whose path was reasonably well identified.

On the other hand, in the years since then, some of the most important and interesting macroeconomic developments and challenges to stabilization policy have stemmed from shocks that originated in the supply side of the economy, shocks that our models and theories do not help us predict. Contrary to the real business cycle *cum* equilibrium models, however, the major stabilization threats posed by these supply shocks stem principally from the fact that they impinge not on a world of rapid market clearing, but on a Keynesian world of sluggish wage and price adjustment.

The first of these supply shocks was the major slowdown in productivity growth that occurred after 1973, and whose causes are still largely shrouded in mystery. Workers' aspirations for real wage growth adjusted downward only very sluggishly to that reduced productivity growth. And so any aggregate demand policy that kept unemployment unchanged would entail a continued rise in inflation, as workers and employers reached nominal wage agreements that were inconsistent with stable inflation.

On top of this development were superimposed the shocks coming from the two rounds of supplier-imposed oil price increases in 1973 and again in 1979–81. I have sometimes seen these shocks modeled as a fall in productivity. And indeed, employer substitution in the production function against energy inputs did reduce productivity. But that was, in fact, a minor problem. The real difficulties came from the way in which the shocks impinged on a Keynesian world. On the one hand, the huge jump in oil prices required that real wages fall. But sluggishly adjusting real wage aspirations produced results similar to and came on top of those induced by the fall in productivity growth. Real wages did fall, but their decline was accompanied by a further rise in inflation. Simultaneously, shifts in real income from consumers to suppliers led, in the short run, to a fall in real aggregate demand. The result was an upward shift in both inflation and unemployment, some temporary combination of which could not have been avoided by any feasible set of policy reactions. (Only a cynic would associate this last conclusion with the fact that my stint at the Council of Economic Advisers came in the middle of these years.) After initial periods of monetary accommodation, the Federal Reserve turned to restrictive policies that raised and for awhile halted, but did not reverse, the prior increase in inflation. The result, in the years up until 1981, was a combination of both higher inflation and higher unemployment.

Ultimately these large and sequential shocks were followed by the era of Paul Volcker. The Fed chairman imposed a massive monetary squeeze of a size sufficient to remove the substantial inflation that remained after the earlier shocks had run their course. Together all of this yielded more than ten years of abnormally poor economic outcomes. While recent economic performance has on most counts been exceptionally good, it probably looks even better than it is because we unconsciously include in our historical base for comparison the uniquely bad 1970s and early 1980s, dominated by unfavorable supply shocks.

Lately we have been surprised by one *benign* supply shock and are possibly in the process of realizing another. Benign they may be, but they nevertheless pose interesting challenges for macroeconomic stabilization policy—for which, these days, read monetary policy. The first of these shocks was the upward shift in the level of potential GDP over the last three to five years, associated with an unanticipated decline in the level of the unemployment consistent with low and stable wage and price inflation. The behavior of productivity growth over the past three years or so holds out the likelihood, even if not yet the certainty, of a second favorable supply shock—an increase in the trend growth of productivity and potential GDP.

Taking advantage of the favorable surprises has posed a major policy challenge for the Fed. Reliance on either old rule of thumb or mainstream models while in the midst of an unpredictable supply-side transition was no longer appropriate. As the Fed began to be aware that something was changing, it responded—to use a term I first heard from Bob Solow—by *probing* cautiously at the edge of the possible. It occasionally reversed course for a time, but then resumed the probing. And while there are indeed lags in the effects of monetary policy, wage and price sluggishness cuts both ways. Inflation in the relatively stable macroeconomic and institutional environment of the United States has never been on a hair trigger, especially after a substantial period of low inflation. And so, with the Federal Reserve having established and periodically reinforced its anti-inflationary credentials, the inflationary risks from possibly overstaying accommodation for one or several open market committee meetings have been small and perceived as such by financial markets.

In sum, I wholeheartedly share Bob Solow's views about the critical importance of distinguishing between aggregate demand and long-run aggregate supply; between stabilization policies and growth policies. But the experience of the last twenty-five years suggests an addition to his proposition: *namely*, that some of the most important and difficult stabilization challenges come from the impact of changes in aggregate supply on a Keynesian world of sluggish wage and price adjustment.

Let me turn to several observations that were stimulated by Solow's comments on growth theory and growth policies. I am going to skip over the more traditional aspects of growth policy having to do with private saving and investment in physical assets and concentrate on investments in human capital and research and development. While the research stimulated by the new growth theory is both exciting and potentially highly valuable, I am not sure whether its empirical findings yet offer much to policymakers seeking guidance about how to speed up growth. In any event, the actual choices facing policymakers at the federal level do not revolve around whether or not to make some generalized and abstract additional investment in human capital or R&D. Rather, policymakers must make choices about very specific policies that typically involve grants-in-aid to state and local governments or tax relief to private industry. In turn, the benefits and costs of these policies depend upon a host of stubborn and often intractable microeconomic and political realities.

Once one begins to cast about for potential growth-promoting investments in this context, three conclusions emerge. First, the range of potentially worthwhile investments narrows substantially. Second, the payoffs by way of increased GDP are likely to be in the same modest range that we became used to from exercising the Solow model. Third, in many cases the critical variable of interest is how political institutions respond to the investment program. Let me illustrate.

Despite wide recognition of the important role of human capital in historical U.S. growth, it was a widely held, although not unanimous view among economists that substantial further increases in financial resources for the U.S. public elementary and secondary school system as currently constituted would not yield much by way of return. More recently, the work of David Card and Alan Krueger stirred new debate on this proposition and gave the optimists some important ammunition.[14] Just recently, Krueger and Diane Whitmore completed an evaluation of the large-scale STAR experiment in Tennessee, which carefully tested the payoff from having children in kindergarten through third grade attend classes of much smaller size (on average, one-third smaller). When the children were reassigned to regular-sized classes in fourth grade and thereafter, the gap between their test scores and those of other students narrowed substantially during the remainder of elementary school, but did not disappear. Moreover, Krueger and Whitmore found that some years later, in high school, students in the treatment group were more likely to take the SAT or equivalent college entrance tests, and therefore more likely to attend college. Further, after adjustment for selection bias, the small-class students scored about one-tenth of a standard deviation higher on the SAT tests. The gain for blacks, on test scores and on the probability of taking the SAT, was twice or more the average gain.[15]

In another paper, Krueger has estimated the potential economic payoff from a reduction in class sizes along the lines of the STAR experiment.[16] Based on a survey of the relevant literature, he estimates the percentage gain in future earnings that would be associated with the increase in test scores produced by a STAR-like reduction in class size. He applies that gain to the age-earnings profile shown in the 1998 Current Population Survey and provides alternate estimates of future payoffs depending on alternate assumptions about the future growth of nationwide productivity and real wages (which affect the base path of the earnings to which the percentage gain is applied). On the cost side, he assumes that the 47 percent expansion in the number of K–3 teachers needed to accommodate the

14. See, for example, Card and Krueger (1992).
15. Krueger and Whitmore (1999).
16. Krueger (1999).

posited reduction in class size would lead to a fully proportionate increase in per pupil educational expenditures. This is a pessimistic but probably realistic assessment. Between 1969–70 and 1996 the number of public elementary and secondary teachers rose by 30 percent; since school enrollment was virtually constant, this translated into a large reduction in average class size. But for every 100 additional teachers added to the payroll, 100 nonteacher personnel were also hired (excluding teacher aides); total costs per student rose, even after allowing for the smaller class sizes. A proportional cost increase would equal almost three times the salary and benefit costs of the added teachers necessary to staff the smaller classes. And the estimated rate of return does not take into account the possibility that substitution effects at the state and local levels could, over time, gradually divert some fraction of additional federal grants-in-aid to noneducational purposes, including tax cuts.

With a productivity growth rate of 2 percent a year, the Krueger calculations show that a 6 percent rate of return could be realized from this educational investment. This is less than the roughly 7 percent rate of return achievable on average from private investment (including residential). From a macroeconomic standpoint, the annual cost of a nationwide program duplicating the one-third reduction in class size for grades K–3 in public schools would amount to about 0.7 percent of net national income. I adapted the Krueger estimates to calculate the potential impact on net national income. If applied over the roughly sixty years necessary to endow the entire labor force with the added human capital, the stream of investments would, by the end of the period, raise the level of national income by about 3.2 percent, implying an average increase of a little over 0.05 percentage point in the annual economic growth rate.[17]

If—with a large dose of optimism—we could assume that a way might be devised to defeat the tendency of total costs to rise proportionately with the additional number of teachers, a larger return per dollar of investment in a STAR-type educational investment could reasonably be expected. For example, if the total incremental costs of the program could be held to, say, two-thirds of the increase assumed by Krueger, the payoff in terms of increased economic output would represent a rate of return a little below 7.5 percent, comparable to that from private investment. And when we take into account the fact that gains for black students in the STAR exper-

17. The growth increase is back-loaded since an investment in human capital at the K–3 level would not begin showing an economic payoff for some ten years.

iment were substantially higher than the average for all students, the social rate of return would be an attractive one.

The moral of the story is twofold. First, an evaluation of the economic return from a large, new educational investment will depend not only on its substantive educational content and its effect on future earnings but also on the political and institutional responses to the influx of new funds and on the extent to which the program can be designed to minimize the excess costs that these responses may induce. Second, while a federal program that would provide an additional $45 billion to $50 billion a year for elementary and secondary education (on the assumption of proportional cost increases) seems like a large public investment in the current political environment, it would probably still add little more than 0.05 percentage point a year to the long-term economic growth rate.

What about national policies for increasing investment in R&D? There is a large body of empirical work that finds that private returns on R&D investment are high and that there are very large positive spillovers. However, it is exceedingly difficult to design federal policies that could actually produce a very large and reasonably well-allocated expansion in the current scale of national R&D.

There are two major kinds of policies: tax subsidies for industry R&D and federal spending for non-defense R&D. Since 1981, there has been a federal tax subsidy to private industry for incremental outlays on R&D that provides a 20 percent credit for expenditures in excess of a moving base period amount. I examined and scaled up to current R&D levels two studies that have been done on the extra GDP provided by this tax credit, one by Martin Baily and Robert Lawrence in 1985 and one by the firm of Coopers and Lybrand in 1998.[18] I then averaged the results. Relying on the findings of a large body of empirical research, both of the studies (which were commissioned by research-oriented industry groups) incorporated very high total returns to R&D investments, substantially in excess of the average return to traditional private investment. Given the average of the user-cost elasticities assumed in these studies, the tax credit was inducing an extra $3 billion to $4 billion in private R&D investment in 1998, around 0.04 percent of GDP. In turn, if this extra investment yielded an average of the various rates of return assumed in the studies, that would produce a contribution of perhaps 0.015 percentage point to the next ten years' growth rate, substantially more, per dollar of resource cost, than the

18. Baily and Lawrence (1985); Coopers and Lybrand (1998).

growth payoff to physical investment. Conceivably the generosity of the tax relief might be doubled to get 0.03 percentage point on the growth rate. But at some stage further increases in generosity would provide very large incentives to game the system and, under an incremental and moving base, to distort the timing of R&D projects. We are dealing with what appear to be large benefit-cost ratios, but quite modest upper limits to the feasible investment increment and therefore to the growth increment.

The federal government might also substantially increase its R&D program. But, at the magnitude it would take to make a real contribution to economic growth, that option too poses major difficulties. Almost two-thirds of all federal spending on nondefense R&D currently goes to health (mainly the National Institutes of Health) and the space program, which have already been pushed to the point where additional resources would be unlikely to yield a high growth payoff (and little of that in *measured* GDP). The remaining federal nondefense budget in 1998 amounted to $12 billion, or 0.14 percent of GDP. Expenditures of triple that amount, with a social rate of return four to five times that from traditional investment, might contribute something like 0.15 percentage point to the medium-term growth rate.

Conceptually one could make a reasonable case for a very large increase in the current level of federal support at the precommercial stage for applied research with potential economic payoffs. But when one starts to think through the practical consequences of designing a federal program that would sharply expand the current $12 billion, much of which would necessarily have to be allocated among particular firms, difficulties begin to appear. Not the least of them is the likelihood of large amounts of political pork larded throughout such a program. Here the problem is not the lack of potential supernormal returns, but the political and institutional factors that would be likely to limit the scale of efficient investments. I do not mean to suggest that this is necessarily an insurmountable problem. It might be possible to devise a grantmaking mechanism to allocate the funds with acceptable efficiency. But it highlights the kind of institutional and political factors that lie at the heart of making good policy in this area.

In sum, while the macroeconomic evidence may suggest the possibility of broad categories of investment that promise significant spillovers, it is no easy matter in advanced countries to find specific and feasible governmental policies of a type and scale that would yield substantial increments to national growth. Indeed, if such policies were lying around waiting to be picked up, we would all be a lot richer by now.

References

Baily, Martin Neil, and Robert Z. Lawrence.1985. "The Need for a Permanent Tax Credit for Industrial Research and Development." Paper commissioned by the Coalition for the Advancement of Industrial Technology (February).

Card, David, and Alan B. Krueger.1992. "Does School Quality Matter? Returns to Education and the Characteristics of Public Schools in the United States."*Journal of Political Economy* 100 (February): 1–40.

Coopers and Lybrand.1998. "Economic Benefits of the R&D Tax Credit." Study prepared for the R&D Credit Coalition. Washington (January).

Council of Economic Advisers. 1962. "Annual Report of the Council of Economic Advisers." In *Economic Report to the President, 1962.* Government Printing Office.

Krueger, Alan B. 1999. "An Economist's View of Class Size Research." Paper prepared for a conference entitled, "What Do We Know About How to Make Small Classes Work." Washington, December 6.

Krueger, Alan B., and Diane Whitmore.1999. "The Effect of Attending a Small Class in the Early Grades on College-Test Taking and Middle School Test Results: Evidence from Project STAR." Princeton University, Industrial Relations Section.

Mankiw, N. Gregory, David Romer, and David N. Weil. 1992. "A Contribution to the Empirics of Economic Growth." *Quarterly Journal of Economics* 107 (May): 407–8.

Solow, Robert M. 1962. "Technical Progress, Capital Formation, and Economic Growth." *American Economic Review* 52 (May, *Papers and Proceedings, 1962*): 76–86.

———. 1982. "Where Have All the Flowers Gone: Economic Growth in the 1960s." In *Economics in the Public Service,* edited by Joseph A. Pechman and Norman J. Simler, 46–74. W. W. Norton.

Solow, Robert M., James Tobin, Christian von Weizsäcker, and Menahem Yaari. 1966. "Neoclassical Growth with Fixed Factor Proportions." *Review of Economic Studies* 33 (April): 79–115.

Swan, Trevor. 1956. "Economic Growth and Capital Accumulation." *Economic Record* 32 (November): 334–61.

Tobin, James. 1955. "A Dynamic Aggregation Model." *Journal of Political Economy* 63 (April): 103–15.

———. 1964. "Economic Growth as an Objective of Government Policy." *American Economic Review* 54 (May, *Papers and Proceedings, 1964*): 1–20.

PART II

The United States and the International Economy

RICHARD N. COOPER

5

Foreign Economic Policy in the 1960s: An Enduring Legacy

It is useful at the outset to recall the substantial changes that have taken place in the world economy over the four decades since 1960 and at the same time to recall some fundamental continuities. To understand policy-making in any period, it is necessary to capture the conditions of the period in question and the main issues the policymakers faced. Monday morning quarterbacking is always fun and sometimes reveals important and durable lessons, but it is seldom helpful in understanding the decisions that were actually taken and their motivations. The choices made in the 1960s and the institutional mechanisms established have played out in complex— and occasionally unpredictable—ways in subsequent decades.

The first point to note was that the world economy was much smaller in 1960 than it is today, with far fewer effective players. World population nearly doubled between 1960 and 1998, and gross world product (in constant dollars) more than quadrupled (growth averaged 3.8 percent a year). Per capita world income thus more than doubled during this period—the most rapid and general improvement in material living conditions in the history of mankind. (Table 5-1 presents some figures.)

Economic transactions among countries increased much more rapidly than did real output. It is difficult to review this period without concluding that the rapid increase in international transactions was a significant factor leading to the extraordinary increase in average living standards around the world. (These are world averages. Some places, of course, grew

Table 5-1. *World Economic Growth, 1960–98*

Statistic	1960	1970	1980	1990	1998
Population (billions)	3.0	3.7	4.4	5.3	5.9
Gross World Product					
(trillions of dollars)	1.7[a]	3.6[a]	10.5[a]	22.2	28.9
U.S. price level					
(1992 = 100)[b]	23.3	30.5	60.3	93.6	112.6
GDP per capita					
(1998 dollars)[c]	3,008	3,923	4,882	5,817	6,200
Exports					
(billions of dollars)	118	289	1,901	3,310	5,458
International reserves					
(billions of dollars)	60	93	453	954	1,797
Of which foreign exchange	18	45	373	845	1,635

Sources: Calculated from Maddison (1995); World Bank, *World Development Report* (2000); IMF, *International Financial Statistics* (1990, 1991, 1996, 1999); and *Economic Report of the President* (1976, 1999).

a. Estimates using U.S. price deflator and growth from Maddison.

b. Chain-weighted GDP deflator.

c. Relative figures for 1960–80 taken from Maddison, chained to 1998 *World Development Report* estimate.

more rapidly than others and in a few places—most notably in Africa—recorded output per capita actually declined.)

The period 1960 to 1998 was also the most inflationary period in the (peacetime) history of mankind. The U.S. consumer price level by 1998 was over five times higher than it was in 1960, an increase of 4.6 percent a year; inflation in almost all other countries was even higher. Whether the fact that four decades of the world's most rapid growth overlapped with the decades of most rapid inflation was a mere coincidence or whether there was in fact a deep causal connection between the two is an interesting question.

From the perspective of the early 1960s, the nominal magnitudes that have become common recently would look huge. U.S. GNP at $530 billion in 1960 compares with $8,511 billion in 1998. U.S. exports of goods and services were then $25 billion—not quite 5 percent of GNP—compared with $953 billion (over 11 percent of GDP) in 1998. World merchandise exports rose 10.6 percent a year, from $118 billion in 1960 to $5,458 billion in 1998. Total official international reserves rose from $60 billion to $1,797 billion over the same period.[1] International capital

1. The latter figure values gold reserves at the artificially low book price of $49 an ounce.

movements increased even more rapidly than trade, although it is difficult to tell exactly how much more rapidly because of poor measurement at the global level. U.S. net private exports of capital in 1998 were $286 billion, down from $464 billion in 1997, compared with under $5 billion in 1960. Private foreign entities invested $524 billion in the United States in 1998, net, compared with less than $1 billion in 1960. Worldwide gross direct foreign investment flows increased from $29 billion annually in 1973–78 to $279 billion in 1993–96. Gross portfolio flows increased from $17 billion to $456 billion over the same period.[2]

The rapid growth in international transactions partly reflects significant technological change. The first successful commercial jet aircraft, the Boeing 707, entered service in 1958. By 1996 the United States received 23 million visitors from overseas (that is, not counting Canada and Mexico) and 20 million Americans traveled abroad, up from 0.9 and 1.6 million, respectively, in 1960. In 1960 Americans made 3.3 million overseas telephone calls; by 1996 this number reached 3.5 billion, a thousand-fold increase, and the average call was much longer.[3] International (as well as domestic) communications were greatly facilitated by introduction of the fax and, more recently, by high-speed data transmission and e-mail—both invaluable for crossing many time zones and both unknown in 1960—as was another essential feature of modern government and business, efficient copying of documents (older readers will remember smudgy carbon copies and thermofax copying).

Policy changes have also played an important role. At the end of the Second World War, tariffs and nontariff barriers to trade, as well as exchange controls, stifled international trade and capital movements. In 1947, twenty-three countries committed to reducing trade barriers adopted the General Agreement on Tariffs and Trade (GATT). Governments engaged in five rounds of tariff-reducing multilateral trade negotiations from 1947 to 1961. The item-by-item negotiating approach had run out of steam by 1960. The Marshall Plan was conditioned on sharp reduction of trade barriers within Europe, and in 1961 (de facto, 1959) ten western European countries formally accepted Article VIII of the International Monetary Fund (IMF), making their currencies convertible for all current (but not capital) transactions. In 1960 only ten countries

2. Eichengreen and others (1998, p. 6).
3. The first transatlantic telephone cable was laid in 1958, with a capacity for thirty-six simultaneous conversations. Before then transoceanic telephone calls used short-wave radio.

had formally accepted Article VIII (joined by the ten European countries plus Saudi Arabia in early 1961). By 1998 that number had reached 146. And three exceptionally ambitious multilateral rounds of trade negotiation since 1963—the Kennedy Round concluded in 1967, the Tokyo Round concluded in 1979, and the Uruguay Round concluded in 1994—reduced import tariffs of the rich countries to less than 10 percent of their level of the late 1940s. Developing countries played a significant role in the latter two rounds, and their nontariff barriers to imports were substantially reduced.

The number of national players in the world economy, and in its important economic institutions, has increased substantially. Membership of the United Nations grew from 51 in 1945 to 82 in 1960 to 185 in 1998. Membership in the International Monetary Fund increased from 68 to 182 between 1960 and 1998. The 37 contracting parties to the GATT in 1960 grew to 135 members of the World Trade Organization (plus 36 applicants) in 1998. Some of this growth came through de-colonization, especially during the 1960s. Some came from countries deciding belatedly to join the economic organizations. And some came from the disintegration of several states. Pakistan led the way, becoming two states in 1971. The U.S.-administered Trust Territory of the Pacific Islands became three separate states and a U.S. territory in the 1980s. In the 1990s, the trend accelerated. The Soviet Union became fifteen states in 1991; Yugoslavia became five in 1991; and Czechoslovakia became two in 1993. Along with the division of states, authority has devolved away from central governments over time, including in France, Spain, Canada, Russia, China, and, most recently, Britain—although foreign economic policy generally continues to be run, at least nominally, by central governments.

Against these proliferating tendencies has come the unification of Vietnam in 1975, of Germany and Yemen in 1990, and the re-attachment of Hong Kong and Macao to China in 1997 and 1999, respectively—albeit with separate systems, including separate foreign economic policy.

Within Western Europe, the European Economic Community, initially a customs union, was formed by six nations in 1958. Its membership has grown to fifteen (with at least thirteen additional applicants), and the European Union's scope now embraces freedom of labor and capital movements, and the right of establishment, as well as freedom of trade. Eleven of its members created a monetary union and launched a common currency, the euro, in 1999.

Less ambitious regional economic arrangements have been created, or are in the process of being created, elsewhere, notably the North American

Free Trade Agreement (NAFTA) embracing Canada, Mexico, and the United States; the Mercosur customs union embracing Argentina, Brazil, Paraguay, Uruguay, and soon Chile; and the Association of Southeast Asian Nations (ASEAN) free trade area. The total list is long and growing. All these arrangements have reduced restrictions on merchandise trade, and sometimes also on services, beyond the multilateral liberalization undertaken in the GATT rounds.

While many more countries have currencies that are convertible for current transactions than was true in 1960, the world has moved away from another feature of the Bretton Woods system that created the IMF: fixed exchange rates. The original idea was that each member country would declare a "par value" for its currency and take steps to prevent its exchange rate from varying in the market place by more than a few percentage points. In 1960 only one member—Canada—was in violation of this undertaking. By 1998, 101 countries (out of 182 IMF members) had formally declared that they had floating exchange rates. More significantly, the world's most important currencies—the U.S. dollar, Japanese yen, British pound, German mark (replaced in 1999 by the euro), and Swiss franc—are now all floating against one another, creating the practical problem for those countries that want to fix their exchange rates to decide what exactly to fix them to.

All these developments—the rapid growth of production, trade, and capital movements; the decline in trade barriers; the move to floating exchange rates; and the increase in number of national players—have represented significant changes in the world economy over the past four decades. But there have been important elements of continuity as well. In particular, the basic framework governing relations among nations, established in the aftermath of the Second World War, has continued and indeed strengthened over time. While at the international level, the United Nations system is the locus of political relations, the principal economic institutions are the IMF, the World Bank, and the GATT, transformed in 1995 into the institutionally stronger World Trade Organization (WTO). The World Bank has been augmented with several subsidiaries (IDA, IFC, MIGA), and supplemented by several regional development banks (IDB, ADB, AfDB, EBRD).[4]

4. Specifically, these are the International Development Association (IDA), the International Finance Corporation (IFC), the Multilateral Investment Guarantee Agency (MIGA), the Inter-American Development Bank (IDB), the Asian Development Bank (ADB), the African Development Bank (AfDB), and the European Bank for Reconstruction and Development (EBRD).

Moreover, the key national economic players of 1960 remain important today, and indeed since 1975 have institutionalized their relationship to one another in the annual G-7 summits. In particular, the United States remains the major source of initiative in world economic policy. Japan has replaced Britain in economic importance, but Britain remains more active in framing and shaping new directions than Japan. A collective Europe is slowly emerging, but apart from trade negotiations (which in principle are handled by the European Commission, as they were in 1960) most decisionmaking continues to occur in national capitals. In short, the rapid changes in the world economy have occurred in an environment that has remained institutionally conservative.

Trade Issues in the 1960s

The basic tariff legislation for the United States remains the Smoot-Hawley Tariff Act of 1930. Initially, it had the highest import tariffs in U.S. history.[5] In 1934 with the passage of the Reciprocal Trade Agreements Act, President Franklin Roosevelt persuaded Congress for the first time to delegate tariff-cutting authority to the president. Under that authority, extended in 1945 and renewed at roughly three-year intervals, tariff-reducing bilateral negotiations had been successfully concluded with twenty-nine countries. With the adoption of the General Agreement on Tariffs and Trade (GATT) in 1947, these negotiations became multilateral in character. Five rounds of tariff reductions followed, the last ("Dillon Round") concluding in 1961. But from the time of the Republican Congress of 1946, these negotiations were increasingly hobbled with restrictions and limitations on the president's authority. By 1961 it had become clear that the prevailing approach to tariff reduction—item-by-item negotiation with each "principal supplier," with the results extended to other exporting countries under the principle of most favored nation (MFN) treatment—had been exhausted.

In the meantime, a trading market as large as the United States was being created. The Rome Treaty in 1958 established the European Economic Community (EEC), a customs union among France, Germany (Federal Republic), Italy, and the three Benelux countries, to be phased in

---

5. The arguable exception is the Tariff of 1828, the "Tariff of Abominations," which prompted South Carolina to threaten to secede from the United States.

by 1970. This arrangement required dropping import duties to zero within the EEC while imposing a common external tariff on external suppliers, implying discrimination within a large European market against U.S. (and other foreign) goods.

The president's remaining meager authority to reduce tariffs was due to expire in June 1962. President John F. Kennedy decided to make further multilateral trade liberalization a major thrust of his administration, and what became the Trade Expansion Act of 1962 was the most important legislative initiative of his second year.

The Trade Expansion Act contained two significant innovations. First, in addition to greatly extending the president's negotiating authority, it abandoned the item-by-item approach in favor of broad across-the-board tariff cuts (allowing for exceptions). Thus the president was authorized to reduce tariffs by up to 50 percent of those prevailing at the inauguration of the negotiations. He was further authorized to eliminate tariffs on those goods for which the EEC and the United States together accounted for 80 percent of world exports;[6] to eliminate tariffs on tropical products with little or no domestic production; and to eliminate "nuisance" tariffs of under 5 percent.

Second, for firms or workers that might be hurt by trade liberalization, the act introduced the possibility of "trade adjustment assistance" (TAA), temporary government financial support to the affected workers or firms for retraining, relocation, or restructuring. The "escape clause" provisions, whereby tariff reductions could be reversed, were retained. But trade adjustment assistance provided a significant alternative mode of relief to import de-liberalization, reflecting the notion that policy-driven actions to benefit most citizens should in some way "compensate" those who lose as a result of the action—or at least ease their burden of adjustment to the changed policy.

President Kennedy mentioned his new initiative in his first State of the Union message and sent a special message to Congress in February 1962.[7] He gave seven reasons for this new, major departure in trade liberalization:

—By creating new export opportunities, especially in rapidly growing Europe, it would enhance U.S. economic growth, as it encouraged a shift of resources into the high-productivity, high-wage export industries.

6. At the time the legislation passed, this category included only aircraft and margarine. However, it would have had much wider scope if, as the administration hoped, Britain were to have joined the EEC.

7. Reproduced in Ratner (1972, annex 18).

—By exposing U.S. management and labor to foreign competition, it would encourage them to be cost-competitive, modernize, and enhance productivity, and would help prevent inflation.

—By creating new export opportunities in rapidly growing markets, it would help correct the adverse balance of payments by enlarging the trade surplus, and thus contribute to maintaining U.S. military expenditures abroad.

—By enhancing growth and helping restore payments equilibrium, it would promote the strength and the unity of the West, especially with respect to the large, self-contained communist world.

—By peacefully "tearing down walls" to economic intercourse among nations, it would prove the superiority of free choice.

—By ensuring nondiscriminatory application of all tariff reductions to third countries, it would aid the developing nations of the world and enable them to share the economic rewards of free choice.

—By undertaking the initiative, it would help maintain the leadership of the free world.

With substantial lobbying by the administration, the bill passed the House by 298 to 125 in June 1962 and the Senate by 78 to 8 in September.[8] After discussions with the EEC, whose Commission would have negotiating responsibility on behalf of all its members, the Kennedy Round of trade negotiations was formally launched in May 1964 and concluded three years later. The average reduction in duties was about 35 percent, on about $40 billion of world trade in 1964 (the base year). The United States also reduced or eliminated duties on about $900 million of imports from developing countries, without insisting on reciprocal tariff reductions by those countries. (This act of "generosity" was probably mistaken, given the peculiar political dynamic of import protection in all countries, which is lowered only with the promise of export expansion. But it was a useful political gesture to developing countries, which were then being strongly wooed by the Soviet Union, and it benefited U.S. consumers.) An attempt to reduce the protective nature of the EEC's new Common Agricultural Policy was less overtly successful, although the process of the Kennedy Round may have kept EEC support prices lower than they otherwise would have been.[9]

The Kennedy Round was the first of three grand, ambitious rounds of multilateral trade negotiations, both setting the general pattern and pro-

8. Schlesinger (1965, p. 848).
9. See Preeg (1970) for an evaluation of the Kennedy Round.

viding lessons of what should be avoided. The Tokyo Round took place in 1973–79, with a comparable reduction in tariffs on manufactured goods and several side agreements, including trade in civil aircraft and government procurement. President Lyndon Johnson proposed a major extension of trade-negotiating authority in May 1968. Congress took no action. President Richard Nixon gave a comparable message in November 1969, marking a sharp break with the historical association of the Republican Party with protection against foreign goods. Congress did not act until December 1974, ironically after Nixon resigned from office. The Trade Act of 1974 authorized the U.S. administration to participate in the Tokyo Round, which had already begun; substantially liberalized the criteria for trade adjustment assistance; strengthened the capacity of the president to penalize other countries that engaged in "unfair trade practices" (Section 301); extended discriminatory tariff preferences to most products coming from developing countries (the Generalized System of Preferences, or GSP); introduced the "Jackson-Vanik" amendment requiring liberal emigration from nonmarket (communist) economies in order to qualify for most favored nation treatment by the United States (a provision aimed originally at the Soviet Union, which until June 2000 plagued U.S. trade relations with China); and provided for "fast track" congressional approval of a successfully concluded negotiation. The fast track was necessary because the Tokyo Round was expected to go well beyond tariff cuts into areas that would require detailed U.S. congressional approval, and foreign countries could not be expected to negotiate fully with U.S. officials if the resulting package were to be picked over selectively by Congress. Thus fast track provided for an up-or-down congressional vote on the entire negotiated package, within a specified time frame.

Subsequently, president Ronald Reagan—the first U.S. president to espouse free trade openly, and perhaps the first really to believe in it—inaugurated the Uruguay Round, with still broader coverage, including services, which ran from 1986 to 1994, on the basis of new congressional authorization in 1984. Thus the Kennedy Round set a pattern for negotiations that has continued to the present. President Bill Clinton in 1999 advocated a new round of trade negotiations, dubbed the "millennium round," requiring additional authorization from Congress, something that has been increasingly difficult since Kennedy's success in getting his proposed bill through Congress in only eight months. A WTO ministerial meeting in Seattle failed, however, to agree on the objectives of a new round.

It has been argued that U.S. trade policy from the 1950s sacrificed U.S. economic interests for national security objectives.[10] With the ending of the cold war and the disintegration of the Soviet Union, the United States can tend to its true economic interests without concern for security. Some such concept seems to have informed the early Clinton administration.

It is difficult to sustain that any such economic sacrifice was either consciously decided or in fact made. The broad trade liberalization that has taken place over the past half century has strongly served U.S. economic (as well as security) interests, in the decisive sense that it has increased U.S. standards of living far more than would have been the case if world trade had remained restricted by policies such as those in place in 1945, or 1950, or 1960.

It is noteworthy that Franklin Roosevelt, in requesting extension of the president's trade negotiating authority in March 1945, before the end of the Second World War and certainly before the beginning of the cold war, argued that "trade is fundamental to the prosperity of all Nations. . . . We do better, both as producers and consumers, when the markets upon which we depend are as large and rich and various and competitive as possible. . . . We have tried often to protect some special interest by excluding strangers' goods from competition. In the long run everyone has suffered. . . . All sections of our population—labor, farmers, businessmen have shared and will share in the benefits which increased trade brings."[11]

This does not sound as though Roosevelt believed he was sacrificing U.S. economic interests in negotiating reductions in trade barriers. Similarly, as noted above, in requesting authority from Congress, Kennedy identified seven reasons for trade liberalization: the first three were economic in character, and included competition from imports as well as expansion of exports among the benefits. The Council of Economic Advisers, which has no responsibility for national security, has strongly endorsed trade liberalization over the years, on the grounds that it is good for the U.S. *economy*.

Kennedy recognized that trade liberalization would at least initially hurt some Americans—both workers and firms—and proposed trade adjustment assistance to ease the transition to new employment, to be assured by active pursuit of full employment through macroeconomic management. While the Trade Expansion Act of 1962 introduced the possibility of trade

10. Eckes (1992).
11. Reprinted in Ratner (1972, pp. 151–52).

adjustment assistance, it also set criteria for qualification that proved to be so tight that few qualified for help—a condition that mattered less in the rapid-growth environment of the 1960s than it did in the recession of 1970–71 and the less buoyant 1970s. The criteria were substantially relaxed in the Trade Act of 1974. In particular, qualification was conditioned on imports for whatever reason (not only due to trade liberalization) being a "substantial" (rather than the primary) cause of actual or potential serious injury. Moreover, single units or groups of workers in multiplant firms were made eligible for relief. The result of these changes, and of slower economic growth in the late 1970s, was significant expenditures under the program, particularly for the automobile industry after the 1979–80 oil shock and the marked shift in public preference to small (largely imported) cars. Expenditure under the trade adjustment assistance program rose to $1.7 billion in 1980, compared with annual outlays of around $300 million in preceding years. An alarmed Congress stiffened the criteria again in 1981.[12]

A less savory aspect of trade policy inaugurated by Kennedy was the "voluntary" restraints on exports of cotton textiles (mainly apparel). Other countries were persuaded to accept these restrictions in the framework of the Long-term Cotton Textile Agreement (LCTA), which was gradually tightened and extended. As a presidential candidate, Kennedy had promised the textile industry relief from growing imports, mainly from Japan and other Asian countries. The industry pressed the new president hard to deliver on this promise. The assignment was given to George Ball, new under secretary of state. Ball was constitutionally opposed to the import quotas desired by the industry and negotiated a multilateral framework of growth in cotton textile and apparel trade within which importing countries could persuade exporting countries to restrain the growth (to 5 percent, and zero in exceptional cases) of particular products that had shown exceptionally rapid growth.[13]

The industry kept up its pressure, and candidate Nixon in 1968 also promised further relief from imports. The Long-term Cotton Textile Agreement was tightened in various ways over the years, most importantly by being extended to woolen and synthetic fibers as the Multi-Fiber Agreement (MFA) in 1974.[14] One of the results of the Uruguay Round, a condition for developing country agreement on intellectual property and

12. See Aho and Aronson (1985, p. 69).

13. Ball (1982) and Cline (1990).

14. As a result of Kennedy's experience in 1960 and Nixon's experience in 1968 with campaign commitments concerning textiles, which the textile industry used to press vigorously for presidential

other issues, was to phase out the MFA by 2005 and thereafter to rely only on tariffs to limit textile imports.

It is noteworthy that employment in the textile and apparel sectors actually grew until 1973, despite rising imports. It declined gradually thereafter, at a rate of 1 percent a year over the entire period 1960–96. Given average job tenure of 3.5 to 4 years throughout the U.S. economy, it can be inferred that virtually the entire labor force of these two sectors was renewed several times. Thus positions and profits, not people, were protected, despite the rhetoric from interested firms, union leaders, and trade associations emphasizing human hardship. Moreover, immigrants, both legal and illegal, made up a consequential fraction of the apparel labor force by the 1990s. On the other hand, trade was not throttled by the restraints: U.S. imports of apparel grew from 2 percent of apparent consumption in 1960 to 6 percent in 1970 to 33 percent in 1997, by value; the import share for textiles was roughly unchanged throughout the 1960s at 4.5 percent, but rose thereafter to nearly one-third.[15] Thus while the MFA and its predecessor LCTA may have restrained the rate of growth of imports, they permitted substantial growth. Their main effect was to restrain exports from the most cost-efficient foreign suppliers, such as Hong Kong, and thus permit higher cost developing countries to export apparel to the United States.

Balance of Payments Issues in the 1960s

Europe emerged from the Second World War and immediate reconstruction with an acute "dollar shortage." European countries did not have and could not earn as much hard currency as they wished to feed their people, rebuild their capital stock, and replenish their financial reserves. By 1958 this period had passed; European currencies became de facto convertible

---

action, I strongly advised candidate Jimmy Carter in 1976 to make no strong or specific commitments to the textile—or to any other—industry. He did not, and was spared the experience of Kennedy and Nixon in this regard. Kennedy and Nixon each wanted new trade negotiating authority, whereas Carter was concluding a negotiating round begun under Nixon. It is possible that Congress would not have granted new negotiating authority without some special treatment for textiles and apparel, given the industry's relatively wide distribution of production sites and employment. But the candidates' election promises made some special treatment difficult to avoid even without this political consideration.

15. Cline (1990, pp. 35 and 40).

for current account transactions by the end of the year (formal acceptance of the IMF's Article VIII had to wait until 1961). Foreign exchange reserves, held mainly in dollars (not counting the sterling balances left over from the war), had risen substantially, and in 1958, $2.3 billion of those reserves were converted into gold at the U.S. Treasury, an exclusive privilege of foreign monetary authorities since the United States demonetized gold in 1934. The U.S. balance of payments deficit jumped sharply in 1958 (as the economic consequences of the late 1956 Suez crisis receded) and remained high in 1959–60.

The payments deficit and the loss of gold left the U.S. and foreign business and financial communities nervous. John F. Kennedy was not greatly loved by the American business and financial communities and was seen as potentially dangerous on what the Kennedy brothers called the gold question. Shortly after his inauguration, President Kennedy sent a message to Congress on his balance of payments program, mainly to reassure an anxious financial community at home and abroad that he would not change the $35 per ounce price of gold or introduce exchange controls on trade or capital flows. Rather, to improve the balance of payments he would promote U.S. exports; encourage foreign tourism in the United States; reduce duty-free allowances for returning U.S. travelers (from $500—about $2,500 in today's dollars—to $100); review expenditures abroad by government agencies; exempt foreign central bank deposits from interest rate ceilings; and issue special bonds to foreign monetary authorities. He canceled the Eisenhower plan to return dependents of overseas military personnel to the United States.[16]

Balance of payments issues plagued the U.S. government throughout the 1960s, finally to be resolved, after a fashion, by President Nixon's closure of the gold window in August 1971, the subsequent two depreciations of the dollar, the floating of other major currencies in 1970–73, and the sharp increase of (dollar-based) oil prices in 1974.

The main economic focus of the Kennedy administration was on economic recovery and enhanced growth. Recovery started in 1961, but Kennedy proposed a series of measures, including an investment tax credit (proposed in April 1961, enacted in October 1962), and a more general tax reduction (proposed in January 1963, enacted about a year later). The administration wanted to manage the balance of payments without compromising its main objectives.

16. Solomon (1982, p. 40).

A word needs to be said about exactly what the "balance of payments problem" was, since that is not self-evident, either then or now. The most obvious manifestation was the irregular declines in U.S. monetary gold stocks (at that time still legally required to back 25 percent of Federal Reserve deposit and note liabilities). The U.S. gold stocks fell from $22.1 billion at the end of 1956 to $13.8 billion at the end of 1965. The largest annual drop, $2.3 billion, occurred in 1958. Monetary gold was withdrawn from general circulation in the United States in 1933, but foreign monetary authorities continued to have the right to convert their dollar holdings into gold at the U.S. Treasury; indeed the rules of the International Monetary Fund were built around this gold convertibility of the U.S. dollar. By the end of 1947 the United States held over 70 percent of the world's monetary gold stock, so some redistribution was necessary and welcome. But the sharp drop of 1958, followed by a marked worsening of the U.S. trade balance in 1959, caused alarm in financial circles on both sides of the Atlantic. In fall 1960 prices on the London gold market rose briefly to $40, prompting central banks (including the United States) to sell gold into the market, an arrangement later formalized as the "gold pool"; this lasted until 1968. President-elect Kennedy is reported to have said to his advisers that the two things that worried him most were nuclear war and the payments deficit, a measure of its gravity in the political mind, if not in reality.[17] (George Ball suggests that a lot of Kennedy's concern arose from having to answer to his conservative father on his financial policies and results.)[18]

But the United States also posted a "deficit" in its balance of payments accounts that averaged $3.7 billion a year from 1958 to 1960 and a reduced but still substantial $2.3 billion from 1961 to 1965. This deficit, reported quarterly, provided at regular intervals an occasion for much handwringing by bankers, financial journalists, politicians, and even some economists. The deficit, or liquidity deficit as it later came to be called, failed to count foreign purchases of U.S. Treasury bills (a favorite vehicle for foreign central and commercial banks, as well as some large firms) and foreign deposits in U.S. banks as U.S. receipts, but counted U.S. deposits abroad or purchases of short-term foreign securities as payments. The rationale for this asymmetric treatment was that foreign monetary authorities could convert their holdings into gold on demand, and nonofficial for-

17. Schlesinger (1965, p. 129).
18. Ball (1982, p. 205).

eign holdings of dollars could be converted into local currencies at fixed exchange rates at short notice, and thereby augment the potential claims of central banks. Of course, so long as the United States played a growing role of banker to the rest of the world, accepting deposits from foreigners and re-lending them abroad, it was bound indefinitely to show a "deficit" measured in this way; that is what mainline banking is all about. Indeed, the United States had registered a "deficit" every year since 1950 (except in 1957), right through the period of so-called dollar shortage.

At the same time, however, the United States recorded a substantial and generally growing current account *surplus,* except in 1959 (see table 5-2). The surplus on goods and services reached its peak of $8.5 billion in 1964, before beginning to decline with the attainment of full employment and the inflationary pressures associated with the buildup in military expenditures for Vietnam. Thus the payments "deficit" was due to net capital outflows, "net" defined to exclude the short-term inflows noted above. Robert Solomon argues that the strong show of concern about the deficit by the late Eisenhower and incoming Kennedy administrations probably increased speculative capital movements, out of the dollar into gold and the German mark, and thereby actually aggravated the problem; "benign neglect" would have been more sensible.[19]

But President Kennedy did not believe that option was available. Over the course of the next few years the administration tied foreign aid more tightly to U.S. procurement; increased the price differential required for foreign bidders to win U.S. government contracts (from the 6 percent established by Eisenhower in 1954); expanded the lending authority of the Export-Import Bank; and introduced in July 1963 an "interest equalization tax" on foreign bond issues in the United States and U.S. purchases of foreign equities (extended in 1965 to cover bank lending abroad, all with stipulated exceptions).[20] But in general the measures, while perhaps misguided, were relatively modest—too modest for the taste of many European financial officials. And some measures emphasized the affirmative objectives of the administration. The investment tax credit aimed to improve productivity and enhance growth. The multilateral trade negotiations sought to reduce tariff barriers to U.S. exports in rapidly growing markets, particularly Europe and Japan. Under Operation Twist (started in 1961), the Federal Reserve undertook

19. Solomon (1982, p. 37).

20. For an early evaluation of the interest equalization tax, which concluded that it affected the form but not the total magnitude of U.S. capital outflows, see Cooper (1965). A later examination by Hewson and Sakakibara (1975) reached broadly the same conclusion.

Table 5-2. *U.S. Balance of International Payments, 1959–73*

Billions of dollars

Year	Merchandise exports	Current account balance	Official reserve transactions balance
1959	16.5	−1.3	...
1960	19.7	2.8	−3.4
1961	20.1	3.8	−1.4
1962	20.8	3.4	−2.7
1963	22.3	4.4	−1.9
1964	25.5	6.8	−1.5
1965	26.5	5.4	−1.3
1966	29.3	3.0	0.2
1967	30.7	2.6	−3.4
1968	33.6	0.6	1.6
1969	36.4	0.4	2.7
1970	42.5	2.3	−9.8
1971	43.3	−1.4	−29.8
1972	49.4	−5.8	−10.4
1973	71.4	7.1	−5.3

Source: *Economic Report of the President,* 1976, 1999.

some of its open market operations in longer-term securities, with the aim of twisting the yield curve clockwise to encourage longer-term investment while discouraging short-term capital outflows. Another measure (not enacted) proposed to relieve the pressure on monetary policy to combat recessions by giving the president limited discretionary power to reduce income taxes. Throughout this period the Council of Economic Advisers argued—sometimes against the Treasury Department—for the pursuit of sensible policies, and against economically costly actions in the name of improving the balance of payments. Countless proposals for restrictions on imports and other payments (such as overseas travel by Americans), in the name of improving the balance of payments, were properly rejected by both the Kennedy and the Johnson administrations.

Throughout the 1960s the U.S. economy grew by 4.6 percent a year. Unemployment dropped from 5.5 percent in 1960 to 3.5 percent in 1969.

Inflation (consumer price indexes) increased from 1.7 percent to 5.4 percent over the same period. The current account surplus rose from $2.8 billion in 1960 to $6.8 billion in 1964 and then declined to $0.4 billion in 1969; the merchandise trade balance registered its first deficit since 1888 in 1971.

U.S. private capital outflows accelerated sharply in the declining-interest recession of 1970–71 (much of it repayment of U.S. bank borrowing in the Eurodollar market during the tight-money year of 1969). Meanwhile, private foreigners liquidated some of their claims on the United States. The two resulted in a $27 billion increase in foreign central bank holdings of U.S. dollars—and increasing signs of restlessness among foreign central bankers. The gold pool was abandoned in 1968 in the face of large purchases (and rumors of even larger purchases emanating from France).[21] By mid-1971, market gold prices in London and Zurich had risen to nearly $44 an ounce—a 26 percent premium over the official $35 price.

This was the context when President Nixon, on August 15, 1971, dramatically introduced his "New Economic Policy," involving a ninety-day freeze on wages and prices, a 10 percent surcharge on dutiable imports, and suspension of gold convertibility for foreign monetary authorities. Other countries were thus confronted with the decision whether to continue to accumulate nonconvertible dollars, to allow their currencies to float upward, or to impose strict controls on capital inflows. They pursued diverse strategies. Canada and Germany floated (Canada had already floated its currency in May 1970, in violation of the then-prevailing IMF rules). Japan floated—but with heavy intervention to brake appreciation of the yen. France tightened its capital controls. Most developing countries maintained their peg to the dollar. There were heavy protests against the import surcharge, which violated GATT undertakings, and efforts, particularly by Canada and developing countries, to obtain exemption from it.

John Connally, who had become U.S. secretary of the treasury early in 1971, obviously relished his new international notoriety. He was in no evident hurry to reach a cooperative settlement that must involve the removal of the import surcharge and perhaps restoration of gold convertibility (possibly at a new price) in exchange for currency appreciation by the major countries and perhaps reductions in their barriers in imports. But what started as a balance of payments crisis quickly became a major foreign policy crisis with America's closest allies, and by November Nixon indicated that he wanted a settlement. The Camp David meeting at which the August 15

21. Solomon (1982, p. 114).

package of actions was worked out involved economic officials and Chairman Arthur Burns from the Federal Reserve Board; no foreign policy officials were present, neither National Security Adviser Henry Kissinger nor anyone from the State Department. After several efforts to elevate the issue to the political level, Kissinger managed to get it on the agenda of a meeting between Nixon and President Pompidou of France in early December.[22]

At that meeting Nixon privately agreed to raise the official dollar price of gold to $38 an ounce but not to restore gold convertibility, thus giving France a symbolic but economically meaningless victory, and implying an appreciation of the French franc against the dollar by 8.6 percent. France had been a major obstacle to earlier agreement with the Europeans. This agreement laid the basis for a settlement in mid-December, in which the United States publicly agreed to remove the import surcharge and other Group of Ten countries agreed to appreciations of their currencies against the dollar ranging from 16.9 percent (Japan) to 7.5 percent (Italy and Sweden). The band of permissible exchange rate variation was also increased from 2.0 to 4.5 percent. Nixon modestly pronounced this Smithsonian Agreement "the most significant monetary agreement in the history of the world."[23]

The United States had desired an improvement in its current account position of $13 billion, a number other countries viewed as much too high. By a Federal Reserve calculation, the Smithsonian Agreement would have resulted in an improvement by $8 billion, but Treasury officials thought this an exaggeration of the impact. In any event, the U.S. payments deficit continued throughout 1972 (partly because of vigorous economic recovery), and in February 1973 the United States negotiated another modest devaluation of the dollar. But exchange markets did not settle down, so Japan and the European countries allowed their currencies to float against the dollar in March 1973. The dollar depreciated about 11 percent against other major currencies during 1973. With major currencies floating against one another, and no currency convertible into gold, the Bretton Woods era—or, more accurately, two central features of it—came to an end.

Some have suggested, then and since, that the dollar should have been devalued much earlier. There are several reasons why devaluation could not have occurred much sooner. First, President Kennedy was unalterably

22. I was in Europe on August 15. On my return, Francis Bator, Robert Hormats, and I drafted a long memorandum to Kissinger indicating how damaging the new policy was to our relations with Europe, suggesting how the issue might be resolved through negotiation, and indicating several occasions at which President Nixon might signal his willingness to reach a cooperative solution.

23. As quoted in Solomon (1982, p. 208).

opposed to it. Although one notable economist, Paul Samuelson, suggested that the dollar was overvalued even before 1961, Kennedy indicated that he did not want any administration official to mention it outside the Oval Office, Theodore Sorenson reports.[24]

More substantively, the United States operationally had no way to devalue the dollar. It could change the official price of gold, although that required congressional action. But unlike other countries it could not simply alter its intervention price in foreign exchange markets, since it did not generally intervene in foreign exchange markets. Changing the price of gold any time in the early 1960s would with virtual certainty have led other countries to do the same, thus increasing the currency value of gold reserves but leaving exchange rates unchanged.

Throughout the 1960s the United States ran a current account surplus, not a deficit. Mercantilistic sentiments remained strong in almost all countries, reflecting in part an appreciation of the merits of export-led growth. Moreover, some Europeans, led by French president De Gaulle, objected in principle to American direct investment in Europe. Dollar devaluation would have enlarged the U.S. trade surplus to finance American investment abroad. Such a strategy was not within the bounds of general acceptability in other countries.

So dollar devaluation was not a realistic option until the U.S. current account position had obviously deteriorated badly; and even then Europeans objected to the modest devaluation proposed by U.S. officials. Unhappily, it probably could not have occurred except under the duress of the import surcharge or some analogously offensive action. As John Connally is said to have told his foreign colleagues at the time, "The dollar is our currency but your problem."

The International Monetary System

Kennedy held out the possibility in his February 1961 message on the U.S. balance of payments that the United States might draw on its substantial credits at the International Monetary Fund. [25] But there was a potential

24. Sorenson (1965, p. 405).

25. As with the previous section, I have relied heavily on Robert Solomon's excellent and authoritative history of the period (Solomon, 1982), both to refresh my memory and to learn afresh. See also Bordo and Eichengreen (1993), especially the comprehensive survey of academic research by Michael Bordo and the essay by Maurice Obstfeld on the adjustment process.

technical problem here: the IMF did not have enough usable currencies to honor a substantial U.S. request and still carry on its normal operations, since its loans to member countries were overwhelmingly in U.S. dollars. Newly convertible European currencies were available in principle, but several of the countries, most notably Britain and Italy, did not themselves have strong payments positions, and France was just emerging from a long bout of balance of payments difficulties.

"Obviously" if the United States had a payments deficit, some other countries must have payments surpluses that could be recycled through the IMF to the United States. This point, in fact, was not obvious at all, given the asymmetric method the United States used to calculate its deficit at the time. The usable currency problem was dealt with by an agreement among the ten largest trading countries, plus Switzerland (not then a member of the IMF), to lend to the IMF up to $6 billion under certain stipulated circumstances (subsequently raised to $48 billion when augmented by the New Arrangements to Borrow, concluded in 1998). Thus was born the Group of Ten, of which seven were European countries (eight of eleven counting Switzerland), whose ministers of finance and their deputies were most prominent in discussion of the international monetary system in the decades following.

The international monetary system exhibited asymmetries deeper than this. One concerned the international role that the U.S. dollar had come to play; another concerned the balance of responsibility between countries in payments deficit and those in payments surplus to correct the imbalances. These themes recurred in discussions of the international monetary system throughout the 1960s and 1970s and in some respects down to the present.

Yale economist Robert Triffin identified a major flaw in the international system in his 1960 book, *Gold and the Dollar Crisis,* based on essays written two years earlier.[26] He drew attention to what became known as the "Triffin dilemma." Demand for international reserves in a growing world economy grew more rapidly than could be supplied by new gold production less industrial demands for gold. The incremental demand for reserves was satisfied by adding U.S. dollars, mainly interest-earning Treasury bills, a process that occurred voluntarily and willingly throughout the 1950s. Dollars held by monetary authorities were convertible into gold. Yet sooner or later the gold-convertibility of the dollar would inevitably come into question, since under the postulated circumstances the dollar liabilities of

---

26. Triffin (1960).

the United States to other monetary authorities would necessarily grow relative to U.S. monetary gold stocks—even if the United States owned most of the world's monetary gold. The dilemma involved a choice between slowing world economic growth (because of a shortage of reserves, and national actions to limit perceived payments problems) or facing a financial crisis as the gold convertibility of the dollar came increasingly into question.[27]

Triffin was a member of a transition team of specialists, under the chairmanship of George Ball, who advised President-elect Kennedy on the positions he should take on issues of foreign economic policy. Triffin's concerns found their way into Kennedy's February 1961 address on the balance of payments, where the president observed that the world could not always rely on gold and dollars (and sterling, still held in the reserves of many countries) to provide world reserves. Kennedy instructed his (not very enthusiastic) Secretary of the Treasury Douglas Dillon to explore ways with his foreign counterparts to furnish needed increases in reserves, to provide "the flexibility required to support a healthy and growing world economy."[28]

The Council of Economic Advisers, with help from Carl Kaysen in the White House, took the lead in keeping this issue alive in the Kennedy administration, but it did not mature until Henry ("Joe") Fowler succeeded Dillon as secretary of the treasury. With strong encouragement and assistance from Francis Bator, who succeeded Kaysen as the senior economist on the staff of the National Security Council, Fowler proposed and negotiated to its successful conclusion in 1968 the possible creation, by the International Monetary Fund, of Special Drawing Rights (SDRs for short), a nationality-neutral man-made medium for international reserves to be held by central banks. The SDR was to be created to meet the secular increase in demand for international reserves. Later in the 1970s, as gold was dethroned, SDRs were designated to become the "principal reserve asset" of the monetary system. They were specifically not meant to be created for normal operations of the IMF, or even when financial conditions in one or more countries threatened the international monetary system, although that is a future possibility in the continuing evolution of the system.

Boom conditions and tight money in the United States in 1968–69 led to a decline in foreign dollar reserves for the first time in many years. This

27. The logical possibility of a smooth worldwide price deflation (thus raising the real value of gold reserves) while maintaining full employment of resources was not envisaged as possible, against the background of the 1930s.

28. As quoted in Solomon (1982, p. 40).

created the conditions for the first allocation of the SDRs, which occurred in 1970–72 in the amount of 9.3 billion SDRs (equal to $9.3 billion at the time). SDRs were again allocated in 1979–81, cumulating SDR 12.1 billion in this period. There have been no other allocations.[29]

The SDR was a good idea that came too late. The Triffin dilemma matured in 1971 in the particular conditions of that year; the cessation of gold convertibility and the subsequent move to floating exchange rates shifted emphasis away from reserve growth, perhaps mistakenly.

Negotiating the SDR was not easy. Despite official French animus against the "privileged" role of the dollar in the system, the French strongly resisted the creation of a man-made nationality-neutral substitute for the dollar in its reserve asset role, for the simple reason that they preferred to restore gold to the central position, necessarily at a higher price. Exactly why this was the French view will probably forever remain a mystery. The French position was dictated by President Charles De Gaulle, allegedly on this issue under the influence of the economist Jacques Rueff.[30] Gold had history on its side, but a careful reading of that history suggests that gold would be completely unacceptable to democratic countries committed to policies of economic growth and full employment (and to fixed exchange rates).[31] An appropriate rise in the price of gold (but how to determine what was "appropriate"?) could assure enough monetary gold for awhile. However, except for accidents of discovery or technical improvement in extraction, the shortage of gold would inevitably arise again and again in the future, requiring further price increases. But if the price of gold is to be adjusted from time to time as a matter of (international) policy, why not instead create an international fiat money subject to similar decisions? This would avoid the real economic costs of hoarding a useful metal and the real economic disruptions that would inevitably attend both the prospect and the occasional fact of sharp increases in the price at which central banks purchase gold?[32]

29. In the late 1990s, the SDR is defined as a fixed combination of U.S. dollars, Japanese yen, German marks, British pounds, and French francs. With floating rates among these currencies, it changes value daily. At the end of December 1998, one SDR equaled $1.408.

30. His finance minister Valery Giscard d'Estaing, later president of France, had a much more nuanced view of gold and of the proper functioning of the monetary system. Perhaps as a consequence, he was dismissed and replaced by hard-liner Michel Debré.

31. On the operation of the gold standard before 1914 and from 1925 to 1933, see, respectively, Cooper (1982) and Eichengreen (1992).

32. Gold still holds fascination for many people, including officials. In the 1990s several central banks finally decided that their gold holdings were an unnecessary and costly relic from the past, and some sales were made by the central banks of Australia, Belgium, the Netherlands, Switzerland, and the

One motive for the French position was suspected to be the existence of large private holdings of gold in France, acquired during earlier periods of domestic monetary instability. Another motive may have been simply to cross the United States, which De Gaulle had resented since his wartime days in London, and which he considered all too influential in post-war European affairs. Some of this influence was assumed by De Gaulle (and many other otherwise intelligent Frenchmen) to emanate from the international use of the dollar. In fact it emanated from the relative size and character of the U.S. economy and the liquidity of its financial markets, from which widespread foreign holding of dollar assets in turn derived. The *independent* contribution to U.S. flexibility arising from the international role of the dollar was at best negligible—and arguably negative, given the excessive consternation it created in successive U.S. administrations, from Eisenhower to Carter.

The other major topic in discussions on international monetary reform concerned how to distribute the burden of adjustment to imbalances between countries in payments deficit and countries in surplus. "Burden" usually meant who should take the initiative for action, and hence political responsibility—not the quite different question of how the real economic costs of adjustment, if any, should be shared (although in official and journalistic discussion, the former issue was usually mistaken for the latter). This paper is already too long to go into this complex but not very fruitful debate in detail. The economically efficient answer requires taking a collective view of the condition of the global economy relative to what it should be, and agreeing on what it should be. It elevates to the global level a debate over macroeconomic policy common within national economies. The IMF is a natural place for such discussion, guided by its staff. However, it persistently shirked the role until the oil crises of the 1970s, and even then it entered the fray only cautiously. Discussions in the Organization for Economic Cooperation and Development (OECD) were much more to the point, partly because they directly involved senior officials and even ministers from member countries.

It is often said that excessive monetary expansion—and inflation—in the United States caused the breakdown of the Bretton Woods system in

---

United Kingdom. But proposals to sell a small portion of the IMF's large gold holdings to help highly indebted developing countries were blocked, mainly by Europeans. (Instead, the IMF will by subterfuge simply revalue some of its gold holdings.) In September 1999 fifteen European countries agreed not to sell any more official gold, beyond sales already announced, for five years. The depression of market prices is of legitimate concern to any seller of an asset—and to producers (who vigorously protested the sales)—but a five-year moratorium seems greatly excessive.

1971–73. That is at best a half-truth. U.S. inflation rose in the late 1960s, but remained below that of most other countries. Of course, the statement could merely be tautological: some degree of monetary contraction in the United States would have been sufficiently severe to reduce inflation, restore the U.S. trade surplus, and attract foreign capital into U.S. interest-bearing securities. There was a whiff of that in late 1968 and 1969, when taxes were increased, money was tightened, and U.S. banks borrowed heavily abroad.[33] That in turn generated the recession of 1970–71 (unemployment, a lagging indicator, rose from 3.5 percent in 1969 to 5.9 percent in 1971), with its attendant weakened demand for imports but also a decline in interest rates. As it happened, Germany and Britain then wanted tighter monetary policy. The result was a huge flow of yield-seeking funds out of the United States, including large repayments of U.S. bank borrowing, which were not subject to the restrictions on new bank lending abroad. In addition, there were large conversions of foreign private holdings of dollars, also not subject to U.S. restrictions on capital outflows, into foreign currencies. This increased U.S. liabilities to foreign central banks by $7 billion in 1970 and $27 billion in 1971. Total dollar holdings of foreign central banks grew even more because of dollar creation in the London-based eurodollar market, as dollars held there rather than directly in the United States were re-lent, thus providing a source for increases in world dollar holdings independent of the U.S. payments deficit.[34]

But there had been earlier periods of U.S. monetary expansion, as great relative to GNP as in 1970. They did not lead to collapse of the Bretton Woods arrangements. By the early 1970s, however, the international mobility of capital had risen to the point (despite attempts to limit capital movements) at which it strained to the breaking point an already fragile and fundamentally flawed system, one that depended critically on low mobility of capital. So while events in the U.S. economy, in conjunction with those in Europe, precipitated the breakdown in 1971–73, a breakdown would have come later if it had not occurred when it did.

33. All major countries except Canada, Germany, Switzerland, and the United States maintained systematic controls on capital movements in the late 1960s, but mainly on outflows. Germany and Switzerland both introduced measures to discourage unwanted inflows. The United States starting in 1963 introduced and gradually extended tax restrictions on U.S. purchases of foreign securities, and starting in 1965 restricted U.S. bank lending abroad. But the euro-dollar market in London fell outside the British exchange control system.

34. To avoid dollar creation not associated with U.S. payments deficits, central banks of the G-10 had agreed to hold their dollars directly in the United States, but the agreement did not apply to other central banks.

Much of the "burden-sharing" issue has gone away with the general floating of exchange rates, although it still exists within the European Union and can be found residually in quarrels over who should take responsibility for intervening in foreign exchange markets when such intervention is thought to be desirable. And of course the condition of the world economy is still relevant for determining how countries collectively should respond to domestic imbalances; for example, whether monetary conditions should be eased or tightened, on average.

What is noteworthy for its absence in the early 1960s, particularly in view of subsequent events, is how little systematic discussion there was of an appropriate exchange rate regime, and in particular consideration of alternatives to the par value system of Bretton Woods. There were few exchange rate adjustments of major currencies during the 1960s. The German mark and Netherlands guilder were revalued by 5 percent (generally judged to be too little) in 1961. The British pound was devalued by 14 percent in 1967, after major efforts to avoid it. In a surprise move, the French franc was devalued by 11 percent in 1969, and the German mark appreciated by 9 percent later that year. During the period, capital moved more freely. In particular, Germany was swamped by inflows in 1968 and again in mid-1969. Of course, serious adjustment by many countries could be avoided so long as the United States was running deficits (implying other major countries had surpluses) and other countries were willing to accumulate dollars without limit. But the political unacceptability of this arrangement became increasingly evident and was reinforced by widespread disapproval, particularly in Europe, of U.S. actions in Vietnam and hence of U.S. budget and overseas expenditures to sustain its activities in Vietnam.

Just as experience during the 1920s and 1930s cultivated a distaste for exchange rate flexibility, experience during the 1950s and 1960s cultivated increasing antipathy, at least in academic circles, to the Bretton Woods version of fixed exchange rates: that is, rates fixed beyond narrow bands of permissible variation, but adjustable if necessary to correct a "fundamental disequilibrium" in international payments, in the words of the IMF Articles of Agreement. It became clear that national authorities held on to their fixed rates for too long, and that by the time a fundamental disequilibrium was evident to them, it was also evident to everyone else. This arrangement created a mechanism for periodic transfers of public wealth, held in the form of foreign exchange reserves, to private parties who speculated successfully on a discrete change in exchange rates, selling before an expected devaluation and repurchasing afterward. Even with pervasive controls on capital movements, determined firms and individuals could move much capital legally through manipulating the "leads and lags" of commercial payments and other loopholes in the control system; and of course funds also moved illegally with bribes or misrepresentations of trade invoices or elsewhere.

This prospect in turn inhibited authorities from changing exchange rates, hoping that the payments difficulties were temporary, or led them to impose and increasingly tighten controls on international transactions in order to reduce payments deficits—thus thwarting the very purposes for which a well-functioning payments system is desired.

Observing this excessive rigidity, as well as the growth in both the possibilities for and the magnitude of international capital movements, many economists increasingly came to favor greater flexibility in exchange rates. Numerous proposals for introducing greater flexibility, short of full floating, were put forward. Some concentrated, like Keynes in the 1920s, on giving greater freedom for differences in national monetary policies, by widening the band of permissible variation around central parities. Others concentrated on providing for gradual secular changes in exchange rates, via a "crawling peg" or "gliding parity," without provoking massive speculation around prospective discrete changes.[35] Of course, numerous combinations of the two approaches were possible.[36]

The functioning of the international monetary system was the topic of a series of meetings from 1964 between a group of academics and central bankers dubbed the "Bellagio Group," under the collective leadership of Fritz Machlup, William Fellner, and Robert Triffin. Of particular interest were exchange rate arrangements and adequate provision of international liquidity. This group exposed key central bankers to the evolution in academic thinking and may have played some role in persuading central bankers that flexible exchange rates were workable, or at least would not be more troublesome than the fixed exchange rate system with which they were then having to cope—and thus paved the way for floating in the 1970s.

Elements of Continuity, or Déjà Vu Yet Again

The U.S. balance of payments "problem" never seems to go away. It was perceived to exist in the 1960s, in the 1970s, and in the 1980s. In the late

35. See, for example, Williamson (1965); Cooper (1968a); Gordon (1968).

36. Useful compendia on academic thinking in the late 1960s can be found in Federal Reserve Bank of Boston (1969) and Halm (1970).

1990s people are again asking about the sustainability of the U.S. payments deficit. With floating exchange rates among major currencies, the focus is now on the large U.S. current account deficit, over 3 percent of GDP in 1999—offset, of course, by equally large net capital inflows.[37]

Moreover, foreigners, especially Europeans, continue to complain about U.S. macroeconomic policy. Even nearly a decade of respectable growth with low inflation evokes concern, as reflected in the 1999 *World Economic Outlook* published by the International Monetary Fund, where the United States is simultaneously urged to restrain its rate of growth to forestall inflation and to trim its large trade deficit.[38] Exactly what action the United States is supposed to take is unclear: tighter monetary policy would restrain growth and inflation, but would also lead to further appreciation of the dollar and eventually worsen the trade balance. Tighter fiscal policy could help but is difficult (impossible?) to engineer when the U.S. government is running the largest budget surpluses in memory and the administration is struggling to limit tax reduction. Moreover, the IMF is properly concerned about the negative impact of a significant depreciation of the dollar on weakly recovering economies elsewhere. Should restrictions on inward movement of capital be introduced or import restrictions tightened? Either action would certainly evoke loud complaints.

In the meantime, the U.S. dollar is in greater demand abroad than ever, by monetary authorities as well as by private parties, despite the general move to floating exchange rates. The widespread view among economists that floating exchange rates would greatly reduce demand for official reserves has proven far from the mark. Roy Harrod, almost alone among leading economists in the 1960s, believed that a move to floating exchange rates would increase demand for reserves, as countries increased their precautionary holdings to counter unwanted market movements, because they could not count on borrowing abroad when they most needed the funds. In fact, total international reserves held by central banks around the world have fallen relative to world imports, but only modestly, from 39 percent in 1965 to 31 percent in 1997. Gold (valued in 1997 at SDR 35, equal to $48 per ounce) has dropped to the bottom of usable reserves, and SDRs exist in only modest amounts. Thus the bulk of the substantial growth in demand for reserves has been satisfied, as in the 1950s, by U.S. dollars, supplemented by German marks and smaller amounts of yen and other currencies.

---

37. For a balanced discussion, concluding that the large U.S. deficit can persist for several years but probably not for a longer period, see Mann (1999).

38. International Monetary Fund (1999, p. 1).

Dollars are wanted, not because of their long-abandoned convertibility into gold at the U.S. Treasury, but because of their high liquidity and attractive yields. Some countries—most notably Japan (whose foreign exchange reserves at the end of 1998 amounted to $203 billion, 11 percent of the world's total, up from $10 billion in 1973)—have acquired dollars not because they are desired per se, but as a by-product of preventing unwanted appreciation of the domestic currency; that is, as a consequence of particular national choices regarding macroeconomic policy. Even relatively laissez faire, floating-currency Switzerland has added $33 billion (perhaps mostly in German marks) to its foreign exchange reserves since 1973, raising its reserve-to-import ratio from 14 to 36 percent.

In sum, the legacy of U.S. foreign economic policy in the 1960s can still be felt. This is most clear in the case of trade policy. As enduring is the policy of striving for prosperity despite alleged balance of payments difficulties—even if those difficulties have translated into financial market anxieties. By contrast, the international monetary system differs greatly from the system that prevailed in the 1960s—and even from the system envisioned in the 1960s for the future.

COMMENT BY
Francis M. Bator

As a postscript to Dick Cooper's illuminating paper, I would like to add a few words about what things looked like from 1965 to 1967 from inside the black box and what we thought we were doing.[39] I'll comment briefly at the end about who the "we" were and cite the relevant evidence.

By mid-1966, it appeared probable that:

—The dollar was overvalued, and very likely becoming more so.[40]

—Without a substantial change in cross rates, fiscal measures that would suffice to assure *internal* balance, however desirable on their own terms, might not suffice to bring about *external* balance, especially if the many inefficient microeconomic restraints on current and capital transac-

---

39. During that time, I served as deputy national security adviser to President Johnson, with staff responsibility for U.S.-European relations and for foreign economic policy.

40. For a May 1966 description of the payments situation that led to that conclusion, see Duncan, Patterson, and Yee (1998, item 95). For a more optimistic assessment six months earlier, see item 79.

tions were lifted.[41] Relying mainly on very tight money to bring about both internal and external balance without help from a cheaper dollar would have been thought much too hazardous ("grabby brakes," and all that, to recall Arthur Okun's phrase).[42]

—Without a precipitating crisis (such as a cessation of U.S. gold sales, perhaps in response to one or more major central banks joining in a bear raid on the dollar), the major surplus countries would not sit still for a substantial one-time dollar devaluation, whether negotiated over a weekend or achieved by means of a (large) one-time increase in the price of gold. The economic and political advantages afforded by an undervalued currency—export-led growth and a large payments surplus (widely thought of as a sign of virtue)—were too appealing to give up voluntarily. I leave aside the satisfaction afforded by the opportunity to lecture the United States about living in balance of payments sin.

—The Bretton Woods rules then in force were likely to give rise to serious economic trouble, irrespective of whether the U.S. international accounts were in deficit or surplus or in balance (however defined). With fixed exchange rates the norm and devaluation of a major currency considered both a mark of political failure and an economic gamble (in the case of the dollar, probably unacceptable to the others); with reserves consisting largely of gold, dollars, and sterling, and gold the only external source of new net reserves for the world as a whole; and with the United States required to keep the dollar convertible into gold at *some* fixed price, it seemed likely that there did not exist *any* gold price, or any configuration of U.S. payments, that would save the rules from causing trouble—even aside from the problems that would be posed by the rapid prospective increase in capital mobility. Reform, it was thought, would have to provide for continuous controlled growth in the supply of reserves in line with growth in activity. It would have to address the instability-confidence problem—the Triffin problem—endemic to widespread reliance on two or more reserve assets, each with a different risk-return profile. Perhaps most important, to facilitate adjustment—or so some of us reluctantly

41. By internal balance, I mean the outermost aggregate demand-output trajectory that, in combination with the wage-price guideposts and in the absence of supply-price shocks, would not give rise to a continuing increase in the underlying inflation rate.

42. According to the static textbook large-country story with perfect capital mobility, the extra induced capital inflow would in any case have been only a one-time event. In a conversation, Richard Cooper suggested that with capital controls, long lags, and long-term saving-investment portfolio effects taken into account, analysis of the likely dynamics would show that there would have been a "permanent" effect.

assumed—the rules would eventually have to allow for endogenous movements in exchange rates, at least much wider bands and "crawling pegs."[43]

In the near term—once actual output had caught up with potential output—pretty much everyone, including President Johnson, thought that the situation called for a large tax increase that would curb the consumption of the nonpoor and thereby free up the resources slated for the Vietnam War and for the increased consumption of Great Society transfer recipients. Along with a snug monetary policy, it would also help reduce—though probably not eliminate—the payments deficit. The debate was about whether we should pay the price that a reluctant Congress and a very reluctant Ways and Means Committee would exact to enact a tax increase.

Until 1967, the president thought the price too high. He would not follow Henry Fowler's advice to call it a "war tax" and appeal to Congress and the country in his role as commander in chief. In private conversation, Johnson gave three reasons. First, he believed it would start a divisive national debate that would wreck both the civil rights and the other Great Society legislation (he thought "the war on poverty" a major part of his civil rights strategy and vice versa). Second, he was convinced it would make it even harder for him to hold off the proponents of a wider war—he sometimes referred to them as the "crazies"—who were urging him to invade North Vietnam, close off the Ho Chi Minh Trail, and bomb up to the Chinese border, never mind the risk of Chinese intervention. Last, he feared that in both Moscow and Washington it would strengthen the many bitter opponents of his attempt to thaw the Cold War. It was the "bridge-building" policy spelled out in his October 1966 speech on Europe that made possible the Non-Proliferation Treaty and helped encourage West Germany's shift from a rigid "re-unification or nothing" stance vis-à-vis the Warsaw Pact countries (the so-called Hallstein Doctrine) to Chancellor Willy Brandt's ameliorative "Ostpolitik." It led to a serious face-to-face conversation between Johnson and Soviet Chairman Alexei Kosygin in Glassboro, notably about the arms race. Had it not been for the brutal, panic-driven suppression by the Kremlin of liberal reforms in Czecho-

43. For contemporary statements on the need for reform, see Duncan, Patterson, and Yee (1998, item 64) and Bator (1968a, b). On the possible shape of a reformed system, see Bator (1968b, especially pp. 59–63). For how U.S. policy on all this evolved, see Brittain (1975, pp. 128–32) and Odell (1982, pp. 130–64). Odell (1982, pp. 138–44) also contains a good account of what various dramatis personae thought about flexible exchange rates. For a fine 1968 discussion of all this, see Cooper (1968b). For the foreign policy context vis-à-vis Europe, see Bator (1968c).

slovakia in August 1968, it might well have led to a full-fledged summit in Moscow with both the antiballistic missile (ABM) and multiple independent reentry vehicles (MIRVs) on the agenda.[44]

Absent fiscal restraint (and very likely even with such restraint), we thought there were three choices, roughly speaking.[45] First, by grossly inefficient microeconomic means, we could drastically compress the various debit components in the accounts, and boost the credit items, so as to eliminate the deficit, or at least reduce it enough to rule out a payments deficit–induced dumping of dollars that might cause the major central banks to try to convert a substantial part of their dollar holdings into gold. Generally speaking, that was the policy favored by the balance of payments hawks in the government. This group included Treasury Under Secretary Robert Roosa and, perhaps a shade more reluctantly, Treasury Secretary Douglas Dillon before they left office; Federal Reserve Board Chairman William McChesney Martin and Defense Secretary Robert McNamara; and inescapably, "ex officio" as it were, Treasury Secretary Henry Fowler (in April 1965, just before the really serious deterioration began, it became *his* job to fix the deficit). In their view, changing the price of gold, or cutting the dollar-gold link, would have been a calamity ("nuclear war," one said, obviously meaning it only metaphorically).

Alternatively, we could try to solve the problem once and for all by cutting the link—as President Nixon and Treasury Secretary John Connally would do in 1971, without the chest thumping and the surcharge. The dollar would be allowed to float indefinitely, or until the rest of the world agreed to change the Bretton Woods rules in ways that would facilitate adjustment in a sticky-price environment, assure adequate liquidity, and contain instability—changes that would shift the balance of power away from the surplus-prone, Bundesbank-minded countries.

The idea had a lot of appeal for anyone who thought that, under the right circumstances, cutting the dollar loose—far from a disaster—might even help speed agreement on sensible reform.[46] We thought it almost cer-

---

44. In a recent conversation, Charles Schultze said that he thought the second reason was decisive. It appears that President Johnson was not alone in his concern about arousing the public's then-hawkish inclinations. While searching for evidence on all this, I was startled to find a November 1965 memorandum of mine urging the president for just that reason *not* to adopt the Fowler "commander and chief" tactic in connection with the 1966 balance of payments program. See Duncan, Patterson, and Yee (1998, item 79).

45. Duncan, Patterson, and Yee (1998, item 94, esp. pp. 272–73); Bator (1968b, pp. 63–67).

46. See Duncan, Patterson, and Yee (1998, item 95, par. 10, and item 100, esp. par. 3 and 8). See also Sampson (1995, item 193) and Bator (1968b, pp. 66–67).

tain, however, that—except, conceivably, as a patently defensive response to a large-scale demand for gold by the major central banks—a U.S. decision to close the window would have wrecked both the Kennedy Round and the SDR negotiations (which we thought would remain important even in a Bretton Woods II regime with endogenous exchange-rate movements). Very likely it would have also derailed such non-narrowly economic enterprises as the so-called "Trilateral Negotiations" among the Germans, British, and Americans concerning force deployments and burden sharing—the negotiations that followed the De Gaulle withdrawal from NATO (the organization) in March 1966.[47] Anyone involved in advising the president on foreign policy generally would also have thought that as long as there was a chance for negotiating reform collaboratively, the United States should avoid taking drastic unilateral action except in response to a serious bear raid or the threat of one by the major central banks.[48]

The third approach was to continue pretending that we would eliminate "the" deficit, but do only enough in the way of *relatively* low-cost microeconomic actions, one-time cosmetic bookkeeping, and preventive persuasion to avoid a dollar crisis *for the time being,* thus protecting the ongoing negotiations, while avoiding any actions that might endanger them directly or do other lasting economic or foreign policy damage.[49]

Scrutiny of the president's decisions—what actions he approved and did not approve—makes clear that by early 1966, when it became apparent that the payments situation was deteriorating, this third approach was the one he adopted. Given the stakes and the *external* constraints, I still think that it was the feasible first best choice. While in public—and sometimes, especially in larger meetings, even to one another—we pretended otherwise, I do not think that any of us thought, at least by mid-1966, that the

47. For the background of the president's decision to engage London and Bonn in a bottoms-up negotiation on force deployments and burden sharing as a function of an agreed assessment of the military threat, see Sampson (1995, item 193, esp. pp. 445 and 448; item 197, esp. pp. 454–56; and items 198, 211, 216, 218, 224, 230, 237–43, 248, and 249).

48. See Bator (1968a, esp. p. 624); Bator (1968b, esp. p. 62).

49. It is fair to say that the advocates of the third approach—balance of payments doves like me—were inclined to be quite hawkish when it came to restrictions on private capital outflows. We thought that the interest equalization tax (IET), for instance, might play a useful role even in a reformed system. See, for example, Duncan, Patterson, and Yee (1998, item 77, esp. p 222; and item 83, par. 3). For the foreign policy argument for restricting private direct investment, see Bator (1968b, p. 65, par. 3). For examples of one-time cosmetic fixes, see Duncan, Patterson, and Yee (1998, item 94, attachments A and C, and item 98). For examples of preventive diplomacy, see ibid. (item 94-V) and Sampson (1995, item 249, attachment 4-II).

actions we took would suffice to eliminate the deficit or even come close. The decision was in effect to live with a substantial residual deficit at least for the time being; in other words, to take a (small) chance that, even before the ongoing negotiations had concluded, we might be faced not merely by recurrent flurries of private speculation but a raid on the dollar, with some major central banks joining private speculators in a scramble for gold. The point of all the talk about fixing the deficit, the churning, and the endless meetings was to position the United States politically in relation to the financial markets, the media, the Congress, foreign governments, and central banks in such a way as to calm nervous dollar holders, strengthen the U.S. position in the ongoing negotiations, and perhaps, just perhaps, give a gradual, collaborative process of reform a chance.[50]

When, at the Brookings meeting in honor of Art Okun, I told Paul Samuelson why I thought the third approach was the feasible first best choice, he replied, "Well, it worked." It did. During the spring and summer of 1967 we successfully completed the Trilateral Negotiations, the Nonproliferation Treaty, the Kennedy Round, and the SDR negotiations. On sterling, the British held out until November. We managed to hold off a gold crisis until the following March, when in collaboration with the other six governments that participated in the London gold pool, we took the first big formal step to demonetize gold (the "two tier" agreement).

Now about the "we" and the evidence bearing on what we thought. The two most important figures in all this were President Johnson himself—he made the critical decisions on balance of payments policy, in fact as well as in principle—and secondarily, Henry Fowler. Before I describe their more complicated views, let me first say that I am pretty sure that by early 1966 both Gardener Ackley, chairman of the Council of Economic Advisers, and Art Okun, then the Council member covering international monetary matters, viewed the situation more or less the way I described it above. And all three of us were inclined to favor the third, or soft, approach.

I learned Gardener's views by what he said and did not say in lots of small ad hoc meetings with the president during 1965 and 1966 (during those summers it seems we had a crisis every weekend concerning the possible devaluation of sterling), and also, in a more guarded way, at meetings of the Cabinet Committee on the Balance of Payments (I formally replaced McGeorge Bundy as the White House staff member sometime during

---

50. See Duncan, Patterson, and Yee (1998, item 95) and, for a revealing example of the president's choices, see item 114.

August or September 1965). And I know Art Okun's views because, quite apart from dozens of meetings of the Deming Group from 1965 to 1967 and a number of small meetings with the president himself—and because he often accompanied and sometimes substituted for Gardener at the Cabinet Committee meetings—he and I spent a lot of time talking about these things.[51] Last, I know what I thought because many of the memoranda I wrote from 1965 to 1967 on these and related subjects have now been published in the State Department's *Foreign Relations of the United States* (FRUS) series for 1964 to 1968.[52] It happens also that shortly after leaving the White House in September 1967—and while still involved part-time as special consultant to Fowler and a member of the President's Advisory Committee on International Monetary Arrangements (the Dillon Committee)—I wrote down what I thought, first for the American Economic Association meetings that December, and then for a talk at the Council on Foreign Relations.[53]

About President Johnson's views, I can testify because from 1965 to 1967 I had many opportunities to talk with him about all this, because I could tell from how and what he decided in response to what I wrote him (those generally were the pieces of paper off which he worked on these matters), and by staffing and participating in most of his small meetings on international economic issues and on European policy. By late 1965, I had become a pretty fair predictor of what he would and would not approve.

Of course, LBJ would not have described things the way I have described them. But his questions, comments, and decisions implicitly reflected at least a tentative, if occasionally reluctant, acceptance of the

51. The Deming Group, as it came to be known, was the inter-departmental committee charged with advising the president and the secretary of the Treasury on international monetary reform and other international financial matters. Set up by presidential instruction in June 1965, it was chaired by Under Secretary of the Treasury for Monetary Affairs Frederick Deming. Its other members from 1965 to 1967 were Assistant Secretary of State Anthony Solomon, Federal Reserve Board Governor Dewey Daane, Art Okun, and myself. For details, see note 18 below.

52. See Duncan, Patterson, and Yee (1998) and Sampson (1995). A full set is available in the LBJ Library.

53. For the mildly sanitized *American Economic Review* and *Foreign Affairs* versions, see Bator (1968a, b). I say mildly sanitized because, for obvious reasons, it would have been inappropriate for me to use scare words like "overvalued" to characterize the dollar, even though what I wrote amounted to saying the same thing in a slightly more roundabout way. For a carefully researched academic account, see Odell (1982, pp. 130–60). Odell's account reminds me of a paper on flexible exchange rates that Seymour Harris asked me to give in 1962 at a Treasury consultants' meeting with Dillon, Roosa, and Fowler. I have not managed to find the paper, but Odell has me making the standard case both for and against, and that sounds right. I do remember being beaten at by both Charlie Kindleberger and Gottfried Haberler and concluding that I must have got it about right.

above view, as well as some powerful intuitions about U.S. priorities. Specifically, I know that he did not think that a run on the U.S. gold stock that led to a cessation of convertibility would be a first order national disaster, to be avoided at all cost. Obviously, he would not have welcomed a financial crisis: what president would? But he did not react negatively when on a number of occasions I explained my "not-the-end-of-the-world" view of the matter.[54] While at times he sounded like a deficit hawk, he invariably refused to approve drastic corrective action. On one occasion that sticks in my mind he said gruffly (and I thought a bit incautiously) to a startled Bill Martin something to the effect that "I will not deflate the American economy, screw up my foreign policy by gutting aid or pulling troops out, or go protectionist just so we can continue to pay out gold to the French at $35 dollars an ounce." (He had observed Dillon and Roosa using the threat of a run on gold to put pressure on President Kennedy to delay a tax cut. I suspect he did not much like it, and was not about to let anything like that happen to him. He had very definite views about relations between presidents and cabinet officers, and the difference between advice and pressure.)

A related Johnson intuition concerned our efforts to keep British prime minister Harold Wilson from devaluing the pound. The president realized that a sterling devaluation might conceivably start a chain reaction of competitive devaluations that could lead to an even more overvalued dollar or a run on the U.S. gold stock, or both—not a happy prospect. But he clearly did not buy the notion that the $2.80 pound mattered more to us than the Wilson government's pending decisions about British military deployments east of Suez; or about trimming the British army on the Rhine, especially as it might affect his ability to defeat Senator Mike Mansfield's resolution calling for large cuts in U.S. forces in Europe, cuts that would badly unsettle German politics already unsettled by the French withdrawal from NATO (the organization); or even what line London would take in the Kennedy Round and the SDR negotiations—all choices powerfully affected by the health of the British economy.

There was a personal point too. He simply did not like being put in a position akin to that of a majority leader pressuring a senior committee chairman on a matter that was obviously of far greater consequence for the

---

54. See, for example, Duncan, Patterson, and Yee (1998, item 95, par. 10, and item 100, par. 3 and 8). In relation to major U.S. political concerns vis-à-vis Germany and NATO, see Sampson (1995, item 193, esp. pp. 446–47).

other fellow, especially when he needed the latter's support on other issues. Obviously he would not have welcomed a financial blowup. But he had a clear sense of what he thought were U.S. priorities, and maintaining the sterling exchange rate or avoiding a run on the U.S. gold stock, though important, were not at the top of his list of what mattered most.

As McGeorge Bundy once observed, Johnson was a very majority leader-like president. Not as some historians have asserted, in his relations with his own cabinet officers or staff: he regularly overruled the whole lot—McNamara, Fowler, Secretary of State Dean Rusk (who was very careful about disagreeing with him), and the others—whenever he thought they were mistaken about something that mattered. But I think he thought of his opposite numbers—Wilson, Ludwig Erhard, Kurt Kiesinger, even De Gaulle, and to a degree even Kosygin—the way he had thought as Senate leader about Everett Dirksen, Russell Long, and Wilbur Mills. He was prepared to be attentive to their problems, as long as they were attentive to his. In our alliance relations, as in relations with Moscow, I think it worked remarkably well, but that is a long story that has not yet been written—another casualty of Vietnam. (The September 1966 contretemps with Erhard about the foreign exchange offset arrangement that is usually cited as evidence to the contrary proves the point. By then Erhard was a politically crippled lame duck. Johnson knew it. No majority leader will show his cards and make a bargain with a committee chairman who cannot deliver.)

The administration's point man in international finance, Henry Fowler, had the task of persuading the financial and political community that we meant what we said about fixing the deficit. Perhaps he meant it; the possibility of a dollar-gold crisis certainly scared him. But one has to wonder. An empirically minded political man of gentle, moderate temper—a Virginia democrat of progressive bent—he knew perfectly well by early 1966, when it became evident that the deficit was growing not shrinking, that many of his colleagues on the Cabinet Committee, and very likely the president too, felt that harsh medicine would be worse than the disease. He certainly had no use for a gold-based system. Immediately upon taking office on April 1, 1965, he boldly took up the president's call in the latter's February 10 message to Congress on the balance of payments to "press forward with our studies and beyond, to action" to create a new kind of reserve asset.[55] He went ahead in the face of widespread skepticism within

---

55. National Archives and Records Service (1966, p. 177).

the Fed, on Wall Street, and within his own department (his cheerfully enthusiastic, ever-optimistic monetary under secretary Fred Deming notably excepted). To be sure, he called it "contingency planning" to prepare for an impending dollar shortage. It was a brilliant negotiating tactic of his own designing, ideally calculated to defang hard money opposition in Europe. But I am quite sure he thought it a tactic.

As an aside, the call to "action" in the president's message had been opposed by Treasury senior staff and was thought much too adventurous by some Federal Reserve governors, and generally within the top reaches of the financial community. In a late evening conversation at his house—I had brought out the draft message for his final clearance—Douglas Dillon, slated to leave the Treasury within a few weeks, agreed to overrule his department. He had strenuously opposed moving forward a month or so earlier, when he called the recommendations in the report of the external Foreign Economic Policy Task Force "just more of the same old Tobin, Kaysen stuff." When I muttered something about Bob Roosa having been a member of the task force and gone along with the report, he said something like "you bamboozled him." As chairman of the president's and Fowler's external advisory committee, Dillon—he was a marvelous chairman—soon became an invaluable supporter. So did Roosa. (In a side conversation soon after Fowler's initiating Virginia Bar Association speech in July 1965, Henry Wallich, the Fed governor who had been until recently responsible for international matters, accused me of having recklessly plotted to engage the United States in a losing venture. "No way the Europeans will go along if we have not first eliminated the deficit.")

One other revealing point about Fowler. Aware that Okun and I were balance of payments doves, and that I might be whispering dangerous thoughts about sterling and gold into LBJ's ear, he nevertheless invited not just advice but our active involvement in what had traditionally been a jealously guarded Treasury preserve. Overriding his own people, he welcomed the president's instruction to set up what came to be known as the Deming Group and the comprehensive marching orders that came with it.[56] He included us in critical private meetings with other min-

56. "I should like you to organize a small high-level study group to develop and recommend to me—through you, and the other principals directly concerned—a comprehensive U.S. position and negotiating strategy designed to achieve substantial improvement in international monetary arrangements. The Study Group should consist of appropriate senior officials from the Treasury, the State Department, the Council of Economic Advisers, the Board of Governors of the Federal Reserve System, and the White House. I understand that you would have in mind that it would be chaired by

isters.[57] He made a point of my joining him on the European tour designed to get the SDR negotiations going,[58] at the Chequers mini-summit,[59] and the climactic August 1967 G-10 Ministers' meeting at Lancaster House at which we succeeded, after hours of wrangling, first to isolate the French and then to get unanimous agreement on the establishment of SDRs.[60] And he seemed to welcome my participation in his private meetings with the president on international matters.[61] He clearly liked having someone on the president's foreign policy staff who knew what he was up to, thereby perhaps making it more likely that the president's agenda, and those of State and Defense, would take into account his agenda.[62] But whatever his reasons, the point about Joe Fowler is that he cared not about his own or his department's prerogatives, but about doing what was good for the United States. In that cause, he welcomed help wherever he could get it.[63]

I would like to end by saying that Art Okun's companionship during those years in the international money business meant a lot to me. I loved working with him, learned a lot from him, and felt honored by his friendship.

COMMENT BY

Maurice Obstfeld

Dick Cooper offers a wide-ranging and masterful overview of U.S. international trade and monetary policy during and since the 1960s. As Cooper

---

the Under Secretary of the Treasury for Monetary Affairs. . . . The Study Group should be small and it should work in the strictest secrecy. . . . I should like to receive a progress report on the work of the Study Group by August 1, 1965, and. . . . I shall expect periodically to meet with you and the other officials concerned." For the full text of the instruction, including the "marching orders," see Duncan, Patterson, and Yee (1998, item 64). On the membership of the Deming Group, see note 13 above; note 3 in item 64 pertaining to membership is incorrect. The president was so proud of this memo that he reprinted it in full in his memoirs, *The Vantage Point* (1971, pp. 597–98). For the history, see Brittain (1975) and Odell (1982).

57. See Duncan, Patterson, and Yee (1998, item 129) for an account of a remarkable small working dinner at Fowler's house with West German Economic Minister Karl Schiller.

58. The president, who disapproved of junkets by his staff, refused to let me go except for a couple of days in London at the end.

59. See Duncan, Patterson, and Yee (1998, items 113, 115, and 116).

60. Duncan, Patterson, and Yee (1998, item 141).

61. See, for example, Duncan, Patterson, and Yee (1998, items 79, 90, 95, and 138).

62. See Miller (1999, item 211); Duncan, Patterson, and Yee (1998, item 120–attachment B, 128, 129, and 130); Sampson (1995, item 240).

63. Personal Postscript. My operational involvement ended on September 1, 1967. From then on, Edward Fried in collaboration with Walt Rostow did the President's work on Europe and on most for-

notes, the world economy was much smaller forty years ago than today, and trade-related activity a much smaller proportion of that period's global product. U.S. leadership helped set in train both an unprecedented era of growth and an ongoing trend of opening to international transactions. The paper suggests, but does not address, questions about the U.S. response to the current antiglobalization backlash. For example, is it likely that America's promotion of trade liberalization will proceed in the future as vigorously and successfully as it had through the completion of the Uruguay Round? The paper's focus, which is descriptive rather than ana-lytical, provides little basis for prediction.

The bulk of the paper is devoted to monetary questions. At center stage in the 1960s was the growing preoccupation of U.S. policymakers with balance of payments issues. The period was a critical one since the tensions that arose and intensified during the decade eventually led to the break-down of the Bretton Woods system of fixed exchange rates. Under that system, the world economy successfully recovered from the devastation of war and attained unprecedented prosperity on the basis of growing world trade. The reasons behind the system's demise, which are also covered in Barry Eichengreen's paper, are essential to understanding both the constraints on U.S. policy and the subsequent course of world monetary history.

The central problem of America's role in Bretton Woods was the sys-tem's failure to provide for dollar devaluation despite the certainty that as the war receded into history, significantly different productivity trends would govern the economic evolution of the United States and its trading partners. Figure 5-1 shows the 1955–75 development of key bilateral real exchange rates against the dollar (an upward movement is a real deprecia-tion of the dollar). Visible in the figure is a secular real U.S. depreciation. In the late 1960s the process slows down vis-à-vis Japan, reverses mildly vis-à-vis Germany, and temporarily reverses sharply vis-à-vis the United Kingdom as sterling is devalued (in 1967). As Eichengreen notes in his paper, trends such as those in figure 5-1 might not represent equilibrium trends if differential productivity growth called for sharper real dollar

eign economic matters. Edward Hamilton, one of my two invaluable junior colleagues, continued to cover Africa and foreign aid generally. The other, the young Lawrence Eagleburger, went back to the State Department as an assistant to Nicholas Katzenbach. (I went back for a few days to try to help out when the Wilson government decided to devalue, and once again during the gold crisis the following March. As a part-time consultant to Fowler and a member of the Dillon Committee, I tried to stay in touch. But for really knowing what was going on, that is not the same.)

Figure 5-1. *The Development of Key Bilateral Real Exchange Rates against the Dollar, 1955–75*[a]

Index (1955 = 100)

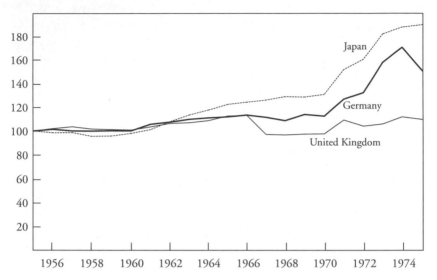

Source: International Monetary Fund, International Financial Statistics.
a. Real exchange rates are based on relative CPIs.

depreciation than actually occurred. The result of such disequilibrium would have been deflationary pressure in the United States and inflationary pressure abroad—pressures that would have made currency realignment an attractive response. In fact, the Balassa-Samuelson effect hinges not on overall productivity growth gaps but on relative differential productivity growth in tradables as compared with nontradables. As I document in a 1993 study, America's major trading partners had much higher productivity growth in tradables compared to nontradables than did the United States.[64] Japan accepted significantly higher inflation than did the United States and avoided revaluing the yen until the 1970s. Germany and some other countries, in contrast, struggled against higher equilibrium inflation through the consistent sterilization of external payments surpluses and, eventually, capital inflow controls.

The difficulty of devaluing the dollar in the face of inconsistent desires by the United States to avoid deflation and by many of its trading partners

64. Obstfeld (1993).

to avoid inflation was bound to lead to a crisis. Here, the relatively slow pace of overall U.S. growth was important. It made the "natural" adjustment process more lengthy and painful than otherwise. Speculative anticipations of dollar devaluation, which erupted with full force after the 1960s closed, led to portfolio shifts into foreign-currency assets and—given the dollar's reserve currency status—upward pressure on foreign money supplies. The underlying tension over the dollar's exchange rate fueled imported inflation abroad even in the absence of sharply higher U.S. money growth.

The other striking trend over the 1960s was the more or less relentless fall in U.S. gold reserves (see figure 5-2). Was this a major problem? In my view, despite its very real impacts on policymakers' perceptions and on policy, it was something of a sideshow, a symptom of more consequential woes. The $35 per ounce gold price at the center of the Bretton Woods system certainly was not helpful, but it was not what brought the system down either. It was a historical accident. It led to the Triffin problem because the United States was unwilling to subjugate its monetary policy to a gold standard.

It was inevitable that European countries would accumulate progressively higher levels of dollar reserves as the world economy grew in the 1950s and 1960s. Increases in money demand outside the United States, other things equal, led to higher official claims on the United States, claims that were supposedly as good as gold. A growing stock of official dollar claims on America was thus a natural feature of the system, one that need not have been incompatible with a fixed dollar price of gold had the United States, counterfactually, been willing to devote monetary policy to that end. Finally, in 1968, the major industrial countries simply created the two-tier gold market, thereby abandoning the Bretton Woods system's nominal anchor. The conflict between the United States' domestic monetary goals and its commitment to the international system was resolved by a sharp immediate increase in the private market price of gold, while the fictitious official price remained at $35 per ounce.

The selection of gold's price as a nominal anchor had adverse repercussions beyond the Triffin dilemma, however. In the end, the market gold price was cut free in 1968 quietly and without political outcry because the public had no attachment to gold and little idea of the link between the gold standard and price stability. By and large, electorates of the 1960s viewed gold as an esoteric feature of high finance, with little direct relevance to their daily lives. When the gold peg was abandoned, they collec-

Figure 5-2. *U.S. Gold Reserves, 1948–98*[a]

Billions of dollars

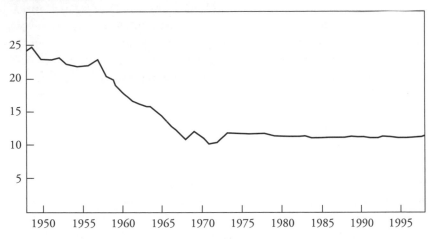

Source: International Monetary Fund, *International Financial Statistics*, 1948–96.
a. Gold figures are at national valuation.

tively shrugged their shoulders. They had little appreciation that countries had taken the first step into what would eventually be a quite inflationary period.

In Britain the gold standard was still anathema in the mid-1940s, and John Maynard Keynes was forced to defend the Bretton Woods plan in the House of Lords. His defense was that exchange rates would be adjusted to accommodate national price levels, rather than vice versa, so that for countries in Britain's position no gold standard constraint would bind. The one country for which this defense could not be invoked was the United States; thus it was predictable that the dollar devaluation problem should eventually become a central one for the stability of the international monetary order. It is hard to see, however, how the Bretton Woods system's design could have avoided a gold anchor once the Keynes plan for an international clearing union gave way to the U.S. plan for what eventually became the International Monetary Fund. At that point, some sort of gold standard probably was inevitable.

As a practical matter, the dollar had to commence its life at the center of the Bretton Woods system linked to *something* in the real economy. In the 1940s, it would have been politically infeasible to introduce a system modeled on the de facto arrangements from 1968 on, in which countries pegged their currencies to the dollar while the United States was constrained only by a vague presumption that it would conduct monetary policy in the interest of international economic stability. Remember that as of 1944, there was no real experience of durable price stability under a fiat monetary standard. There had been periods of unbacked paper currency, often culminating in high inflation or hyperinflation. There had been the gold standard, associated with price level stationarity, if not stability. But the modern notion of defining price stability explicitly in terms of an inflation target is, indirectly, a product of the 1960s and of the decade of inflation that followed. We have now learned that a country can maintain 2 percent inflation per year over the medium term under a fiat standard, provided the political will is present. This is a new development in world monetary history.

In the mid-1940s, the gold standard was still viewed in influential quarters as a safeguard against hyperinflation. That concern won the day, so the Bretton Woods system was saddled with an internal contradiction: the United States ultimately would have to decide between the nominal anchor and deflation. It should have been clear at the outset, Triffin dilemma or no, how the conflict would be decided.

Europeans were increasingly disconcerted by the evolution of the world monetary system during the 1960s. The recently realized European monetary unification initiative can be traced to that epoch. Under Bretton Woods, all currencies were pegged to the dollar with a narrow fluctuation margin, and the margins for European cross rates therefore were twice as broad. Both the European Economic Community's Common Agricultural Policy and the desire for further economic integration within Europe made movements in European cross exchange rates problematic. From this problem the 1970 Werner Plan for European monetary integration was born. Interestingly, some Europeans believed that a single European currency, by economizing on the need for intra-EEC international liquidity, would help alleviate the perceived world liquidity problems of the 1960s. A perceptive statement by Giscard d'Estaing, reproduced in the book by Francesco Giavazzi and Alberto Giovannini, suggests that when Europeans spoke of gold some were really speaking metaphorically of a single European currency, which might reduce the need for large official dollar holdings.[65] Giscard's ideas probably were atypical—as Cooper points out, his views got him fired as France's finance minister—and I suspect that in truth, when the French spoke of gold, they meant gold.

65. Giavazzi and Giovannini (1989, p. 21).

It would have been interesting to see more discussion in this paper of how events in the 1960s influenced the subsequent explosion in international financial transactions. One of the great ironies of the Bretton Woods system and complementary initiatives is that their very success in promoting world trade helped to create the capital account instability that ultimately ended fixed exchange rates in the early 1970s. The Bretton Woods era made clear that one cannot have growing world trade without growing opportunities to move funds across national borders in disguised forms. Growing world trade required more extensive credit facilities and enhanced the possibility of leads and lags in trade-related payments. In this setting, the maintenance of adjustably pegged exchange rates became untenable. These developments, combined with the macroeconomic and foreign policy difficulties the United States was experiencing by the late 1960s, created an explosive mixture that finally blew apart in 1973.

In a throwaway line early in his paper, Cooper remarks that the four decades from 1960 to 1998 were characterized by historically high levels of both output growth and peacetime inflation, as measured by the Consumer Price Index. He raises the question of the causal relationship, if any, between these two developments. It would have been interesting indeed to plumb that relationship, which is multifaceted and involves social and political developments as well as purely economic ones. Unfortunately, the topic is not covered in the present volume. One basic and provocative fact is that on a year to year basis, real output growth and CPI growth are negatively, not positively, correlated since the late 1940s. Certainly, the Bretton Woods experience showed how some form of precommitment in monetary policy might be consistent with relatively low inflation and rapid real growth. For the United States and several other countries, the decade of the 1990s furnishes another example. That empirical record certainly throws doubt on the simplest Phillips-curve accounts of the unemployment-inflation link, which rightly did not survive long after the 1960s.

References

Aho, C. Michael, and Jonathan David Aronson. 1985. *Trade Talks: America Better Listen!* New York: Council on Foreign Relations.

Ball, George W. 1982. *The Past Has Another Pattern: Memoirs.* W. W. Norton.

Bator, Francis M. 1968a. "International Liquidity: An Unofficial View of the U.S. Case." *The American Economic Review,* vol. 58 (May): 620–24.

————. 1968b. "The Political Economics of International Money," *Foreign Affairs*, vol. 47 (October): 51–67.

————. 1968c. "The Politics of Alliance: The United States and Western Europe." In *Agenda for the Nation*, edited by Kermit Gordon, 335–72. Brookings.

Bordo, Michael D., and Barry Eichengreen, eds. 1993. *A Retrospective on the Bretton Woods System: Lessons for International Monetary Reform*. University of Chicago Press.

Brittain, W. H. Bruce. 1975. "Two International Monetary Decisions." In *Commission on the Organization of the Government for the Conduct of Foreign Policy*, vol. 3 (June), 127–38. Government Printing Office.

Cline, William R. 1990. *The Future of World Trade in Textiles and Apparel*, revised ed. Washington: Institute for International Economics.

Cooper, Richard N. 1965. "The Interest Equalization Tax: An Experiment in Separation of Capital Markets." *Finanz Archiv* 24(August).

————. 1968a. *The Economics of Interdependence: Economic Policy in the Atlantic Community*. McGraw-Hill.

____. 1968b. "The Dollar and the World Economy." In *Agenda for the Nation*, edited by Kermit Gordon, 475–508. Brookings.

————. 1982. "The Gold Standard: Historical Facts and Future Prospects." *Brookings Papers on Economic Activity* 1:1982, 1–45

Duncan, Evan, David S. Patterson, and Carolyn Yee, eds. 1998. *Foreign Relations of the United States, 1964–68*, vol. VIII, *International Monetary and Trade Policy*. Government Printing Office.

Eckes, Alfred E. 1992. "Trading American Interests." *Foreign Affairs* 71(Fall): 135–54.

Eichengreen, Barry. 1992. *Golden Fetters: The Gold Standard and the Great Depression, 1919–1939*. New York: Oxford University Press.

Eichengreen, Barry, and others. 1998. "Capital Account Liberalization: Theoretical and Practical Aspects." Occasional Paper 172. International Monetary Fund.

Federal Reserve Bank of Boston. 1969. *The International Adjustment Mechanism*.

Giavazzi, Francesco, and Alberto Giovannini. 1989. *Limiting Exchange Rate Flexibility: The European Monetary System*. MIT Press.

Gordon, Kermit, ed. 1968. *Agenda for the Nation: Papers on Domestic and Foreign Policy Issues*. Brookings.

Halm, George N., ed. 1970. *Approaches to Greater Flexibility of Exchange Rates*. Princeton University Press.

Hewson, John, and Eisuke Sakakibara. 1975. "The Impact of U.S. Controls on Capital Outflows on the U.S. Balance of Payments: An Exploratory Study." *IMF Staff Papers* 22(1): 37–60 (March).

International Monetary Fund. 1999. *World Economic Outlook*. Washington: International Monetary Fund (September).

Johnson, Lyndon Baines. 1971. *The Vantage Point: Perspectives of the Presidency, 1963–1969*. Holt, Rinehart, and Winston.

Maddison, Angus. 1995. *Monitoring the World Economy, 1820–1992*. Paris: Organization for Economic Cooperation and Development.

Mann, Catherine L. 1999. *Is the U.S. Trade Deficit Sustainable?* Washington: Institute for International Economics.

Miller, James E., ed. 1999. *Foreign Relations of the United States, 1964–68, vol. XV, Germany and Berlin*. Government Printing Office.

National Archives and Records Service. 1966. *Public Papers of the Presidents of the United States: Lyndon B. Johnson 1965, Book 1*. Government Printing Office.

Obstfeld, Maurice. 1993. "The Adjustment Mechanism." In *A Retrospective on the Bretton Woods System*, edited by Michael D. Bordo and Barry Eichengreen, 201–68. University of Chicago Press.

Odell, John S. 1982. *U.S. International Monetary Policy: Markets, Power, and Ideas as Sources of Change*. Princeton University Press.

Preeg, Ernest H. 1970. *Traders and Diplomats: An Analysis of the Kennedy Round of Negotiations under the General Agreement on Tariffs and Trade*. Brookings.

Ratner, Sidney. 1972. *The Tariff in American History*. New York: Van Nostrand.

Sampson, Charles S., ed. 1995. *Foreign Relations of the United States, 1964–68, vol. XIII, Western European Region*. Government Printing Office.

Schlesinger, Arthur M., Jr. 1965. *A Thousand Days: John F. Kennedy in the White House*. Boston: Houghton Mifflin.

Schott, Jeffrey J. 1994. *The Uruguay Round: An Assessment*. Washington: Institute for International Economics.

Solomon, Robert. 1982. *The International Monetary System, 1945–1981*. Harper and Row.

Sorenson, Theodore. 1965. *Kennedy*. Harper and Row.

Triffin, Robert. 1960. *Gold and the Dollar Crisis: The Future of Convertibility*. Yale University Press.

Williamson, John. 1965. "The Crawling Peg." Reprinted in *The International Monetary System: Highlights from Fifty Years of Princeton's Essays in International Finance*, edited by Peter B. Kenen, 49–69. 1993. Boulder, Colo.: Westview Press.

BARRY EICHENGREEN

6

From Benign Neglect to Malignant Preoccupation: U.S. Balance of Payments Policy in the 1960s

The title of this paper, taken from an April 1971 *Newsweek* column by Paul Samuelson, summarizes the conventional wisdom regarding U.S. balance of payments policy in the 1960s.[1] Over the course of the decade the U.S. international financial position moved from strength to weakness; the balance of payments, which had previously been treated with neglect, became a growing concern. The 1960s was the first peacetime period for more than a quarter of a century when the external constraint mattered for the United States. The country emerged from World War II in a position of unrivaled strength, and the 1950s had presented no balance of payments challenges; U.S. monetary gold reserves at the beginning of 1958 were even larger than ten years before.[2] In contrast, the net liquidity balance, the most widely cited contemporary measure of the external position, was in deficit throughout the 1960s, while the more conventional official settlements balance was in deficit every year except 1966 (when it was essentially zero) and 1968–69. (Figure 6-1 displays both the net liquidity and official settlements balances, together with a third contemporary concept of the external position, the basic balance, or the sum of current account and private long-term

For research assistance, I am grateful to Julian De Giovanni, Amy Huang, Intaek Han, and Chris Nekarda. Maury Obstfeld generously helped with data. George Perry, Robert Lawrence, and Jeffrey Sachs provided helpful comments.
1. Paul A. Samuelson, "The Shaky Dollar," *Newsweek*, April 19, 1971, p. 106.
2. As Raymond Mikesell (1970, p. 6) put it, "Neither the U.S. government nor the informed public expressed concern about the U.S. balance of payments before 1959."

185

Figure 6-1. *Three Measures of the U.S. Balance of Payments, 1958–70*

Billions of U.S. dollars

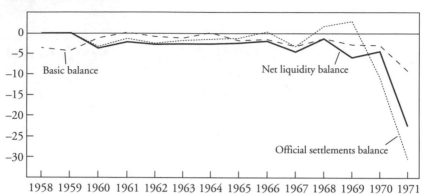

Source: Bureau of Economic Analysis, *Survey of Current Business* (various issues).

capital flows.)[3] U.S. gold stocks, which had once seemed all but unlimited, had fallen to dangerously low levels by the end of the 1960s. The dollar shortage had become a dollar glut, rendering the currency overvalued.

Given the commitment to peg the dollar to gold at $35 an ounce, these balance of payments developments were regarded with growing concern as the decade progressed. It became impractical to treat the external position with neglect—benign or otherwise. But neither was there a readiness to subordinate other economic and political goals to the maintenance of external balance. Other objectives—the New Society and the Vietnam War, but above all the pursuit of demand-driven growth—took precedence. The Kennedy, Johnson, and Nixon administrations resorted to a series of indirect policy initiatives—differential tax treatment of domestic and foreign investments, reductions in the value of the goods American tourists could bring into the country, tied foreign aid, and finally an across-the-board import surcharge—in an effort to remedy the balance of payments problem and free up monetary and fiscal policies for the pursuit of domestic objectives.[4]

3. The net liquidity balance excluded both private short-term capital flows and U.S. government foreign borrowing from the credit side of the balance of payments ledgers, the rationale being that such flows could reverse direction quickly. The official settlements balance, adopted in the mid-1960s, was a comprehensive measure that defined the overall balance as the change in U.S. foreign exchange reserves minus the increase in official foreign claims on the United States.

4. As the Council of Economic Advisers put it (referring to the voluntary foreign direct investment program of 1965), "Compared with reliance solely on restrictive general monetary measures that might

These expedients, however, failed to address the fundamental conflict between internal and external objectives—in particular, between "external pressures for higher [interest] rates and the needs of the domestic economy for monetary expansion," as the point was put in the report of the President's Task Force on Foreign Economic Policy in 1964.[5] And insofar as financial capital became more mobile over the course of the 1960s, these jury-rigged policies to limit U.S. capital outflows were neutralized and overwhelmed. Thus the microeconomic and structural expedients to which successive administrations resorted in an effort to reconcile the monetary and fiscal policies desired for domestic purposes with the external constraint were rendered ineffectual. And in the absence of a reconciliation to the policy conflict, it became inevitable that the dollar would come crashing down.

This now traditional interpretation has informed a number of influential accounts of U.S. balance of payments policy in the 1960s.[6] Yet there are also aspects of the period that do not fit so neatly into this tidy historical framework. For one, it is not obvious that the balance of payments problem in fact grew progressively worse as the period progressed. The first crisis of the dollar occurred at the beginning of the decade, in 1960. Could the policy conflicts of the Johnson and Nixon administrations have been at the root of the problem, given that payments pressures manifested themselves before either president took office? As figure 6-2 makes clear, references to terms like "gold outflows," "trade deficits," and "balance of payments" in the "Record of Policy Actions" of the Federal Open Market

---

conceivably hold down capital flows to the same extent, [these measures] have the obvious advantage of allowing monetary policy to respond to the needs for domestic credit, as well as to affect that 5–10 percent of total credit that flows abroad." Council of Economic Advisers (1966, p. 168). In addition, this was the period (starting in March 1961) when first the Treasury Department and then the Federal Reserve began to engage in sterilized intervention in the foreign exchange market, in what can be understood as an effort to influence the direction of gold and capital flows without having to alter the stance of monetary policy.

5. Reprinted in Duncan, Patterson, and Yee (1998, p. 39). The point carries over to attempts to alter the macroeconomic policy mix to better reconcile internal and external objectives. Stimulating domestic investment meant adopting a mix of loose monetary and tight fiscal measures, according to the prevailing policy orthodoxy of the 1960s, while strengthening the external accounts meant adopting precisely the opposite mix. Thus the Bank for International Settlements in its annual report for 1962 urged the United States to tighten monetary policy while loosening fiscal policy (and repeated the recommendation annually). Hence efforts to adjust the policy mix did not finesse the fundamental conflict between internal and external balance. The same can be said of Operation Twist, the effort to limit the rise in long-term interest rates while at the same time tightening monetary policy to address balance of payments concerns (as I explain below).

6. See, for example, Willett (1980); Gowa (1983).

Figure 6-2. *References to Balance of Payments Considerations in the Federal Reserve's Statement of Policy Actions, 1959–71*

Number of citations

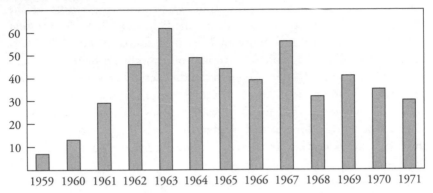

Source: Board of Governors of the Federal Reserve System (various years), "Records of Policy Actions." For details, see text.

Committee (FOMC) peak in 1963 and 1967, not at the end of the decade.[7] And the characterization of U.S. policy toward the balance of payments as benign neglect is difficult to reconcile with increases in Federal Reserve discount rates in 1963, 1965, and 1967, all taken in response, at least in part, to concern over external balance.

Second, there are some uncomfortable facts about U.S. economic performance. For one thing, the payments position strengthened at the end of the 1960s, rather than deteriorating as the crisis approached. For another, U.S. inflation did not exceed foreign inflation; in fact the opposite was true. Nor did the rate of growth of the monetary base accelerate significantly as the crisis approached. It shot up only in 1972—that is, after the dollar had been devalued.[8]

Third, and related to the above, there are reasons to question that U.S. policy was responsible for the country's payments problems in the sense that even significantly different policies would have produced significantly different outcomes. In particular, there is Robert Triffin's argument that the

7. See Board of Governors of the Federal Reserve System (various years). Figure 6-2 is a count of references in this Fed publication to "gold outflow(s)" and "outflow(s) of gold," "gold loss(es)" and "loss(es) of gold," "balance of payment," and "balance of payments" and "trade deficit." (Whenever "trade" and "deficit" appeared within ten words of one another, they were counted as a reference.)

8. A point emphasized by Richard Cooper in Bordo and Eichengreen (1993, pp. 104–07).

country's external deficit reflected not excessively expansionary domestic policies but rather the appetite of an expanding world economy for dollar reserves, an appetite that could be satisfied only if other countries ran surpluses vis-à-vis the United States.[9] The 1960s was a decade of rapid expansion in Europe and Japan, the regions on which contemporary discussions of the U.S. balance of payments focused. These countries needed additional international liquidity to buffer their economies from trade-related shocks, and given capital controls and tight domestic financial regulations outside the United States, accumulating reserves meant accumulating dollars. Foreign claims on the United States exceeded U.S. monetary gold reserves as early as 1960, and that excess widened as the period progressed (see figure 6-3). The United States was acting as banker to the world, importing short-term capital while investing long term abroad, providing a function necessary for the operation of the Bretton Woods system.[10] But while essential to the functioning of the Bretton Woods system, this behavior was also a source of financial fragility, since foreign holders of dollars could "run on" U.S. gold reserves at any time. In this view, the fundamental conflict was not between the domestic and foreign economic policies of the United States but between the liquidity needs of an expanding world economy and the unresponsiveness of global gold supplies. The problem was less that the dollar was fundamentally overvalued relative to the yen and the European currencies; it was more that the dollar was increasingly overvalued relative to gold, reflecting the inelasticity of monetary gold supplies and the growing overhang of foreign dollar balances.

In the remainder of this paper I will argue that these observations can in fact be reconciled with the traditional interpretation. I will emphasize that the 1960s was a decade of secularly declining U.S. international competitiveness. These were the years when European and Japanese producers, having moved up the product ladder and improved their marketing and quality-control techniques, first emerged as serious competitors for U.S. basic industries.[11] These trends are evident in the steady deterioration of

9. Triffin (1947).

10. Emile Despres, Charles P. Kindleberger, and Walter Salant, "The Dollar and World Liquidity: A Minority View," *Economist*, February 5, 1966, pp. 526–27.

11. This is when they first became a serious competitive presence in markets like those for U.S. motor vehicles and steel. In the case of steel, these pressures culminated in the 1968 voluntary steel quotas, under which foreign producers agreed to limit their shipments to the U.S. market. In the case of autos, there was, working in the other direction, the 1965 U.S. auto pact with Canada, under whose provisions U.S. companies could shift component production and assembly north of the border, again reflecting the realities of cost competition.

Figure 6-3. *International Liquidity Position of the United States, 1955–71*

Billions of U.S. dollars

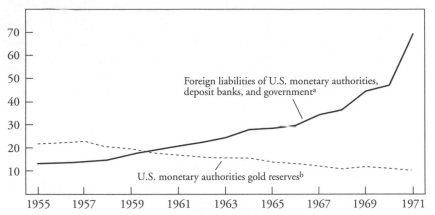

Source: International Monetary Fund, *International Financial Statistics* (various years).

a. Country Table, United States—Monetary authorities, foreign liabilities; Commercial Banks, foreign liabilities; Government Finance, debt held by foreign and international.

b. Country Table, United States—International Liquidity, gold (ounces).

the U.S. current account balance, from a surplus of $1 billion–$2 billion in the mid-1960s to a deficit of $1 billion–$2 billion in the early 1970s. A close look at inflation rates and unit labor costs is consistent with this view. This intensification of competitive pressures rendered the dollar increasingly overvalued. At the same time, the framers of U.S. monetary and fiscal policies remained reluctant to counter the trend. The problem in 1970–71 was not so much that monetary and fiscal control was lost; it was that monetary and fiscal policies remained on hold. As the modern literature on balance of payments crises shows, it is not necessary to point to a sudden increase in the rate of growth of the monetary base to explain the timing of a speculative attack. Even without it, a secular deterioration in competitiveness can precipitate a sudden crisis, leading to large capital outflows like those observed in 1970–71.

That this trend was not universally appreciated reflected the fact that the external accounts strengthened in 1965–66 and 1968–69, suggesting to some that the country had successfully adjusted to the more competitive international economic environment. However, these improvements were temporary. They were engineered by exceptional macroeconomic policy responses that were sustainable neither economically nor politically and by microeconomic and structural expedients whose effectiveness was at best transitory. Once their effects wore off, the external crisis returned, and with a vengeance.

Thus the key factor setting the stage for the 1971 run on the dollar was real overvaluation created by monetary and fiscal policies that were fundamentally inconsistent with the external constraint.[12] To be sure, the inelasticity of world gold supplies and the dependence of the world economy for meeting its growing liquidity needs on foreign dollar holdings also played a role. The accumulation by foreign central banks and markets of short-term dollar claims rendered the United States vulnerable to a loss of confidence on the part of its foreign creditors. A shared interest in the stability of the international system prevented foreign central banks from rushing to convert their dollar balances into gold. This shared interest in regime-maintenance, buttressed by veiled U.S. threats of retaliation against governments that converted their dollars into gold, allowed the system to stagger on for longer than it would have otherwise, as foreign authorities absorbed ever larger dollar balances in an ultimately futile effort to prevent Bretton Woods from falling apart. While the Bretton Woods system was flawed in ways that required international cooperation for it to survive even for the short twelve years from the restoration of convertibility at the end of December 1958 to the denouement in 1971, the fact is that awareness of those flaws led it to be sustained, in the face of the U.S. government's unwillingness to adjust, for even longer than would have been the case otherwise.

But it could not survive indefinitely. The overvaluation of the dollar against foreign currencies raised the costs of regime-maintenance to America's European and Japanese allies. And private investors could force the issue: no shared interest in regime-maintenance deterred them (or, for that matter, U.S. residents) from selling dollars as the currency became increasingly overvalued, requiring the authorities to buy all the dollars they sold. The two-tier gold market created in 1968 prevented the private sector from converting their dollars into U.S. gold, but there was still nothing to prevent them from swapping their dollars for other currencies. While private investors had every reason to hold liquid dollar claims so long as they believed that others were inclined to do likewise—indeed, to increase their holdings as the world economy grew—they also had an incentive to

12. In terms of the theoretical literature, the kind of model Krugman (1979) used for balance of payments crises, in which the run on reserves results from the pursuit of macroeconomic policy incompatible with the exchange-rate commitment, would appear to explain much of what needs explanation.

scramble out of dollars if they thought others were preparing to do likewise and that the currency would be devalued.

The last seven words are critical: the denouement could have been averted by a sharp rise in U.S. interest rates or massive unsterilized intervention by foreign central banks. But the fact that the U.S. payments position had deteriorated, while U.S. unemployment and European inflation had risen, meant that these responses were unattractive. Given the weakness of the position, effective support would have required a drastic course correction by the Federal Reserve, or ongoing intervention by foreign central banks. But U.S. officials could not credibly attach priority to external stability relative to internal balance. Stability therefore hinged on the continued provision of support by foreign central banks and governments. And the latter were unwilling to indefinitely accept the inflationary consequences of supporting the dollar, collective interest in the maintenance of the Bretton Woods regime or not. Once they signaled their reluctance, the run was on. Closing the gold window became unavoidable.[13]

The Problem and Its Setting

In this section I set the stage for the analysis to follow by reviewing the U.S. balance of payments problem and its setting.

The Setting

The setting for this problem was the international monetary arrangement agreed to by delegates from forty-four countries in Bretton Woods, New Hampshire, in 1944. The Bretton Woods system was a peculiar hybrid of pegged exchange rates and adjustable exchange rates, of gold-based and fiat money regimes. It can be understood as a compromise between the competing objectives of the United States and the United Kingdom, given concrete form in the plans drawn up by Harry Dexter White and John Maynard Keynes.

13. As these veiled and overt references to the notions of multiple equilibria and coordination games imply, a full explanation for the dollar crisis thus also requires referring to the sort of second-generation model of speculative attacks analyzed by Eichengreen and Jeanne (1998). One of the principals, Francis Bator (1968, pp. 58–59), appears to have anticipated the key point when he wrote, "In part because $35 was a credible floor, it became an increasingly non-credible ceiling, and in this sort of situation non-credibility tends to be self-confirming."

That compromise had a number of key features for the problem at hand. First, it was a compromise between Keynes' proposal for an International Clearing Union with the power to create and issue international reserves as a way of meeting the liquidity needs of the expanding world economy, and White's vision of a world in which every country would float on its own bottom (and the financial obligations of the United States would be minimized). Resources could be transferred from surplus to deficit countries through the International Monetary Fund (IMF) only to a limited extent. Critically, the IMF would not have the power, and did not acquire the power until very late in the Bretton Woods period, to create international reserves.[14] This meant that the only way for countries needing additional international reserves to smooth fluctuations in their trade and payments was by accumulating foreign exchange.

Second, the Bretton Woods Agreement split the difference between the U.S. desire for currency convertibility, which would advance the country's dual objectives of nondiscrimination and expanding international trade, and the British desire for insulation from international financial pressures, which could inhibit the use of macroeconomic policy to counter unemployment. The compromise, of course, was the provisions in the IMF Articles of Agreement mandating the restoration of currency convertibility on current account but authorizing (and, tacitly, encouraging) countries to retain controls on capital-account transactions. As a result, all the major economies except the United States retained controls on capital flows for extended periods—in more than a few cases, into the 1990s. This meant that currencies other than the dollar were slow to acquire an international role. And in turn this left central banks seeking to acquire foreign exchange reserves few alternatives to acquiring dollars.

Third, Bretton Woods was a compromise between the British desire for monetary freedom of action, a priority which led British officials to regard the gold standard as anathema, and the U.S. desire for a system rooted in traditional values and capable of inspiring investor confidence. Both in the 1920s and in wartime, fiat money had meant inflation, which had been demoralizing to investors; gold was still the obvious confidence-inspiring alternative. Hence the famous Bretton Woods compromise in which the dollar was pegged to gold, as under a traditional gold standard, but other currencies were pegged to the dollar. Changes in currency pegs were per-

14. This situation changed in 1969 with the issue of Special Drawing Rights, but this was too late and much too little to shape the financial dynamics discussed below.

missible in the event of "fundamental disequilibria," whatever that meant, but the asymmetry in the way the dollar and other currencies were pegged created uncertainty about whether the United States could change the dollar exchange rate. While other countries could devalue against the dollar, the United States could only raise the dollar price of gold. And if concerns for their competitiveness, lobbying by export interests, or other considerations rendered other countries reluctant to see their currencies appreciate, they could prevent this from happening by doing nothing—in other words, simply by maintaining their par values expressed in terms of the dollar. There was a question, in other words, of whether the United States could use the exchange rate to address its balance of payments.

This was the background against which the U.S. postwar payments position developed. The U.S. balance of payments in the 1960s has a peculiar cast to an observer schooled in the currency crises of the 1990s. There was no trade deficit, no current account deficit, and no large capital inflow to fuel a domestic credit boom, reverse suddenly, and precipitate a crisis. The payments problems of the 1960s were of a different sort. The U.S. trade balance had been in surplus continuously since World War II.[15] The merchandise trade surplus peaked at $10 billion in 1947, reflecting the exceptional import needs and limited export capacity of Europe's war-torn economies and the fact that the United States was the principal source of supply for traded goods. The European economies were being run under high pressure of demand, and U.S. foreign aid, under the provisions of the Marshall Plan and successor programs, financed other countries' deficits. European growth accelerated further once postwar reconstruction was complete.

The Statistics

Reflecting strong demand abroad, the U.S. trade balance strengthened further at the beginning of the 1960s and remained in strong surplus through the first half of the decade. In the second half of the decade, however, the situation began to shift. The merchandise trade balance fell toward zero in 1968 and remained at low levels in 1969 and 1970 (see figure 6-4).[16] The dominant interpretation was that this reflected "soaring [domestic] demand, approximately full employment, and rising prices in the United States."[17]

15. Indeed, U.S. merchandise trade had been in surplus in every year since 1936.
16. Note that figure 6-4 shows goods and services, not just merchandise.
17. Federal Reserve Bank of Philadelphia (1970, p. 9).

Figure 6-4. *Merchandise Balance of the United States, 1960–71*[a]

Billions of U.S. dollars

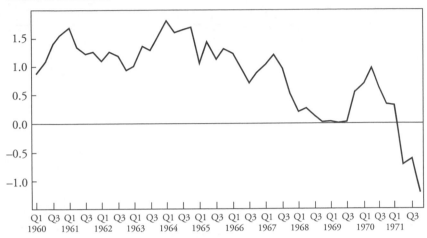

Source: Datastream National Government Series.
a. U.S. Merchandise Balance is series "USVSMERCB" of Datastream.

U.S. trade in services was also in surplus in this period, the main credit item being net interest earnings on foreign investments, which rose from $3 billion in 1960 to $6 billion in 1970. But the swing in the current account was limited by growing imports of transportation and travel services and rising military expenditures abroad (see figure 6-5).

Superimposed on this was the steady outflow of U.S. long-term investment, which made the absence of a substantial current account surplus problematic. In the immediate postwar period, international financial transactions had been dominated by foreign aid, after which U.S. capital exports fell to low levels. The restoration of current account convertibility in Europe and the relaxation of statutory restrictions on international capital flows then stimulated increases in U.S. foreign lending. Public and private outflows both rose (as shown in figure 6-6), the former reflecting U.S. military and economic aid to developing countries, the latter attracted by a growing range of attractive investment opportunities. Thus the maintenance of external balance required continued short-term capital inflows into the United States—equivalently, the continued accumulation by foreign central banks and residents of short-term liquid claims on the United States.

Figure 6-5. *U.S. Direct Military Expenditures Abroad and Imports of Travel and Transportation Services, 1959–70*

Billions of U.S. dollars

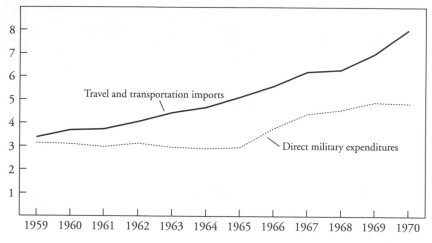

Source: U.S. Bureau of the Census (1975).

The capital account deficit peaked in 1963–64, not at the end of the 1960s when pressure on the dollar mounted. The improvement following the difficulties of 1963–64 was driven by the decline in private capital outflows after 1964 and a rise in inflows after 1965. The authors of one widely circulated study of balance of payments trends conjectured that this indicated a structural shift in the capital account, as the obvious opportunities for foreign direct investment by U.S. corporations were exhausted and investors overseas began to access this country's relatively advanced and efficient securities markets.[18] This, however, was not to be.

The Policies

The fact that both the trade and current accounts remained in surplus all through the 1960s (with the exception of two quarters in 1968 and 1969) and that the current account strengthened rather than weakened in 1969 is invoked by those who deny the existence of a competitiveness problem. In fact the current account had trending downward, quarter by quarter

18. Federal Reserve Bank of Philadelphia (1970).

Figure 6-6. *U.S. Capital Flows, 1945–70*

Billions of U.S. dollars

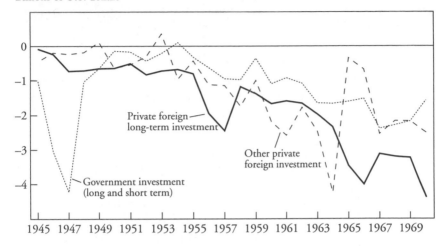

Source: U.S. Bureau of the Census (1975), table U1–25, p. 866.

almost without interruption, from its peak in 1964 through 1968. Extrapolating its trend from mid-1964 to mid-1968 leads to a deficit of $1 billion–$2 billion in 1972, which is the level that in fact obtained.[19] That there was confusion about this projection in the late 1960s and early 1970s is hardly surprising. In 1969 U.S. import demands were compressed by the onset of recession. And in 1971 they were stimulated as importers scrambled to beat the price increases that would result from devaluation. The actual current account oscillated increasingly wildly around its underlying trend.

Monetary and fiscal policies can largely explain these exceptional movements in the current and capital accounts. The continued deterioration in the external accounts through 1967 reflected the pressure of demand as the budget deficit widened in the face of the Vietnam War, monetary policy was reigned in only modestly, and the labor market tightened. Their subsequent improvement mirrored the policy's turn in a more contractionary direction, which in turn reflected fears that the economy was overheating. Fiscal policy was tightened in 1968, as the income tax surcharge intended

19. Meltzer (1991) shows that the underlying trend remained unchanged—that the 1972 deficit lay on an extension of the straight line drawn through the 1964–70 balances. This is readily apparent in figure 6-4.

to finance the country's growing social and military expenditures came into effect, and a cap was placed on government spending.[20] Federal spending stopped rising by the end of 1968 and fell in real terms by 7 percent from the last quarter of 1968 to the last quarter of 1969.[21] The constant employment budget balance shifted from a deficit of $11 billion in 1967 to a surplus of $12 billion in 1969. Monetary policy was tightened in response to mounting inflationary pressures. The Fed Funds rate was ratcheted up from less than 4 percent in mid-1967 to 6 percent in mid-1968 and 9 percent in 1969.

Higher taxes and interest rates had the obvious effect of compressing U.S. import demands. In addition, higher interest rates encouraged U.S. banks, which had placed funds abroad in higher-yielding eurodollar deposits, to repatriate these balances (accounting for an inflow of nearly $2 billion in 1968) and foreign banks and investors to deposit their liquid balances in New York. Foreigners continued to pour money into U.S. financial markets, so long as bond yields remained high and the stock market held up. This last effect was particularly important; the net inflow of foreign capital nearly tripled between 1966–67 and 1968, which by itself accounted for the shift of the capital account from deep deficit to balance (see table 6-1). David Morawetz attributes these changes in U.S. merchandise and capital imports in large part to the country's tighter monetary policy.[22]

The result of these restrictive monetary and fiscal impulses, aside from their balance of payments consequences, was, predictably, a growth slowdown. The growth of constant-dollar GNP decelerated from 4.4 percent in 1968 to 2.6 percent in 1969 and turned negative in 1970 for the first time in more than a decade.[23] 1970 was not too soon, the Watergate tapes reveal, for President Nixon to be thinking about reelection.[24] The idea that tight

20. The tax surcharge became law in June 1968, retroactive to April 1 for individuals and January 21 for corporations. Government spending restraint was the quid pro quo demanded by congressional Republicans in return for agreeing to the Johnson administration's request for a tax increase.

21. Solomon (1982, p. 107).

22. Morawetz (1971). In the interest of balance, it should be admitted that this is not the entire story. In addition to the level of interest rates, the capital account was strengthened by capital flight from Europe, reflecting political unrest in France and the movement of Soviet troops into Czechoslovakia. In addition, there were a variety of exceptional U.S. measures to discourage capital outflows, to which I return below.

23. *Economic Report of the President, 1976*, p. 173.

24. As Donald Kettl (1986, p. 121) put it (citing a Nixon phone call to White House Chief of Staff John Ehrlichman in late 1969), "Nixon focused single-mindedly on economic growth high enough to bring unemployment down to the 1972 election, even if that meant higher inflation."

Table 6-1. *Balance on Capital Flows, 1946–68*[a]

Billions of U.S. dollars

	Net outflow U.S. capital		Net inflow	
Year	Government[b]	Private	foreign capital	Balance
1946	5.3	0.4	–1.0	–6.7
1947	6.2	1.0	–1.3	–8.5
1948	4.9	0.9	0.6	–5.2
1949	5.8	0.6	0.2	–6.1
1950	3.7	1.3	1.9	–3.1
1951	3.3	1.0	0.6	–3.7
1952	2.5	1.2	1.7	–2.0
1953	2.2	0.4	1.1	–1.5
1954	1.7	1.6	1.3	–2.0
1955	2.4	1.3	1.4	–2.3
1956	2.5	3.1	2.5	–3.1
1957	2.7	3.6	1.1	–5.2
1958	2.8	2.9	1.3	–4.4
1959	2.2	2.4	3.6	–1.0
1960	3.0	3.9	2.1	–4.7
1961	3.0	4.2	2.5	–4.7
1962	3.3	3.4	1.7	–5.0
1963	3.8	4.5	3.0	–5.3
1964	3.8	6.6	3.3	–7.1
1965	3.8	3.8	0.4	–7.2
1966	3.8	4.3	3.3	–4.8
1967	4.7	5.7	6.9	–3.5
1968	4.7	5.4	9.4	–0.4

Source: Author's calculations based on data from U.S. Bureau of the Census (1975), table U1-25, p. 866.

a. Includes short-term capital.

b. Includes certain special government transactions.

monetary and fiscal policies would be maintained in the face of a serious recession was as inconceivable on political grounds as it was undesirable on economic ones. The 10 percent tax surcharge was allowed to expire in the first half of 1970. The Nixon administration pressed Federal Reserve Board Chairman Arthur Burns, in both public and private, to get the Fed to adopt a more expansionary policy.[25] Monetary policy shifted in a more expansionary direction after February: short-term interest rates were allowed to fall in the first half of the year and were joined by long-term

25. Kettl (1986, pp. 124–25).

rates in the second. The fact that fiscal policies were turning in more stim-
ulative directions implied that commodity imports would recover along
with the rest of the economy. And lower U.S. interest rates implied that the
exceptional capital inflows of 1968–69 would not be sustained.
Predictably, these fell back in 1970, as U.S. banks returned the money they
had borrowed in the eurodollar market. And with this return to macroeconomic normalcy, equally predictably, the balance of payments problem
reemerged.

While the stance of fiscal policy is not in dispute, the stance of monetary policy is. The reference here is to the conclusion of a 1983 study edited
by Michael Darby and others that Fed policy was too expansionary to be
compatible with the exchange-rate constraint.[26] Richard Cooper and
Ronald McKinnon both dispute the facts.[27] Cooper observes that the growth
of the U.S. monetary base did not accelerate sharply in the years leading up
to 1971. McKinnon similarly suggests that the data on U.S. monetary aggregates do not display a big enough jump in the late 1960s to explain the
timing of the crisis. Other commentators have further observed that U.S.
inflation was persistently below foreign inflation, consistent with the skeptical view of the role of monetary policy.

There is reason to think that the role of monetary policy is not so easily
dismissed. For one thing, there was a noticeable increase in the rate of
growth of the base in the months leading up to the crisis (as shown in figure 6-7). In any case, it is not just the base that is relevant for balance of
payments outcomes, but also broader monetary aggregates. Those broader
aggregates may not be under direct control of the authorities, but their
evolution is still something to which they should respond. While the
strong cyclical fluctuation of the rate of M1 growth in figure 6-7 compli-
cates interpretation, the upward trend over the course of the decade is
unmistakable. One might argue that the accelerating rate of growth of the
money supply was justified by the accelerating growth of the economy, but
in fact the *excess* growth of the broader aggregates—defined by Michael
Bordo, in a 1993 study, as the rate of growth of M1 minus the rate of
growth of real GNP—rose sharply after 1969.[28] To be sure, the sharp
increase in excess money supply growth after 1969 reflected the recession
into which the U.S. economy plunged (most of the action in Bordo's

---

26. See Darby and others (1983).
27. See their discussion of the issue in Bordo and Eichengreen (1993, chapters 1 and 13).
28. Bordo (1993).

Figure 6-7. *U.S. M1 and Monetary Base Growth, 1960–71*

Percent

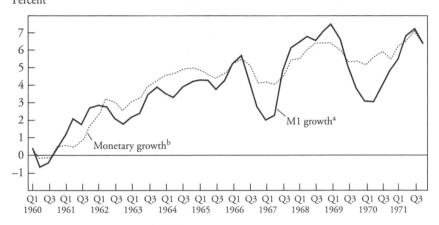

Source: Datastream National Government Series.
a. Four-quarter change. Calculated from series "USM1...B" of Datastream.
b. Four-quarter change. Calculated from series "USMONBASB" of Datastream.

measure of excess growth, in other words, reflects the fall in GNP rather than the rise in money supplies). However, the fact that the Fed directed monetary policy toward the imperatives of internal rather than external balance (allowing this measure of excess monetary growth to rise) created a conflict with the external constraint. And the owners of internationally mobile capital were surely more alarmed than they would have been otherwise because this behavior took place against the backdrop of a secular acceleration in the rate of excess M1 growth starting in 1966.

U.S. money supply growth must be considered in relation to that prevailing in the rest of the world. Hans Genberg and Alexander Swoboda, upon undertaking the relevant analysis using a two-region model of the world economy, reach exactly the same conclusion in a 1993 work.[29] They show how the demand for money in the United States fell significantly between 1967 and 1970 relative to money demand in the rest of the world, while money supplies in the United States (here, a broad measure reflecting both changes in the base and changes in the multiplier) rose sharply relative to those in the rest of the world. Again, it would appear that monetary policy was looser than necessary for the maintenance of external balance.

29. Genberg and Swoboda (1993).

Moreover, modern models of balance of payments crises do not suggest, contrary to the suggestions of Cooper and McKinnon, that an acceleration in the rate of growth of the monetary aggregates needs be observed prior to a sharp deterioration of the capital account. To the contrary, an unchanged monetary (and fiscal) policy can precipitate a run on reserves.

Finally, that U.S. inflation was lower than foreign inflation does nothing to undermine this emphasis on trends in monetary policy. Foreign countries, most notably Japan but also the western European nations, were still in the process of catching up to the United States. Faster growth and higher incomes meant faster rates of inflation through the operation of the Balassa-Samuelson effect. Thus the fact that U.S. consumer prices were falling relative to foreign consumer prices does not rule out the existence of a problem. A better measure of international competitiveness, free of Balassa-Samuelson bias, is export prices.[30] Between 1963 and 1969, these rose by 15 percent in the United States but only a third that fast in Germany and Japan.[31] And contemporaries were well aware of these facts.[32]

One can argue that this statement that U.S. monetary policy was too expansionary for the maintenance of external balance is uninteresting, even tautological. U.S. interest rates were not raised sufficiently, after all, to avert the dollar crisis. I disagree with the critique; the observation is important because it places in relief the proximate source of the imbalance. And this in turn directs attention to the more fundamental underlying political factors constraining policy.

Short-term Expedients

There is no stronger support for the theme of this paper—that the U.S. authorities were fundamentally unwilling to subordinate monetary and fis-

30. Or, more precisely, export unit values, since data on actual export prices were not yet gathered by the U.S. government. Given the rough-and-ready nature of export unit values as a proxy for export prices, their movement too should be taken with a grain of salt.

31. Further evidence of mounting inflationary pressure can be found in the fact that the ratio of the U.S. CPI to a trade-weighted index of foreign CPIs—which had been falling from 1960 through 1965—reversed direction in 1966 and trended upward through the remainder of the decade. Another piece of evidence is the rise in unit labor costs relative to the country's trading partners, again starting in 1968–69. To be sure, as foreign countries closed the per capita income gap vis-à-vis the United States and the Balassa-Samuelson effect was played out, one would expect to see some normal deceleration in the decline in the ratio of U.S. to foreign CPIs. One would not, however, expect to see the ratio reverse direction as dramatically as it did.

32. See, for example, Sohmen (1963, p. 13).

cal policies to the imperatives of defending the dollar peg—than the expedients to which they resorted to avoid having to direct macroeconomic policies at the balance of payments problem.

European Support for U.S. Military Commitments

On the current account side, steps were taken to reduce the deficit associated with U.S. military expenditures abroad. The U.S. military, starting in 1960, was instructed to reduce its foreign purchases and to repatriate dependents of U.S. servicemen abroad. The Defense Department simultaneously began giving preference to domestic goods in meeting foreign procurement requirements.[33] Under pressure from the Kennedy administration, various European countries, led by Germany and Italy, agreed to purchase military hardware from the United States to offset the impact on the U.S. balance of payments of U.S. military expenditures there. In the summer of 1962 the Defense Department instituted a Buy American program, under which price preferences for U.S. goods were raised to 50 percent.[34]

The Buy American program reduced the Defense Department's foreign purchases by $78.5 million in 1963–64, Norman Fieleke calculates.[35] But lower U.S. purchases abroad meant lower foreign exchange receipts for other countries, reducing other U.S. exports. Assuming standard multipliers, Fieleke estimates that the program strengthened the balance of payments in 1963–64 by less than $50 million.[36] Allan Meltzer suggests that even this effect was neutralized by inducing additional business support for stationing American troops in these European countries.[37]

33. This last measure was instituted by the Eisenhower administration but reversed by Kennedy upon taking office.

34. The extra cost in terms of Defense Department operations was factored into the military budget (and referred to as the Department's "gold budget"). In 1963 the 50 percent rule was extended to all government agencies except the U.S. Agency for International Development (USAID), which discriminated even more heavily against foreign goods.

35. Fieleke (1969, pp. 10–12).

36. This number may have risen somewhat in subsequent years, but at considerable welfare cost, since the U.S. military was purchasing unnecessarily expensive goods. The estimates of Morawetz (1971, p. 426) suggest a smaller effect insofar as two-thirds of any reduction in U.S. military purchases abroad was offset by reductions in U.S. exports. Fieleke's estimate (1969, p. 12) of the welfare cost is roughly $26 million in 1963–64. Hitch (1965, p. 176) suggests that the budgetary cost at this time was even higher, in the range of $30 million–$40 million.

37. Meltzer (1991). The more extreme policy of stationing troops at home rather than abroad was not pursued, owing to the even higher welfare losses that would have been associated with the budgetary costs of increased sealift capacity (Fried, 1971).

Tied Foreign Aid

U.S. aid was tied, formally and informally, to purchases of American goods. From the early 1960s, new aid commitments were limited to countries that agreed to spend the dollars on commodities in the United States.[38] Additionality provisions ensured that aid funds were not merely substituted for non-aided purchases in the United States that the recipient country would have made anyway. In 1966 nine of every ten dollars of recipient countries' commodity spending financed by USAID went to U.S. suppliers, up from four or five of every ten dollars prior to the program.[39] C. Fred Bergsten estimates that as a result of extensive tying, the balance of payments cost of U.S. foreign aid was at most 20 cents on the dollar.[40] Morawetz's econometric estimates suggest an even smaller effect.[41] But since foreign aid was only a small share of U.S. overseas expenditures, the overall balance of payments impact of even such extensive tying was negligible.

Tighter Rules for Tourists

On the import side, the value of the duty-free goods American tourists were allowed to bring into the country was cut from $500 to $100. Insofar as such measures discouraged foreign travel, their effects would have been magnified. The expected impact was to reduce spending abroad by $50 million–$100 million a year.

Operation Twist

Starting in 1961, the Treasury Department, in cooperation with the Federal Reserve, attempted to "twist" the yield curve, purchasing Treasury bonds and selling Treasury bills as a way of reconciling the imperatives of internal and external balance. The rationale was that financial capital flows were responsive to short-term interest differentials, while the domestic investment plans on which economic activity and productivity growth

38. In addition, U.S. contributions to multilateral development banks and institutions such as the Inter-American Development Bank were tied; the country's contributions to the bank's Fund for Special Operations were subject to restrictions that made it difficult to use them for purposes other than purchasing U.S. merchandise.

39. Hyson and Strout (1968, p. 64).

40. Bergsten (1975, p. 296).

41. Morawetz (1971).

depended were responsive mainly to long-term rates. Twisting the yield curve would thus make it possible to use higher interest rates to produce a stronger capital account without at the same time slowing recovery from the 1960–61 recession.

The resulting changes in the term structure were disappointing. Long rates fell slightly from 3.81 percent in February 1961 to 3.73 percent in May but then rose as high as 4.06 percent in December. Short rates fluctuated, rising from 2.41 percent in February to 2.62 percent in December. In 1962 short rates rose slightly, by 11 basis points from January through December, while long rates fell by 21 basis points. Both short and long rates rose in 1963, the former by 61 basis points, the latter by 26. The only general statement that can be made about these movements in the yield curve is that none of them was large.

Anthony Campagna concludes on the basis of these relatively small changes that "Operation Twist could be considered only a very modest success at best."[42] Meltzer argues that it was ineffective "since the market for government securities is very active and highly competitive," allowing "participants. . . [to] reverse any temporary change in interest rates achieved by the twist."[43] It is not clear what he means; private agents could not issue Treasury bonds and bills themselves in response to changes in relative interest rates. Perhaps he means that Treasury bonds and bills were close substitutes for one another, so that the "very active and highly competitive" market prevented the Treasury and the Fed from significantly shifting the slope of the yield curve. Perhaps he means that Operation Twist was undone by the close substitutability of private and government paper and of bonds and time deposits and by the incentive for the corporate sector to change the mix of corporate bonds and commercial paper it issued and for households to shift from bonds to time deposits in response to changes in the yield curve.[44] This was Arthur Okun's conclusion: that Treasury bills and bonds were very close substitutes for one another, and that changes in their mix would have only a modest impact on the term structure of interest rates and hence on the short-term capital flows associated with a given long-term rate.[45]

42. Campagna (1987, p. 285).
43. Meltzer (1991, p. 59).
44. Campagna (1987) notes that households did in fact shift from securities into time deposits in response to the initial upward move in bond prices, consistent with this view.
45. Okun (1963).

Above all there was the fact that the Fed's purchases of bonds remained limited. Chairman William McChesney Martin had to be leaned on continuously not to revert to the Fed's traditional "bills only" policy.[46] More fundamentally, increasing the supply of interest-bearing government securities that were relatively close substitutes for money threatened to excite inflationary fears. The basic problem was not that Operation Twist was conceptually flawed but that the policy, though designed to address balance of payments problems in a manner consistent with other goals, still created a conflict with the Fed's overriding domestic objectives. The policy might have been more effective had it been pursued more aggressively, but—consistent with the central theme of this paper—this was not something that the Fed was prepared to countenance for domestic reasons.

The Interest Equalization Tax

The Interest Equalization Tax (IET) was designed to discourage long-term lending to foreign countries.[47] A tax equal to a 1 percent rate of interest was imposed in 1963 on foreign bonds sold in the United States.[48] The obvious limitation of the measure was that it applied only to certain types of foreign assets and encouraged substitution from taxed to untaxed investments. There was an obvious incentive to purchase short-term foreign securities with a maturity of less than a year and to substitute bank loans for bonds. Martin Prachowny estimates that such substitution completely neutralized the IET in a matter of months.[49] In response, the tax was extended in 1965 to bank loans to foreigners with a maturity of more than one year.

Allan Meltzer concludes that even these more comprehensive measures had little effect.[50] For one thing, restraints on foreign lending by U.S.

---

46. Kettl (1986).

47. Loans to Canada and the World Bank were exempted.

48. The policy was kept in place until 1973. Simultaneous with the announcement of the IET, the United States announced that defense spending abroad would be reduced by $1 billion and that it had obtained a $500 million standby credit from the IMF. (The United States drew $300 million of this in 1965.) The administration followed up with a White House conference on export expansion, at which the president and various Cabinet officials spent more than three hours exhorting business to sell more products abroad.

49. Prachowny (1969). The IET also had a major positive impact on foreign investment in the months between its announcement and imposition (Johnson, 1966).

50. Meltzer (1966).

banks discouraged those same institutions from funding themselves by attracting foreign deposits.[51]

Agreements with U.S. Companies

In addition, a series of voluntary agreements with U.S. companies was concluded starting in 1965 with the intent of limiting the deficit on the long-term capital account. Each company was asked to submit a "corporate balance of payments account" and to suggest means of improving its balance by 15 to 20 percent. Late in 1965 company-by-company ceilings were set for the subsequent calendar year.[52] In 1966 such agreements were drawn up for some 900 major corporations. From 1968 the program was made mandatory and administered by the Office of Foreign Direct Investment (OFDI).

The Commerce Department tabulated the early results of the program on the basis of a sample of 233 participating companies in early 1966, concluding that the estimated improvement of the credit balance of these companies was 13 percent.[53] At the same time, there were signs that U.S. corporations, in order to satisfy the agreement, had simply pushed their 1965 foreign investments into 1966.[54] In addition, much of the reported improvement was achieved not by less foreign direct investment (FDI) by U.S. firms but rather by more intense efforts on their part to finance that investment on foreign markets.

In response, the government doubled the target for the desired reduction in foreign direct investment, doubled the number of participating companies, and added targets for reductions in the foreign short-term assets held by U.S. companies and their foreign affiliates. The results for 1966 suggested that the program delivered perhaps a third of the targeted improvement in the U.S. balance of payments. Harry G. Johnson reluctantly concluded that the program had some effect, though firms found various ways of limiting the reduction in foreign investment to lower levels than mandated by government.[55]

51. This is the heterodox Kindleberger-Salant view, also endorsed to an extent by Bergsten (1975), that U.S. banks and the U.S. economy generally were acting as banker to the world, borrowing short and lending long.

52. A *Business Week* article referred to this program as an administrator's nightmare (*Business Week*, October 9, 1965, p. 53).

53. Johnson (1966, pp. 173–74).

54. Treasury Secretary Henry Fowler, having initially promised that the restraints would be temporary, said that in any case they would not extend beyond two years (Johnson, 1966, p. 176).

55. Johnson (1966).

The program was also applied to U.S. banks from 1965. Because the Fed's ability to exercise moral suasion over the banks exceeded the Commerce Department's influence over corporations, it was never necessary to make the guidelines for the banks mandatory. Each bank was asked not to let its lending at the end of 1965 exceed 105 percent of that outstanding at the end of 1964. Largely as a result of this program, U.S. financial transfers abroad declined by $2.8 billion between 1964 and 1965. A similar ceiling was set for end-1966 lending, this time at 109 percent of 1964 levels. Again, however, substitution from controlled to uncontrolled channels cast doubt over the long-term effectiveness of the program. From 1966, nonbank financial institutions were also requested to limit the rate of growth of their foreign investments, to limit the scope for further substitution. The effectiveness of these guidelines is less clear, since the Fed had less leverage over nonbank institutions.

While all these studies considered impact effects, it is worth recalling that less foreign investment now meant lower foreign earnings later. Given estimated rates of return on foreign direct investment by U.S. manufacturing in the 10 to 20 percent range in the first half of the 1960s, this offset could have been substantial.[56]

The Gold Pool

A final initiative designed to contain the pressure on the dollar was the London Gold Pool. As early as March 1960, the price of gold rose above $35 an ounce on the London gold market. Policymakers worried that a rise in the free market price would lead to a drain of U.S. gold reserves. Foreign central banks would have an incentive to convert their dollars into gold at the U.S. Treasury and resell that gold at higher market prices. Even if they could be induced to resist the temptation to engage directly in arbitrage, any central bank with extra gold would obviously prefer to sell in the market, while those wishing to buy gold would have every reason to come to the United States.[57] Hence until 1968, it was viewed as essential to prevent the London gold price from rising significantly above $35.

From late 1960, European central banks agreed to refrain from buying gold in the London market for monetary purposes when the price rose

56. See Lindert (1971, p. 1096, table 2).
57. Solomon (1982, p. 115).

above $35.20, the official U.S. price plus costs of shipping and insurance. In 1961 this agreement was succeeded by the creation of the gold pool. The United States and seven European governments undertook to jointly supply the gold needed to keep the price in London from rising above $35.20.

Over its lifetime, the United States provided $1.6 billion of the $2.5 billion of net gold sales by the members of the pool on the London market. Clearly, the existence of the gold pool did not eliminate the pressure on U.S. monetary gold reserves. What it did was give the other members a shared sense of responsibility for preventing the market price of gold from rising. It was a mechanism whereby the United States could exert moral suasion for their central banks and governments to sell gold and accumulate dollars instead of the reverse.

The pool functioned until March 1968, when a surge of private buying led to its suspension and to the creation of a two-tier gold market with significantly higher prices for private than for official transactions. That buying surge can be understood in terms of declining confidence in the dollar peg. The 1967 devaluation of sterling had telegraphed the message that no reserve currency was immune from market pressures. France terminated its participation in the gold pool out of dissatisfaction with U.S. monetary policy, a fact that became publicly known following sterling's devaluation, leading to fears that other countries would also withdraw. And the fact that the official price of gold had not been changed over a period of many years of secular inflation created the perception of a one-way bet. When Senator Jacob Javits issued a statement at the end of February 1968 calling for the suspension of dollar convertibility, the gold rush was underway, and the gold pool was history.[58]

Evidence from the Behavior of Interest Differentials

A number of these policies—including the Interest Equalization Tax and voluntary restraint agreements with U.S. banks not to increase their lending overseas—were designed to break the link between domestic and foreign monetary policies and give the U.S. authorities more room to tailor interest rates to domestic conditions without having to worry so much about the balance of payments. If these policies were less easily evaded than

58. Javits (1968).

suggested in the third section above, then one should expect to see a change in the behavior of U.S. and foreign interest rates following their imposition in 1963 and 1965.

I therefore analyzed short-term interest rates for the United States, Canada, West Germany, and the United Kingdom from early 1960 through August 1971.[59] These are end-of month rates in each case. I was interested in how quickly a gap between U.S. and foreign rates tended to close once it opened up.

I started by testing whether it is possible to reject the hypothesis of a unit root in the interest differential and then turned to the question of convergence speed. It seems implausible that there should be a unit root in the interest differential, as opposed to the individual interest rate series themselves, given the incentives for arbitrage. The interest differentials plotted in figure 6-8 appear consistent with the hypothesis of mean reversion. Nonetheless, the augmented Dickey-Fuller test does not speak loudly. The null of a unit root can be strongly rejected for the United Kingdom; however, one barely fails to reject at the 10 percent level for Canada, and one fails to reject by a wide margin for Germany. The problem, as Graham Elliot and John Rogers have observed, is that the test has low power for short time spans.[60] Daily or weekly interest rate data would not help, since the power is increasing in the length of the time span, not the number of observations. Following Andrew Levin and Chien-Fu Lin, who suggest that panel estimation can dramatically increase the power of the test, I ran the augmented Dickey-Fuller test for the panel of three countries.[61] Now, the null of a unit root in any of the three interest differential time series could be decisively rejected.

To examine speed of convergence, I posited a zero-mean AR(1) process and regressed the change in the interest differential on the lagged level of the interest differential and four lags of the dependent variable.[62] I then looked for changes over time in the coefficient on the lagged level of the interest differential by plotting the recursive coefficient estimates obtained by first estimating the relationship on a small sample and then adding addi-

---

59. The interest rate series are from the OECD database distributed with RATS. I used Treasury bill rates for the United States, Canada and the United Kingdom, and three-month loan rates for Germany.

60. Elliot and Rogers (1999).

61. Levin and Lin (1992).

62. Four lags are sufficient to deal with serial correlation in the residuals, according to Durbin's H test.

Figure 6-8. *Interest Differentials: Canada, Germany and the United Kingdom vis-à-vis the United States, 1960–71*[a]

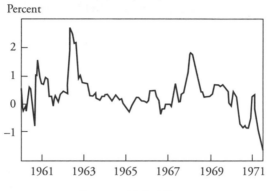

Canada–United States

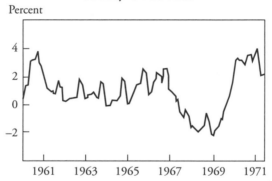

Germany–United States

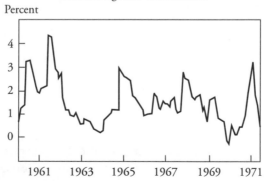

United Kingdom–United States

Source: Author's calculations based on data from OECD database distributed with RATS.
a. Treasury bill rates are used for the United States, Canada, and the United Kingdom, and three-month loan rates are used for Germany.

tional data points one by one. The full sample estimates are shown in table 6-2, the recursive coefficient estimates in figure 6-9. Speed of adjustment is fastest for the United Kingdom–United States interest differential and slowest for the Germany–United States differential, with Canada in the middle.[63] These coefficients imply half-lives of approximately four months for the United Kingdom–United States differential, five months for the Canada–United States differential, and eleven months for the Germany–United States differential.

The recursive coefficients show their standard instability at the beginning of the period, when the data set is still short. For Canada and the United Kingdom, they show essentially no movement thereafter. For Germany, there is a decline in adjustment speed in 1967–68. But the timing is wrong for it to be attributable to U.S. balance of payments initiatives. A more likely explanation lies in the 100 percent reserve requirements that the Bonn government slapped on Deutsche mark deposits held by non-residents in 1968.[64] In any case, the fall in speed of adjustment is small relative to the two standard-error band. A variety of stability tests fail to reject the null of a constant convergence coefficient.

These findings are consistent with the skeptical view of the effectiveness of the various non-macroeconomic expedients to which the United States resorted to address its balance of payments problem. There is no sign of a decline in the speed of adjustment to interest differentials, as would have been the case had initiatives like the Interest Equalization Tax and mandatory restraints on foreign investment succeeded in throwing significant sand in the wheels of international finance. It is possible, to be sure, that the constancy of the estimated speed of adjustment conflates two offsetting trends: on the one hand, the tendency for capital mobility to rise over the course of the 1960s; and on the other hand, the tendency for these policy initiatives to slow adjustment. Be that as it may, there is no evidence of what U.S. officials sought, namely, greater policy autonomy.

Limited Policy Options

This discussion assumes that the U.S. payments imbalance was a policy problem caused by inadequate international competitiveness and that it was solvable by devaluation of the dollar, revaluation of foreign currencies,

---

63. As could have been inferred from the country-by-country Dickey-Fuller tests.
64. See Bakker (1994).

Table 6-2. *Convergence Speed, 1960–71*[a]

Independent variable	Canada	West Germany	United Kingdom
Constant	0.04	0.069	0.245
	(1.11)	(1.31)	(2.90)
Excess over U.S. interest rate	–0.139	–0.075	–0.168
	(2.44)	(2.32)	(3.38)
Dependent variable (–1)	0.279	0.155	0.161
	(2.98)	(1.78)	(1.82)
Dependent variable (–2)	–0.162	0.072	0.104
	(1.76)	(0.86)	(1.16)
Dependent variable (–3)	0.002	–0.237	0.054
	(0.02)	(2.87)	(0.61)
Dependent variable (–4)	0.052	0.266	0.045
	(0.60)	(3.02)	(0.49)
S.E. of regression	0.34	0.52	0.46

Source: Author's calculations based on data from OECD database distributed with RATS.
a. Dependent variable is change in excess over U.S. interest rates; *t*-statistics are in parentheses.

or the adoption of more restrictive domestic policies. The dilemma was that, to a large extent, all three options were ruled out. To be sure, Germany revalued the mark by 9.3 percent in October 1969. But revaluation by one country could not solve a global financial problem. Reaching a wider agreement to revalue required surmounting collective-action problems, since individual countries seeking to steal a competitive advantage had an incentive to free ride, and not all countries other than the United States were in a strong international position. Indeed, the United Kingdom and France could plausibly argue that the shoe was on the other foot. And engineering a blanket revaluation of European currencies was all the more difficult when first the British and then the French currencies came under pressure and ultimately had to be devalued, eroding the competitive position of their neighbors. Even in the strong-currency countries, powerful lobbies opposed revaluation. As the *New York Times* put it in an editorial, "Washington underestimated the resistance of foreign business and farm groups that saw their interests being hurt by currency changes as well as the bitterness of foreign governments over what they regarded as a crisis bred by the United States but foisted upon them."[65]

65. "Solving the Payments Riddle," *New York Times,* May 8, 1971, p. A28.

Figure 6-9. *Recursive Coefficient Estimates of Speed of Convergence*

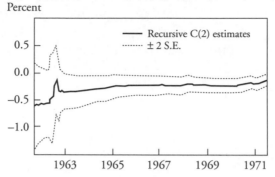

Canada–United States interest differential

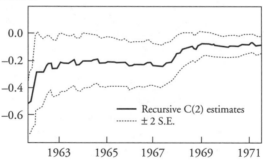

Germany–United States interest differential

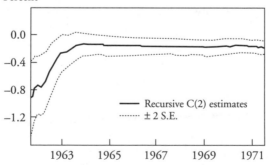

United Kingdom–United States interest differential

Source and notes: See figure 6-8.

Dollar devaluation was debated by academics and discussed by officials but similarly ruled out by policymakers. Here too there were free-rider problems. Under Bretton Woods, the United States declared a par value for the dollar in terms of gold, while other countries declared par values vis-à-vis the dollar. While the United States could raise the dollar price of gold, nothing guaranteed that other countries would simultaneously alter the dollar price of their domestic currencies, owing to the aforementioned "resistance of . . . business and farm groups." To prevent their currencies from appreciating against the dollar, they would buy gold using their domestic currency, which would further undermine the stability of the Bretton Woods system. George Shultz, a member of Nixon's kitchen cabinet, suggests that this was a real and pressing concern.[66] On the basis of interviews with the principals, Joanne Gowa reports that this fear was shared by members of the Volcker Group (made up of high-ranking representatives of the Department of the Treasury, the Federal Reserve, the Council of Economic Advisers, the State Department, and the assistant for National Security Affairs).[67]

Beyond that was the danger that raising the dollar price of gold would prompt other foreign central banks and market participants suffering capital losses on their dollar balances—including even those prepared to see their currencies revalued against the dollar—to convert those dollar reserves into gold in order to protect themselves against further losses at the hands of the United States. Dollar devaluation, in other words, threatened to damage the credibility of the gold-dollar system. Thus the fact that the international system was still a gold-dollar system, with a fixed dollar link to gold, discouraged the United States from solving the problem the way it ultimately did after 1973.

The two-tier gold market, which obviated the need for the United States to sell gold from its reserves to prevent a rise in the market price, and the Gentlemen's Agreement, under which foreign central banks and governments agreed to refrain from converting their existing dollar holdings into U.S. monetary gold, were the responses taken to relieve the pressure on the dollar. These responses can be understood in terms of collective interest in the preservation of the system. Specifically, Gowa concludes that the other industrial countries acceded to the two-tier market in response to a warning by Chairman Martin that, absent such an agreement, the United States

---

66. Shultz and Dam (1977, p. 114).
67. Gowa (1983, p. 74).

would be forced to close the gold window.[68] But U.S. pressure could be even more direct. Thus the U.S. government implied to its German ally that conversions of the German government's dollars into gold would jeopardize the future of American troops stationed in Germany, which elicited a letter from Karl Blessing, the president of the Bundesbank, that Germany would abstain from further conversions.[69] It was made clear to Canada and Japan that the preferential treatment they enjoyed under the provisions of U.S. government programs to restrain capital exports was linked to similar restraint.[70]

But insofar as these measures succeeded in relieving that pressure, they also weakened the incentive for the United States to adjust. If dollars could no longer be converted into gold, there was one less constraint on the ability of the United States to pump dollars into the international system. Events like those of 1967–68, when the monetary gold holdings of national authorities had declined as private investors shifted from dollars to gold in anticipation of an increase in the dollar price, could not recur. And so long as foreign central banks could be depended on to hold any additional dollars supplied by the United States that were not absorbed by private investors, the pressure for adjustment was minimal. This was the basis for the advice of experts like Lawrence Krause that the United States adopt a posture of benign neglect toward its balance of payments.

But this overestimated the insulation the dollar enjoyed. In fact, nothing about the two-tier gold market or the Gentlemen's Agreement prevented private market participants, either Americans or foreigners, from converting their dollars into other currencies. With the development of European financial markets, the range of assets available to investors had expanded greatly compared to, say, ten years before. Market participants therefore had the same opportunities to speculate on a dollar devaluation as in any system of pegged exchange rates and open capital markets.

In this environment, the liquidity of foreign dollar holdings exposed the United States to the threat of a bank-run-like crisis. If private investors converted their claims on the United States into foreign currencies *en masse,* the dollar would come tumbling down. This, of course, was the problem that the creation of Special Drawing Rights was designed to address. But by the time the decision to issue SDRs was taken in 1969,

---

68. Gowa (1983, p. 53).
69. Hirsch and Doyle (1977, p. 41 and passim).
70. Block (1977, p. 184); Gowa (1983, p. 54).

short-term foreign dollar balances massively exceeded U.S. gold reserves. The creation of SDRs held out hope for limiting future problems, but they did not remove the financial inheritance.

Whether investors rushed for the exits depended on the strength of their belief that central banks would defend the dollar. So long as market participants were confident that the United States would hike interest rates if they sold dollars or that other central banks would purchase the dollars they sold, there was no incentive to sell dollars in the first place. The credibility of the commitment to support the dollar would be both necessary and sufficient for stability. But in 1970, with the rise in U.S. unemployment, doubts deepened that the Fed had the stomach to raise interest rates to whatever levels were needed to defend the dollar. And as foreign inflation accelerated, it became less credible that other central banks would purchase however many dollars market participants sought to sell. The 1968 Gentlemen's Agreement obligated foreign monetary authorities to hold onto their inherited dollar balances but not to absorb all additional dollars they acquired as a result of capital flight from the United States, especially if these fueled unacceptable rates of inflation.

In early 1971 there were signs that the united front was breaking down. The Netherlands and Belgium exchanged dollars for gold toward the beginning of the year. Germany made known its desire to buy $500 million of U.S. gold in a step that was technically consistent with the Gentlemen's Agreement (on the grounds that Germany had sold this same amount of gold to the United States in 1969)—but hardly confidence-inspiring. France demanded the conversion of dollars into gold in May, and in early August the press reported that it was preparing to ask for $191 million in gold to make a repayment to the IMF. The last straw was on August 13, when Britain also requested gold. Flight from the dollar rose to high levels. Reluctant to use monetary or fiscal policy to defend the currency and conscious that European central banks had reached the end of their rope, the United States was left with no alternative to closing the gold window.

Devaluation as a Non-Option

Given the perspective developed in this paper, devaluing the dollar was the obvious way of squaring the circle. Devaluation would have enhanced the competitiveness of U.S. exports, improved the trade balance (given sufficient time), and altered the direction of foreign investment flows by raising the profitability of domestic production relative to foreign production. This solution would not have required higher interest rates or budgetary economies that would have jeopardized the pursuit of the country's other economic and military objectives. Contemporaries were aware of the argument: unilateral devaluation was one of three policy options submitted to President Nixon by the Volcker Group in 1969. Similar arguments had been placed before President Johnson during the final years of his administration.

Why then was the option shunned? One explanation is fear that devaluation would damage the credibility of the Bretton Woods system and, perhaps of more relevance to U.S. officials, of the dollar itself. A government that devalued revealed itself to be less than fully committed to the maintenance of its currency peg. If its priorities came to be questioned, investors would run at the first sign of trouble, and trouble would proliferate. The French and British governments, having caved in to pressure for devaluation, were saddled with just such a reputation. If the dollar fell under the same cloud as sterling and the franc, suffering from chronic weakness and being devalued repeatedly, the very *raison d'etre* for the Bretton Woods system, in which other countries pegged to the dollar so as to achieve a semblance of international monetary stability, would be destroyed, and the system likely along with it.

Unilateral devaluation therefore would have antagonized the United States' allies and trading partners, who saw themselves as possessing a collective interest in the maintenance of this international monetary system, which offered them a favorable climate for export-led growth. Germany and Japan, to cite only two examples, had predicated their entire postwar recoveries on this export-led strategy. In both countries, exporters were key supporters of the political status quo. An attempt by the United States to solve its domestic economic problems—not to mention to pursue its controversial foreign policy aims and to establish beachheads for American multinationals in places like France—at the expense of European exporters would not have been well received. It would have frayed the Western alliance at a time when cold war tensions were high. It would have thrown a wrench in the works of ongoing GATT negotiations. For all these reasons it was unacceptable.

Finally, there was the possibility that if the U.S. government raised the dollar price of gold, which was the only instrument it in fact controlled, other governments would also raise the domestic-currency price of gold, leaving exchange rates and U.S. international competitiveness unchanged.

Europe and Japan, for all the aforementioned reasons, were reluctant to see the competitiveness of their exports erode. Export interests would scream if their governments acquiesced in policies with this effect, and they were too important to ignore. Germany might agree, under the most intense pressure, to revalue, but only to a limited extent. Moreover, the structure of the Bretton Woods system made more than their mere acquiescence necessary; positive steps were required in order for the dollar to be devalued against their currencies, given that they had declared par values in terms of the dollar. If the dollar depreciated against gold, nonaction on their part meant that their currencies would depreciate along with the dollar. There would be no benefits for U.S. competitiveness. And given their domestic political situation, nonaction was the likely outcome. That was what Treasury Secretary Fowler meant when he said that "the U.S. under the present rules cannot change its own parity."[71]

To be sure, a higher price of gold, even if achieved in this way, was not without benefits. It would raise the dollar value of U.S. monetary gold relative to foreign dollar liabilities, reducing the likelihood, ceteris paribus, of a run on U.S. gold reserves. By increasing the value of the world stock of monetary gold, it would limit the need for foreign central banks and governments desperate for additional reserves to further augment their claims on the United States. It would be easier, in other words, for the United States to reduce its payments deficit without at the same time starving the rest of the world of international liquidity. No longer having to import reserves, those governments would be encouraged to stimulate demand. And more demand abroad would be unambiguously good for the U.S. balance of payments. Because the reduction in the deficit would be brought about by foreign expansion, not U.S. contraction, this approach was compatible with domestic objectives.

But a one-time increase in the dollar price of gold offered only a one-time source of relief. The shock to confidence would mean that every effort had to be made to reassure investors that it would not be repeated. This was easier said than done. And if the relief was only temporary, reasonable people could question whether the risk was worth taking.

Framing the problem this way makes clear that dollar devaluation was simply not feasible in this context. The structure of Bretton Woods meant that it required foreign cooperation that was unlikely to be forthcoming. It meant that it would damage systemic stability. The economic policy strate-

71. Cited in Duncan, Patterson, and Yee (1998, p. 604).

gies and domestic politics of America's European allies meant that they would be antagonized, and the cold war context rendered this price unacceptable. That the Soviet Union was one of the world's two leading gold producers (and South Africa was the other) compounded the problem. So did the fact that the policy would penalize countries that had cooperated by accumulating dollars, while rewarding others like the French who had insisted on acquiring gold.

All this meant that devaluation was beyond the pale. Francis Bator's 1968 summary cannot be improved on: "Raising the price of gold was judged by the U.S. Government, rightly I think, a medieval expedient, inefficient in providing for the need (which is for a continuous, relatively smooth expansion in reserves); inequitable in its first-round benefits; and last, given the history, politically out of the question."[72] At least it was beyond the pale until 1971, when the United States had its back against the wall—when the policy could be portrayed as the only remaining choice. And, even then, negotiating a limited realignment of the dollar against the other major currencies required months of acrimonious negotiations. As early as 1973 it was clear that the modest exchange rate changes agreed to at the Smithsonian had been grossly inadequate.

Further Issues

In this section I consider some potential qualifications and extensions of the aforementioned arguments.

The 1960 Crisis

The first U.S. balance of payments crisis occurring in the years covered by this paper was in 1960. Capital outflows became increasingly worrisome as the year progressed. The London price of gold shot up to $40 in October, alarmingly higher than the U.S. Treasury's $35 selling price.

Is the 1960 crisis consistent with this paper's interpretation of the roots of U.S. balance of payments problems? After all, the competitiveness problems emphasized here had not yet reached serious proportions by the early 1960s. The U.S. current account actually moved from deficit to surplus between 1959 and 1960, U.S. exports of merchandise rising by 20 percent.

---

72. Bator (1968, p. 1).

Admittedly, there were concerns in 1958–59 that military and economic aid to other countries was becoming a structural drain on the U.S. balance of payments, although this too was small relative to subsequent years. And 1960 was the first year when foreign claims (private plus official) exceeded U.S. monetary gold reserves.[73] But references and, by implication, concern on the part of the Federal Open Market Committee (FOMC) to gold losses, trade deficits, and the balance of payments were minimal in 1959–60. It is hard to believe that there had yet developed a strongly held belief that the U.S. external position was unsustainable.

The simple explanation for this crisis, consistent with the theme of this paper, is the belief that Kennedy might take unilateral action to devalue the dollar as a way of removing the constraint on policy initiatives to reduce unemployment. The president-elect had campaigned on a promise to get the economy moving again, it having been becalmed in recession for much of 1959–60. If Kennedy was going to raise the dollar price of gold, market participants and, for that matter, foreign central banks had obvious incentives to sell dollars for gold and foreign currencies in anticipation.[74]

Kennedy was not the first presidential candidate ever to have campaigned on a promise of implementing policies to stimulate economic growth. But it is important to recall that the last newly elected Democratic president, facing similar concerns, had devalued the dollar within weeks of taking office. Anticipation of that policy had precipitated the 1933 financial crisis.[75] Seen in this historical light, it is not surprising that fears that Kennedy might devalue the dollar were taken seriously. And, in turn, recollections of 1933 led Kennedy to issue a strong, unambiguous statement to reassure the markets, something that in 1932–33 FDR had failed to do.[76] When the new president followed up on these statements with his first comprehensive balance of payments program, signaling his concern

73. Although this gold overhang was tiny by the standards of subsequent years.

74. Thus purchases by foreign central banks were responsible for some $2 billion of U.S. monetary gold losses in the second half of the year.

75. Wigmore (1987).

76. Kennedy devoted an entire speech, in Philadelphia on the eve of the election, to the balance of payments. The famous passage was "we pledge ourselves to maintain the current value of the dollar. If elected President I shall not devalue the dollar from the present rate. Rather I shall defend the present value and its soundness" (Roosa, 1967, p. 268). Subsequently, Kennedy rejected the advice of the majority of his advisers to request legislation to repeal the gold cover requirement of the Federal Reserve Act, which required the Fed to hold gold certificates in an amount equal to at least a quarter of its deposit and note liabilities—a requirement that immobilized much of the U.S. monetary gold stock. Apparently, Kennedy was convinced that repeal would frighten domestic and foreign markets, which were still suspicious of his commitment to a strong dollar.

with the external value of the dollar, the pressure on the currency subsided. The fact that his public statements caused the pressure on the dollar to evaporate is the strongest evidence that it was temporary uncertainty about policy priorities that lay behind this episode.

Fed Policy and the Balance of Payments

The Fed's concern with the external position reached a peak three times during this period: in 1963, 1965, and 1967. In each instance the balance of payments was cited as a rationale for the decision to raise interest rates. This raises the question of whether it is accurate to interpret U.S. monetary policy in the 1960s as taking an attitude of benign neglect toward the balance of payments.

In fact, the first two decisions were resisted and criticized by the administration, intensifying the pressure on the Fed to reverse direction sooner rather than later. In contrast, the third one, taken in a period of high employment and accelerating inflation, was desired on domestic as well as international economic grounds.

In July 1963, concern with the balance of payments led the Fed to raise the discount rate from 3 to 3.24 percent and to increase the interest rate on time deposits payable in ninety days to one year to enable U.S. banks to better compete with foreign banks for funds. Even within the Fed, there were fears over the domestic economic impact; a "healthy minority" of FOMC members worried that the rise in the discount rate could "set off a reaction that . . . might possibly choke off business expansion."[77] As the FOMC papered over the dispute in its "Record of Policy Actions," "there was extensive discussion . . . about the proper course of monetary policy in the light of the serious and persistent balance of payments deficit and the urgent need for additional measures to deal with it. At the same time it was recognized that the domestic economy was not expanding at a rate sufficient to bring about full employment soon and that a more rapid rate of growth was highly to be desired."[78] One dissenting governor, George Mitchell, publicly argued that tighter monetary policy was likely to damage the domestic expansion and suggested greater reliance on taxes on capital outflows to address the balance of payments deficit. The president's advisers reportedly were furious that the Fed had raised short-term interest

77. *Business Week,* July 20, 1963, p. 25.
78. Board of Governors of the Federal Reserve System (1963, p. 41).

rates without at the same time reaffirming its commitment to somehow keep long-term rates from rising, as required for the effectiveness of Operation Twist. Walter Heller wondered in a memo to Kennedy "whether we're getting the twist or the screw."[79] Heller convened further meetings of the Quadriad (made up of the chairman of the CEA, secretary of the Treasury, chairman of the Board of Governors, and director of the budget) to intensify the pressure on the Fed. Leaks to the press suggesting that the administration was upset with its action further ratcheted up the pressure on the central bank.

Concern mounted over the course of 1965 about the U.S. balance of payments. Responding to alarmingly large gold losses, in December the Federal Reserve Board raised the discount rate from 4.0 to 4.42 percent. (The earlier increase to 4 percent, in December 1964, had also responded to balance of payments considerations, namely, an increase in the Bank rate by the Bank of England designed to attract financial flows from the United States and other countries.) This tightening elicited an angered response from the administration, which argued that the Fed should have waited for the release of the budget for 1966 in January and for evidence that fiscal measures had succeeded in redressing the balance of payments and inflation problems.[80] The president himself was said to be furious.[81] The financial press portrayed the Fed as "defying" the Johnson administration.[82] This was the famous episode when Chairman Martin was called to the LBJ ranch and bounced around in a jeep in an attempt to coax him toward a more accommodating policy.[83]

The third such instance was December 1967, when the Fed raised the discount rate from 4.18 to 4.5 percent in response to Britain's devaluation of the pound and the resulting pressure on the dollar. U.S. gold reserves fell by $1 billion, to just $1.3 billion above the 25 percent cover ratio required by the Federal Reserve Act. This was the only one of the three episodes when resistance to the measure was not severe; signs of domestic overheat-

79. Kettl (1986, p. 100).

80. The Fed's move occurred against the backdrop of criticism by Wright Patman, chairman of the House Banking and Currency Committee, who proposed to radically scale back the independence and autonomy of the Federal Reserve Board.

81. Kettl (1986, p. 104).

82. See, for example, "What's New Today?" *Wall Street Journal,* December 6, 1965, p. 1.

83. Kettl (1986, p. 94) tabulates the number of meetings between Chairman Martin and the president each year from 1953 through 1968 (Quadriad meetings plus private meetings, excluding social occasions and official events) and finds that these peaked in 1965.

ing were rampant, and business investment initially resisted the damping effects of the tax surcharge. Thus this episode offers confirmation that the only times when monetary policy could be used to address payments problems in a sustained way were when the imperatives of internal and external balance coincided.

The Brookings Report

In 1962 the Council of Economic Advisers commissioned a team of Brookings experts (led by Walter Salant, and with the participation of Emile Despres, Lawrence Krause, Alice Rivlin, William Salant, and Lorie Tarshis) to analyze the prospects for the U.S. balance of payments. Its report, *The United States Balance of Payments in 1968*, transmitted to the Council in January 1963, projected the disappearance of the country's external problem by 1968. (Specifically, it forecast that the basic balance— current account plus government payments plus long-term capital flows— would have moved into a $1 billion–$2 billion surplus.)[84] It thus provided some justification for the policies of benign neglect pursued in this period.

The assumptions underlying the Salant Committee's forecasts are shown in table 6-3. The key assumptions were that U.S. GNP would grow faster than Western European GNP over the period 1960–68 and that unit labor costs would rise only half as rapidly in the United States.[85] Moreover, not only was aggregate supply projected to increase more rapidly in the United States than in Europe, but with the European economy continuing to be run under high pressure of demand and higher European incomes finally translating into an increased demand for non-traded goods, an increasing share of European investment would be devoted to sectors producing personal and housing services. The implication for Europe was that the supply of exports would grow more slowly than GNP, while the opposite would be true in the United States. The other side of the same coin was that unit labor costs would grow by 1.5 percent each year in the United States, but by 3.2 percent in Western Europe. Higher unit labor costs would be passed through to higher prices, implying a shift in the relative prices of U.S. and European goods

---

84. Salant and others (1963, appendix table 10).

85. Thus real GNP was projected to grow by 4.8 percent each year in the United States but by only 4.3 percent in the United Kingdom, West Germany, France, and Italy.

that would create the requisite demand for the additional U.S. output of traded goods.[86] This is how the committee saw the relatively rapid increase in U.S. exports being absorbed by international markets. The bottom line was a stronger U.S. trade balance. Indeed, the U.S. balance of payments would strengthen even more dramatically than the trade accounts, since slower growth, lower profits, and a higher labor share in Europe would make U.S. direct foreign investment less attractive.

The growth forecasts of the Salant Committee were very close. Its forecast of U.S. economic growth (adopted from the Council of Economic Advisers) was dead on: where it had forecast that U.S. GNP would be 45.5 percent higher in 1968 than 1960, it actually rose by 45 percent. So too was its estimate for industrial Western Europe. GDP was 37 percent higher in 1968 than 1960 in West Germany, 56 percent higher in Italy, and 52 percent higher in France, compared with forecasts of 38, 55 and 48 percent.[87] The phenomenon was general; in Belgium, Denmark, and Norway, all relatively poor performers in the 1950s, there was a sharp acceleration in the 1960s. With respect to the United Kingdom, the "sick man" of Europe, the committee's pessimism was justified; there output rose by only 27 percent (almost exactly as forecast), contributing to that country's own balance of payments problems.

The good performance in continental Europe was driven by a combination of wage moderation and high investment, to whose delivery Europe's corporatist institutions were ideally suited. The growth of labor supplies was sustained by the movement of workers to the industrial regions from Mediterranean Europe and North Africa. Wage growth remained considerably more subdued than the 9.0 percent a year forecast for France and Germany, 7.6 percent for Italy, and 6 percent for the United Kingdom. Investment rates rose further from the levels of the 1950s in every European country (except in Norway, where overall investment remained stable—although investment rates net of residential construction rose even there), and the countries of Western Europe remained net importers of capital. Much U.S. foreign investment in Europe was associated with technology transfer in chemicals, computers, and transport

86. To some extent, reductions in capital's share of national income could limit the pass-through from higher unit labor costs to higher prices, but the Salant Committee saw limits on how radically capital's share could be compressed. At the same time, a somewhat higher labor's share nonetheless would mean lower profits and lower investment, validating the expectation of slower European growth.

87. These forecasts were arithmetic averages of the high and low target figures submitted by the four countries to the OECD.

Table 6-3. *Evolution of Selected Variables on Salant Committee Assumptions, 1960–68*

Percent

Component	United States	United Kingdom	France	West Germany	Italy	France, West Germany, Italy	United Kingdom, West Germany, France, Italy
GNP in constant prices							
Average	4.8	3.3	5.0	4.1	5.6	4.75	4.3
Cumulative	45.5	29.7	47.75	37.9	54.6	45.0	40.2
Labor force							
Average	1.71	0.48	0.70	0.35	0.64	0.54	0.52
Cumulative	14.5	3.9	5.7	2.8	5.2	4.4	4.2
Employment in years							
Average	1.87	0.48	0.83	0.35	0.91	0.64	0.60
Cumulative	15.9	3.9	6.8	2.8	7.5	5.2	4.9
Hours worked per week							
Average	0	−0.93	−1.0	−1.02	0	−0.80	−0.84
Cumulative	0	−7.2	−7.7	−7.9	0	−6.2	−6.5
Employment in hours							
Average	1.87	−0.45	−0.18	−0.67	0.91	−0.17	−0.25
Cumulative	15.9	−3.6	−1.4	−5.5	7.5	−1.3	−1.9
Output per hour							
Average	2.9	3.8	5.2	4.8	4.6	4.9	4.6
Cumulative	25.5	34.5	49.8	45.9	43.8	46.9	42.9

Labor cost per hour							
Average	4.4	6.0	9.0	9.0	7.6	8.7	7.9
Cumulative	41.3	59.4	99.3	99.3	79.7	94.9	83.7
Labor cost per unit of output							
Average	1.5	2.1	3.6	4.0	2.8	3.6	3.2
Cumulative	12.6	18.5	33.0	36.6	25.0	32.7	28.6
Labor cost as a percentage of price							
In 1960	68.9	71.3	60.7	62.0	59.0	60.9	64.1
In 1968	68.9	71.3	63.2	65.3	62.0	63.8	66.4
Price of output							
Average	1.5	2.1	3.1	3.3	2.2	3.0	2.75
Cumulative	12.6	18.5	27.7	29.7	19.0	26.7	24.1

Source: Salant and others (1963), p. 283.

equipment. And Europe's patient bank-based financial system and low-turnover labor market were ideally suited for adapting these known technologies.[88]

Where the Salant Committee projected a decelerating rate of growth of U.S. foreign direct investment abroad and growing foreign direct investment (FDI) flows into the United States, net long-term capital outflows in the private sector (the vast majority of which were accounted for by FDI) actually ran at double the rate forecast for 1968.[89] The Committee failed to appreciate the importance of trends making for continued strong FDI, namely, the role of U.S. multinationals as technological leaders, and of improvements in information and communications technologies in diminishing problems of corporate control of foreign branch plant operations.

Conclusion

U.S. balance of payments problems in the 1960s, I have argued, had two aspects and must be understood using a framework encompassing both. On the one hand, there was a growing problem of real overvaluation, evident in the erosion of the current account and aggravated by the reluctance of U.S. policymakers to adjust monetary and fiscal policies. Occasional half-hearted responses to balance of payments pressures were made by the Fed, the executive branch, and Congress, but there was no systematic willingness to assign monetary and fiscal policies to external targets or to subordinate domestic political and economic objectives to balance of payments goals. The markets were aware of this fact, and the level of international capital mobility was high enough for them to act upon it. This was the crux of the U.S. balance of payments problem in the 1960s.

Elsewhere I have argued that the conjuncture of these two facts—high capital mobility together with political democracy that makes it unrealistic to ask governments to assign priority to exchange-rate targets over and above all other goals—is what is distinctive about today's international

---

88. As opposed to developing the kind of radical innovations pioneered by the United States in earlier (and subsequent) decades. The argument that the U.S. constellation of flexible labor markets and securitized finance is ideally suited for an environment with opportunities for radical innovation, while Europe's bank-based finance and low-turnover labor markets have a comparative advantage in environments dominated by incremental innovation, is developed by Soskice (1996).

89. Salant and others (1963, pp. 147–49). Where the Committee had projected $2.1 billion, the actual long-term outflow in 1968 was $4.3 billion, of which $3.2 billion was FDI.

monetary environment.[90] It is what has compelled a growing number of countries to accept greater exchange rate flexibility. From this point of view, U.S. balance of payments policy in the 1960s and the floating of the dollar in 1971–73 can be seen as harbingers of future trends.

The U.S. payments problem was further aggravated by its systemic aspect, that the main source of international liquidity for the expanding world economy was dollar balances, which created the potential for instability. Despres, Kindleberger, and Salant rightly emphasized that the role of the United States in this system was to act as banker to the world, borrowing short and lending long. But they were not right that this situation rendered benign the U.S. deficit on net liquidity balance. Just like a bank providing liquidity transformation services to its customers, the United States was vulnerable to a "depositor run." So long as foreign central banks, concerned about preserving the Bretton Woods system of pegged budget-adjustable exchange rates, stood ready to support the dollar, they provided the equivalent of deposit insurance. But unlike a classic lender of last resort, their willingness to do so was limited—collective interest in the maintenance of the Bretton Woods regime or not. And when that limit was reached in 1971, the system collapsed in a heap.

This ancient history may not be irrelevant to our day. Today, the apostles of the "new economy" reassure us that foreign direct investment inflows will continue to painlessly finance the U.S. current account deficit, now running at more than $300 billion and projected to rise further, because productivity growth in the United States will continue to outstrip productivity growth abroad. Given U.S. dominance of the burgeoning field of information technology, foreigners, it is said, will continue to find such investment irresistible. In 1963 the Salant report similarly predicted that our external deficit was not a problem: that the deficit would shrink and the direction of foreign direct investment would reverse (or at least, U.S. foreign direct investment would decline significantly) as U.S. productivity surged relative to European productivity. In fact, U.S. productivity did not surge relative to foreign productivity, and the balance of payments problem, rather than gradually disappearing, brought the dollar down with a crash. This is a cautionary tale for those who invoke the mantra of the new economy whenever the fact of the U.S. current account deficit is raised.

90. This is the theme of Eichengreen (1996).

COMMENT BY
Robert Z. Lawrence

In a well-written and well-argued paper, Barry Eichengreen defends the conventional wisdom that over the course of the 1960s, the U.S. balance of payments became an increasingly important problem that American policymakers refused to fix with fundamental macroeconomic policy actions. Instead, their efforts involved an ill-fated set of poor, expedient, and malign policies that were ultimately ineffective in staving off the demise of the Bretton Woods system.

Barry convincingly rebuts evidence that could call this characterization into question. While some reject the view that the balance of payments problem became progressively worse because there was a crisis in 1960, Barry argues that the episode in 1960 was unique and not related to the more fundamental problem of a progressive loss of competitiveness that emerged over the decade. (This problem was disguised by tight macroeconomic policies in the late 1960s, but emerged with a vengeance when President Nixon sought to resume growth in the early 1970s.) While others point out that monetary policymakers paid heed to the balance of payments when hiking rates in 1963, 1965, and 1967, Barry notes the first two of these episodes were exceptions that were soon reversed and actually proved the dominance of domestic policy considerations, while tightening in 1967 was compatible with domestic stabilization. While some discount the view that the dollar was overvalued by pointing out that U.S. inflation was no higher than foreign inflation, Barry notes that relative export prices, which are more relevant, tell a story of progressive decline. While some note the absence of rapid U.S. monetary expansion, Barry stresses that the evidence is more ambiguous and in any case that this is not necessary for a competitiveness problem to engender a crisis. Finally, while some question whether the U.S. role in providing liquidity was a problem, Barry argues that America's role as banker did create pressures, which became more powerful as capital markets developed.

I agree with Barry's argument about a fundamental and progressive decline in U.S. competitiveness, at times disguised by macroeconomic policies. Indeed, with the benefit of hindsight, it is clear just how far out of line the dollar had actually become. Even the devaluation of the dollar of about 12 percent that was engineered in 1971 was insufficient. Another 10 percent decline took place in March 1973 and an additional devaluation proved necessary in the late 1970s.

Moreover the notion that the relationship was progressive was well captured by the regressions that Hendrik Houthakker and Stephen Magee ran in the late 1960s, which obtained significantly different income elasticities on U.S. exports and imports.[91] Indeed, this continues to be a property of trade regressions fitted through the 1990s. While interpreting these specifications as structural equations requires making some quite strong assumptions, they have proven remarkably robust. They indicate a tendency for the trade balance to decline with similar growth rates at home and abroad and suggested the need, given the growth rates actually recorded in the 1960s, for a real exchange rate depreciation.

(In this regard, however, it is noteworthy that the serious underestimation made by the Salant Commission of the potential for European economic growth should have led them to predict an even stronger U.S. trade balance than they did. In other words, they were actually helped by this forecast error.)

I would make even more out of this issue of dollar overvaluation than Barry does. The system did have well-appreciated difficulties. These were the liquidity problem (providing sufficient international reserves) and the confidence problem (in the dollar's convertibility into gold). In fact, the United States was able to solve the confidence problem by simply abandoning the commitment to convert the dollar into gold. And steps were taken to deal with the issue of international reserves by creating the SDR.

But the crucial flaw in the system, in my judgment, turned out to be the problem of adjusting to a fundamental current account deficit in the pivotal country—the United States. The system dealt asymmetrically with surplus and deficit countries. Deficit countries were forced to adjust because they ran out of reserves. However, although there were some efforts in the IMF Articles to force surplus countries to adjust, these were not effective and the surplus countries could accumulate reserves indefinitely (as long as they are able to sterilize them). Thus in the late 1960s the weaker currencies such as sterling and the franc devalued, and the Deutsche mark adjusted too little; given the secular decline in U.S. competitiveness, the dollar was left seriously overvalued. Since there was no mechanism to devalue the dollar unilaterally, the United States had to declare a "force majeur" and impose an adjustment of rates at the Smithsonian Conference in 1971 (which actually proved to be insufficient).

---

91. Houthakker and Magee (1969).

The paper makes enjoyable reading because it is something like watching a tragedy when we in the audience, who know how the story must end, feel superior as we ponder the follies of the characters struggling to deny their inevitable fate. There were indeed numerous internal contradictions in the Bretton Woods system, and inevitably one of these was going to bring the system down. But actually dealing with the contradictions was too painful or impossible to do while preserving the system, so the participants sought refuge in a variety of smaller measures that were ineffective. And the numerous measures that Barry recounts do look like they were something akin to rearranging the deck chairs on the Titanic. But before we bandy about the notion that these were "malign" policies, we need to consider the counterfactual. Would the world have actually been better off if the United States had been willing to take more decisive actions to deal with its balance of payments problems?

Presumably these actions could have taken one of three forms: adjustments in exchange rates, or changes in macroeconomic or microeconomic arrangements. One option would have been to direct U.S. monetary or fiscal policy more forcefully to meet the requirements of external balance. But first recall the Triffin dilemma, which pointed to the central clash between the requirement of maintaining confidence in the convertibility of the dollar into gold on the one hand, and providing sufficient liquidity to a growing world economy on the other. This dilemma implied that the United States would inevitably cause difficulties. If it acted to reduce its balance of payments deficit dramatically, it would deprive the world of reserves. If it continued to run large deficits, it would undermine confidence in the dollar's convertibility into gold. More decisive adjustment on the part of the United States would have meant fewer reserves in the system. In combination with the system's asymmetries, this would actually have forced other deficit countries to adjust more rapidly.

Moreover, it is now clear that to maintain the fixed dollar exchange rate, as of the late 1960s, the United States would have had to have a real depreciation of a significant order of magnitude. Some combination of much lower U.S. inflation and much higher foreign inflation would have been required under fixed rates. Perhaps making some of this adjustment in the mid-1960s would not have been such a bad idea for domestic reasons, but as Barry notes, there were strong political reasons why this did not take place. Had the adjustment been applied by the late 1960s, it would have required macroeconomic policies that were even tighter than those applied and would probably have meant a very deep recession in the early 1970s.

The alternative was to have higher inflation abroad. But there were already considerable inflationary pressures in the early 1970s (from 1968 to 1970, European inflation accelerated from 3.22 to 5.0 percent).

The second option was to let the exchange rate move earlier and not wait until 1971, when the United States was forced to make a move. Of course, this would not have been easy. But would the late 1960s have been a more prosperous period if the floating rate system had existed earlier? It is hard to imagine that. A weaker dollar would surely have meant initially more inflationary pressures in the United States and required tighter policies in the United States to offset this. Would the rest of the world have been prepared to supply more domestic stimulus in response to their stronger currencies? To be sure, the case for a weaker dollar was stronger in 1970 once the U.S. economy had slowed down and European inflation had accelerated.

The third choice was actually to try to do more in the way of interfering with international trade or capital movements. Indeed, there were those in the United States who advocated additional and tighter controls. Again, as is now clear, these controls might have had to become progressively tighter. Surely the best thing that can be said about the measures that were adopted is that they were not particularly effective. Making them more effective would have required the United States to become increasingly protectionist, and the good thing about this period, as Dick Cooper notes in his paper, was the progress in trade liberalization that was made at the Kennedy Round. Indeed the term "malignant preoccupation" best applied to the actions of John Connaly in unilaterally violating U.S. GATT commitments with a 10 percent import surcharge.

In sum, I think it worth stating that the outcome was not all that bad. *'T wasn't really a tragedy after all.* The Bretton Woods system had serious flaws, but it gave the world two very prosperous decades. Even at the time, its weaknesses were appreciated. The United States could play a crucial role at the center of that system, but only as long as the flaws remained manageable. It was inevitable, however, with even the most benign of U.S. policies, that the system would fail once private markets were freed to override official forbearance.

Finally I think the paper might also have noted that U.S. policymakers did devote considerable effort to trying to patch up the system. Most of the work, of course, went into dealing with the issue of reserves, rather than the adjustment mechanism. But those efforts do suggest that U.S. policymakers who played a major role in the discussion and implementation of the

SDR were actually less neglectful than might have been implied in Barry Eichengreen's paper.

COMMENT BY
Jeffrey Sachs

One is bound to learn a lot of history in a paper by Barry Eichengreen, and this one is no exception.[92] Eichengreen takes us on a veritable blow-by-blow account of the U.S. balance of payments in the 1960s and the policy debate surrounding it, in order to illuminate the devaluation of the dollar in 1971 and the collapse of the Bretton Woods par value system. As the judicious economic historian that he is, Eichengreen finds that several factors played into the ultimate collapse of the dollar: growing real overvaluation, excessive monetary expansion compared with U.S. trade partners, unwillingness of the United States to subordinate its domestic policies to balance of payments considerations, and fundamental weaknesses of the Bretton Woods par value system. Indeed, if I have any complaint with the paper, it is overjudiciousness: as all hypotheses are allowed their due, too little is done to test the *relative importance* of the various explanations. To my own taste, Eichengreen overemphasizes U.S. competitiveness factors and underemphasizes the fundamental weakness of the dollar-gold system that lay at the heart of the Bretton Woods arrangements.

The Bretton Woods system that collapsed in August 1971 had two main features. First, it was an adjustable-peg exchange rate system, in which the exchange rates were expected to be stable most of the time, and to change only on extraordinary occasions. Second, the world's nominal aggregates (price level, money supplies, and so forth) were anchored loosely by gold, in the sense that the U.S. dollar was to remain stable in terms of gold at $35 per ounce, while all other currencies were to remain stable vis-à-vis the U.S. dollar. There were three main points of vulnerability of this system. First, the relative fixity of exchange rates, except in extraordinary circum-

---

92. It is a great privilege to participate in this memorial volume for Arthur Okun, who was mentor, inspiration, and deeply valued friend in my early days in the economics profession. One of my first dreams in studying economics as a freshman at Harvard College was that someday I might be able to publish a paper in Art Okun and George Perry's *Brookings Papers on Economic Activity.* That dream came true early on in my career, and I am forever grateful.

stances that could be met by devaluation or revaluation, meant that real exchange rate pressures (coming, for example, from differences in productivity growth or shifts in global demand) had to be resolved mainly through differential inflation rates of the various countries rather than through changes in the nominal exchange rates. A country with an overvalued currency in real terms was generally expected to slow the economy, and reduce price inflation, relative to its competitors. Devaluation was a last resort.

The second vulnerability was the one identified by Robert Triffin and discussed briefly, but too briefly, in Eichengreen's paper. A growing world economy, with at least modest price inflation on average, would have a growing demand for money related to the growth of nominal incomes. This would require a growth of the U.S. money supply and a growth in foreign demand for U.S. monetary reserves, both in the private sector and in the central banks charged with maintaining par values of the currency. The U.S. dollar, in turn, was still expected to be convertible into gold by foreign governments at the fixed rate of $35 per ounce. Triffin early on noted that there was no reason to expect that the physical stock of monetary gold, valued at the fixed price of $35 per ounce, would grow at a sufficient rate to support the secular rise in demand for monetary assets. He expected, indeed, that the U.S. money stocks would grow faster than gold, putting into doubt the convertibility of the dollar into gold.

The third vulnerability, linked to the second, was the asymmetric position of the U.S. dollar in the system. Since gold supplies would not automatically keep up with monetary demand, steps were taken from the earliest days to weaken the gold-dollar linkages, while not abandoning it altogether. Most notably, the United States did not undertake to convert private dollar holdings into gold. It also discouraged its trading partners from actually drawing upon the U.S. gold stocks through conversions of dollar reserves. And eventually, albeit briefly, the United States and Europe tried to separate more completely the private markets for gold and the official rights of dollar-gold exchange by allowing the private market price of gold to rise well above the $35 per ounce set in the Bretton Woods system. But to the extent that the dollar was implicitly or explicitly severed from gold, the asymmetry meant that it was the United States alone that set the monetary anchor, or lack of anchor, for the world. The United States could in effect ratchet up the world's inflation rate at will, by running an expansionary U.S. monetary policy untethered by a strong commitment to convert dollars to gold.

Eichengreen essentially argues that all three problems grew in the 1960s, and somehow came to a collective head in 1971, putting most weight (and I think excessive weight) on the first factor relative to the other two. The United States was becoming more and more overvalued in real terms, meaning that the dollar would have to depreciate or that foreign inflation would have to be significantly higher than in the United States. Gold stocks were under pressure, signaled by the tendency of the private price of gold to rise above $35 per ounce all through the 1960s. And the asymmetric ability of the United States to set the monetary tone for the world became more evident, and more troubling, as the U.S. inflation rates tended to rise in the late 1960s, prompting Germany to revalue the currency at the end of the 1960s.

I think it would have added to the pith of the paper to have scrutinized these alternatives more sharply for their relative contributions. It matters. The breakup of the Bretton Woods system was very costly, and the resulting floating rate system in which we operate has clear limitations as well. Could the breakup of a par value system have been avoided by one or more technical fixes, or was it fundamentally flawed? Was the problem basically the antiquated reliance on gold, which might have been resolved by introduction of a truly man-made monetary standard, such as the SDR if it had not arrived so late in the day? Was the problem basically that real exchange rates between major trading regions need the freedom to change, so that flexible exchange rates are the least costly way to achieve those changes? Was the problem the excessive power accorded to the United States under the Bretton Woods system to set the world's monetary conditions, in which case the SDR or some variant might also have achieved a more balanced set of arrangements (though this begs the question of whether the United States would have agreed to live under such constraints)?

By telling the story so much in terms of the specific conjunctural features of the late 1960s, Eichengreen gives us critical evidence on these issues, but does not leave us with the bigger picture. The issues are not going away, to be sure. The large swings between the dollar, the euro, and the yen, seemingly untethered in many cases to fundamentals, continue to suggest that the current arrangements could be improved upon. Eichengreen's paper takes us part of the way toward understanding what went wrong the last time a global system was constructed, but it does not take us as far as we need to go.

References

Bakker, Age. 1994. "The Liberalization of Capital Movements in Europe: The Monetary Committee and Financial Integration, 1958–1994." Ph.D. dissertation, University of Amsterdam.

Bank for International Settlements. 1962. *Annual Report.* Basle.

Bator, Francis M. 1968. "The Political Economics of International Money." *Foreign Affairs* 47 (October): 51–67.

Bergsten, C. Fred. 1975. *The Dilemmas of the Dollar: The Economics and Politics of United States International Monetary Policy.* New York University Press.

Block, Fred L. 1977. *The Origins of International Economic Disorder: A Study of United States International Monetary Policy from World War II to the Present.* University of California Press.

Board of Governors of the Federal Reserve System. (Various years). *Annual Report.*

Bordo, Michael D. 1993. "The Bretton Woods International Monetary System: An Historical Overview." In *A Retrospective on the Bretton Woods System,* edited by Michael D. Bordo and Barry Eichengreen, 3–108. University of Chicago Press.

Bordo, Michael D., and Barry Eichengreen, eds. 1993. *A Retrospective on the Bretton Woods System.* University of Chicago Press.

Campagna, Anthony S. 1987. *U.S. National Economic Policy, 1917–1985.* Praeger.

Cooper, Richard. 1993. "Comment." In *A Retrospective on the Bretton Woods System,* edited by Michael D. Bordo and Barry Eichengreen, 104–107. University of Chicago Press.

Council of Economic Advisers. 1966. *Economic Report to the President, 1966.* Government Printing Office.

Darby, Michael R., James R. Lothian, and others. 1983. *The International Transmission of Inflation.* University of Chicago Press.

Duncan, Evan, David S. Patterson, and Carolyn Yee, eds. 1998. *Foreign Relations of the United States, 1964–1968, vol. VIII, International Monetary and Trade Policy.* Government Printing Office.

Eichengreen, Barry. 1996. *Globalizing Capital: A History of the International Monetary System.* Princeton University Press.

Eichengreen, Barry, and Olivier Jeanne. 1998. "Currency Crisis and Unemployment: Sterling in 1931." Working Paper 6563. Cambridge, Mass.: National Bureau of Economic Research (May).

Elliott, Graham, and John H. Rogers. 1999. "Borders and the Persistence and Volatility of Relative Prices." University of California at San Diego and Board of Governors of the Federal Reserve Board System, Division of International Finance.

Federal Reserve Bank of Philadelphia. 1970. *Defending the Dollar.* Philadelphia.

Fieleke, Norman S. 1969. "The Buy-American Policy of the United States Government: Its Balance-of-Payments and Welfare Effects." *New England Economic Review* (July/ August): 2–18.

Fried, Edward R. 1971. "The Financial Cost of Alliance." In *U.S. Troops in Europe: Issues, Costs, and Choices,* edited by John Newhouse, 102–44. Brookings.

Genberg, Hans, and Alexander K. Swoboda. 1993. "The Provision of Liquidity in the Bretton Woods System." In *A Retrospective on the Bretton Woods System,* edited by Michael D. Bordo and Barry Eichengreen, 269–306. University of Chicago Press.

Gowa, Joanne S. 1983. *Closing the Gold Window: Domestic Politics and the End of Bretton Woods.* Cornell University Press.

Hirsch, Fred, and Michael W. Doyle. 1977. "Politicization in the World Economy: Necessary Conditions for an International Economic Order." In *Alternatives to Monetary Disorder,* edited by Fred Hirsch, Michael W. Doyle, and Edward L. Morse, 9–64. McGraw Hill.

Hitch, Charles J. 1965."Testimony." In *Balance of Payments–1965.* Hearings before a Subcommittee of the Committee on Banking and Currency, United States Senate, 89 Cong. 1 sess., Part 1, pp. 1–10. Government Printing Office.

Houthakker, Hendrik S., and Stephen P. Magee. 1969. "Income and Price Elasticities in World Trade." *Review of Economics and Statistics* 51 (May): 111–25.

Hyson, Charles D., and Alan M. Strout. 1968. "Impact of Foreign Aid on U.S. Exports." *Harvard Business Review* 46 (January-February): 63–71.

International Monetary Fund. 1966. *Annual Report.* Washington: IMF.

Javits, Jacob. 1968. "Steps to Strengthen Confidence in the Dollar." *Congressional Record* 114, part 4, pp. 4548–52 (February 28).

Johnson, Harry G. 1966. "Balance-of-Payments Controls and Guidelines for Trade and Investment." In *Guidelines, Informal Controls, and the Market Place: Policy Choices in a Full Employment Economy,* edited by George P. Shultz and Robert Z. Aliber, 165–82. University of Chicago Press.

Kettl, Donald F. 1986. *Leadership at the Fed.* Yale University Press.

Krugman, Paul. 1979. "A Model of Balance-of-Payments Crises." *Journal of Money, Credit and Banking* 11 (August): 311–25.

Levin, Andrew, and Chien-Fu Lin. 1992. "Unit Root Tests in Panel Data: Asymptotic and Finite-Sample Properties." University of California at San Diego.

Lindert, Peter H. 1971. "The Payments Impact of Foreign Investment Controls." *Journal of Finance* 26 (December): 1083–99.

McKinnon, Ronald I. 1993. "Bretton Woods, the Marshall Plan, and the Postwar Dollar Standard." In *A Retrospective on the Bretton Woods System,* edited by Michael D. Bordo and Barry Eichengreen, 597–604. University of Chicago Press.

Meltzer, Allan H. 1966. "The Regulation of Bank Payments Abroad, Another Failure for the Government's Balance-of-Payments Program." In *Guidelines, Informal Controls, and the Market Place,* edited by George P. Shultz and Robert Z. Aliber, 183–206. University of Chicago Press.

———. 1991. "U.S. Policy in the Bretton Woods Era." *Federal Reserve Bank of St. Louis Review* 73 (May/June): 54–83.

Mikesell, Raymond F. 1970. *The U.S. Balance of Payments and the International Role of the Dollar.* Washington: American Enterprise Institute.

Morawetz, David. 1971. "The Effect of Financial Capital Flows and Transfers on the U.S. Balance of Payments Current Account." *Journal of International Economics* 1 (November): 417–28.

Okun, Arthur M. 1963."Monetary Policy, Debt Management and Interest Rates: A Quantitative Appraisal." In *Stabilization Policies, A Series of Studies Prepared for the Commission on Money and Credit,* 331–80. Prentice Hall.

Prachowny, Martin F. J. 1969. *A Structural Model of the U.S. Balance of Payments.* Amsterdam: North Holland.

Roosa, Robert V. 1967. *The Dollar and World Liquidity.* Random House.

Salant, Walter S., and others. 1963. *The United States Balance of Payments in 1968.* Brookings.

Shultz, George P., and Kenneth W. Dam. 1977. *Economic Policy Beyond the Headlines.* University of Chicago Press.

Sohmen, Egon. 1963. "International Monetary Problems and the Foreign Exchanges." *Special Papers in International Economics* 4. Princeton University, International Finance Section, Department of Economics.

Solomon, Robert. 1982. *The International Monetary System 1945–1981.* Harper & Row.

Soskice, David. 1996. "German Technology Policy, Innovation, and National Institutional Frameworks." Discussion Paper FSI 96–319. Berlin: Wissenschaftszentrum Berlin für Sozialforschung.

Triffin, Robert. 1947. "National Central Banking and the International Economy." *Postwar Economic Studies* 79: 46–81.

U.S. Bureau of the Census. 1975. *Historical Statistics of the United States, Colonial Times to 1970.* Government Printing Office.

Wigmore, Barrie A. 1987. "Was the Bank Holiday of 1933 Caused by a Run on the Dollar?" *Journal of Economic History* 47 (September): 739–55.

Willett, Thomas D. 1980. *International Liquidity Issues.* Washington: American Enterprise Institute.

PART III

Labor Markets and Distribution

ROBERT HAVEMAN

7

Poverty and the Distribution of Economic Well-Being Since the 1960s

M y, how things change! In the mid-1960s, America was experiencing a period of sustained economic growth, rising real wages, and low unemployment; the fruits of prosperity were widely visible. It was after the Korean War and before the Vietnam War had heated up. One of the nation's primary public policy issues was "poverty," and numerous pieces of legislation backed by appropriations were making their way through Congress and on to the president's desk.

Today, at the beginning of a new millennium, the nation is again experiencing a period of sustained prosperity. However, unlike the mid-1960s, such issues as easing capital gains taxation, reducing the marriage penalty, granting broad-based tax relief, enforcing work for low-income benefit recipients, and ensuring that social insurance and medical benefits for the older population are maintained, occupy center stage. The nation's poverty problem is off the table, and economic inequality seems of little concern, despite its dramatic increase.

This paper revisits issues about which Arthur Okun felt deeply and wrote elegantly. *Equality and Efficiency: The Big Tradeoff* addressed a subject

Gary Burtless and Larry Katz provided very insightful comments; the paper is improved because of them. The helpful research assistance of Jonathan Schwabisch and Michael Oakleaf is gratefully acknowledged, as is the typing support of Dawn Duren and the editorial assistance of Jan Blakeslee. The Institute for Research on Poverty and the La Follette School of Public Affairs provided supportive intellectual environments.

broached by few mainstream economists at that time. Blending values and analytical rigor, its message and relevance are no less important today than they were then; it stands as a classic.[1]

In this paper, I review the evolution of thinking on and policy toward the problems of poverty and inequality over the last forty years. I begin by discussing the facts of changing poverty and inequality patterns since the 1960s (and some of the factors underlying these changes). Then, in the second and third sections, I review the changes in "received wisdom" regarding the poverty problem and in the evolution of social policy over this period.

Although economic performance played an important role in reducing poverty before the mid-1970s, it lost its bite during the two decades that followed. Has the recent expansion again led to a decline in poverty? I present some recent evidence on this question in the next-to-last section. I conclude with a few comments about the future: the issues that the nation is likely to face in this area and some possible approaches to them.

Changing Poverty and Inequality Patterns since 1960: The Facts

The nation's declaration of a "War on Poverty" in 1965 came during a long period of postwar economic growth, with rising productivity and wages and declining inequality. This section reviews trends in the prevalence of poverty in the nation since 1960, as well as how changes in society and the labor market have affected these trends.

The Trend in Poverty since 1960

As figure 7-1 shows, in the years preceding announcement of the War on Poverty, the poverty rate had been falling in line with this growth and prosperity.[2] The War on Poverty initiative started fast, and progress was made.

---

1. Okun (1975).

2. These figures are based on the official national definition of poverty in which a family's cash income is compared to a cutoff line designed to reflect the consumption needs of families of various sizes and structures. The official poverty line in 1998 was $16,660 for a family of four; the cutoffs for larger families are greater than this value and are less for smaller families. Because the poverty thresholds are only updated annually for inflation based on changes in the Consumer Price Index, the 1998 value has essentially the same purchasing power as that for 1959 ($2,973). See Citro and Michael

Figure 7-1. *People in Poverty, 1959–98*

Percent in poverty

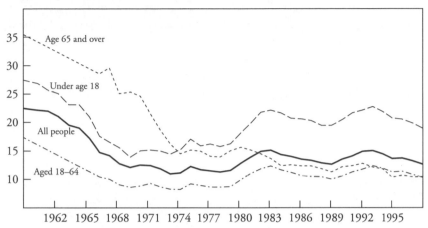

Source: U.S. Census, *Historical Poverty Tables*, 1959–98.

The overall poverty rate fell from 17.3 percent in 1965, when the War on Poverty was declared, to 11.1 percent in 1973. In that year, roughly 23 million Americans were poor, 42 percent fewer than in 1959. This decrease in the overall rate was fueled by the decreased poverty rate for the elderly, which declined faster than that for the other groups identified in figure 7-1 (children and those aged 18 to 64). The elderly poverty rate fell from about 35 percent in 1959 to about 25 percent in 1970, and to 16 percent by 1973.

Since 1973, however, the nation's overall poverty rate has never again reached the low 11.1 percent level attained in that year. By 1975, the overall rate had increased to 12.3 percent, and then oscillated around 11.6 per-

---

(1995, chapter 1) for a more detailed description of the official measure. A recent National Academy of Sciences (NAS) panel report on the measurement of poverty recommends a new measure based on a more comprehensive measure of a family's access to resources—including adding the money refunds from the earned income tax credit and some in-kind public benefits to, and subtracting taxes from, resources available for consumption. See Citro and Michael (1995). Short, Garner, Johnson, and Doyle (1999) have experimented with a number of variants of a new poverty measure based on the NAS proposals. In general, the adjustments that are reflected in these measures do not substantially alter the overall poverty trends described below, though the reduction in poverty in the post-1993 period is somewhat greater than reflected in the official measure.

cent during the remainder of the 1970s, as real wage and productivity growth virtually came to a halt after the oil crises. This stagnation in the overall rate reflects quite divergent trends in the rates of the population subgroups in the figure. The elderly poverty rate continued falling throughout the 1970s, while the children's rate and that for prime-aged adults drifted up over the period.

In the early 1980s, the most severe recession since the 1930s occurred, and the overall poverty rate rose to 15.2 percent. The increase in the poverty rate for children was discouraging during this period; by 1985, it exceeded 20 percent. The rate for prime-age citizens also rose substantially during the first half of the 1980s.

Following the recession of the early 1980s, employment rose and civilian unemployment fell (from 9.7 percent in 1982 to 5.6 percent in 1990). However, the real wages of low- and medium-skilled males continued the erosion that had begun in the mid-1970s. In 1985, the inflation-adjusted income of the typical full-time male worker was below the level it had been in 1970. Among educated and skilled workers, however, wage rates and earnings grew rapidly, resulting in an increase in earnings inequality (see below).

While the poverty rate edged down following the recession, it stood at more than 13 percent when the recession of the early 1990s set in. The children's poverty rate remained stalled at around 20 percent for the entire decade from 1985 to 1995.

During the recession of the early 1990s, the overall poverty rate rose again, reaching the 15 percent mark in 1993. Between 1973 and 1992, the number of people officially classified as poor increased from 23 million to 38 million persons. During this entire period, the poverty rate for the elderly continued to edge down, falling from about 13 percent in 1985 to about 11 percent by the mid-1990s. After the mid-1980s, the poverty rate for the elderly was lower than the overall national rate, and by the mid-1990s it had fallen below the rate of working-age people.

During the prolonged expansion following 1992, the overall poverty rate and the rates of the subgroups drifted down steadily; the overall rate stood at 12.7 percent in 1998, the last year for which data are available.[3]

---

3. In spite of the recent decrease in the nation's overall poverty rate since the early 1990s, there is some evidence that the rate of "deep poverty" families—primarily, mother-only families living below, say, one-half of the poverty line—has actually increased during the current expansion. See Primus and others (1999).

The poverty rate for both the elderly and the working-aged was slightly in excess of 10 percent, while the children's poverty rate still hovered around the 20 percent level.

Social and Economic Trends since 1960 and the Prevalence of U.S. Poverty

This evolution in the nation's official poverty rate since 1960 reflects a wide variety of social, economic, and policy developments that occurred along the way. Understanding these changes, and their effect on the official measure, is necessary in accurately interpreting the nation's progress against poverty over this period.

CHANGES IN EARNINGS AND INCOME INEQUALITY. Beginning in the early 1970s—and accelerating after 1980—all indices of inequality in male wage rates and earnings increased substantially, a phenomenon that ran counter to both past experience and expectations and led to a search for explanations.[4] The earnings spread among working-age males increased by over 17 percent during the 1973–91 period, as revealed by analyses using the variance in the log of earnings as the indicator of inequality.[5]

Year	Variance in Logarithm of Earnings
1973 (peak)	1.11
1975 (trough)	1.18
1988 (peak)	1.29
1991 (trough)	1.30

In addition to the overall increase in earnings inequality, the gap between workers with more and less education and skill also increased, as did the gap

---

4. Evidence supported some role for each of a large number of changed institutions or environments that could have led to an increasing relative demand for high-education and high-skill workers. These included the declining influence of trade unions, the reduced manpower demands of the military, the growth in the demand for high-skill workers induced by changes in technology and the spread of computers, an increase in trade and global competition, the rapid growth of the female and immigrant work forces, and the perceived declining quality of U.S. elementary and secondary schooling. Studies that have documented and attempted to explain this post-1973 increase in wage and earnings inequality are Levy and Murnane (1992); Burtless (1990); Moffitt (1990); Karoly (1993); Heckman, Lochner, and Taber (1998a); and Haveman and Buron (1999).

5. See Haveman and Buron (1999).

between younger and older workers. This was the period when the baby boom generation entered the work force, and as it did, older workers prospered while younger workers saw their relative earnings fall. The earnings premium received by a college graduate, relative to a worker with a high school degree or less, increased from about 30 percent in the 1970s to over 60 percent by the early 1990s. This focus on gaps, however, masks the absolute deterioration of earnings for those workers with few skills or low education. Since the early 1970s, the hourly wage rate for a man with a high school degree but no more has fallen in real terms by about 35 percent.

Moreover, in a quite distinct break from the early postwar period, when the average production worker's real hourly earnings grew about 2.1 percent per year, the hourly earnings of the average worker actually *fell* by about 0.3 percent per year from 1973 to 1991.[6] The increase in male work patterns and joblessness from 1973 to the early 1990s reinforced these real wage and inequality patterns.[7] Clearly these labor market developments play an important role in understanding the floor that the poverty rate seemed to encounter after the early 1970s.

THE INCREASED "ATOMIZATION" OF U.S. HOUSEHOLDS. Over the past forty years, living alone or in family arrangements other than the two-parent family with children has become increasingly prevalent. The growth of mother-only families with children is only one prominent aspect of this change (see below). Apart from any real effect of this change on people's well-being, this trend has a statistical effect that is reflected in the overall

6. The basic cause of the sharp decline in average earnings growth is the fall in the rate of productivity growth, to which gains in average compensation are ultimately tied. From 1948 to 1973, output per worker in the U.S. business sector increased nearly 2.9 percent per year; from 1973 to the early 1990s, the average gain has been about 1 percent per year. While this pattern explains why average earnings growth has been so anemic, it leaves unanswered the question of why the rate of productivity growth has stagnated since the early 1970s. A number of studies have attempted to determine the causes of the productivity slowdown; however, there has been no general agreement among them. The factors identified range from aggregate economic conditions to structural considerations such as the two oil crises in the 1970s, the changing demographic composition of the labor force, changes in education, training and R & D expenditures, changes in international trade patterns, and the increased costs imposed on private activities because of public regulations, especially in the environmental area. See Denison (1985).

7. See Haveman and Buron (1999). During this period, joblessness among working-age males increased from 7.4 percent to 13 percent. About 50 percent of out-of-school youth aged 16 to 24 years old without a high school degree were not employed in 1991. There was also an increase in the prevalence of part-time work, both among year-round and part-year workers. Whereas in 1973 about 13 percent of all working-age males were either not working or working part-time, by 1991, 22 percent of all males were either jobless or working part-time.

poverty trend. Because of the way the official poverty measure reflects the consumption needs and sizes of families, the separation of a nonpoor family into two households may result in one or both of them being counted as poor.[8] Thus the "atomization" trend among U.S. households contributes to the stagnation of the poverty rate over the last three decades.

THE EFFECT OF INCREASED IMMIGRATION. Along with the changes in family size and structure has come a substantial change in the demographic composition of the nation's population, especially those at the bottom of the economic ladder. Perhaps the most prominent such change relates to the rapid growth of the foreign-born population. Since 1970, the United States has admitted approximately 20 million immigrants; in addition, several million more illegal immigrants have entered the country.[9] These recent additions to the nation's population have less education and fewer skills than earlier immigrants, and a high proportion—up to one-quarter by some estimates—of them are recorded as officially poor. This growth of the immigrant population, and their concentration at the bottom of the nation's income distribution, has also contributed to the slow official progress against poverty since the early 1970s.

POLICY SHIFTS AND THE OFFICIAL POVERTY MEASURE. Large shifts in public policy toward the poor are also reflected in the official poverty trend (see below). The rapid decrease in the poverty rate during the 1960s and early 1970s reflected the focus of national attention on the nation's elderly population. Social Security retirement benefits became more generous in real terms, and the coverage of many of the nation's poorest elderly expanded. Disability benefits were introduced in the 1950s, and both benefits and coverage from this source also expanded. At the same time as War on Poverty measures were put into place in the mid-1960s, cash support to single parents through traditional welfare programs was liberalized, and take-up rates grew rapidly. However, after the mid-1970s, these trends stopped short and cash assistance actually eroded. While some elements of

---

8. The poverty lines in the official measure incorporate "economies of scale" in living arrangements that reflect the fact that living together requires less than twice as much as living apart. The specific scales used in the official measure indicate that the combined incomes of the former spouses of a divorced couple who live separately would have to rise by at least 50 percent (and be divided equally) in order to maintain their standard of living.

9. This compares to about 7 million immigrants admitted to the country in the four decades before 1970.

income support continued to grow, by and large these provided help in the form of in-kind benefits; food stamps and Medicaid are two prominent examples. While these programs provide support for the nation's poor, their benefits are not in the form of cash and hence are not reflected in the poverty rate. While the substitution of in-kind for cash benefits to low-income families may not adversely affect the overall well-being of the poor, it would lead to an increase in the number of families captured by the official statistical measure. This policy twist has also contributed to the stickiness of the nation's poverty during the past three decades.[10]

Winners and Losers: 1960–97

The persistence of poverty since the early 1970s camouflages substantial changes in the composition of poverty over the period.[11] Demographic changes, the uneven changes in production processes and factor markets, and changes in public policy have reduced poverty for some groups, while driving the incomes of other groups below the poverty line.

In the paragraphs that follow, I first discuss the two primary groups that experienced declines in the official poverty rate. Then I discuss three groups whose economic position deteriorated over this period. The changes in the poverty rates of these groups explain the primary shifts in the composition of the nation's poor population over this period. Many of these patterns are summarized in table 7-1.

THE WINNERS. While several socioeconomic groups have moved up in the nation's income distribution, prominent among the recent winners are the elderly and African Americans who live in intact families.

The elderly. The economic plight of the elderly in the 1960s was an important catalyst for the War on Poverty effort. Because of low earnings during working years, negligible accumulated savings, virtually nonexistent private pension plans for low-wage workers, and a Social Security system

10. A further issue in the nation's official poverty measure is the price index problem. Recent estimates, culminating in the report of the Boskin Commission, have indicated that the official consumer price index may overstate the actual rate of price increase by at least one 1 percentage point per year, especially during the past twenty-five years. See U.S. Senate, Advisory Commission to Study the Consumer Price Index (1996). Because the official poverty thresholds are annually adjusted by the consumer price index, they may be increasing faster than the "true" poverty lines, biasing upward the trend in the official poverty measure.

11. The discussion in this section updates that in Haveman (1988).

Table 7-1. *Economic Status of Various Groups, 1959–97*

Economic status by group	1959	1967	1970	1980	1990	1997
Poverty Rates						
Elderly	35.2	29.5	24.6	15.7	12.2	10.5
African American intact						
family	n.a.	31.3	n.a.	15.5	14.3	9.0
Mother-only with children	59.9	44.5	43.8	42.9	44.5	41.0
Children	27.3	16.6	15.1	18.3	20.6	19.9
Youth						
Unemployment rates[a]	n.a.	n.a.	3.4	3.4	3.5	3.6
Earnings[b]	n.a.	37	32	29	23	23

Source: U.S. Census Bureau, *Historical Poverty Tables—People*, table 3 [www.census.gov/hhes/poverty/histpov/hstpov3.html]; *Historical Poverty Tables—Families*, table 4 www.census.gov/hhes/poverty/histpov/hstpov4.html]; *Statistical Abstract of the United States* (various years), Civilian Labor Force—Employment Status by Sex, Race and Age; Current Population Survey microdata.

n.a. Not available.

a. Ratio of black male, aged 20 to 24, to aggregate male unemployment rates.

b. Ratio of mean earnings of full-time–full-year males, aged 15 to 24, to mean earnings of full-time–full-year males, aged 45 to 54.

that was far from universal in its coverage of new retirees, the elderly of the 1960s had low incomes and very high poverty rates.[12]

As figure 7-1 indicates, by the mid-1980s this was no longer the case; indeed, the average Social Security benefits of a retired worker grew from about $420 per month in 1970 to about $722 per month in 1984 (in 1997 dollars).[13] By then the poverty rate of elderly people had fallen below the national rate. It has remained there since. In 1997, the poverty rate of the elderly stood at about 10.5 percent. Although some elderly subgroups, notably nonwhite older people and widows, still experience higher poverty rates than the national average, no longer are the elderly considered to be one of the nation's vulnerable or insecure population groups. These gains in the economic status of the elderly can be attributed to the deliberate and rapid increases in public benefits largely through the Social Security retirement program targeted toward older people.

African American intact families. While the levels of insecurity and poverty remain far higher for African Americans and Hispanics than for

12. In 1966, for example, the poverty rate of the elderly was twice that of the overall national rate and the poverty rate for the black elderly was nearly four times the national rate.

13. Monthly benefits have remained virtually constant in real terms since 1984.

whites, there is a striking—though often overlooked—success story for racial minorities, especially those living in intact families. Take African Americans, for example. While they still earn less than whites in comparable positions, the gap between them has narrowed considerably. While the median African American male full-time-full-year worker earned only about 60 to 62 percent of the average white male worker in 1960, today the figure stands at about 75 percent. The gain is also dramatic for females.

These earnings gains have carried over to the income levels of families, in particular intact families with two potential earners. In 1960, average income for African American two-parent families stood at 64 percent of that of white intact families; today it is nearly 80 percent. From 1967 to 1980, the poverty rate for intact African American families with children fell from over 30 percent to about one-half of this level; by 1997, the poverty rate for these families stood at less than 10 percent, a figure that is below the overall national poverty rate.

These gains are impressive; progress has been made. Among the several factors that have contributed to these gains, the decreasing gaps in schooling attainment and in the quality of the schooling appear to be among the most important, accounting for at least one-half (and up to 80 percent) of the decrease in the earnings gap between African American and white males over this period.[14]

A second important factor in explaining this gain is the strong economic growth from the start of the 1960s to the late 1970s. Although historically racial minorities have been on the fringe of the labor market, this period was a relatively good one for them. Economic growth was strong, and many found jobs paying a wage that reflected their growing levels and quality of education. Although progress faltered after the late 1970s, the record of the 1960s and 1970s stands as a period of solid gains for racial minorities with a high school degree or some college.

Disparities in regional growth, and the willingness of racial minorities to respond to them, have also played an important role in the gains experienced by African Americans. During the 1950 to 1970 period, the northern states and their large cities tended to have stronger economies, more rapid growth, and smaller racial earnings differences, and many African

14. For example, African American men aged 26 to 35 had an average of 9 years of schooling in 1960, while the schooling level attained by young white men was 11.5 years, a 2.5-year difference. Today, white prime-aged men have an average of only about one-half-year more schooling than do their African American counterparts. On the effect of this reduction of education gaps on earnings, see Smith and Welch (1986).

Americans (and Hispanics) migrated to them. This also contributed to the overall narrowing of racial earnings differences.[15]

THE LOSERS: THE NEW POOR. The exit of the elderly and racial minorities (especially those living in intact families) from the bottom tail of the income distribution has left a vacuum that has been filled by other groups. These "new poor" are composed primarily of mother-only families, children, and youths (especially minority young men).

Families headed by single mothers. Families headed by single mothers form the most rapidly growing group living in poverty. By 1996, poor persons living in mother-only families constituted 42 percent of non-aged poor people, even though persons living in mother-only families are only about 15 percent of the nation's population. Indeed, today more than half of all poor families are headed by a single parent, nearly always a woman.[16]

Several factors explain the increase in the share of the poor that can be accounted for by these families. The most important reason is the rapid increase in the number of mother-only families over the past few decades, in line with the increase in both divorce rates and the rate of out-of-wedlock childbearing.[17]

With few exceptions, a mother-only family has but one potential wage earner. While two-parent families have supplemented the husband's (often eroding) earnings by the wife's increased work, this option is not open to mother-only families.[18] Even when the mother is working full-time, female earning stand at about two-thirds of male earnings; hence, the earning

15. The effect of civil rights legislation—affirmative action, in particular—on the earning power of racial minorities is unresolved among researchers. However, most now agree that a decline in discrimination, whether attributable to antidiscrimination policies or to other fundamental economic and social changes, has been an important factor in reducing racial income differences. See Smith and Welch (1986).

16. Over two-thirds of African American children who live in mother-only families are poor, and nearly 80 percent of all black children in poverty live only with their mothers.

17. The prevalence of teen nonmarital childbearing has been described as the nation's "most serious social problem," notably by President Bill Clinton ("State of the Union Message," 1995, http://web.lexis-nexis.com/universe/). More than one-half million children are now born to U.S. teenagers each year: about 13 percent of all births and nearly one-quarter of all African American births. This trend has been reinforced by the increasing trend in the number and rate of divorces. The 1960 divorce rate of 2.2 (per thousand) had increased to 3.5 in 1970 and to 5.2 in 1980, and it has remained about constant at 4.7 until the present. By 1997, nearly 25 percent of all families with children were mother-only families, up from less than 11 percent in 1970 (*Statistical Abstract*, various issues).

18. Indeed, the percentage of intact families with children who have two workers increased from 44 percent in 1967 to about 70 percent today. The percentage for African American intact families is nearly 80 percent.

power of a typical mother-only family is no more than half that of a similar intact family. Additionally, single mothers are burdened by child care responsibilities. When child care costs are subtracted from the earnings of single mothers with low education and few skills, there is little left for other necessary expenditures.[19] The effect of the rapid growth in the number of mother-only families on the national poverty rate has been the subject of several studies, not always with consistent findings.[20]

The erosion of the public safety net after the mid-1970s is another cause for the increase in the prevalence of poverty among mother-only families. Although the rhetoric of the 1960s was to offer the poor "a hand up" and not a "handout," the reduction in poverty in the late 1960s and early 1970s was due in large part to increased public spending on income transfers.[21] However, after 1973, real cash welfare benefits (Aid to Families with

19. Burtless (1994a, figure 4.5, p. 84) has estimated that the upper-bound of the market earnings of single mothers with the characteristics of those who have received welfare benefits is about $12,000 to $14,000 (in 1991 dollars), even if they were to work full-time-full-year. (In 1991, the poverty threshold for a family of four was $13,924.) This estimate is consistent with the findings of numerous recent studies that have tracked the earnings of single mothers who have left welfare after the 1996 welfare reform legislation.

20. Adopting a rather simple technique of assuming that poverty rates within categories of families described by marital status remain constant over a period of analysis, studies have found that these changes in family structure account for a large proportion of the increase in poverty from 1970 to the present. See Eggebeen and Lichter (1991) and Lerman (1995). Other studies have concluded that changes in family structure have not had a substantial effect on the poverty rate, especially relative to the changes in the labor market. One of the most detailed studies of the factors accounting for the increase in the number of poor persons during the 1980s (1979 to 1991) concluded that the overall increase in population accounted for 32 percent of the increase in the number of poor persons; changes in the race and headship structure of the population accounted for 26 percent; and decreases in the generosity of public transfer programs accounted for 28 percent. The remaining 14 percent was attributed to adverse changes in the receipt of private market income and federal tax policy changes. See U.S. House of Representatives, Committee on Ways and Means (1993, p. 113). More sophisticated approaches have attempted to measure the effect of changes in marital and headship patterns on the poverty rate, simultaneously controlling for the income and childbearing patterns related to these changes. In this research, researchers simulated marriages and the induced earnings responses to marriage. The results of these studies are, if anything, stronger than those of the more straightforward estimates—virtually all of the rise in the children's poverty rate during the 1970s and 1980s is attributed to the trend away from marriage among parents. See Gottschalk and Danziger (1993) and Lerman (1995). While both these studies focused on the effect of changing family structure on the rate of children's poverty, similar results, though perhaps slightly less strong, would have been found if the dependent variable being analyzed was the aggregate national poverty rate. It should also be noted that demographic factors and economic changes (unemployment and job loss, for example) are likely to be simultaneously determined. Treating either as exogenous could lead to biased estimates.

21. Public income transfers decreased the poverty gap by 53 percent in 1965 and by 64 percent in 1972. See Plotnick and Skidmore (1975, pp. 139–40). The poverty gap is defined as the total amount of money required to bring the income of every poor family up to the poverty line. Because income transfers have incentives that lead to reduced work effort, and because the poverty gap is based on a

Dependent Children, or AFDC) began to erode, and the erosion acceler-ated after 1980 (see below). Although the trends in other cash benefits tar-geted toward the poor were not as stark as those in the AFDC program,[22] the drop in public cash income support complements the effect of the atomization of families and the low earnings capabilities of mother-only families in explaining their increased prevalence among the poor.[23]

Children. These discouraging trends for mother-only families account for much of the growth in the number and percentage of the nation's chil-dren who live in poverty. When the War on Poverty began, the poverty rate of children younger than 18 was not much above that of the rest of the population (about 18 percent). Like the national poverty rate, the chil-dren's poverty rate fell until the early 1970s, when it reached a low of about 15 percent. Since then, there has been a steady increase in the children's poverty rate. By 1980, children were about 40 percent more likely to be liv-ing in poverty than the rest of the population; by 1997, the children's poverty rate stood at around 20 percent, about 150 percent of the national rate. Indeed, nearly 40 percent of the nation's poor are children.[24]

Low-education youths, especially minorities. The third group making up the "new poor" is youths, especially minority males aged 18 to 24. While it is not surprising that both earnings and employment levels for youths are below those of older workers, this pattern has become accentuated over the past two decades. In particular, wage-earnings profiles have become sub-stantially steeper over time.[25]

---

comparison of post-transfer income with a poverty line, this calculation may overstate the effects of transfers in reducing poverty.

22. While Supplemental Security Income (SSI) benefits dipped slightly during the early 1980s, substantial increases were recorded since the early 1970s. Rapid rises in both food stamp benefits (except for the retrenchment during the 1980s) and the earned income tax credit (EITC) also tended to offset the erosion in AFDC benefits over the post-1973 period (see below).

23. The failure of the court-administered U.S. child support system to effectively secure payment of awards made to single mothers has also contributed to the concentration of mother-only families in the poverty population. See Garfinkel and McLanahan (1986); Ellwood (1988); McLanahan and Sandefur (1994); Sorenson and Halpern (1999).

24. Children's poverty is not evenly distributed across the population; it is concentrated in partic-ular racial and family-type categories. For example, in 1997, when the poverty rate for all children was about 20 percent, the rate for African American and Hispanic children living in mother-only families was about 50 percent. For white children living in single-parent families, the rate was nearly 38 percent. Using data from the Luxembourg Income Study and a common poverty standard similar to the offi-cial U.S. norm, Timothy Smeeding (1992) found the children's poverty rate in the United States to be about three times that in other OECD countries, and trending in the opposite direction.

25. See Haveman (1988). For example, the earnings of full-time white male workers aged 18 to 24 who failed to complete high school relative to the earnings of similar workers aged 45 to 54 fell from 61 percent in 1960 to about 30 percent in 1996. (It must be recognized, however, that high school

These trends apply only to those who made it—those who actually got jobs. Over the past twenty-five years, a large and growing group of youths have been unsuccessful in the labor market. From 1970 to 1997, the unemployment rate of 16- to 19-year-old black men increased from 32 to 37 percent, or by nearly 16 percent. Over the same period, the unemployment rate for young white men edged up from 14 to 14.3 percent. Similar racial disparities are observed for young men aged 20 to 24.

Numerous factors have interacted to account for the deteriorating labor market performance of youths relative to adults—changes in the economy and the labor market, demographic trends, the attitudes and characteristics of youths, and the incentives that they confront. Disentangling the effect of these factors is devilishly difficult.

Youth are far more sensitive than adults to swings in labor demand; just entering the work force, they are a marginal group. For this reason, the fall in the relative economic position of youths has been accounted for in large part by the deterioration of the low end of the labor market since 1973.

While the demographic and labor force bulge created by the baby boom is often cited as a cause of the worsening earnings and unemployment experience of youth, this factor does not appear to have seriously affected the relative employment prospects of youths.[26] Two other demographic factors, however, may be relevant: new waves of immigration and the increasing labor force participation rates of women. There is some evidence that each of these influences has had an adverse effect on both the wages and the employment prospects of youths, especially on lower education and minority youths.[27]

A third factor contributing to the decline in youth labor market prospects comes from a surprising source—the military. The nation's military is dominated by young males, especially racial minorities. Since the

---

dropouts are a smaller share of the population today than in 1960, and probably a more negatively selected group. This could account for some of the decrease in this percentage over the period. However, for workers with a high school degree in these age groups, the ratio fell from 57 percent in 1960 to about 45 percent in 1990.)

26. See Betsey and others (1985); Freeman and Wise (1982); Freeman and Holzer (1986).

27. Legal immigration to the United States has increased from about 3.3 million in the 1961–70 decade, to 4.5 million in the 1971–80 decade, to 7.3 million in the 1981–90 decade. Currently, more than 1 million people immigrate to the United States each year. The composition of the immigrants has also changed radically. In the 1950s, 45 percent of immigrants came from Latin America, Mexico, and Asia; by the1980s, immigrants from these areas accounted for more than 90 percent of immigrants. In addition, there has been a major increase in the number of refugees and undocumented immigrants over the past decades. Most studies have concluded that immigration has adversely affected the labor market opportunities of other low-skilled workers, but that these effects are not substantial. See Tienda and Laing (1994), who review the research literature on the economic effects of immigration.

Vietnam War, and especially since the fall of communism, the size of the military has been reduced significantly, releasing many young minority males to the private labor market.[28]

Fourth, the relative shift of the job distribution toward high-tech jobs—skill-biased technological change—has adversely affected the wage and earnings prospects of those youths with less than a college education. Finally, the relatively adverse family, social, and neighborhood environments of many minority youth should be recognized as one of the important reasons why their labor market experiences have lagged behind those of equivalent majority youths. Minority youths are much more likely to come from families in which the parents have low education levels, low income, and a higher incidence of single parents, all of which appear to adversely affect youth performance.[29] Many are also disadvantaged by the broader social culture and high crime environments of the urban ghettos in which they grow up; over the past four decades the nation's poor have become increasingly concentrated in central cities.[30] At the same time, crime rates in these inner-city neighborhoods have risen (until recently), the quality of schools has eroded, and the levels of joblessness and dependency have increased. The impact of these changes on minority youth has been devastating; by the early 1990s, over 600,000 black men in their twenties (23 percent of the age group) were "under the control of the criminal justice system—in prison, in jail, or on probation or parole," and the homicide rate among black men is six to seven times higher than the rate among white men.[31]

"Received Wisdom" and the Poverty Problem

Since 1960, the views of scholars and other observers regarding the nature, causes, and cures of poverty have changed, sometimes radically. In some

28. See Freeman and Wise (1992); Freeman and Holzer (1986).

29. Evidence on the effects of family and neighborhood on the education and economic activity outcomes of young adults is found in Haveman and Wolfe (1994). William Julius Wilson (1987) has emphasized the "catastrophic" increase of behavioral problems and unproductive choices of African American youths that has grown out of the disintegration of racial enclaves in large U.S. cities. See also Freeman and Wise (1992), who found a variety of important links among attitudes, aspirations, the payoffs for criminal activities, and ultimate economic success.

30. In 1959, less than 27 percent of poor persons lived in central city areas; by 1998, over 43 percent of the poor were concentrated in central cities. This urban concentration of the poor has been documented by Jargowsky (1997).

31. The statistics on the prevalence of contact with the criminal justice system are from Duneier (1992, p. 25), who quotes the New York Times, "One in 4 Young Black Men is in Custody, a Study Says," October 4, 1990, p. 6.

cases, these views preceded developments in the nature of the poverty problem and antipoverty policy; in others, the received wisdom followed social and policy developments. In the following sections, I discuss the evolution of thought regarding the poverty problem since 1960.

The 1960s

During the 1960s, Americans seemed convinced that government could combine scientific thinking and resources to solve pressing national problems. For a complex set of reasons, poverty became one of those problems, and the federal government set out to wage war on it. The problem was identified, the best minds were gathered to address it, measurements of number and composition of the poor population were made, and a legislative agenda was prepared.[32] Assessing and understanding the War on Poverty effort was to occupy economists and other social scientists for decades.

There was no single prevailing doctrine that drove the antipoverty effort, as economists, sociologists, and other social scientists all had their say in the process. Although most observers saw economists as dominating the debate and formulating policy proposals, there was no unified economic point of view.

Perhaps the best characterization of economists' thinking was offered by Robert Lampman at the American Economics Association meetings in December 1964.[33] Lampman saw the poverty problem as multicausal, deriving from some combination of three main factors. First are *events external to individuals* (such as illness/disability, family dissolution, death of family breadwinner, unemployment). Second are *social barriers in the form of caste, class, and custom* (such as racial and gender discrimination, employer hiring procedures, union rules). Third is the *limited ability to earn* (such as inadequate skills needed for the market). Viewing the problem as multicausal led to a multipronged set of proposed policy interventions, and it is here that economists became separated.

---

32. As part of the antipoverty initiative, an income poverty line was set and made official and the federal government made the elimination of poverty a national target. As Lampman (1974) emphasized, the existence of the poverty line raised the question, "What does it do for the poor?" to a test for national policy. A case can be made—and indeed, has been—that the most important contribution of the War on Poverty era was the establishment of an official national poverty line. As James Tobin (1968, p. 83) put it, because of this official measure "[a]dministrations will be judged by their success or failure in reducing the . . . prevalence of poverty. . . . no politician will be able to . . . ignore the repeated solemn acknowledgments of society's obligation to its poorer members."

33. Lampman (1965).

The prevailing point of view among economists (and one that Lampman shared) was that external events were the major culprit, and among them unemployment was chief.[34] For most economists, then, improved macroeconomic performance could abolish cyclical unemployment and hence was the primary instrument for reducing poverty and securing widely distributed economic gains. Inflationary pressure that might be associated with expanding the economy was not given much attention, as the Phillips curve was viewed as relatively elastic.[35] Moreover, pressures leading to price increases could be reduced through complementary education and training efforts and regional measures, which would reduce the imbalance between available skills and employer demands ("structural unemployment").

Consistent with this perspective, any remaining poverty is beyond macroeconomic performance, the market, and education and training interventions, and hence a comprehensive income support system is also required. For economists from both ends of the political spectrum, the negative income tax was the program of choice.[36] The potential disincentive effects of generous income transfers tended to be dismissed by some[37] and fretted about by others.[38]

However, some economists (primarily labor economists) argued that the economy confronted serious structural imbalances, and hence that education and training measures should be the primary policy instrument. They were a distinct minority and tended to be derided by the majority.[39] The conflict between the two perspectives was reflected in the Office of

34. Lampman (1965, p. 525) stated, "Among the important events in this context the one most relevant to public policy . . . is excessive unemployment."

35. Edmund Phelps (1974, p. 31), in reviewing the 1960s, described the prevailing attitude among economists as reflecting the view "that within wide limits the norm of 'full employment' was what the nation wished to make it."

36. See Friedman (1962); Tobin, Pechman, and Mieszkowski (1967).

37. Harry Johnson (1965, pp. 544–45) emphasized the importance of "maintaining full employment," but went even further advocating generous use of transfers to the poor. "Such payments . . . would not seriously strain the resources of an economy as affluent as this one. . . . It is true that they would generate some waste, by [reducing work and encouraging fraud]; but waste is one of the main uses of resources that an affluent society can and does afford. . . ." He took Lampman to task for proposing a negative income tax with a low income guarantee, claiming to be "skeptical about the empirical" evidence on work disincentives that inhibited Lampman.

38. Rolph (1967).

39. Harry Johnson (1965, p. 544) stated, "[T]he stress now laid on education as the key to the poverty problem . . . is both seriously handicapped and forced into deviousness by the requirement that this . . . be accomplished in ways consistent with middle class morality."

Economic Opportunity (the federal antipoverty agency) and in the heavy emphasis on education and training measures in antipoverty legislation proposed by the Johnson administration.[40]

The 1970s

Less than a decade after the War on Poverty was initiated, the perspective of macroeconomists had shifted. By the mid-1970s, driving down the unemployment rate was seen to have potentially serious inflationary dangers; the Phillips curve, it seems, had become steeper. This revision in outlook was attributed in part to changes in labor force composition (including the rapid increase of women, teenagers, and those without prior work experience in the work force), which increased the natural rate of unemployment. Moreover, empirical research had indicated a lack of employer responsiveness in adjusting to changing labor market circumstances, and this undermined the view that labor markets with flexible wages would adjust quickly and smoothly to changes in the mix of skills supplied.

The advent of dual or radical theories of the labor market (with their emphasis on internal labor markets, job ladders, secondary labor markets, and other institutional constraints) supported these findings.[41] This erosion of faith in the flexible and smooth adjustment of labor markets seemed to fit the facts of the combination of high unemployment and high inflation that characterized the last half of the 1970s (the era of "stagflation"). The case that a consistent tradeoff relationship existed between unemployment and price changes became more difficult to make.

This focus on the difficulties of simultaneously attaining multiple goals was reflected in the microeconomic thinking of this period as well. In 1975, Arthur Okun's *Equality and Efficiency: The Big Tradeoff* appeared, and it carried much the same message. There is "no free lunch" in the quest for more equality; efficiency costs will be reaped and they must be recognized and confronted.

---

40. The basic strategy of the War on Poverty legislation was premised on the view that while economic growth would reduce poverty, the problem was primarily one of low labor market productivity. Hence the Job Corps, the Neighborhood Youth Corps, Head Start, Upward Bound, Follow Through, the National Teachers Corps, Neighborhood Health Centers, and Medicaid. The Community Action and Legal Services programs were established to restructure the social institutions by which the poor gained access to jobs and goods and services. See Plotnick and Skidmore (1975); Aaron (1978); Haveman (1987).

41. See Cain (1976) for both an exposition and a critique of this perspective.

During this era, the theme of "structural unemployment" was empha-sized by numerous pundits and commissions.[42] Most economists, however, viewed high and sticky unemployment as less a problem of certain groups being unable to find jobs (long-term, structural unemployment), and more a problem of job changes and long waiting periods of new entrants. The economists' view tended to undermine the case for education and training measures. The support for these policies was also undermined by the numerous evaluations of training interventions that found some success for a few groups, but little if any employment and earnings impacts for most groups. Benefit-cost tests were passed, but not by much.

During the 1970s, however, the economists' perspective on the merits of a universal, comprehensive transfer system as a replacement for the cate-gorical and piecemeal welfare system began to take hold. In 1969, the President's Commission on Income Maintenance Programs (the Heineman Commission) had recommended "a universal income supplement program to be administered by the Federal government."[43] At the start of the decade President Nixon had proposed his Family Assistance Plan (FAP), a negative income tax with a low income guarantee. The election of 1972 was in part fought over Democratic candidate George McGovern's proposal to replace existing welfare programs with a demogrant of $1,000 for each person. McGovern and his plan were roundly rejected, and the Family Assistance Plan failed in the Senate (having passed the House) because it was too con-servative for liberals and too liberal for conservatives.[44]

The defeat of FAP was overseen in the Senate by Russell Long of Louisiana. Long had another view of how support to low-income people should be provided; public support should be given only if people worked and earned. He called his proposal an earnings subsidy. In legislation, it was referred to as the earned income tax credit (EITC), and it was adopted in 1975 as an alternative to FAP.[45]

However, the basic idea of a minimum income guarantee did not die. President Carter resurrected it in his 1977 Program for Better Jobs and

42. These ranged from the U.S. Chamber of Commerce on the right, through a variety of labor economists, to the Ad Hoc Committee for the Triple Revolution on the left. See Aaron (1978), who discusses this concern with structural unemployment.

43. As reprinted in Marmor (1971, p. 183).

44. Another study by Aaron (1973), documenting the high cumulative marginal tax rates that would have existed with FAP, highlighted the growing concern with the labor supply effects of univer-sal income maintenance programs.

45. See Haveman, Mirer, and Lurie (1974); Haveman (1975).

Income (PBJI). Like FAP, it too ultimately failed after prolonged congressional debate. PBJI was the "last hurrah" for universal income maintenance proposals featuring a minimum income guarantee if no other income is available.

Although the economists' vision failed in the world of practice, policies toward poor families developed rapidly during the 1970s. By the end of the decade, the food stamp program—a minor half billion dollar effort to stabilize and support farm prices in 1970—had grown to a major program of assistance to all low-income families, regardless of their work status or the cause of their meager income. The coverage and benefits of Medicaid expanded, and real expenditures more than doubled from 1970 to 1980. Housing assistance for low-income families grew tenfold during the decade, and tax expenditures on the EITC increased rapidly (see below).

The 1980s

By the end of the 1970s, the conventional policy wisdom of the prior twenty years—that a combination of low unemployment, programs to provide training and education, and more generous income support would lead to a decrease in poverty—seemed to have little support. The nation was ready for a new view of the nature of the problems of poverty and inequality and the operation of the labor market. It did not have to wait long.

Already in the late 1970s, negative critiques of public redistribution and other social policy interventions had begun to strike a resonant chord. The disincentives that were incorporated in these programs (as well as the tax measures to support them) were seen by many as having adverse supply-side effects. In 1980 President Reagan was elected, citing "welfare queens," touting large work effort and savings gains from improved incentives and lower taxes, and promising to end stagflation by "getting the government off our backs."

In 1981 this revisionist view of the nature of poverty and government's approach to it appeared more formally as George Gilder's *Wealth and Poverty.*[46] In Gilder's view, the social policies enacted in the 1960s and 1970s undermined the functioning of the nation's basic institutions—family, church, community, and the workplace. They encouraged permissiveness and dependence, leading to marital breakup, nonmarital child-

46. Gilder (1981).

bearing, the substitution of institutional child care for that of mothers, youth joblessness, and the erosion of individual initiative and respect for others. Not long after, Charles Murray and Lawrence Mead added their support, emphasizing the incentives incorporated into social programs that encourage these dysfunctional behaviors.[47] In their view, those who have been assisted become alienated, and those who work but remain near-poor come to view themselves as "chumps."

These views had some support in research findings. In a 1984 study that was widely cited in support of retrenchment, Edgar Browning and William Johnson concluded that upper-income groups bearing the costs of taxes would sacrifice $349 for every $100 that the poor gained.[48] At the end of the 1970s and early in the 1980s, the results of large-scale social experiments designed to reliably measure the work effort and other behavioral effects of negative income tax–type plans began to be released and reviewed. Analyses of the data from the New Jersey, rural, and Seattle-Denver experiments (SIME-DIME) indicated that the labor supply reductions of low-income families covered by the plans were not trivial.[49]

SIME-DIME also tested the effectiveness of education and training vouchers given to low-income family heads. While the vouchers had some effect on the level of schooling and training, there was no observed payoff in the job market. Similarly, a number of other large-scale experiments of the impacts of education and training programs were undertaken at this time, with equally discouraging findings.[50]

47. See Murray (1984); Mead (1986).

48. Browning and Johnson (1984, p. 199). It was not until the end of the decade that these results were seriously challenged. Charles Ballard (1988, p. 1026), in a well-specified numerical general equilibrium model, calculates that when taxes are raised on only those in the highest portion of the income distribution and transfers are received by only those in the bottom, it would cost $114 to transfer $100. Robert Triest (1993, p. 26) estimated the efficiency costs of expanding a program like the EITC and finds that the cost of redistributing $100 would be $116 under his central parameter estimate.

49. The first of these experiments, the New Jersey Income Maintenance Experiment, found small (and statistically insignificant) labor supply reductions for the husbands of the families, but large and statistically significant work reductions for the wives in the families. Family labor supply reductions fell into the 5 to 10 percent range (Watts and Rees, 1977). The results from the larger Seattle-Denver Income Maintenance Experiment (SIME-DIME) trickled out in the early 1980s and revealed substantially larger labor supply reductions. Prime-age men reduced their annual hours of work by 9 to 10 percent in response to the plans; their spouses by 17 to 20 percent; and single mothers with children by more than 20 percent. A negative income tax plan with an income guarantee equal to three-fourths of the poverty line and a marginal tax rate of 0.5 was estimated to reduce earnings by 50 cents for each dollar of net governmental cost. See Robins (1985, pp. 577–79).

50. For example, the National Supported Work Demonstration, a random-assignment program providing carefully designed work experience to individuals with severe employment problems, found

The nature of the economic growth following the deep recession of 1982–83 raised still other questions regarding the effect of technological change and the structure and operation of the labor market. While the economy expanded, wage rates of low- and medium-skilled male workers did not, but the earnings of those in the upper tail of the distribution grew rapidly. The growing inequality of the 1980s prompted numerous references to the failure of rising tides to raise all boats during that decade.

Public support to the poor during the decade of the 1980s reflected these concerns; this was the era of retrenchment. In 1981 President Reagan proposed a program of mandated work for able-bodied welfare recipients combined with an increase in the benefit reduction rate to 100 percent (and elimination of allowed amount of income that could be disregarded in computing benefits) for those recipients who found paid employment. Congress approved the latter of these changes in the 1981 Omnibus Budget Reconciliation Act (OBRA). This fundamental change in the structure of the AFDC program, together with legislative encouragement for states to establish narrowly focused work requirement programs (known as "welfare-to-work"), signaled a new culture of work expectations for single mothers with children. Indeed, states took this signal and targeted AFDC benefits as a source of budget savings.[51]

Employment programs also came under attack during this period. The Comprehensive Employment and Training Act (CETA), enacted in 1973 to provide public service jobs and on-the-job training to disadvantaged workers in place of earlier classroom training programs, was terminated in 1983.[52] It was replaced with a job training and search assistance program, which was smaller and less well funded.[53] Only selected in-kind programs—primarily food stamps and Medicaid—showed any growth during this decade.[54] Total real means tested spending on state welfare programs increased by 33 percent

---

some success in increasing earnings for long-term welfare recipients, but trivial or no effect for recently released convicts, former drug addicts, and young school dropouts with a delinquency record. See Hollister, Kemper, and Maynard (1984). Subsequent randomized evaluations of training and education interventions also produced disappointing results. See Danziger and Weinberg (1986).

51. Real monthly median state welfare benefits (for a family of four, in 1992 dollars) fell from about $760 in 1980 to about $460 in 1990; welfare became a much less attractive option than it had been before.

52. See Haveman (1980). In the late 1970s, CETA supported over 1 million people in public service jobs and offered training assistance to 1.3 million low-skilled workers.

53. Rebecca Blank (1994) provides a more detailed discussion of program retrenchments during the 1980s.

54. These programs grew because of inflation-adjustments (especially for Medicaid) and increased participation (in part because of the recession of the early 1980s), in spite of tightened eligibility standards imposed during the early 1980s.

during the 1980s, as compared to an increase of 113 percent during the 1970s.[55]

The 1990s

New themes came to dominate policy discussions in the 1990s. One was macroeconomic, the other the dominance of value-driven policymaking.

On the macroeconomic front, the explicit Keynesian policymaking of the 1960s, and the large-deficit Keynesian-like policies of the 1970s and 1980s, gave way to a new orthodoxy—namely, that long-run economic growth demands increased saving and investment. Fiscal restraint (with fixed deficit targets or balanced budgets) was seen as the recipe for attaining this goal.[56] Fiscal expansion, with its potential to achieve equity objectives, was sacrificed to the primacy of a monetary policy designed to balance stable prices with continued expansion.[57] With the prolonged expansion that followed the recession of the early 1990s, deficits have fallen and surpluses have been realized (perhaps to continue as far as the eye can see), all this along with falling unemployment, high economic growth (and a decrease in underlying estimates of the unemployment rate at which the rate of inflation would begin to accelerate).[58] The test will be to see if this new austerity orthodoxy now sustains prolonged growth and prosperity.

Simultaneous with this changed macroeconomic perspective came a new moral standard for judging individuals and their behavior, with implications for the role of the state in social policy. This standard emphasizes the merits of individual self-reliance. In this view, the real problem of poverty is the substitution of welfare for income generated by people's own efforts, fostering the creation of a dependent and dysfunctional social class.[59]

---

55. See Burtless (1994b, table 3.1, p. 57).

56. This perspective was advocated by many fiscal economists, though some prominent critics did not subscribe to this view. An example of advocacy in support of the position is presented by Joseph Minarik and Rudolph Penner, who state, "The federal budget deficit is like a debilitating disease. . . . If left untreated, the deficit disease could become very painful" (1988, p. 279).

57. A subcurrent to this new macroeconomic perspective is the conjecture that the rapid development of computer and information technology has ushered in a new era of high productivity—and hence, potential economic growth—reducing concern with potential inflation. A corollary of this view is that monetary policy need not keep such a tight rein on policy and that structural surpluses need not be sustained.

58. This "nonaccelerating inflation rate of unemployment" is known as the NAIRU.

59. Through its emphasis on individual responsibility, this point of view implicitly rejects the basic concept of cash income (including government transfers) on which the official poverty measure rests.

The standard of "self-reliance" motivated the 1996 welfare reform legislation entitled Temporary Assistance for Needy Families (TANF); its primary goal is to move recipients from reliance on cash transfers into work and earning.[60] The new standard also underlies proposals for the privatization of the Social Security retirement program, medical savings accounts as a replacement for Medicare benefits, shifts from defined benefit to defined contribution pension plans, and the emphasis on loans rather than grants to cover the rising costs of higher education.

During the 1990s, trends in social policy continued to reflect the initiatives that were begun in the 1980s. Before the 1996 welfare reform legislation was enacted, average AFDC benefits continued to drift lower, and states obtained federal waivers from AFDC regulations that permitted them to experiment with policy changes that would promote work, responsibility, and self-reliance.[61] The word went out that, irrespective of their skills, training, or home demands, single parents and low-skill families had to learn to "get by on their own." Enforcement of child support payments, begun in the 1980s, was accelerated in the 1990s, and payments did increase (though not by as much as had been hoped).[62] As a result of TANF, states have emphasized "diversion" from benefit receipt into work and have tightened the enforcement of work standards; welfare caseloads have fallen by over 40 percent nationally.

However, offsetting the erosion in welfare support, programs providing in-kind support to low-income families—primarily food stamps and Medicaid—expanded. The signal development in the nation's safety net was the substantial (phased-in) expansions of the earned income tax credit in 1990 and 1993. For a family with two children, the maximum credit went from $953 in 1990 to $1,384 by 1992 to $2,528 in 1994. In 1998, it stood at $3,756.[63] The increased generosity of the EITC removed some of the sting from the 1996 TANF legislation.

Indeed, to advocates of self-reliance, the official measure is but an indicator of failed social policy based on communitarian objectives.

60. TANF eliminated the receipt of public transfer benefits by single-parent households as an entitlement and imposed firm limits on the period that eligible families could receive support. It enabled states to restructure their own programs through the awarding of a block grant but imposed numerous rules that the restructured program had to meet.

61. Hundreds of welfare waivers were granted, ranging from measures to increase work incentives through reducing marginal tax rates, to time limits on the receipt of benefits, to reducing benefits if the behavior of recipients (for example, having additional children, failing to meet work requirements, school truancy of recipient children) did not meet requirements. See Greenberg and Shroder (1997).

62. See Sorenson and Halpern (1999).

63. See Hotz and Scholz (forthcoming).

The Evolution of Public Policy Affecting Low-Income People

Table 7-2 shows the level of total real federal and state expenditures on programs that are targeted toward low-income families—both elderly and working-age—through the several legs of the nation's social welfare system for several years since 1960.[64] A companion table, table 7-3, estimates the extent of this total spending on poor families that is allocated to nondisabled working-age families, primarily families with children. Because the focus of antipoverty policy has been on working-age families since the early 1970s, the discussion that follows concentrates on the latter table.[65]

Consider the first column of table 7-3, describing expenditures in the nation's primary cash income support program for working-age poor families, Aid to Families with Dependent Children (AFDC). When the number of recipients peaked in 1994, AFDC provided cash income support conditioned on family size to about 14 million people in 5 million families (primarily those headed by mothers only). About 5.5 percent of the nation's population lived in these recipient families, up from about 4.1 percent of the population in 1970.[66] During the mid-1970s, up to 80 percent of the nation's children who lived in poor families were assisted; because of increasingly restrictive eligibility requirements, this share had decreased to about 60 percent by 1994.

During the 1960s and up to 1973, monthly AFDC benefits grew rather steadily. However, after 1973, real cash welfare (AFDC) benefits began to erode, and the erosion accelerated after 1980.[67] Some states simply allowed inflation to erode the real value of benefits; others enacted cuts in benefits.

---

64. Because the table reflects programs that are targeted at low-income families, it excludes the Social Security retirement and disability insurance programs. As the discussion above indicates, these social insurance programs have grown rapidly since 1960 and have been responsible for the bulk of the reduction in poverty among the elderly.

65. Several assumptions were made in deriving the estimates in table 7-3; they are described in the note to the table.

66. In August 1996, as the TANF legislation was passed, the number of families on AFDC had declined significantly to 4.4 million.

67. A congressional report described the reduction in public cash and near-cash income support in the post-1980 period as follows: "During the 1982 recession, Federal changes to the [AFDC] program removed some 1.2 to 1.5 million individuals (mainly female-headed families who were working) from the welfare roles. In addition, real AFDC and Food Stamp benefits declined 15 percent in the median state between 1979 and 1983. In 1980, combined AFDC and food stamps removed a mother and two children with earnings equal to 50 percent of poverty from poverty in 21 states. By 1984, this same family would have income above poverty in only 2 states." See U.S. House of Representatives, Committee on Ways and Means (1993, pp. 33–34).

Table 7-2. *Public Sector Spending on Transfer Programs Targeted at Low-Income Families, 1960–96 (Selected Years)*
Billions of 1996 dollars

Year	AFDC/ TANF	Food stamps	SSI	EITC	Medicaid	Housing benefits	Education aid	Social services	Jobs and training	Other	Total
1960	5.4	n.a.	12.2	n.a.	n.a.	n.a.	n.a.	n.a.	n.a.	n.a.	n.a.
1970	16.5	n.a.	11.9	n.a.	19.6	n.a.	n.a.	n.a.	n.a.	n.a.	n.a.
1973	24.7	8.0	12.1	n.a.	32.2	n.a.	n.a.	n.a.	n.a.	n.a.	n.a.
1979	21.4	12.5	15.3	4.4	47.0	17.4	10.0	8.6	20.2	35.6	196.3
1983	20.8	18.5	14.8	2.8	55.1	19.5	12.7	6.6	5.5	41.9	200.8
1989	20.3	15.4	18.6	8.3	77.5	20.1	16.5	7.2	4.9	46.0	238.4
1990	22.3	17.6	19.9	9.0	87.0	21.1	17.3	7.8	5.1	47.4	255.8
1992	24.9	24.5	24.8	14.6	132.1	23.0	17.9	9.6	6.2	48.9	327.6
1996	20.4	23.5	28.2	25.9	162.0	27.2	16.3	10.1	4.6	52.6	372.8

Sources: Author's calculations, based on U.S. House of Representatives, Committee on Ways and Means, *Green Book* (various years and 1998, pp. 264, 402, 927, 968–69, 1421); *Statistical Abstract of the United States* (various years), "Cash and Non-Cash Benefits for Persons with Limited Income," Consumer Price Index.
n.a. Not available.

Table 7-3. Public Sector Spending on Transfer Programs Allocated to Nondisabled Working-Age Families, 1960–96 (Selected Years)

Billions of 1996 dollars

Year	AFDC/ TANF[a]	Food stamps[b]	SSI[c]	EITC[d]	Medicaid[e]	Housing benefits[f]	Education aid[g]	Social services[h]	Jobs and training[g]	Other[g]	Total	Total as percent of GDP
1960	5.4	n.a.	0.4	n.a.	n.a.	.7	n.a.	n.a.	n.a.	n.a.	n.a.	n.a.
1970	16.5	5.0	0.4	n.a.	7.3	1.6	n.a.	n.a.	n.a.	n.a.	n.a.	n.a.
1975	24.5	9.9	0.5	3.6	13.7	5.1	n.a.	n.a.	n.a.	n.a.	n.a.	n.a.
1978	25.5	12.4	0.5	2.5	15.2	11.3	10.1	8.0	23.5	20.3	129.2	2.34
1980	22.0	12.8	0.5	3.8	14.8	14.9	9.7	6.9	16.6	20.1	122.0	2.29
1990	22.3	14.4	1.2	9.1	22.4	17.9	17.3	7.0	5.1	32.7	149.4	2.14
1992	24.9	18.9	2.2	14.6	31.0	19.5	17.9	8.6	6.2	36.2	180.0	2.55
1995	22.7	19.0	4.1	26.7	37.1	23.9	16.6	10.5	5.6	39.3	205.4	2.70
1996	20.4	16.9	4.1	25.9	40.6	23.1	16.3	9.1	4.6	37.7	198.7	2.54

Sources: See table 7-2.

n.a. Not available.

a. Assumes that all AFDC benefits were allocated to nondisabled working-age families.

b. Assumes that 72 percent of total food stamp benefits were allocated to nondisabled working-age families. (Between 1980 and 1995, the share of benefits supporting households with either an elderly head or an elderly member ranged from 17 to 23 percent. Assuming the average benefit paid to these families equals that paid to non-elderly families, 80 percent of the benefits are estimated to be paid to working-age families. Of these benefits, 90 percent are assumed to support the food consumption of nondisabled families.)

c. Assumes that the benefits from SSI to nondisabled working-age families are those supporting children who are disabled and living in poor families. Benefits are allocated in proportion to the number of recipients. (Through 1980 approximately 3 percent of beneficiaries were under the age of 18. This percentage rose to 6.1 in 1990, 9.4 in 1992, 14.0 in 1995, and 14.4 in 1996.)

d. Assumes that all EITC benefits were allocated to nondisabled working-age families.

e. Assumes that Medicaid program expenditures are allocated to recipients by virtue of their being dependent children under age 21, adults in families with dependent children, or recipients in other Title XIX-eligible categories. In 1995, Medicaid expenditures allocated to these families totaled about one-third of all Medicaid expenditures.

f. Assumes that 85 percent of all housing benefits to low-income families were allocated to nondisabled working-age families.

g. Assumes that all education, jobs and training, and other expenditures were allocated to nondisabled working-age families.

h. Assumes that 90 percent of all social services expenditures were allocated to nondisabled working-age families.

Monthly AFDC benefits averaged $644 per family in 1970 (in 1992 dollars), but eroded steadily in the subsequent twenty-five years; by 1994 the value of real monthly family benefits was about $350—about 55 percent of their value in 1970. Trends in other cash benefits targeted toward the poor were not as stark as those in the AFDC program.[68]

Because of the decline in monthly benefits, total real spending on AFDC drifted down from its 1978 peak of over $25 billion (1996 dollars) to about $20 billion in 1996 (the year of the major reform in welfare policy), in spite of the increase in beneficiaries.

The second element in the pre-TANF system is the food stamp program. As the second column in table 7-3 indicates, food stamps have grown from a small program in 1970 to a major source of income support today. Real expenditures allocated to nondisabled working-age families increased from about $5 billion (1996 dollars) in 1970 to $19 billion in 1995. Currently, the average recipient family of four secures a booklet worth about $280 per month for food purchases, and about 10 percent of the nation's population receives benefits—about 27 million people.

The Supplemental Security Income (SSI) program provides cash benefits to poor people who are aged, blind, or disabled, and to disabled children. A comparison of tables 7-2 and 7-3 indicates that the bulk of benefits from SSI accrue to the elderly and disabled adults; disabled children receive a small share of expenditures from this program. Many AFDC recipients have their welfare checks supplemented by SSI. Unlike AFDC, SSI benefit generosity did not erode over the post-1970 period. Largely because of an increase in the number of recipients, SSI real expenditures on disabled children grew from less than $0.5 billion (1996 dollars) before 1975 to over $4 billion in 1996.

The fourth leg of the stool is the earned income tax credit (EITC).[69] In 1996, about $26 billion in credits were paid to 18 million working-age

68. Burtless calculates that the total value of means-tested programs, including both cash and in-kind benefits (such as food stamps, Medicaid, and housing benefits), per pre-transfer poor person has remained virtually constant since the late 1970s at about $3,800–$4,000 (in 1990 dollars). See Burtless (1994b, figure 3.2, p. 56).

69. See Hotz and Scholz (forthcoming). The EITC is available to all low-income working taxpayers but is targeted at those with dependent children. The credit is determined by a schedule which (in 1998) subsidized incremental annual earnings at a 40 percent rate up to about $9,400 for a family with two children (for a credit of more than $3,756 per year). The credit is refundable and available to the taxpayer only after filing a return in year x, which records income and tax liabilities for year $(x-1)$. The maximum credit is available until annual earnings of the two-parent family reach about $11,500, after which it is reduced at a rate in excess of 21 percent. No EITC is available for families with income in excess of about $31,000.

families with earners, for an average credit of about $1,400 per year; nearly 85 percent of the credits were refunded after tax filing. As table 7-3 indicates, the size of the program increased almost threefold from 1990 to 1996, reflecting the large expansion in generosity during this period.

The *Medicaid* program is the final leg of the nation's social support stool and provides health care benefits to poor elderly people, families on welfare, and children living in low-income families (even those in two-parent families). The benefit package is quite generous; average expenditures for a single mother with three children in 1995 were about $350 to $400 per month. Medicaid costs have grown rapidly because of rapid increases in health care prices, as well as expanding coverage. As table 7-2 indicates, by 1996 Medicaid expenditures totaled about $162 billion (1996 dollars), up from $32 billion in 1973. However, the bulk of Medicaid benefits are allocated to the elderly and to disabled people; families with children receive a relatively small share of them. Table 7-3 indicates that Medicaid benefits allocated to nondisabled working-age families expanded from about $7 billion (1996 dollars) in 1970 to over $40 billion in 1996.[70]

In addition, a variety of other public programs provide benefits to low-income, working-age families. These include housing benefits (such as public housing), education aid (such as Pell grants), social services, and jobs and training programs (see the middle columns of tables 7-2 and 7-3). With the exception of jobs and training programs, all these efforts have expanded since 1980, though rather slowly. Public spending on labor market programs targeted at low-income families fell in real terms from over $23 billion (1996 dollars) in 1978 (the end of the CETA program, described above) to less than $5 billion in 1996.[71]

In total, expenditures on programs targeted at nondisabled, low-income working-age families have grown substantially since 1978—from about $130 billion (1996 dollars) to about $200 billion in 1996. The bulk of this growth is accounted for by expansions in the EITC and Medicaid programs. However, as a proportion of the nation's Gross Domestic Product

70. Passage of the federal children's health insurance program (CHIP) in the mid-1990s has generated a substantial recent expansion in coverage of children in low-income families, and in some states coverage has been extended to all low-income families. Ceilings on eligibility set at 200 percent of the poverty line are common among states today.

71. The decline in wage rates of low-skilled workers and the increase in wage inequality that has accompanied it suggest the potential for policies designed to both increase the formation of skills by these workers and reduce inequality. These declining budgets suggest that this opportunity has not been pursued. Heckman, Lochner, and Taber (1998b) and Heckman and Lochner (forthcoming) present evidence on the net benefits of pursuing these options.

(GDP), this support to the nation's poor working-age families has barely grown at all, hovering between 2.1 and 2.7 percent throughout the entire period. As the comparison of tables 7-2 and 7-3 reveals, the proportion of total expenditures on low-income people (table 7-2) that are allocated to nondisabled working-age families (table 7-3) has decreased from about 65 percent at the end of the 1970s to about 53 percent by 1996.

This constellation of existing transfer and tax programs improved the lives of the nation's most disadvantaged families. Given the post-transfer cash income basis of the official poverty measure in the United States, this system has led to official poverty rates that are substantially below what they would have been without these programs. In 1995, the official poverty rate would have stood at about 21 percent if these programs had not existed. With the benefits that they provide, the poverty rate was 13.8 percent, representing a nearly 30 percent reduction in the number of poor people in these families.

The Poverty-Economic Growth Relationship: Does a Rising Tide Lift All Boats?

One of the most striking patterns noted in the first section of this paper is an apparent floor under the poverty rate since the mid-1970s. It was not always so. For much of the 1950s and 1960s, rapid growth and full employment were accompanied by a declining poverty rate. A growing and prosperous economy was believed to be the nation's most effective antipoverty policy instrument, and research studies documented this relationship.[72] In the 1960s, real GDP grew by almost 50 percent, the male unemployment rate fell from 6.4 percent in 1961 to 2.8 percent in 1969, and the poverty rate dropped from 21.9 to 12.1 percent for the same period. Many economists argued that economic growth was the nation's most effective antipoverty policy instrument, echoing President Kennedy's oft-stated claim that "a rising tide lifts all boats."[73]

---

72. Aaron (1967).

73. See, for example, the debate between Lowell Gallaway (1965) and Henry Aaron (1967). Gallaway had taken issue with the Council of Economic Advisers, which was projecting that economic progress alone would reduce family poverty in 1980 to only 10 percent (assuming 1947–56 levels of economic activity). See *Economic Report of the President, 1964* (chapter 2) for the first statistical analysis of the problem of poverty in America and the potential of economic growth for poverty reduction. Gallaway himself, using the same assumptions but different methods, projected a rate of 6.4 percent.

Overall Economic Performance-Poverty Patterns Since 1960

Beginning in the early 1970s, however, the economic terrain became rockier, and the apparently robust relationship between economic growth and poverty began to erode. While real GDP grew by about 35 percent during the 1970s, the poverty rate dropped only slightly, from 12.6 percent in 1970 to 11.7 percent in 1979.

During the 1980s, the link between economic growth and the poverty rate became even less apparent. Despite the recession of the early 1980s, real GDP grew about 30 percent over the entire decade. The poverty rate rose steeply during the recession; during the recovery that followed, however, it receded very slowly, and in 1989 stood at 12.8 percent. During the rocky period from 1973 to 1992, while real GDP per capita grew by 32 percent, the poverty rate *increased* by nearly 4 percentage points.

THE PERSISTENCE OF POVERTY IN THE 1970S AND 1980S. The failure of economic growth to erode poverty during the 1970s and 1980s suggested that the formerly robust relationship between macroeconomic performance and poverty had experienced a serious breakdown. One of the first systematic studies of this conjecture was undertaken in 1986 by Rebecca Blank and Alan Blinder, using time-series data from 1959 to 1983.[74] Their approach involved time-series regressions that estimated the relationship between the nation's poverty rate and a variety of factors that describe important aspects of a changing macroeconomic environment, including the unemployment rate and the inflation rate. Following this empirical approach, in 1991, David Cutler and Lawrence Katz extended the analysis through 1989, using statistical time series also examined by Blank when she revisited the issue in 1993. The most recent study is that by Elizabeth Powers, who extended the time-series data through 1992.[75]

All these studies reaffirmed a strong and statistically significant effect of macroeconomic performance on the poverty rate during the years before the mid-1970s. However, all of them also found that the relationship between economic growth and the poverty rate was quite different after that date than it was earlier.[76] Blank concluded that if the historical rela-

---

74. The first estimates of a statistically robust relationship between economic growth and poverty found in the literature are in Anderson (1964).

75. Blank and Blinder (1986); Cutler and Katz (1991); Blank (1993); Powers (1995b).

76. The study by Blank and Blinder (1986) produced time-series regression estimates using annual observations from 1959 (the first year official poverty rates were calculated) to 1983, with the nation's

tionship between poverty and macroeconomic indicators had continued on the path it followed before 1970, the poverty rate in 1989 should have stood at 9.3 percent; instead, it was 12.8 percent.[77] The diminished response of personal income to prosperity held across the population, among groups whose incomes derive primarily from private sector employment, where earnings were historically more responsive to economic growth, as well as among those who rely on public transfers or employment, which have historically been less responsive.

A variety of factors could have led to this break in the relationship between economic performance and poverty. A potentially important factor was the increase in male earnings inequality that began in the mid-1970s and accelerated in the 1980s (see above). This trend is unambiguous in its effect on the poverty rate; the increasing earnings inequality during the 1970s and 1980s has blocked the benefits of that growth from trickling down to those with the least education and the fewest skills.

If this trend toward increasing labor market inequality had been accompanied by growth in average earnings, poverty rates could have kept falling during the 1970s and the 1980s. However, the hourly earnings of the average worker failed to rise from 1973 to 1991. Moreover, increasing numbers of working-age males were either jobless or working less than full-time-full-year (see above). In addition to these labor market changes, a number of demographic changes during the 1970s and 1980s have contributed to the ineffectiveness of economic growth in reducing poverty. The surge in divorce and out-of-wedlock births in the 1970s and 1980s resulted in a poverty population that is heavily dominated by mother-only families (see

---

poverty rate (for families and for individuals) as the dependent variable. The explanatory variables were chosen to reflect a variety of aspects of the macroeconomic environment thought to affect the poverty rate. The prime-age male unemployment rate and the inflation rate were included as standard macroeconomic variables thought to differentially affect higher- and lower-income people, and these were the central focus of the study. The ratio of total government transfers to persons to GNP was included to capture the effect on the poverty rate of rapid expansion of government transfers, especially during the period before 1980. Also included were the ratio of the poverty line (for a family of four) to mean household income to reflect the fact that an absolute poverty line "falls relative to mean income in times of real growth, an effect that almost by definition will decrease poverty"—as explained on page 188 of the study—and the lagged poverty rate to capture the dynamic effects of macroeconomic shocks. A 1 percentage point change in the unemployment rate was related to a 0.7 percentage point change in the poverty rate and was statistically significant. The models were not viewed as measuring causal relationships, or as reflecting a structural economic model of the determination of the poverty rate (p. 187).

77. Blank (1993, p. 24).

above) and hence relatively unresponsive to changes in overall labor market conditions.

Finally, the decreases in public cash income support have also worked to retard the antipoverty effectiveness of economic growth (see above). Powers reports that although real transfers grew at an average annual rate of 6 percent from 1960 to 1979, annual growth fell to 2 percent in the 1980s.[78]

Blank examined a number of potential factors that might account for the failure of the poverty rate to respond to economic growth, including problems with the actual measurement of poverty, regional differences in where the poor lived and where economic expansion was occurring, government policy under the Reagan administration, the changing demographic composition of poor households, and reduced labor market activity among poor families. She found little evidence that they could account for the "stickiness" of the poverty rate and concluded, "The slower income growth among families at the bottom of the income distribution was almost entirely due to a decline in the responsiveness of earnings among family unit heads to the macroeconomy. In turn, this decline in earnings responsiveness was almost entirely due to the lack of responsiveness of real wages to the macroeconomic growth of the 1980s."[79]

---

78. See Powers (1995a). It is possible to indicate—at least roughly—the effect of this retrenchment of income support benefits on poverty by calculating the "antipoverty effectiveness" of these public transfers. Considering both social insurance and other cash benefits (those benefits that contribute to reducing official poverty), the poverty rate was reduced from 19.2 to 11.6 percent in 1979—a reduction of 40 percent. However, because of the erosion in these benefits during the 1980s, by 1990 they accounted for a reduction in poverty income from 20.5 to 13.5 percent, or by 34 percent. There seems little doubt then that the decline in the generosity of public income support also contributed to the increase in official poverty during the 1980s.

Another effect of the pattern of erosion of public welfare benefits is seldom noted, although it too eroded the effectiveness of economic growth in reducing the poverty rate. As real AFDC benefits fell throughout the 1970s and 1980s, larger percentage (and, hence, absolute) reductions occurred in those states with the highest benefits. For example, between 1970 and 1994, the average percentage reduction in real benefits for a three-person family among the ten highest benefit states as of 1970 (excluding Alaska and Hawaii) was 47.1; the percentage reduction in real benefits among the ten lowest benefit states as of 1970 was 34.6 percent. As a result, the dispersion in real benefits among the states was substantially lower by 1994 than it was in 1970. While benefit levels in the lowest benefit states were so low as to move virtually no pretransfer poor families from below to above the national poverty line, the larger reductions in the higher benefit states caused large numbers of poor families who had been removed from poverty by benefits in 1970 to drop below the poverty line by 1994. This reduction in the variation in benefits among states reinforced the effect of the overall decline in benefits in reducing the antipoverty "punch" of economic growth.

79. Blank (1993, p. 51). These conclusions were supported in later studies by Blank and Card (1993) and Tobin (1994). The authors of both studies argued that marked changes in the operation of the labor market over the 1980s—in particular wage rate stagnation combined with growing wage

THE 1990S: A RETURN TO NORMALCY? At the end of 1999, the United States is basking in an unbroken six-year record of economic growth, in which the macroeconomic indicators bear a distinct resemblance to the prosperous years of the 1960s and the 1980s (after 1983). Is there continuing evidence that the break in the relationship between macroeconomic performance and the poverty rate observed during the 1970s and 1980s has persisted into the 1990s, or has the traditional relationship apparent in the 1960s again been reestablished?[80]

Consider the following estimates, based on time-series data through 1998. In these analyses, I broke the period after 1960 into a standard set of subperiods that characterize the U.S. economy. The period from 1960 to 1972 is lumped into a single period, suggesting that the oil price increases of the early 1970s separate it from the "stagflation" years, 1973–81. I break the years after 1981 into two periods: 1982–92, reflecting the growth years between the major recession of the early 1980s and that of the early 1990s, and the most recent period of expansion from 1993 to 1998.

In some of the earlier studies, the persistence of poverty in the 1980s was explored by introducing a trend variable for the period from 1982 on into the time-series regression estimates. If the coefficient on this variable was positive, it would indicate that the poverty rate during this period drifted up, after accounting for macroeconomic factors such as the unemployment rate. These studies found evidence for an upward drift of about 0.2 percentage point a year in the poverty rate during this period.[81] Using time-series data through 1998, I estimated a similar "drift" model, using the unemployment rate as an indicator of macroeconomic performance. The estimates from this model also suggest that from 1982 to 1992 the poverty rate drifted up by about 0.18 percentage point a year above what the model would predict—a finding nearly identical to that of David Cutler and Lawrence Katz. But the estimate of the drift for the years after 1992 is substantially smaller, about 0.11 percentage point a year. This sug-

---

inequality—accounted for the changed effect of macroeconomic factors on poverty. "I confess," said Tobin (1994, p. 161), "I come to conclusions of this kind reluctantly. In the past I have been skeptical of periodic structural explanations of higher unemployment rates and higher poverty rates. I have thought that the American people are very mobile and adaptable and that the U.S. economy adjusts quickly to sectoral shocks, provided an overall macroeconomic climate of prosperity has been maintained. . . . In my experience, structural hypotheses have usually been excuses for policymakers to do nothing to stimulate the economy."

80. This section is based on Haveman and Schwabish (2000).
81. See, for example, Cutler and Katz (1991); Powers (1995a).

gests that the strong, unpredicted upward trend in the poverty rate so evident during the 1980s has been muted or eliminated since 1992.

It is possible to test the effect of macroeconomic performance on the poverty rate over different periods by estimating both the overall relationship of the unemployment rate and the poverty rate, and a set of separate relationships between these two variables during the three specific periods of interest (see table 7-4, column 1). When these separate period effects are taken into account, the rising unemployment rate over the entire period went hand-in-glove with a growing poverty rate. Each one point increase in the unemployment rate resulted in an increase in the poverty rate of nearly 0.65 points (see the 0.648 coefficient on the unemployment rate, in bold), nearly identical to that found in Blank's 1993 work and Powers's 1995 study.[82] This suggests that, if the poverty rate was, say, 14 percent, an increase in the unemployment rate from 6 to 9 percent would imply an increase in the poverty rate to about 16 percent—about a 14 percent increase. The coefficients on the interaction variables indicate that, relative to the early period (1959–72), the relationship of the unemployment rate to the poverty rate was greatly diminished during both the 1970s and the 1980s (the coefficients are –0.440 and –0.536, respectively, both of which largely offset the coefficient on the entire-period unemployment rate variable of 0.648).[83] However, for the most recent period, the coefficient on the interaction variable (–0.197) is much smaller than those on the subperiods from 1973 to 1992. The sum of the coefficients on the unemployment rate (0.648) and the unemployment rate interacted with the dummy variable for the period after 1992 (–0.197) is 0.451, indicating that in this recent period a 1 percentage point decrease in the unemployment rate leads to a 0.45 percentage point decrease in the poverty rate. The difference between the effect of the unemployment rate during the 1970s and 1980s and that during the most recent period is striking.

I also estimated a model that included both the unemployment rate and the lagged GDP growth rate as macroeconomic determinants of the poverty rate (see table 7-4, column 2). The unemployment rate is positively associated with the poverty rate (0.458). However, during the two sub-periods between 1973 and 1992, the unemployment rate again

82. Blank (1993); Powers (1995a).

83. The coefficients on the interacted variables are to be interpreted as "adjustments" to the overall coefficient on the unemployment rate. Hence, negative coefficients on the interaction variables indicate a reduced effect of the unemployment rate during the specific period relative to the overall coefficient on the unemployment rate.

Table 7-4. *Unemployment, Lagged GDP Growth, and the Poverty Rate, 1959–98*[a]

Variable	Coefficient	Coefficient
Constant	−13.710	−13.850
	(3.089)	(3.619)
Poverty line/Mean income[b]	0.658	0.636
	(0.099)	(0.124)
Lagged poverty rate[c]	0.143	0.232
	(0.105)	(0.122)
Inflation rate[d]	-0.017	−0.025
	(0.041)	(0.052)
1973–81 dummy	1.195	. . .
	(0.474)	
1982–92 dummy	2.243	. . .
	(0.749)	
1993–98 dummy	1.614	. . .
	(1.149)	
Government transfers/GDP[e]	-0.506	−0.465
	(0.252)	(0.276)
Unemployment rate[f]	**0.648**	**0.458**
	(0.184)	**(0.196)**
UR * 1973–81 dummy	**−0.440**	**−0.219**
	(0.125)	**(0.098)**
CUR * 1982–92 dummy	**−0.536**	**−0.223**
	(0.114)	**(0.101)**
UR * 1993–98 dummy	**−0.197**	**−0.026**
	(0.167)	**(0.135)**

appears to have little effect on the poverty rate. For both the 1973–81 and 1982–92 periods, the negative coefficients on the unemployment interaction variable (−0.219 and −0.223, respectively) are about one-half the value of the overall coefficient, suggesting a much diminished relationship of the unemployment rate to the poverty rate during the 1973–92 period. However, for 1993–98, the negative offset seen for the 1973–92 period has disappeared. During this most recent period, the poverty rate decreased by 0.43 percentage point for each 1 percentage point decrease in the unemployment rate. Figure 7-2 summarizes these changes in the unemployment–poverty rate relationship over the various periods and

Table 7-4. *Unemployment, Lagged GDP Growth, and the Poverty Rate, 1959–98*[a] *(continued)*

Variable	Coefficient	Coefficient
Lagged GDP growth	. . .	**−0.077**
		(0.064)
Lagged GDP growth * 1973–81	. . .	**0.108**
		(0.061)
Lagged GDP growth * 1982–92 dummy	. . .	**0.128**
		(0.069)
Lagged GDP growth * 1993–98 dummy	. . .	**−0.006**
		(0.158)
Entire period trend	0.186	0.218
	(0.032)	(0.035)
Number of observations	39	38
Adjusted R^2	.992	.986

Source: Author's calculations. Data for poverty, income, and unemployment are from *Statistical Abstract of the United States* (various years); Powers (1995b); Current Population Survey, March Supplement (1999). Data for government transfers are from Bureau of Economic Analysis, "Selected NIPA Tables," table 3.2, "Federal Government Receipts and Expenditures." Data for GDP are from Bureau of Economic Analysis, table 1, "Gross Domestic Product." Data for inflation are from *Economic Report of the President, 1998*; Powers (1995b).

a. Estimates referred to in the text are in bold; *t* statistics in parentheses.

b. Poverty line is the weighted average poverty threshold for a family of four. Mean family income is income of families, all races, in 1996 dollars.

c. Poverty rate is the percentage of persons living below the poverty line.

d. Consumer Price Index for all items (CPI-U).

e. GDP is real GDP in billions of dollars deflated by 1992 GNP price deflator.

f. Unemployment rate for males, all races, aged 24 to 54.

shows the return of the robust effect of economic performance on the nation's poverty rate in the period since the early 1990s.

Results for the GDP growth interaction variable are similar; the coefficients for the two periods from 1973 to 1992 (0.108 and 0.128, respectively) more than offset the opposite-signed overall coefficient (−0.077). However, the coefficient on the interaction variable for the 1993–98 period is very small and negative (−0.006), indicating a negative relationship between GDP growth and the poverty rate in the recent period similar to that in the period prior to 1973. The sum of the interaction coefficient for this period and the overall coefficient on the GDP growth variable suggests

Figure 7-2. *Changes in the Unemployment-Poverty Rate Relationship,*
1959–98[a]

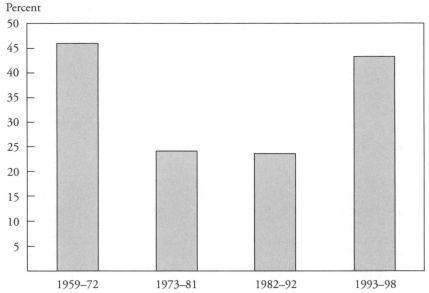

Source: Author's calculations.

a. The figure shows the percentage point change in the poverty rate from a 1 point decrease in the unemployment rate.

that in recent years, a 1 percentage point increase in the GDP growth rate is associated with a decrease of 0.08 percentage point in the poverty rate.[84] The coefficient on the entire-period trend variable again indicates an upward drift of the poverty rate of slightly more than 0.20 percentage point per year over the entire period. Figure 7-3 shows this period-specific relationship between the growth rate of GDP and the poverty rate and also suggests the return of the expected relationship during this most recent expansion.

These estimates suggest that the historically strong relationship between macroeconomic performance and the poverty rate had eroded during the 1970s and 1980s. They also suggest, however, that this relationship may well have reestablished itself. Again, strong economic growth and

84. Note that I used the GDP growth variable for the year prior to the year of the poverty rate to reflect the fact that it is last year's growth that is likely to affect this year's poverty rate.

Figure 7-3. *Change in the GDP Growth Rate–Poverty Rate Relationship, 1959–98*[a]

Percent

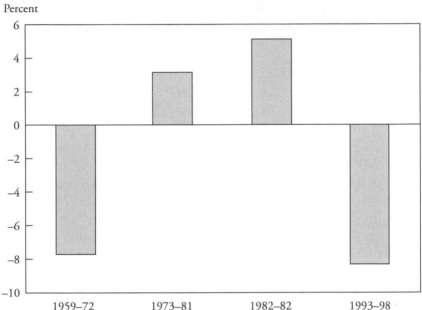

Source: Author's calculations.

a. The figure shows the percentage point change in the poverty rate from a 1 point increase in the GDP growth rate.

high employment may be the nation's most effective antipoverty policy instrument.

While such a conclusion may be reassuring, it rests on a relatively small number of observations in the post-1992 period, and this period may itself be an aberration. Moreover, future developments may again offset the ability of the tide of economic growth to raise all boats. Technological change focused on educated workers could contribute to growth that generates little in the way of increased earnings for low-skilled workers. Continued increases in labor force participation of youths, immigrants, and others with relatively low experience could also restrain wage growth in entry-level jobs. Persistent growth in female-headed families, and especially the movement of many of them from welfare to work associated with the 1996 welfare reform legislation, could also counteract the antipoverty effect of economic growth. Finally, when the value of cash welfare benefits (which enter directly into the numerator of the poverty measure) decline or disappear—as this legislation envisions—their contribution to poverty reduction will also evaporate. These factors mean that economic growth may have to work against strong countercurrents in reducing poverty. In the face of such trends, the relationship that again seems to apply may not persist.

Conclusion: What Might the Future Hold?

As we stand at the beginning of a new millennium, most Americans find things to be about "as good as it gets." Employment is full, prices are stable, the stock market is high, wages are growing in line with productivity, important gender and racial gaps among people have been narrowed, the growth in earnings inequality has slowed, and the poverty rate is edging down.

This was not always the case, and a look backward is instructive. During the 1970s and 1980s, the poverty rate seemed to have bottomed out, in spite of economic growth. Earnings and income inequality rose, overall earnings stagnated, and corporate restructuring left many feeling insecure. While people at the top of the distribution prospered, folks in the bottom half did not. The nation substituted faith in collective action for a return to a market philosophy and a message of self-reliance that accompanied it. Public concern and intervention waned, and this benevolent offset to the vagaries of the market was blunted; much of the reduction in government has been targeted at those with low skills and low incomes. At the end of the 1980s, homelessness was a national issue, crime and drugs were seen as undermining the nation, and schools and the health care system were generally viewed as broken. The age of self-reliance seemed unwilling to muster the collective action necessary to effectively address these concerns. Interestingly, it took just a few years of growth and prosperity to suppress these concerns and sweep them off the table.

Yet the current prosperity is fragile. Maybe we have entered a new era of sustained growth that will truly counter this legacy, but then again probably we have not. If recession strikes, these old problems will again be with us. More important, because of the eroded social support system that has accompanied welfare reform, their return may well be with some vengeance. This reform has opened the nation up to a set of potential consequences about which we know very little. What will happen in the long run to the children of former welfare recipients who are now forced to work full-time to get by? How will society deal with those women facing high barriers to work, without a public sector last resort jobs program and no financial support when the time limit has expired? Can the nation thrive when the poor become increasingly segregated in high-crime and dysfunctional inner-city areas?

As Frank Levy has effectively reminded us, continued national progress rests on three variables: "the rate of productivity growth, the economy's level of skill bias, and the quality of our equalizing institutions."[85] Each of us has our own best guesses regarding future trends in the nation's productivity and the degree to which new technology will work to the disadvantage of those without skills. Unfortunately, no one will tell us whose forecast is the most reliable.

However, the tale of the last forty years cannot give us comfort regarding the strength of the nation's equalizing institutions. Indeed, trends in educational policy, in retirement policy, in the strength of worker organizations (especially relative to the economic and political power of shareholders), in the financing of higher education, in the access to health care, and in the erosion of the nation's safety net all testify to the prevailing view that each family must rely on its own resources, and that self-reliance has replaced social support. When things are "as good as they get" these trends become camouflaged—yet they are real and ready to raise their head if given a chance. If the economy falters, the poor and the unskilled are not likely to fare well.

If there is any truth in this observation, then the nation needs now to place on its agenda the strengthening of institutions and policies that are able to cushion the impact of a reversal of fortunes on those who are already disadvantaged. Such institutions are "social insurance" writ large. Proposals for the restructuring or creation of such institutions are not lacking and include labor market reforms (in the form of employee- and employer-based work subsidies, or public employment measures), enforcement of support by absent parents for their own children, expansion of work-oriented income support (such as the earned income tax credit or child care subsidies), the subsidization of asset accumulation for low-income families, increased investments in early childhood, nontraditional training programs, and the extension of medical care support for those

85. Levy (1998, p. 188).

unable to pay for it on their own.[86] The absence of consensus among experts regarding the most promising among these options is not surprising and is no different than it was in the 1960s. What is different—and dangerous—is the apparent national disinterest with this erosion of its equalizing institutions, and the failure of those who are concerned to place the issue back on the nation's table.

COMMENT BY

Gary Burtless

Robert Haveman divides his story into four main slices, each of them easily digestible.

—First, he describes the overall trend in poverty over the past forty years, indicating who has gained and who has lost ground over various subperiods and explaining why those groups have gained or lost out.

—Then he surveys economists' received wisdom on the poverty problem. He shows how economists' understanding has evolved over time, in part because the set of facts to be explained has changed.

—Third, he summarizes the four-decade shift in public policies toward the poor, noting some of the main changes in federal programs targeted at the low-income population.

—Finally, he considers the relationship between economic progress in general and the economic progress of the low-income population in particular.

Pedants and ideological purists may have nits to pick with Bob's summary of recent history, but I do not have any important ones. He gets the main facts right. His summary of the shifting "received wisdom" on poverty strikes me as compact, accurate, and balanced.

I want to focus on the fourth slice of Bob's cake: his analysis of the relationship between overall economic growth and improvements in well-being at the bottom. Economists have had different opinions about this relationship at different points in time. In the 1960s and early 1970s it was easy to be optimistic. It looked as though strong growth could reliably produce robust income and consumption gains for the poor. Bob cites John Kennedy's famous—though later disproved—remark that "A rising tide

---

86. See, for example, Haveman (1988); Danziger, Sandefur, and Weinberg (1994); Blank (1997); and Heckman and Lochner (forthcoming).

lifts all boats." Kennedy is also credited with the remark "Life is unfair," which has almost the opposite implication.[87] Kennedy's second remark has stood the test of time a lot better than his comment about tides and boats.

One thing we have learned since the 1960s is that a rising tide can lift some boats and sink others. It is now clear that the link between growth and poverty is much more complicated than the relationship between tides and boats.

Bob cites his own research and that of Alan Blinder, Rebecca Blank, David Cutler, and Larry Katz to show that the relationship between economic progress and poverty reduction has been anything but constant over time. Poverty plunged in the fourteen years after 1959 (the poverty rate fell in half, from 22.4 percent to 11.1 percent). But that trend did not persist after 1973. The poverty rate has actually edged up since the early 1970s. It was 11.1 percent in 1973 and 12.7 percent in 1998.

Given the trend in per capita income, one would think America should have done better than this. To be sure, per capita income growth fell off noticeably after 1973. In the fourteen years from 1959 to 1973, per capita real GDP increased 2.9 percent a year. In the twenty-five years after 1973, per capita GDP rose just 1.7 percent a year.[88]

Still, 1.7 percent a year is a lot better than 0 percent. It means that per capita output increased about 50 percent in the last twenty-five years. Surely, a 50 percent jump in average income should cause a reduction in the fraction of people who are poor. But this has not been the case.

One might argue that the economy was weaker in 1998 than it was in 1973. But this would simply show ignorance of the statistics. The unemployment rate was almost a half point lower in 1998 than it was in 1973, and the employment to population ratio was 6.3 points higher in the later year.

The regressions at the end of Haveman's paper provide a way of quantifying the size of the poverty rate "mystery" in different subperiods. This presumes, of course, that the poverty reductions that occurred from 1959 to 1973 represent some kind of benchmark for what should be expected of the "normal" relationship between the economy and poverty. But just as the trend in productivity growth over the early postwar period offered an unreliable benchmark for predicting productivity growth after 1973, poverty reductions in the 1950s and 1960s proved a poor guide for forecasting poverty changes after the mid-1970s.

87. *Public Papers of the Presidents* (1963, p. 259).
88. I measure GDP with chained 1992 dollars.

In the case of poverty, unlike the case of productivity growth, econo-mists are in a good position to explain *why* the experience of the 1950s and 1960s was so different from that of the 1970s, 1980s, and 1990s. Whereas analysts can account for no more than one-half—and probably less than one-third—of the productivity fall-off after 1973, they can explain a much bigger share of the "surprise" in the relationship between the economy and the poverty rate. This does not mean the "surprise" would have been any smaller to a person thinking about this relationship in the mid-1970s. But unlike the case of the productivity surprise, economists in 2000 can mechanically account for most of the poverty "surprise" after 1973.

The explanation has just a few elements:

—Mismeasurement;

—Policy change;

—Increased wage inequality;

—Immigration; and

—Household "atomization."

Consider the mismeasurement of poverty. Americans are classified as poor if their incomes fall below a threshold that is fixed in terms of pur-chasing power. But there is a problem in the way the official statistics mea-sure the resources available to American families.[89] In the mid-1960s, around the time the poverty measure was developed, most Americans' resources could be easily measured in cash. Almost all government transfers provided to people with low incomes were provided as cash. The official poverty measure reflected this fact. Only cash income (on a pretax basis) was included in countable resources.

The situation changed dramatically after 1970. The government spent ever-increasing amounts on programs that gave noncash benefits to poor families—food stamps, subsidized housing, and free medical insurance. In the 1980s and 1990s, the nation boosted spending on a refundable tax rebate program—the EITC—which is ignored when considering whether people have enough money to reach the poverty threshold. By the end of

---

89. There is also a problem in the way analysts measure how much the threshold changes from one year to the next. Analysts have historically adjusted the threshold in line with changes in the Consumer Price Index (CPI). Most economists believe this index overstated price change before 1997. If the Census Bureau had used the CPIUX1 price deflator instead of the CPIU price deflator between 1967 and 1996, for example, the official poverty rate would have increased by 1.5 percentage points less over this period and the 1996 poverty rate would have been 12.2 percent instead of 13.7 percent. If it had used even newer techniques for measuring price change, such as those adopted by the Bureau of Labor Statistics over the past four years, the increase in the nominal poverty threshold, and the official poverty rate, would have been even smaller.

the 1990s, more than 80 percent of income-tested transfers were noncash or were refundable tax rebates, up from just 17 percent of transfers in the mid-1960s. This means that almost all of the new government transfers that have been added since 1974 are ignored when statisticians calculate the resources available to the poor. Using the most expansive definition of resources—while retaining the existing poverty thresholds—would reduce measured poverty in the late 1990s by about one-third. No one knows how a more expansive definition of resources would have changed the poverty rate in 1973 because the Census Bureau did not measure the distribution of subsidized insurance and noncash income in 1973.

In addition, a rising percentage of labor compensation since 1973 has been paid as fringe benefits, notably, as employer contributions for employee health insurance. These fringe benefits are not counted in family resources available to meet the poverty threshold, even though they help pay for a large and growing percentage of family consumption.[90]

Part of the mystery about why poverty has not declined since 1973 is easily resolved. It probably has declined if income is measured appropriately (or if a consumption standard rather than income is used to determine who is poor). Haveman might note that the decline in poverty after 1973 is still much smaller than would be predicted based on the experiences of 1959–73, and he is right. But still, some progress against poverty is better than a humiliating retreat, which is what the official poverty statistics imply.

Second, a lot of progress in poverty reduction in the 1950s and 1960s can be explained by changes in public policy. Many of those changes improved the well-being of people whose incomes are not much affected by the state of the economy. The aged, the disabled, and mothers rearing children without the help of a spouse enjoyed significant improvements in their cash incomes between 1950 and 1973. Social security disability insurance was introduced in the mid-1950s. Social security retirement and disability benefits became much more generous and covered many more of the frail and elderly over the same period. Cash welfare benefits for single

90. Since 1979 the Census Bureau has attempted to track the impact of taxes, noncash income sources, and fringe benefits on the distribution of income and on the poverty rate. Its calculations show that even under a broad definition of countable income, the poverty rate and income inequality would have increased by approximately the same proportional amount as the official statistics show for the period from 1979 to 1997. I suspect, however, that the surge in government-financed noncash transfers in the late 1960s and in the 1970s would push down the poverty rate under a broad definition of income faster than shown in the official poverty statistics.

parents were liberalized in the 1960s and early 1970s, and cash public assistance was substantially increased for the aged and disabled poor in 1974.

The idea that poverty reductions in the 1960s were driven mainly by tight labor markets and rapid wage increases is flatly incorrect for many segments of the population. The big reductions in old-age poverty that Haveman documents in table 7-1 did not occur because of tighter labor markets. The elderly and disabled actually reduced their employment rates over the whole period from 1960 to 1985, partly in response to bigger public pensions. The low-income elderly were less poor in 1985 than in 1960 because Uncle Sam took better care of them, not because fatter paychecks helped old folks take better care of themselves.

This suggests a second explanation for the sluggish response of poverty to overall income growth after 1973. The welfare state stopped growing more generous—or at least stopped growing more generous in ways that are captured by official poverty measures.

The third explanation for slower progress is widening wage inequality. This phenomenon has been documented in enough academic articles to fill a telephone book—the one for Manhattan, not the one for Madison. Some of the articles are cited in Haveman's paper, and a couple of excellent ones were written by Haveman himself.

The idea that "a rising tide lifts all boats" rests on the notion that the sea level rises by roughly similar percentage amounts for everyone with an oar in the water. That is not strictly true for tides, and it is far from true for wages. Sometimes wages grow by similar percentage amounts for all skill classes (as in the 1960s), and sometimes they do not (as in the 1940s and 1980s). In the 1940s, there was a compression of U.S. wages; in the 1980s and 1990s, wage disparities increased sharply.

Many economists based their ideas about the relationship between poverty and the economy on the experiences of the 1960s and early 1970s. These experiences shed little light on what would happen if average earnings increased sluggishly but grew less equal—precisely the combination that occurred from the late 1970s through the early 1990s. It is now obvious what happens under these circumstances. Low-wage breadwinners see their earnings sink, and many more of them slip into poverty. Since low-wage breadwinners are disproportionately young, it would not be surprising if the poverty rate increases disproportionately among families containing young children, because such families have the youngest breadwinners.

The fourth part of the explanation for increased poverty in the midst of increased affluence is immigration. In the forty years before 1970, the

United States admitted about 7 million legal immigrants; in the twenty-nine years after 1970 it admitted almost three times as many—more than 20 million legal immigrants. Five to seven million immigrants entered the country illegally and stayed after 1970. In 1997, 22 percent of people in immigrant households were poor, but just 12 percent of people in non-immigrant households were poor. According to one recent calculation, all of the increase in poverty under the official definition since the late 1970s has been due to the increased presence of immigrants in the population and to the increased prevalence of poverty among immigrants. The prevalence of poverty has not increased among the native born. Immigrants in 2000 are poorer than immigrants in 1973 because on average they have fewer skills than earlier immigrants. Of course, many poor immigrants would not be poor using the standards of their country of origin, but they are poor by the standards of the United States. One result of increased immigration is that U.S. poverty statistics have worsened even though the incomes of the immigrant poor have dramatically improved compared with what those incomes would have been if U.S. immigration policy had remained as restrictive in the 1980s and 1990s as it had been in the 1960s and early 1970s.

Finally, the idea that steady economic progress will lift a steadily increasing percentage of people out of poverty rests on the premise that people will share their incomes in ways that are similar to ways Americans have shared their incomes in the past. But that has not turned out to be the case. American households are increasingly atomized. People are less likely to live in big households. In a big household, the income shocks suffered by one adult are often buffered by the earnings or incomes of other adults. Americans are now more likely to live alone or in households headed by a single person who is raising minor children.

As households grow smaller, it takes more income to support people at the same "equivalent" income level.[91] To take a simple example, according to the official poverty guidelines it takes 56 percent more money to support two people living apart than it does to support the same two people if they live together.[92] That means when a couple with an income just above the poverty line splits up, the couple's combined income would have to increase 56 percent and be divided equally in order for both people to

91. "Equivalent" income is calculated so that the well-being of two households with different family sizes can be compared. If it takes twice as much income for a family consisting of six members to live as comfortably as a family containing two members, then a six-member family with $30,000 would be considered to have the same "equivalent" income as a two-person family with $15,000.

92. Dalaker (1999, p. A4).

remain above the poverty line. The same is true if a couple with one or two children splits up. More money is needed—and the money must be divided just right—if both parts of the atomized family are to retain the same "equivalent" income.

This is a very simple point, but it is one that is missed surprisingly often. If families are atomized into smaller units, there is usually an increase in the variance of the "equivalent" incomes of the resulting family units. Unless actual incomes increase at the same time that families split up, the "equivalent" income of an average family member declines. It follows that the atomization of American families, holding actual incomes constant, has both reduced the average "equivalent" income and increased the variance of "equivalent" income. This combination must push up the poverty rate.

I suspect the atomization of families is partly the result of rising incomes. As U.S. affluence and security have increased, adult Americans have less and less reason to put up with the disagreeable habits of an irritating partner. Experience suggests that living alone, like bowling alone, is a superior good.

Whatever the reasons for household atomization, the trend has had a profound impact on the way Americans share their income with others. The percentage of Americans who live in married-couple families is shrinking steadily. Between 1980 and 1997 it shrank from 74 percent to less than 65 percent of the population.[93] This trend increases the amount of actual income that is needed to support an average person at the same "equivalent" income level. It increases the variance of equivalent income. Both these effects of atomization boost the measured poverty rate.

Over the long haul, the country is witnessing a race between rising average incomes and increased household atomization. Atomization goes a long way toward explaining why 1.7 percent growth in per capita GDP each year over the past twenty-five years has not produced much progress against poverty.

COMMENT BY

Lawrence F. Katz

Robert Haveman has produced a thoughtful paper summarizing the evolution of poverty and antipoverty policy in the United States over the last

93. Burtless (1999, p. 864).

forty years. First, Haveman documents the key facts concerning U.S. poverty and inequality since 1960: substantial progress against poverty in the 1960s; a surprising persistence of measured poverty since 1973; and a sharp increase in earnings and family income inequality in the United States since the 1970s. Second, Haveman points out the changing face of U.S. poverty: tremendous progress in improving the living standards of the elderly since 1960; rising poverty for children since the early 1970s; increased concentration of poverty in single female-headed households; and the deteriorating labor market position of less-skilled workers, particularly young and less-educated minority males. Third, Haveman provides a useful summary of the evolution of the academic "conventional wisdom" on the causes of poverty and the implications for antipoverty policy. Finally, Haveman examines the extent to which the relationship between macroeconomic performance and the changes in the official poverty rate has changed over time.

I have few basic disagreements with Haveman's useful survey. Thus I will use this comment to elaborate briefly on some issues raised by Haveman.

First, I think an understanding of recent (and possibly future) trends in the distribution of U.S. economic well-being requires more emphasis on the shifting geographic distribution of poverty in the United States. As Haveman points out, poverty has become increasingly concentrated in the central cities of U.S. urban areas. Although the overall U.S. poverty rate declined from 22.4 percent in 1959 to 12.7 percent in 1998 (and real per capita income more than doubled over this period), the poverty rate in central cities has shown no improvement in forty years.[94] In fact, the poverty rate in central cities actually increased slightly from 18.3 percent in 1959 to 18.5 percent in 1998. And the share of the poor residing in central cities has also increased substantially from 26 percent in 1959 to over 43 percent in 1998, even though rapid suburbanization meant an actual decline in the overall share of the population living in central cities over this same period. Furthermore, as William Julius Wilson has hypothesized and as Paul Jargowsky has documented, the geographic isolation of the poor in metropolitan areas has greatly increased since 1970. The share of people living in inner-city poverty census tracts—those with rates of poverty of over 40 percent—is rising, and broader measures of

---

94. U.S. Bureau of the Census, 1999, *Historical Poverty Tables—People*, tables 2 and 8, www.census.gov/hhes/poverty/histpov/.

residential segregation by economic status are also showing substantial increases.[95]

We need a better understanding of the causes and consequences of the growing concentration of U.S. poverty in inner-city areas. A recent study by Edward Glaeser, Matthew E. Kahn, and Jordan Rappaport explores the possible role of U.S. transportation policies in this pattern.[96] High crime rates and school problems in central cities clearly exacerbate these initial conditions in the growing sorting among neighborhoods by economic status. The implications of such increased sorting are disturbing, given growing evidence of possibly substantial effects of neighborhood conditions on the current well-being of residents and the long-run outcomes for children.[97]

The second issue I would like to address is the role of macroeconomic factors in the persistence of measured poverty since 1973. Haveman presents some interesting evidence suggestive of the changes in the efficacy of macroeconomic growth in affecting the poverty rate. I am somewhat skeptical of the ability of the limited annual time series to sort out such changes. But I do think it is reasonable to conclude that the sharp slow-down in the rate of economic growth from the 1959–73 period to the 1973–98 period goes a substantial distance to explaining the sharp decline in poverty in the first period and the lack of progress over the second. Nevertheless, my own research indicates that the actual overall and child poverty rates observed since the mid-1980s are much higher than those predicted by the historical relationship between poverty and standard macroeconomic variables that prevailed prior to 1983.[98] The persistence of high poverty rates over the past two decades appears to also be the result of structural changes in the economy (such as strong labor market shifts against less-skilled workers) that have increased the inequality of economic resources at a given rate of economic growth. Problems in the measurement of poverty are also exacerbated by large shifts in family structure and by the growth in in-kind transfers and the earned income tax credit.

Finally, I believe that we need a better understanding of the political economy of the major shifts in antipoverty policy over the past four

95. Wilson (1987); Jargowsky (1996, 1997).

96. Glaeser, Kahn, and Rappaport (2000).

97. That evidence includes an analysis of the quasi-experimental Gautreaux program (Rosenbaum, 1995) and an investigation of the recent random assignment Moving-to-Opportunity housing mobility demonstration (Katz, Kling, and Liebman, 1999).

98. Cutler and Katz (1991); Katz and Krueger (1999).

decades documented by Haveman. I think several factors have played an important role in the recent shift from a welfare system based on cash assistance to one focusing on work-based support. The rapid increase in labor force participation of married women with young children (under six years of age) from under 20 percent in 1960 to over 60 percent in the late 1990s clearly raised expectations for work and self-sufficiency for single mothers. Second, slow economic growth and growing economic anxiety among middle-class families in the 1970s to early 1990s played a role in reducing public generosity for transfers to those not working. And the growing concentration of poverty in inner-city areas with disproportionate minority populations may also have played a role in reducing views of transfer programs as being universal social insurance and in affecting public and congressional support. An important question is whether the much stronger linkage of government cash and in-kind assistance to employment (that is, to playing by the rules) will reduce the negative political stereotypes associated with the pre-existing welfare system and actually lead to more rapid growth in economic support for those from disadvantaged backgrounds. Given the large real reductions in real welfare benefits for twenty-five years through 1996 in the traditional AFDC system, I believe the old approach clearly did not appear to be very effective or politically viable.

Another important unknown of the new system of work-based support is how such a safety net will operate in periods of economic slowdown. The new time limits and stiffer eligibility requirements for cash assistance are likely to lead to more severe economic hardship for those unable to find work during periods of weak labor markets. But the increases in labor market experience and connections of many low-income individuals in the current long boom may make them more valuable to employers in the future and reduce the incidence of long-run joblessness in the next downturn.

References

Aaron, Henry J. 1967. "The Foundations of the 'War on Poverty' Reexamined." *American Economic Review* (57)5: 1229–40.

———. 1973. *Why Is Welfare So Hard to Reform?* Brookings.

———. 1978. *Politics and the Professors: The Great Society in Perspective.* Brookings.

Anderson, W. H. Locke. 1964. "Trickling Down: The Relationship between Economic Growth and the Extent of Poverty among American Families." *Quarterly Journal of Economics* 78: 511–24.

Ballard, Charles L. 1988. "The Marginal Efficiency Cost of Redistribution."*American Economic Review* 78 (December): 1019–33.

Betsey, Charles L., Robinson G. Hollister, Jr., and Mary R. Papageorgiou, eds. 1985. *Youth Employment and Training Programs: The YEPDA Years*. National Research Council, National Academy Press.

Blank, Rebecca M. 1993. "Why Were Poverty Rates So High in the 1980s?" In *Poverty and Prosperity in the USA in the Late Twentieth Century*, edited by Dimitri Papadimitriou and Edward Wolff, 21–55. Macmillan.

———. 1994. "The Employment Strategy: Public Policies to Increase Work and Earnings." In *Confronting Poverty* edited by Sheldon H. Danziger, Gary Sandefur, and Daniel H. Weinberg, 168–204. Harvard University Press and Russell Sage Foundation.

———. 1997. *It Takes a Nation: A New Agenda for Fighting Poverty*. Russell Sage Foundation and Princeton University Press.

Blank, Rebecca M., and Alan S. Blinder. 1986. "Macroeconomics, Income Distribution, and Poverty." In *Fighting Poverty*, edited by Sheldon Danziger and Daniel Weinberg, 180–208. Harvard University Press.

Blank, Rebecca M., and David Card. 1993. "Poverty, Income Distribution, and Growth: Are They Still Connected?" *Brookings Papers on Economic Activity 2:1993*, 285–325.

Browning, Edgar K., and William R. Johnson. 1984. "The Tradeoff between Equality and Efficiency." *Journal of Political Economy* 92 (April): 175–203.

Burtless, Gary. 1990. "Earnings Inequality over the Business and Demographic Cycles." In *A Future of Lousy Jobs?* edited by Gary Burtless, 77–117. Brookings.

———. 1994a. "Employment Prospects of Welfare Recipients." In *The Work Alternative: Welfare Reform and the Realities of the Job Market*, edited by Demetra Nightingale and Robert Haveman, 71–106. Urban Institute Press.

———. 1994b. "Public Spending on the Poor: Historical Trends and Economic Limits." In *Confronting Poverty*, edited by Sheldon Danziger, Gary Sandefur, and Daniel Weinberg, 51–84. Harvard University Press and Russell Sage Foundation.

———. 1999. "Effects of Growing Wage Disparities and Changing Family Composition on the U.S. Income Distribution." *European Economic Review* 43 (4-6) April: 853–67.

Cain, Glen G. 1976. "The Challenge of Segmented Labor Market Theories to Orthodox Theory: A Survey." *Journal of Economic Literature* 14 (December): 1215–57.

Citro, Constance F., and Robert T. Michael, eds. 1995. *Measuring Poverty: A New Approach*. National Academy Press.

Cutler, David M., and Lawrence F. Katz.1991. "Macroeconomic Performance and the Disadvantaged." *Brookings Papers on Economic Activity 2:1991*, 1–61.

Dalaker, Joseph. 1999. "Poverty in the United States: 1998." Current Population Reports P60-207. Government Printing Office.

Danziger, Sheldon H., Gary Sandefur, and Daniel H. Weinberg, eds. 1994. *Confronting Poverty: Prescriptions for Change*. Harvard University Press and Russell Sage Foundation.

Danziger, Sheldon H., and Daniel H. Weinberg, eds. 1986. *Fighting Poverty: What Works and What Doesn't?* Harvard University Press.

Denison, Edward F. 1985. *Trends in American Economic Growth, 1929–1982*. Brookings.

Duneier, Mitchell. 1992. *Slim's Table: Race, Respectability, and Masculinity*. University of Chicago Press.

Eggebeen, David J., and Daniel T. Lichter. 1991. "Race, Family Structure, and Changing Poverty among American Children." *American Sociological Review* 56 (December): 801–17.

Ellwood, David T. 1988. *Poor Support: Poverty in the American Family*. Basic Books.

Freeman, Richard B., and Harry J. Holzer, eds. 1986. *The Black Youth Employment Crisis*. University of Chicago Press.

Freeman, Richard B., and David A. Wise, eds. 1982. *The Youth Labor Market Problem: Its Nature, Causes, and Consequences*. University of Chicago Press.

Friedman, Milton.1962. *Capitalism and Freedom*. University of Chicago Press.

Gallaway, Lowell E. 1965. "The Foundations of the 'War on Poverty'." *American Economic Review* 55 (March): 122–31.

Garfinkel, Irwin, and Sara E. McLanahan. 1986. *Single Mothers and Their Children: A New American Dilemma*. Urban Institute Press.

Gilder, George F. 1981. *Wealth and Poverty*. Basic Books.

Glaeser, Edward L., Matthew E. Kahn, and Jordan Rappaport. 2000. "Why Do the Poor Live in Cities?" Harvard University, Department of Economics (February).

Gottschalk, Peter, and Sheldon Danziger. 1993. "Family Structure, Family Size, and Family Income: Accounting for Changes in the Economic Well-Being of Children, 1968–1986." In *Uneven Tides: Rising Inequality in America,* edited by Sheldon Danziger and Peter Gottschalk, 167–93. New York: Russell Sage Foundation.

Greenberg, David, and Mark Shroder. 1997. *Digest of Social Experiments,* 2nd ed. Urban Institute Press.

Haveman, Robert H. 1975. "Earnings Supplementation as Income Maintenance Strategy: Issues of Program Structure and Integration." In *Integrating Income Maintenance Programs,* edited by Irene Lurie, 109–46. Academic Press.

———. 1980. "Direct Job Creation." In *Employing the Unemployed*, edited by Eli Ginzberg, 142–59. Basic Books.

———. 1987. *Poverty Policy and Poverty Research: The Great Society and the Social Sciences*. University of Wisconsin Press.

———. 1988. *Starting Even: An Equal Opportunity Program to Combat the Nation's New Poverty*. Simon and Schuster.

Haveman, Robert H., and Lawrence Buron. 1999. "The Growth in U. S. Male Earnings Inequality: Changing Wage Rates or Working Time?" *Journal of Income Distribution* 8: 1–22.

Haveman, Robert H., Thad Mirer, and Irene Lurie.1974. "Earnings Supplementation for 'Working Poor' Families: An Evaluation of Alternatives." In *Benefit-Cost and Policy Analysis–1973,* edited by A. C. Harberger and others, 291–318. Chicago: Aldine Publishing.

Haveman, Robert H., and Jonathan Schwabish. 2000. *Has Macroeconomic Performance Regained its Antipoverty Bite?* Institute for Research on Poverty, University of Wisconsin, Madison.

Haveman, Robert H., and Barbara Wolfe.1994. *Succeeding Generations: On the Effects of Investments in Children*. New York: Russell Sage Foundation.

Heckman, James J., and Lance Lochner. Forthcoming. "Rethinking Myths about Education and Training: Understanding the Sources of Skill Formation in a Modern Economy." In *Securing the Future: Investing in Children from Birth to College,* edited by Sheldon Danziger and Jane Waldfogel. New York: Russell Sage Foundation.

Heckman, James J., Lance Lochner, and Christopher Taber. 1998a. "Explaining Rising
    Wage Inequality: Explorations with a Dynamic General Equilibrium Model of Earnings
    with Heterogenous Agents." *Review of Economic Dynamics* 1(1): 1–58.
————. 1998b. "Tax Policy and Human-Capital Formation." *American Economic Review*
    88(May): 293–97.
Hollister, Robinson G., Jr., Peter Kemper, and Rebecca A. Maynard. 1984. *The National
    Supported Work Demonstration.* University of Wisconsin Press.
Hotz, V. Joseph, and John Karl Scholz. Forthcoming. "Not Perfect, But Still Pretty Good:
    The EITC and Other Policies to Support the U.S. Low-Wage Labor Market." *OECD
    Economic Studies.*
Jargowsky, Paul A. 1996. "Take the Money and Run: Economic Segregation in U.S.
    Metropolitan Areas." *American Sociological Review* 61 (December): 984–98.
————. 1997. *Poverty and Place: Ghettos, Barrios, and the American City.* New York: Russell
    Sage Foundation.
Johnson, Harry G. 1965. "Discussion." *American Economic Review* 55 (March): 543–45.
Karoly, Lynn A. 1993. "The Trend in Inequality among Families, Individuals, and Workers
    in the United States: A Twenty-Five Year Perspective." In *Uneven Tides: Rising Inequality
    in America,* edited by Sheldon Danziger and Peter Gottschalk, 19–97. New York:
    Russell Sage Foundation
Katz, Lawrence F., Jeffrey R. Kling, and Jeffrey B. Liebman.1999. "Moving to Opportunity
    in Boston: Early Impacts of a Housing Mobility Program." Cambridge, Mass.: National
    Bureau of Economic Research (September).
Katz, Lawrence F., and Alan B. Krueger.1999. "The High-Pressure U.S. Labor Market of
    the 1990s." *Brookings Papers on Economic Activity, 1:1999,* 1–65.
Lampman, Robert J. 1965. "Approaches to the Reduction of Poverty." *American Economic
    Review,* 55 (March): 521–29.
————. 1974. "What Does It Do for the Poor? A New Test for National Policy." *Public
    Interest* 34, Winter: 66–82.
Lerman, Robert I. 1995. "The Impact of the Changing U.S. Family Structure on Child
    Poverty and Income Inequality." Urban Institute Press.
Levy, Frank. 1998. *The New Dollars and Dreams: American Incomes and Economic Change.*
    New York: Russell Sage Foundation.
Levy, Frank, and Richard J. Murnane. 1992. "U. S. Earnings Levels and Earnings
    Inequality: A Review of Recent Trends and Proposed Explanations." *Journal of Economic
    Literature* 30 (September): 1333–81.
McLanahan, Sara, and Gary Sandefur. 1994. *Growing Up with a Single Parent: What Hurts,
    What Helps.* Harvard University Press.
Marmor, Theodore, ed. 1971. *Poverty Policy: A Compendium of Cash Transfer Proposals.*
    Chicago: Aldine-Atherton.
Mead, Lawrence M. 1986. *Beyond Entitlement: The Social Obligations of Citizenship.* Free
    Press/Macmillan.
Minarik, Joseph J., and Rudolph G. Penner. 1988. "Fiscal Choices." In *Challenge to
    Leadership,* edited by Isabel Sawhill, 279–316. Urban Institute Press.
Moffitt, Robert A. 1990. "The Distribution of Earnings and the Welfare State." In *A Future
    of Lousy Jobs?* edited by Gary Burtless, 201–30. Brookings.

Murray, Charles. 1984. *Losing Ground: American Social Policy, 1950–1980.* Basic Books.

Okun, Arthur M. 1975. *Equality and Efficiency: The Big Tradeoff.* Brookings.

Phelps, Edmund S. 1974. "Economic Policy and Unemployment in the 1960's." *Public Interest* 34 (Winter): 30–46.

Plotnick, Robert D., and Felicity Skidmore. 1975. *Progress Against Poverty: A Review of the 1964–1974 Decade.* Academic Press.

Powers, Elizabeth T. 1995a. "Growth and Poverty Revisited." *Federal Reserve Bank of Cleveland Economic Commentary,* April 15, 1995.

————.1995b. "Inflation, Unemployment, and Poverty Revisited." *Federal Reserve Bank of Cleveland Economic Review* 31(3): 2–13.

Primus, Wendell, Lynette Rawlings, Kathy Larin, and Kathryn Porter. 1999. *The Initial Impacts of Welfare Reform on the Incomes of Single Mother Families.* Washington: Center on Budget and Policy Priorities.

Public Papers of the Presidents of the United States: John F. Kennedy 1962. 1963. Government Printing Office.

Robins, Philip K. 1985. "A Comparison of the Labor Supply Findings from the Four Negative Income Tax Experiments." *Journal of Human Resources* XX (Fall): 567–82.

Rolph, Earl R. 1967. "The Case for a Negative Income Tax Device." *Industrial Relations* 6: 155–65.

Rosenbaum, James E. 1995. "Changing the Geography of Opportunity by Expanding Residential Choice: Lessons from the Gautreaux Program." *Housing Policy Debate* 6 (1995): 231–69.

Short, Kathleen, Thesia Garner, David Johnson, and Patricia Doyle. 1999. *Experimental Poverty Measures: 1990 to 1997.* U.S. Census Bureau. Current Population Reports, Consumer Income, P60–205 (June).

Smeeding, Timothy M. 1992. "Why the U. S. Antipoverty System Doesn't Work Very Well." *Challenge* 35 (January–February): 30–35.

Smith, James P., and Finis R. Welch. 1986. *Closing the Gap: Forty Years of Economic Progress for Blacks.* Rand Report R-3330-DOL. Santa Monica, Calif.: Rand Corporation (February).

Sorenson, Elaine, and Ariel Halpern. 1999. "Single Mothers and Their Child Support Receipt: How Well Is Child Support Enforcement Doing?" Draft paper. Urban Institute Press.

Tienda, Marta, and Zai Liang. 1994. "Poverty and Immigration in Policy Perspective." In *Confronting Poverty,* edited by Sheldon Danziger, Gary Sandefur, and Daniel Weinberg, 330–64. Harvard University Press and Russell Sage Foundation.

Tobin, James. 1968. "Raising the Incomes of the Poor." In *Agenda for the Nation,* edited by Kermit Gordon, 77–116. Brookings.

————. 1994. "Poverty in Relation to Macroeconomic Trends, Cycles, and Policies." In *Confronting Poverty,* edited by Sheldon Danziger, Gary Sandefur, and Daniel Weinberg, 147–67. Harvard University Press and Russell Sage Foundation.

Tobin, James, Joseph A. Pechman, and Peter M. Mieszkowski. 1967. "Is a Negative Income Tax Practical?" *Yale Law Journal* 77 (November): 1–27.

Triest, Robert K. 1993. "The Efficiency Cost of Increased Progressivity." Working Paper 4535. Cambridge, Mass.: National Bureau of Economic Research (November).

U.S. Census Bureau. *Statistical Abstract of the United States.* Various years. Government Printing Office.

U.S. House of Representatives, Committee on Ways and Means. Various years. *Green Book: Background Material and Data on Programs within the Jurisdiction of the Committee on Ways and Means.* Government Printing Office.

U.S. House of Representatives, Committee on Ways and Means, Subcommittee on Human Resources.1993. *Sources of the Increases in Poverty, Work Effort, and Income Distribution Data.* Government Printing Office (January).

U.S. Senate, Advisory Commission to Study the Consumer Price Index.1996. *Toward a More Accurate Measure of the Cost of Living: Final Report to the Senate Finance Committee.* Government Printing Office.

Watts, Harold W., and Albert Rees, eds.1977. *The New Jersey Income Maintenance Experiment. Vol. 2, Labor-Supply Responses.* Academic Press.

Wilson, William Julius. 1987. *The Truly Disadvantaged: The Inner City, the Underclass, and Public Policy.* University of Chicago Press.

ALAN B. KRUEGER 8

Labor Policy and Labor Research Since the 1960s: Two Ships Sailing in Orthogonal Directions?

Much has changed since the 1960s. The Beatles broke up; the baby boomers grew up; three great leaders were assassinated; women joined the labor force in ever growing numbers; unions waned in the private sector and expanded in the public sector; the microchip, spaceship, and PC were invented; and Jim Crow segregation came to an end. As Bob Dylan says, "the times, they are a-changin'." My assignment for this splendid tribute to Arthur Okun is to describe and evaluate changes in labor market policy and changes in labor economics research since the 1960s. To limit this boundless subject, I focus primarily on the activities of the U.S. Department of Labor (DOL), which is where most of the action has occurred since the 1960s anyway.

My main goals in this essay are to document what the Labor Department does and how it has changed since the 1960s; to summarize

This paper was written while I was on leave at the Center for Advanced Study in the Behavioral Sciences at Stanford University. I am grateful to Diane Whitmore for excellent research assistance; to Orley Ashenfelter, John Donahue, Mary Eccles, Ray Fair, Victor Fuchs, Judy Gueron, Morris Kleiner, Tze Leung Lai, Walter Oi, and Cecilia Rouse for helpful discussions; and to my discussants, James Heckman and Frank Levy, for particularly helpful comments. I also thank Linda Oppenheim, Bill Keisler, and Mark Wichlin for providing data and answering many questions. The Center for Advanced Study in the Behavioral Sciences and the Princeton University Industrial Relations Section provided financial support. The views represented in this paper should not necessarily be attributed to any organization with which I am currently, or have been previously, affiliated.

what labor economists do, and how that has changed since the 1960s; to explore the impact of labor economics research on policy by providing a detailed case study of recent budgetary changes in job training programs; and to offer hypotheses as to why labor market policy has changed since the 1960s.

One of the main findings of the paper is that labor policy has moved away from job training and toward regulation since the 1960s. New regulatory activities are carried out by an alphabet soup of agencies, such as the Occupational Safety and Health Administration (OSHA), the Mine Safety and Health Administration (MSHA), the Office of Federal Contract Compliance Programs (OFCCP), the Pension and Welfare Benefits Administration (PWBA), and the Employment Standards Administration (ESA). The proportion of DOL employees devoted to regulatory activities increased from around one-third of the work force in the 1960s to 60 percent by the end of the 1970s. The figure remains close to 60 percent today. After accounting for inflation, resources devoted to job training are only one-third as large as they were in 1979, and resources for youth job training in particular have declined.

Research in labor economics continues to be dominated by work on unions, although as union membership has declined, the proportion of research on union-related topics has also declined. The shift in emphasis toward regulation of the labor market in policy circles is not noticeably reflected in the research agenda of economists, nor have research findings figured prominently in the design of labor market regulations. Available research in labor economics tends to be mostly reactive; after policies are implemented, they are studied. In some areas, including job training, however, the accumulated research wisdom has influenced the direction of policy reforms.

In the conclusion, I offer some political-economy–type hypotheses to explain the tremendous growth in labor market regulation since the 1960s. Explanations based on long-term secular changes offer the most promise because the scope and scale of regulation expanded under both Republican and Democratic administrations, and during periods of budgetary surplus and deficit. I also argue that labor economists can have a more profound influence on future policy development by devoting greater attention to potential ways of improving the efficiency and efficacy of labor market regulations, and by proposing and evaluating alternative approaches to achieving the same aims as existing labor market regulations.

Survey of Labor Policy Since the 1960s

Major employment legislation enacted since 1960 is summarized in table 8-1. This legislation includes the landmark Civil Rights Act of 1964, workplace safety and health legislation (OSHA and MSHA), and several training bills. The legislation enacted since the 1960s greatly expanded the scope of the Labor Department. Before the 1960s, labor legislation was primarily confined to regulating collective bargaining and union governance, providing unemployment insurance (UI), and mandating that employers pay a minimum wage and time-and-a-half for overtime. After the 1960s, labor legislation added additional mandates on employers (such as family and medical leave, and advance notice of plant closings), required nondiscrimination for all covered employers and affirmative action for federal contractors, and sought to restrict the use of hazardous production techniques.

To provide an overview of the size of the Department of Labor, figure 8-1 reports the department's actual budget outlays in constant 1998 dollars from 1962 through 1998, and the Office of Management and Budget's (OMB's) projected outlays for 1999–2004.[1] The figure indicates that DOL's budget fluctuated between $14 and $18 billion in the 1960s, increased more than threefold to a peak of $65 billion in 1976, fell by almost half in the 1980s, spiked up during the recession of the early 1990s, and returned to its late 1980s level by the end of the 1990s. The Department's outlays also clearly display a countercyclical pattern, typically peaking a year after the trough of a recession. The correlation between year-over-year changes in the Department's real outlays and changes in the unemployment rate is 0.63. The countercyclical pattern is largely driven by spending on unemployment insurance benefits, which naturally rise during a recession, and which currently constitute fully 70 percent of the department's budget.

Figure 8-2 displays DOL's budget as a percent of overall federal budget outlays. Abstracting from cyclical effects, this figure shows that DOL's budget fell gradually relative to the overall federal government in the 1960s, grew sharply in the 1970s, and declined in the 1980s and 1990s. By 1998, DOL's share of the federal budget fell to 1.8 percent,

1. The GDP implicit price deflator was used to adjust for inflation. To adjust the OMB figures for inflation, a 2 percent inflation rate was assumed each year between 1999 and 2004.

Table 8-1. *Major U.S. Labor Legislation Enacted since 1960*

Legislation	Year	Brief description
Manpower Development and Training Act (MDTA)	1962	Identified labor shortages, trained unemployed and underemployed workers.
Equal Pay Act	1963	Sought to assure that women workers received equal pay for the same work as men.
Civil Rights Act (Title VII)	1964	Prohibits discrimination in employment on the basis of race, color, religion, sex, or national origin.
Executive Order 11246 (and amendments)	1965	Requires federal contractors to set goals and time tables for hiring minority workers and women. Established Office of Federal Contract Compliance Programs (OFCCP).
Age Discrimination in Employment Act (ADEA)	1967	Prohibited the use of mandatory retirement in most occupations in the 1980s.
Occupational Safety and Health Act (OSHA)	1970	Established OSHA to set safety standards and inspect workplaces. Established National Institute for Occupational Safety and Health (NIOSH) to study safety.
Comprehensive Employment and Training Act (CETA)	1973	Moved federal employment and training programs to states, counties, and cities.
Employee Retirement Income Security Act (ERISA)	1974	Established Pension and Welfare Benefits Administration (PWBA) to promote and protect pensions, and required nondiscrimination in the provision of certain benefits.

its lowest level in over four decades. OMB projects a small upward increase in the Labor Department's budget in the next five years, which may reflect wishful thinking or the effect of an expected mild rise in unemployment.

The budget gives an incomplete picture of government activity. Table 8-2 summarizes the allotment of DOL employees across various agencies over the last forty years. The selected years correspond to business cycle peaks. In the bottom part of the table, I have grouped employment into four broad functions based on the mission of the agencies. I have tried to fit now-defunct agencies into the current set of agencies, but there are clearly several limitations to the data because some functions have no obvious modern counterpart (such as the Mexican Farm Labor Program), and the functions of some agen-

Table 8-1. *Major U.S. Labor Legislation Enacted since 1960 (continued)*

Legislation	Year	Brief description
Coal Mine Safety and Health Act	1977	Established Mine Safety and Health Administration (MSHA) within DOL to regulate mine safety.
Pregnancy Discrimination Act	1978	Extends Title VII protection against employment discrimination on the basis of pregnancy, childbirth, and related conditions.
Job Training Partnership Act (JTPA)	1983	Replaced CETA; targeted training to economically disadvantaged or dislocated workers.
Worker Adjustment and Retraining Notification Act (WARN)	1988	Requires sixty days advance notice before plant closing or mass layoffs.
Americans with Disabilities Act	1990	Extends Title VII protection against employment discrimination to those with disabilities.
Family and Medical Leave Act	1993	Grants family and temporary medical unpaid leave under certain circumstances for up to twelve weeks.
Workforce Investment Act	1998	Replaced JTPA; established one-stop system for job training and introduced greater flexibility in training.

cies have changed over time.[2] Nonetheless, several shifts in policy are evident from the table. In 1959 the Labor Department employed 5,476 employees; that number nearly doubled in the 1960s, and doubled again in the 1970s to more than 21,000 employees. The increase in employment was necessary to implement the legislation that was passed in the 1960s and 1970s. Employment at the department fell by about 20 percent during the 1980s and by another 7 percent in the 1990s. Per 10,000 employees in the private non-farm work force, DOL employed 1.2 workers in 1959, 2.9 in 1979, and 1.5 in 1999.

Much of the decline in DOL employment has been associated with a decline in training activities. In 1969, 37 percent of DOL employees were

2. For example, in 1969 many of the functions of the Office for Administration and Management were handled by the Secretary's office.

Figure 8-1. *Department of Labor Outlays, 1962–2004*

Billions of 1998 dollars

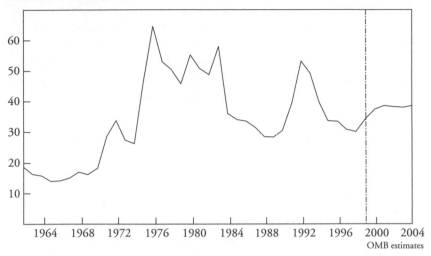

OMB estimates

Source: Nominal outlays are from Historical Table 4.1 from the Budget of the United States Government, Fiscal Year 2001. Data are adjusted to constant dollars using the GDP deflator.

assigned to the Manpower Administration, the predecessor of the Employment and Training Administration (ETA), which is responsible for job training and administering the unemployment insurance system. By 1999 ETA employment had declined to just 8 percent of the Department's total employment. The number of workers employed by ETA fell by half between 1979 and 1989. The training budget has declined substantially since the 1970s, as well. In constant 1998 dollars, spending on training and employment services was $14 billion in 1979 and only $4.8 billion in 1989. Although job training has been a stated priority of the Clinton administration, training and employment services increased by just $0.1 billion between 1992 and 1999.[3] Data are hard to come by, but it appears unlikely that state and local governments, or other branches of the federal government, have made up for the decline in government-supported job training since the early 1980s. The penultimate section of this paper provides a detailed case study of the fed-

3. The 1979 data are from DOL's annual reports. The post-1980 data are from "Historical Summary of Actual Budget Authority" provided by DOL. The figures pertain to "Training and Employment Services." The GDP deflator was used to convert to 1998 dollars.

Figure 8-2. *Department of Labor Outlays Relative to the Federal Budget,*
1962–2004

Percent of government spending

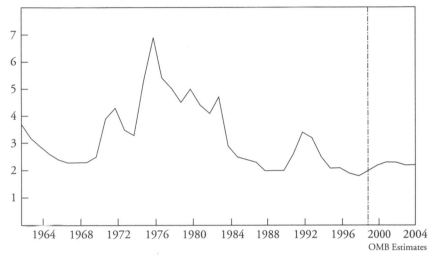

Source: Budget of the United States Government, Fiscal Year 2001.

eral training budget, and the impact of economic research on training
programs.

Table 8-2 further shows that regulatory activities grew while training
programs declined. Between 1969 and 1979, the share of DOL employees
in agencies engaged in some type of regulatory function increased from
33 to 59 percent. Put another way, the number of employees devoted to
regulatory activities nearly quadrupled between 1969 and 1979. The
advent of OSHA and MSHA in this period accounted for 70 percent of
the increase, and the expansion of other regulatory agencies such as the
Office of Federal Contract Compliance Programs (OFCCP) accounted for
the remainder.[4] Changes in budget authority also reflect the expansion of
employment in new and existing regulatory agencies in the 1970s.

The relative magnitude of some of the regulatory agencies raises some
obvious questions. For example, it is noteworthy that MSHA is slightly
larger than OSHA in terms of number of employees.[5] Because mine work-

4. The Interior Department had responsibility for mine safety from 1910 until 1977.
5. It should be noted, however, that a small number of states (including California) operate their
own state OSHA program. State OSHA programs can supersede federal OSHA programs if they are
as stringent as the federal program.

Table 8-2. *Number of Department of Labor Full-Time-Equivalent (FTE) Employees by Agency, 1959–99*[a]

Agency	1959 N	1959 Percent	1969 N	1969 Percent	1979 N	1979 Percent	1989 N	1989 Percent	1999 N	1999 Percent
Employment and Training Administration	1,356	24.8	3,887	37.2	3,507	16.1	1,696	9.6	1,350	8.3
Labor-Management Services and Standards	254	4.6	617	5.9	1,272	5.9	959	5.4	...	...
Employment Standards Administration	1,824	33.3	2,805	26.8	4,991	23.0	4,047	23.0	3,830	23.5
Occupational Safety and Health Administration	...	...	...	...	2,855	13.1	2,270	12.9	2,154	13.2
Mine Safety and Health Administration	...	...	...	...	3,703	17.0	2,671	15.2	2,202	13.5
Bureau of Labor Statistics	958	17.5	1,537	14.7	2,087	9.6	2,097	11.9	2,406	14.7
Solicitor of Labor	329	6.0	462	4.4	818	3.8	722	4.1	689	4.2
International Labor Affairs	...	...	178	1.7	376	1.7	83	0.5	69	0.4
Office of the Secretary	187	3.4	961	9.2	860	4.0	247	1.4	211	1.3
Administration and Management	124	2.3	...	...	1,250	5.8	926	5.3	890	5.5
Inspector General	...	...	...	...	...	...	524	3.0	412	2.5
Veterans' Employment Services	64	1.2	...	...	...	...	267	1.5	254	1.6
Pension Benefit Guaranty Corp. and PWBA	...	...	...	...	...	...	520	3.0	1,432	8.8
Other	380	6.9	...	...	...	...	575	3.3	420	2.6
Total DOL FTE Employment	5,476		10,447		21,719		17,604		16,319	
Summary of DOL FTEs by Function[a]										
Regulation	2,078	37.9	3,422	32.8	12,821	59.0	10,467	59.5	9,618	58.9
Training	1,420	25.9	3,887	37.2	3,507	16.1	1,963	11.2	1,604	9.8
Bureau of Labor Statistics	958	17.5	1,537	14.7	2,087	9.6	2,097	11.9	2,406	14.7
Management, Executive Direction, and Program Development	640	11.7	1,423	13.6	2,928	13.5	2,419	13.7	2,202	13.5
Total	5,096	93.1	10,269	98.3	21,343	98.3	16,946	96.3	15,830	97.0

Source: Author's analysis of DOL Annual Reports 1959–89 and DOL Budget Office unpublished tables, 1999.

a. International Labor Affairs is not classified into a function, and neither is "other." The DOL employment data for 1959 are number of positions; data for all other years are FTEs.

ers make up only 0.3 percent of the work force, this staffing differential implies that it is impossible to enforce safety standards the same way for miners as for other workers. Indeed, every mine in the United States is inspected by MSHA virtually every year, whereas the typical work-site will be visited by OSHA only once every eighty-four years.[6] An important issue for regulatory agencies is how best to target their limited resources. For example, which types of policies for selecting establishments to inspect for OSHA violations will bring about the greatest decline in injury rates? This issue receives relatively little attention in scholarly research.

The expansion of labor market regulatory activities in the Nixon presidency stands out as one of the major changes in labor policy since the 1960s. The trend toward enacting legislation that regulated more aspects of the labor market continued in the 1980s and 1990s. Examples of such legislation include the Age Discrimination in Employment Act, which prohibited mandatory retirement in most occupations in the 1980s; the Americans with Disabilities Act (ADA), which added individuals with disabilities to the groups protected by Title VII of the Civil Rights Act; the WARN Act, which required employers to give sixty days of advance notification prior to a mass layoff or plant closing; and the Family and Medical Leave Act, which mandated unpaid leave in the event of certain medical emergencies. In addition, increasing numbers of employers became covered by existing regulations because of reductions in the minimum size of covered establishments under many standards and the elimination of many industry exemptions.

The fact that the scope and scale of regulation increased without a concomitant increase in the number of employees engaged in regulatory activities raises questions as to whether many regulations are enforced. For example, John Addison and McKinley Blackburn found little evidence that the fraction of laid-off workers who receive advance notice of their layoff actually increased following the enactment of the WARN Act.[7] Although this issue is not discussed much, the lax enforcement of many labor standards may be economically efficient. The standards impose a little pressure on employers to comply, and those who would bear the greatest cost from complying tend to violate the standards.

Without self-congratulation for a policy developed and implemented on his watch, Arthur Okun argued that the Civil Rights Act of 1964

---

6. See Burton (1999). There are seven covered mines for every MSHA employee in 1999.

7. Addison and Blackburn (1994). For earlier evidence on compliance with the Fair Labor Standards Act, see Ashenfelter and Smith (1979).

"enhance[d] both equality of income and efficiency," and calculated that "the narrowing of racial differentials during the sixties implied a gain of nearly one-fifth in the wages and salaries of blacks. That gain approached 1 percent of the nation's income." He argued, "When we can have more justice and more real GNP, society should make the most of it."[8] Much of the labor market legislation put in place since 1960 could be viewed as an attempt to increase both equality and efficiency. Whether this legislation has succeeded, or how much efficiency was sacrificed for how much equality, is a topic for another day.

Labor Policy outside the Labor Department

Many federal government policies and programs outside of DOL impact the labor market. For example, the decline in progressivity in the federal income tax during the 1970s and 1980s has obvious direct implications (of indeterminant sign) for labor supply. The Earned Income Tax Credit is another tax policy that impacts labor supply. The All Volunteer Force fundamentally changed the youth labor market. Preschool programs and welfare reform have less direct but sizable impacts on the labor market, but I will leave these issues for Bob Haveman's paper.

State and local governments often regulate the labor market, as well. Before the advent of OSHA, regulating workplace safety had traditionally been the province of the states. Indeed, workers' compensation insurance, which provides cash and medical benefits for workers who suffer a work-related injury or illness, is a set of independent, state-run programs operating in each of the fifty states. Workers' compensation insurance was the first social insurance program enacted in the United States, with most states implementing programs early in the twentieth century. Total workers' compensation insurance costs to employers in 1995 were $57 billion, more than 2.5 times as great as unemployment insurance costs that same year.[9] A major change in state labor policy that occurred during the 1970s is that state workers' compensation benefits became more generous and uniform.[10] Changes in many states were enacted in large part in response

8. See Okun (1975, pp. 76 and 79). Okun's interpretation of the effect of the Civil Rights Act is also consistent with Ashenfelter (1970), Freeman (1973), and many subsequent studies. Okun also perceptively recognized the "backsliding" in the black-white wage gap in 1973, which he called a "cause for self-examination" (p. 79).

9. See U.S. Bureau of the Census (1999, tables 626 and 629, pp. 396–97).

10. See Krueger and Burton (1990).

to the work of the National Commission on State Workmen's Compensation Laws (1971), chaired by John F. Burton Jr. The commission unanimously recommended that federal legislation set minimum standards for workers' compensation laws if the states did not comply with their essential recommendations. Mary Eccles and Richard Freeman singled out this commission as an example of "a commission whose report had a significant impact."[11] Another noteworthy change in workers' compensation programs is that many states deregulated the industry that sells workers' compensation insurance beginning in the early 1980s.

States also aggressively regulate the labor market by setting and enforcing occupational licensing standards. Teachers, lawyers, and boxers are just a few of the many occupations that require a license or certification by the state to practice one's profession. Eighteen percent of all employees are in occupations that require some form of state licensing, Morris Kleiner estimates.[12] City and county governments also license some occupations, especially in the construction trades. Given the importance of occupational licensing for the labor market—there are currently more workers who are licensed than who are union members—it is unfortunate that databases with which the impact of licensing on earnings, labor supply, and output could be estimated are sparse.[13]

A recent thrust at the local level is that many local governments have pursued "living wage standards," perhaps in response to the decline in the share of workers covered by union contracts. These standards often require companies that do business with the local government to pay a minimum wage that is substantially above the federal minimum wage. Boston, for example, requires city contractors and subcontractors above a specified size to pay a minimum wage of $8.23 per hour.

One key area of labor policy that deserves more attention than I will be able to devote to it is the role of state and federal courts. At the state level, an important development has been the withering away of the employment-at-will doctrine. The common law of the United States permits employers to fire workers for any cause, good or bad. Federal legislation has

11. See Eccles and Freeman (1982, p. 231). They cited the commission's professionalism, development of model legislation that was useful to state programs, and unanimity on key policy recommendations as reasons for its success. I would also add the persistence of the chairman in tracking, prodding, and advising the states to this list.

12. See Kleiner (1990, p. 177).

13. There are, of course, some exceptions. For example, seminal work by Friedman and Kuznets (1945) on doctors and dentists focused on a form of licensing. More recently, Kleiner and Kudrle (1997) examine the effect of licensing standards for dentists on dental hygiene.

gradually restricted that right (for example, making it illegal to fire an employee because of his or her race). In many states, the state court has recognized further exceptions to employment-at-will, such as those embodied in an implicit contract (as specified in a personnel manual, for example) requiring "good cause" for dismissal. One state, Montana, has even passed legislation requiring just cause for dismissal, but limiting employers' liability if they violate that requirement, somewhat akin to workers' compensation legislation.[14]

Federal courts also play an active role in labor policy. The courts, of course, interpret and enforce much labor legislation. The role of the courts has been particularly prominent in the area of equal employment opportunity legislation and affirmative action. Economic research has played a role in the legal process, as the parties to a lawsuit often hire economists to bolster their case, and the judge deciding the case may also hire an economic expert for advice. Indeed, labor economists may have more influence on policy via the legal realm than via the political or administrative realms.

Policies affecting the labor market implemented outside DOL are clearly important, but I suspect most have a smaller effect than the expanding realm of labor market regulation. For example, the Earned Income Tax Credit (EITC) was estimated to have cost $28 billion in 1998, or 0.4 percent of national income—a small amount compared to Okun's estimate that the Civil Rights Act increased national income by 1 percent.[15] As another comparison, the recently proposed OSHA ergonomic standards are estimated to cost business from $3.5 to $18 billion per year; the entire program costs many billions more.[16]

Survey of Labor Economics Research

At the end of World War II, labor economics was dominated by "institutional economists" who believed that non-economic considerations, such as views of fairness and a firm's ability to pay, influenced economic out-

14. See Krueger (1991).

15. U.S. House Committee on Ways and Means (1998, table 13-2, p. 839). Also bear in mind that part of the EITC is meant to replace higher payroll taxes and part may be offset by lower wages.

16. Robert Pear. "After Long Delay, U.S. Plans to Issue Ergonomic Rules." *New York Times,* November 22, 1999, p. A20. The lower figure is from OSHA and the higher one is from the Small Business Administration.

comes in addition to standard economic forces (such as demand conditions). The institutional economists included Sumner Slichter, John Dunlop, Lloyd Reynolds, Clark Kerr, and Richard Lester. In the post-war period, labor economics came to be dominated by economists such as H. G. Lewis, Gary Becker, Jacob Mincer, Albert Rees, and Sherwin Rosen, who adapted and applied neoclassical models to the labor market. This transition was in full swing in the 1960s.

More recently, many labor economists have grown frustrated with the view that labor markets operate as spot markets with perfect information. "Behavioral economics," which recognizes that economic agents often consider fairness and act quasi-rationally, has begun to influence several fields of economics, including labor economics.[17] In an article published posthumously, for example, Albert Rees observed:[18]

> I do not want to be misinterpreted as saying that I now think that neoclassical theory is wrong. It is not, but it is incomplete. The most it can do is to set the stage for players such as personnel directors, union officers, and individual workers. It cannot write their lines. It matters a great deal whether the demand for labor in an industry or occupation is rising or falling and whether or not a particular occupation is in short supply or oversupply. These are the forces with which neoclassical theory deals. But given any configuration of these forces, the individual players usually still have substantial room for maneuver. In their maneuvering, they constantly struggle to preserve fairness as they see it.

A healthy synthesis is currently taking place, in which the best aspects of the older institutional economics and modern labor economics are being forged together.[19] In addition, institutional knowledge has proved essential for identifying natural experiments that have formed the basis for empirical tests of neoclassical models. In my view, what might be called the newly emerging empirical synthesis has found that neoclassical models of some

17. Jim Heckman pointed out to me that Arthur Okun (1981, pp. 26–133) anticipated the importance of search frictions and personnel economics for understanding many labor market phenomena. For example, Okun anticipated Acemoglu and Pischke's (1999) explanation of why employers might pay for general training. See Lazear (1995) for an attempt to model personnel policies in an optimizing framework.

18. Rees (1993, pp. 251–52).

19. See Freeman (1988) for a refreshing analysis of the respective contributions of institutional and neoclassical labor economics.

aspects of the labor market work well, such as human capital, although the standard neoclassical model needs to be amended to take account of search frictions, dynamic monopsony power, fairness considerations, and other market "imperfections" to adequately explain many labor market phenomena, such as the elusive effect of the minimum wage on employment and noncompetitive wage differentials.

Trends in Research Topics

To provide an indication of the quantity of research on various topics in labor economics, I searched over several DOL program names and research topics using *EconLit,* an electronic database of articles assembled by the American Economic Association. The search yielded the number of journal articles that mention the program or topic in their title, key words, or abstract.[20] The results were tabulated separately for each of the last three decades.[21] Table 8-3 summarizes the number of articles published on the selected programs and topics.[22] Although this analysis is crude for several reasons (some articles are more thorough in listing key words than others; *Econ Lit*'s compilation of abstracts and journals changes over time; and, perhaps most important, the volume of journal articles does not necessarily translate into the research interests of those in the field), it nonetheless provides some indication of changes in economists' interests among labor market topics.

The results in table 8-3 indicate that work on unions and collective bargaining continues to dominate research in labor economics, although the fraction of articles published on unions from this set of topics has declined from over two-thirds in the 1970s to less than one-third in the 1990s. The decline in the share of research on unions coincided with a decline in the importance of unions in the U.S. labor market; private sector union membership declined steadily from a peak of over 30 percent in the mid-1950s to less than 10 percent in 1998, with the sharpest decline occurring in the 1970s and 1980s.[23] Interestingly, research on labor supply, labor demand,

20. When the key word search was done on "union or collective bargaining," many more references were found, probably because of studies concerning the Soviet Union or European Union. Consequently, the union search was based on the *Journal of Economic Literature* (JEL) code.

21. Unfortunately, *EconLit* only extends back to January 1969.

22. See Manser (1998, table 1.2) for related evidence. The number of articles covered by the topics in table 8-3 accounted for about two-thirds of all articles in labor economics (JEL codes J1–J7) in the 1990s.

23. In contrast, union membership levels in the public sector increased from 23 percent in 1973 to 37.5 percent in 1998. See Hirsch and Macpherson (1999, tables 1c and 1f).

Table 8-3. *Journal Articles Published on Selected Topics in Labor Economics, 1970–99*[a]

Program or Topic	1970–79 Number	1970–79 Percent	1980–89 Number	1980–89 Percent	1990–99 Number	1990–99 Percent
OSHA	15	0.8	16	0.4	16	0.2
MSHA	1	0.1	1	0.0	0	0.0
Workers' Compensation insurance	7	0.4	23	0.6	73	0.9
Unemployment insurance	122	6.3	222	6.1	634	7.4
Fair Labor Standards Act	3	0.2	2	0.1	6	0.1
Minimum wage	46	2.4	82	2.3	488	5.7
Overtime	7	0.9	25	0.7	53	0.6
Government job training programs	15	0.8	18	0.5	72	0.8
Employment standards	2	0.1	1	0.0	5	0.1
Civil Rights Act or discrimination	29	1.5	46	1.3	138	1.6
Affirmative action	9	0.5	26	0.7	76	0.9
Pensions	69	3.6	177	4.9	601	7.1
Unions or collective bargaining	1,328	68.7	2,373	65.2	2,489	29.2
Earned Income Tax Credit	0	0.0	0	0.0	19	0.2
Occupational licensing	6	0.3	9	0.2	2	0.0
Wage subsidy	3	0.2	1	0.0	4	0.0
Wage inequality or dispersion	3	0.2	16	0.4	165	1.9
Return to education	20	1.0	20	0.5	126	1.5
Job search	55	2.8	95	2.6	1,014	11.9
Labor supply	140	7.2	360	9.9	1,812	21.3
Labor demand	42	2.2	126	3.5	730	8.6
Total	1,932	100.0	3,639	100.0	8,523	100.0

Source: Author's calculations based on searching *EconLit*. Only articles published in journals covered by *EconLit* are included. Data are totals by decade.

a. Searches were conducted for abbreviations as well as full program names. MSHA also includes studies of "mine safety." Government job training also includes searches for JTPA, CETA, Job Corps, and MDTA. The employment standards result also includes "labor management standards." Civil Rights Act and discrimination searches also required a labor market connection. "Unions or collective bargaining" refers to JEL Code J5 in 1990 and after, and JEL Code 830 before 1990.

and job search has increased over time, both absolutely and as a percentage of all work on these categories. Studies on wage dispersion and the returns to education also increased in the 1990s, following a decade of dramatically increasing wage dispersion and returns to education in the 1980s. The lag may reflect time lags in journal publications, or slowness of economists to recognize new trends in the economy.[24]

Research on specific labor market programs is much less common than work on fundamental economic parameters and trends. This is not necessarily a negative reflection on the profession, however, because understanding the operation of the economy is important in its own right, and can obviously lead to better public policies.

The volume of work on various labor market programs appears to me to be only weakly related to the thrust of labor market policies or the importance of those policies. For example, with the possible exception of work on pensions, the shift toward greater labor market regulation is not reflected in the topics that economists research. Despite workers' compensation costs exceeding unemployment insurance costs by 2.5 times, nearly nine times as many studies were published on UI as workers' compensation in the 1990s. And the increase in the number of studies on unemployment insurance since the 1970s exceeded the increase in the number on workers' compensation insurance, despite the more rapid increase in workers' compensation costs and more significant changes in the program. On the other hand, unemployment insurance is the Labor Department's largest budget item, and it has received more attention than any other program listed in the table. I also would add that I think much of this research has deepened the understanding of UI and unemployment, and some of it even has influenced the design of the program.

The quantity of research on the minimum wage grew in the 1990s, after the minimum wage increased in the beginning of the decade and a controversy broke out over the effect of minimum wage increases on employment. Remarkably, the combined number of articles published in the 1990s on the Civil Rights Act or labor market discrimination, affirmative action, overtime, OSHA, MSHA, government job training, the Earned Income Tax Credit, occupational licensing, and wage subsidies was less than the number published on the minimum wage, even though these programs affect far more employees than the minimum wage.

---

24. There are also some exceptions who published on these trends early on, such as Frank Levy (1987) and Bennett Harrison and Barry Bluestone (1988).

Again, I would caution against drawing the conclusion that the allocation of research effort across topics is necessarily a mark against the profession. For example, work on some programs (such as job training) offers greater promise of yielding insight into econometric methods and of developing new methods than work on other programs, even if the programs are not of great importance for the economy. And research on some public policies (such as the minimum wage) has more potential than others for improving economists' understanding of the most appropriate way to model the labor market. Indeed, the increase in research on job search in the 1990s may partly result from findings of minimum wage research. I certainly do not mean to imply that the direction of government policy should set the research agenda of labor economists. Nonetheless, the figures in table 8-3 do suggest to me that a shift toward research on the effects of labor market regulation, and ways of improving the efficiency and efficacy of regulations, would make labor economics more germane to public policy.

Research Methods, Data, and "Consensus" in Labor Economics

Labor economics remains one of the more empirical fields in economics, despite a general shift in economic research toward empirical analysis across all fields.[25] Almost 80 percent of articles on labor economics published in eight leading economics journals in 1994–97 contained some empirical analysis, compared to 56 percent in all fields of economics.[26]

Several studies have documented a shift in the data used by labor economists, and the methods used to analyze the data, since the 1960s. In the second half of the 1960s, for example, 42 percent of labor economics articles in eight leading economics journals used aggregate time-series data, whereas only 6 percent of articles published in 1994–97 used time-series data.[27] Micro panel and cross-section data, by contrast, have become much more prevalent.

The econometric methods and strategies commonly employed in labor economics research have changed as well. Based on his survey of econometric techniques used in articles on labor economics published in eight leading economics journals in 1985–87 and 1995–97, Robert Moffitt con-

25. See Moffitt (1999); Figlio (1994); Angrist and Krueger (1999).
26. Angrist and Krueger (1999).
27. See Angrist and Krueger (1999); Stafford (1986); Manser (1998).

cludes, "Selection bias methods of all types have shown a marked decline over the period. This includes the two-step methods as well as full-information maximum likelihood methods. . . . Moving in the opposite direction are methods using IV [instrumental variables] or two-stage least squares (2SLS), which have grown enormously."[28] He interprets these trends as evidence that "econometric practice in labor economics is shifting toward techniques that are, or at least can be argued to be, less restrictive and more robust than some of those used in the past. Identification of the parameters of econometric models has become a more important focus of attention than it has been historically. This is a trend which would appear to be occurring across many fields of economics, in other social science disciplines, and in fact in the field of statistics itself."[29]

What do labor economists conclude from research in the field? Table 8-4 summarizes and (slightly) extends some of the results in Victor Fuchs, Alan Krueger, and James Poterba's 1996 survey of labor economists at universities whose economics department is ranked among the top forty departments in the United States.[30] The sampled economists were asked to report their best estimate of selected parameters (such as the compensated elasticity of labor demand) and a subjective confidence interval which they were 95 percent confident contained the true economic parameter. The first column of table 8-4 reports the median of the best estimates of each parameter, and the next two columns report the 25th percentile and 75th percentile of the best estimates. The fourth and fifth columns report the median of the lower and upper bounds of the subjective confidence intervals for the parameters, respectively. The sixth column reports the median width of the individual confidence intervals reported by the respondents, which in general does not equal the difference between the median upper bound and median lower bound. The last two rows report results for the male labor supply questions for public finance economists, who were also included in the survey.

As discussed in Fuchs, Krueger, and Poterba, the median of the best estimates accords reasonably well with the findings of mainstream literature reviews (which, of course, does not necessarily imply that the estimates are the true parameters). The median best estimate of the output-constant labor demand elasticity, for example, is exactly equal to Daniel Hamermesh's "best guess" of −0.30 for this parameter based on his comprehensive

28. Moffitt (1999, pp. 1372 and 1369).
29. Moffitt (1999, p. 1369).
30. See Fuchs, Krueger, and Poterba (1998) for a greater description of the survey and a copy of the questionnaire.

Table 8-4. *Labor and Public Finance Economists' Views about Selected Parameters*

| Parameter | Best estimate | | | Subjective confidence interval | | | Disagreement coefficient[a] |
	Median (1)	25th percentile (2)	75th percentile (3)	Median lower bound (4)	Median upper bound (5)	Median width (6)	(7)
Labor economists							
Total labor demand elasticity	-0.50	-1.00	-0.30	-0.90	-0.25	0.50	49.1
Output-constant labor demand elasticity	-0.30	-0.50	-0.20	-0.70	-0.13	0.40	45.0
Marshallian labor supply elasticity (women)	0.30	0.10	0.70	0.10	0.60	0.60	55.1
Compensated labor supply elasticity (women)	0.43	0.20	0.80	0.20	0.75	0.55	50.0
Marshallian labor supply elasticity (men)	0.00	0.00	0.10	-0.10	0.20	0.35	31.3
Compensated labor supply elasticity (men)	0.18	0.08	0.28	0.00	0.30	0.30	34.8
Payroll tax borne by employers (percent)	20	5	33	0	42.5	30	43.3
JTPA earnings effect for youth (percent)	2	0	6	0	8	10	27.6
JTPA earnings effect for men (percent)	2	0	5	0	10	10	28.8
JTPA earnings effect for women (percent)	7	2	10	0	10	12	37.6
Minimum wage effect on teen employment (percent)	-1	-3	0	-3	0	4	49.3
Union wage effect (percent)	15	10	15	5	20	15	16.1
Union productivity effect (percent)	0	0	10	-5	10	15	35.1
Public finance economists							
Marshallian labor supply elasticity (men)	0.05	0	0.1	-0.1	0.3	0.35	31.8
Compensated labor supply elasticity (men)	0.2	0.1	0.3	0.05	0.5	0.4	39.3

Source: Columns 1–3 are from Fuchs, Krueger, and Poterba (1998, table 2); columns 4–7 are author's calculations based on survey data described in Fuchs, Krueger, and Poterba (1998).

a. The disagreement coefficient is the average percentage of best estimates that lie beyond the other respondents' 95 percent subjective confidence intervals. Sample size ranges from 40 to 63.

review of the literature.[31] The median labor supply estimates are consistent with Mark Killingsworth's and John Pencavel's surveys.[32] On the other hand, a wide range of best estimates were reported for many of the parameters. For example, the interquartile range of best estimates for the output-constant labor demand elasticity is 0.30.

One noteworthy pattern of the survey responses is that many of the behavioral parameters are estimated to be quite small. For example, the median best estimate of the male labor supply elasticities (either compensated or uncompensated) is close to zero. Moreover, the public finance economists' assessments of the male labor supply elasticities are quite similar to the labor economists'. In view of some of the large labor supply estimates in the public finance literature, this finding is noteworthy. The female labor supply elasticities are larger, but still well below 1.

The labor economists also reported that they expected modest or negligible effects of a minimum wage increase on employment, consistent with most of the literature. The median labor economist's best estimate was that a 10 percent increase in the minimum wage would lead to a decline in teenage employment of 1 percent, while 30 percent of labor economists expected that it would have no adverse effect on teenage employment. Furthermore, over two-thirds of the labor economists reported confidence intervals that contained no adverse effect within their boundaries. Nonetheless, a small minority of economists predicted large employment effects.

The median of the best estimates for the proportionate effect of participating in the Job Training Partnership Act (JTPA) program on earnings was small: 2 percent for both youth and adult men, and 7 percent for adult women. Many respondents include no effect in their range of plausible estimates. I suspect that the actual average effects of JTPA training are small, but I also suspect they are larger than that reported by the median labor economist. For example, based on the National JTPA Experiment, Bloom and his colleagues find that in the second year after leaving training adult women who participated in JTPA had earnings on average that were 15.6 percent higher than the non-JTPA control group, while adult men had earnings that were 10.5 percent higher.[33] No effect on earnings was found for youth. Interestingly, the pattern of larger percentage effects for women than men and youth was reflected in the survey responses.

31. See Hamermesh (1993, p. 92).
32. See Killingsworth (1983); Pencavel (1986).
33. Bloom and others (1997, p. 562). See Heckman, LaLonde, and Smith (1999) for a comprehensive review of job training programs and related evaluation methods.

Despite—or perhaps because of—the large body of empirical work in labor economics, there is tremendous uncertainty and disagreement about the magnitude of key parameters among labor economists. The relative depth of many of the confidence intervals (as evidenced in the sixth column) reveals a great range of uncertainty at the individual level. Fuchs, Krueger, and Poterba find much collective uncertainty as well: for the typical parameter, the mean best estimate is rejected by 41 percent of the respondents' 95 percent subjective confidence intervals.[34]

The seventh column of table 8-4 reports a new statistic for measuring the disparity of views among members of the profession, which I call the "disagreement coefficient." The disagreement coefficient can be interpreted as the expected probability that a randomly selected economist's best estimate of a parameter is not contained in the confidence interval of another randomly selected economist. The disagreement coefficient was calculated as follows. For each economist denoted i, the percentage of other economists denoted j ($i \neq j$) whose confidence intervals did not include i's best estimate was calculated. This percentage was denoted as d_i. The disagreement coefficient was then calculated as the mean of d_i taken over all economists in the sample.

The disagreement coefficients are high, ranging from 30 to 50 percent for most parameters. The average disagreement coefficient across all questions is 38 percent. As a benchmark for comparison, suppose independent, random samples of a characteristic X are drawn from an infinite, normal population, and a series of sample means are calculated from these samples. Also suppose that 95 percent confidence intervals are formed by adding and subtracting 1.96 times the standard deviation of the distribution of sample means to each sample mean. The expected value of the disagreement coefficient in this scenario (that is, the expected percentage of confidence intervals that exclude the sample means) is approximately 17 percent. Because the best estimates in table 8-4 are not derived from independent draws from a normal population—instead, economists rely on the same literature, discuss parameter estimates with one another, and sometimes bound parameters based on theoretical considerations—one could argue that the disagreement statistics should be smaller than this benchmark. On the other hand, because some economists may have interpreted the survey questions differently than others (for example, labor supply could be measured in terms of hours of work, participation, or work

34. Fuchs, Krueger, and Poterba (1998, pp. 1392–93).

effort), one could argue that the measured disagreement is more apparent than real.[35] It is also possible, however, that some respondents increased the width of their confidence intervals to account for variable interpretations of the questions. In any event, the 17 percent figure provides a benchmark of what to expect under controlled conditions.

For some parameter estimates, such as the extensively researched labor supply and demand elasticities, the disagreement rates are nearly three times greater than the benchmark level. If a randomly selected labor economist were to compare notes with another randomly selected labor economist, there is a 50–50 chance the first economist's best estimate of the female labor supply elasticity would lie outside the other's 95 percent confidence interval. (Based on these results, it is no wonder that "The News Hour with Jim Lehrer" rarely has trouble finding economists who disagree with one another.) As John Gilbert and Frederick Mosteller predicted many years ago, "No matter how much experimentation we do, controversy will still be the order of the day."[36]

The disagreement coefficient is 16 percent for the union wage differential question, which is slightly below the benchmark level. Fuchs, Krueger, and Poterba similarly found that there was considerably more accord on this question than on the others. They attributed this phenomenon largely to the herculean effort H. G. Lewis devoted to reworking, evaluating, and synthesizing most of the estimates in the literature at the time.[37] Lewis narrowed the range of plausible estimates, and many economists appear to have adopted his conclusions.

One of Arthur Okun's enduring metaphors is the "leaky bucket" used to transfer resources from the affluent to the disadvantaged. Okun expected that labor supply responses to taxes would be small, concluding that dozens of studies "have uncovered virtually no significant effects of the present tax system on the amount of work effort of the affluent. Some limited effects of transfer payments have been found on the work effort of secondary earners . . . in low-income families, but virtually none on primary earn-

---

35. Fuchs, Krueger, and Poterba (1998) provide a calculation that adjusts for variability added to the best estimates due to alternative possible interpretations of labor supply (such as weekly hours, annual weeks, annual hours, or participation) and still find a great deal of collective disagreement. It is also worth noting that, across questions, the disagreement rates are essentially uncorrelated with the fraction of respondents who did not answer a question. This is relevant because the question nonresponse rate is probably higher for more ambiguous questions.

36. Gilbert and Mosteller (1972, p. 377).

37. Lewis's work is summarized in two books; see Lewis (1963, 1986).

ers."[38] My reading of the survey results in table 8-4 is that much of the labor economics profession is in agreement with Okun's conclusion. The crucial elasticities that determine the distortionary effects of taxes, transfers, and regulations appear to imply relatively small deadweight losses. Alas, the enhanced earnings and employment prospects of those who receive job training or wage subsidies also appear to be small. The good news is that Okun's bucket has a relatively small leak. The bad news is that it requires many watering trips before the flowers become self-sufficient— more like growing orchids than desert flowers.

Not everyone agrees that the "consensus" estimate among labor economists is that some important behavioral responses are small, or that the available evidence tends to support this conclusion. Gary Becker, for example, while defending the supply-side assumptions embedded in the Dole tax plan, has argued, "Economists should go out of business if they deny that taxes, prices, and costs significantly alter behavior."[39] In view of the high disagreement coefficients in table 8-4, it would be surprising if there were not a wide range of opinion on these issues, as long as the economics profession stays in business.

The Labor Department's Impact on Research

Before turning to the case study of job training, it is worth considering four areas in which Labor Department policy has influenced labor economics research, rather than vice versa. First, as Henry Aaron has argued, "despite our professional pride in determining our priorities, history strongly suggests that the president's priorities will shape the research agenda of economists . . . more than ours will shape his."[40] Administration and congressional initiatives do Granger-cause some research in labor economics. Consider, for example, the outpouring of work on "job lock" due to health insurance around the time that the Clinton health care task force was formed, or the large volume of work on Individual Retirement Accounts (IRAs).

Second, the Bureau of Labor Statistics (BLS) has obviously helped fuel the micro data revolution in labor economics.[41] Much research in labor

38. Okun (1975, p. 97). Okun goes on to note that socially unproductive efforts are devoted to other forms of tax avoidance "as surely as snow is followed by little boys on sleds."

39. Gary Becker, "Why the Dole Plan Will Work," *Business Week,* August 26, 1996, p. 16.

40. See Aaron's (1989, p. 1) Richard T. Ely lecture to the American Economic Association.

41. See Goldberg and Moye (1985) on the history of the BLS.

economics relies on the basic monthly Current Population Survey (CPS), the March Annual Demographic File of the CPS, and supplements to the CPS such as the Displaced Worker Survey.

Third, the formation of the Manpower Demonstration Research Corporation (MDRC), and support for social experiments and data collection more generally, has influenced research. Six government agencies and the Ford Foundation were involved in the formation of MDRC.[42] The Manpower Administration in DOL, and Howard Rosen in particular, played the lead role from the government's side. The Labor Department had authority to conduct experiments and demonstration projects through the Comprehensive Employment and Training Act (CETA). Support for the creation of an organization like MDRC within DOL arose from frustration that the department's training programs had not been adequately evaluated.

Mitchell Sviridoff of the Ford Foundation and Howard Rosen assembled a coalition of scholars, practitioners, and government officials that formed MDRC.[43] In 1974, MDRC was set up to conduct the National Supported Work Demonstration experiment, which has subsequently been the subject of an influential paper by Robert LaLonde.[44] The Ford Foundation and federal government provided the initial financial support. Between 1974 and 1976, DOL contributed $9.9 million in grants to MDRC, which was 56 percent of MDRC's total funding.[45] I suspect that the strategy of establishing an external research organization to evaluate the government's training and welfare programs helped shield the researchers from bureaucratic and political pressures, and has led to more objective research. The Labor Department has subsequently supported several other experimental evaluations, including Job Search Assistance evaluations, the National JTPA Study, and an on-going evaluation of Job Corps. The department has also helped to establish other nonprofit organizations to conduct evaluation research.

The number of labor and related social experiments that were initiated since the early 1960s is displayed in figure 8-3. The figure is based on data

42. This paragraph and the next one draw heavily from Brecher (1978), which tells the story of the founding of MDRC.

43. The committee that oversaw research issues in the National Supported Work Demonstration consisted of Eli Ginzberg (chair), Robert Lampman, Richard Nathan, Robert Solow, Gilbert Steiner, and Phyllis Wallace.

44. See LaLonde (1986).

45. Brecher (1978, p. 22).

Figure 8-3. *Labor-related Social Experiments Begun Each Period, 1962–96*

Number

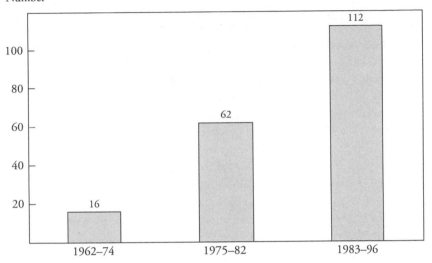

Source: Author's calculations based on Greenberg, Shroder, and Onstott (1999).

reported in a study by David Greenberg, Mark Shroder, and Matthew Onstott.[46] The number of labor-related experiments conducted per year increased from 1.2 in the 1960s and early 1970s to 6.5 in the 1980s and 1990s. Greenberg, Shroder, and Onstott also document that the scale of the experiments increased: the median sample size grew from 401 in the early period to 2,312 in the later period. They also observe that most social experiments have been conducted on persons or families who are somehow disadvantaged. Social experiments have been conducted on negative income taxes, welfare reforms, and job search assistance, but not individual retirement accounts or capital gains tax cuts.[47]

That experimental evaluations initiated by DOL have contributed to labor economics is suggested by the Fuchs, Krueger, and Poterba survey cited earlier. Three-quarters of the labor economists in the survey

46. See Greenberg, Shroder, and Onstott (1999, table 2). The figures pertain to education and training (excluding preschool), obtaining employment, and guaranteed income experiments.

47. One could argue that it is efficient to confine experiments to poor individuals because the costs are lower. However, some have argued that the benefits of treatments that are relevant for high-income populations (such as capital gains cuts) are much larger than their costs. Thus it is unclear which way the efficiency argument cuts.

responded, "To understand the effects of job training, I would give more credence to results coming from studies that employ" randomized assignment as opposed to structural modeling. Ten percent of respondents were indifferent toward the two options, and 15 percent of respondents preferred a structural model. Heterogeneous preferences over methodology may be an important source of disagreement over the value of economic parameters. Nonetheless, I suspect that results of experimental evaluations influence labor economists' and policymakers' views about key economic issues more than most other evidence. Consider, for example, the nearly completed Job Corps experiment currently being conducted by Mathematica, Inc., a nonprofit corporation in Princeton, New Jersey. This is the only experimental evaluation of the program, although there have been nonexperimental evaluations. When results of the evaluation are available, I suspect that economists and policymakers will strongly adjust their views of the effectiveness of the Job Corps in the direction of the findings of the Mathematica evaluation.

A fourth area in which DOL has influenced the development of the labor economics profession involves support for Ph.D. students.[48] Between 1968 and 1981, the Manpower Administration operated a small grants program that provided financial support for more than 500 doctoral students in labor economics and related fields. In 1977, the average grant was $12,500, the equivalent of $30,00 in 1999 dollars. Howard Rosen was also instrumental in developing and implementing this program. Grant recipients were selected by a rotating panel of experts who met quarterly to review and evaluate submissions; DOL set research priorities each year and approved the criteria against which the proposals were judged. The list of participants in this program reads like a *Who's Who* of modern labor economics, including Steven Allen, Francine Blau, Barry Bluestone, Michael Boskin, Sheldon Danziger, Ronald Ehrenberg, Randall Filer, Robert Flanagan, Richard Freeman, James Heckman, Joseph Hotz, Lawrence Kahn, Morris Kleiner, Robert E. B. Lucas, Thomas McCurdy, Stephen Marston, James Medoff, Robert Moffitt, Ronald Oaxaca, Paul Osterman, Harvey Rosen, James P. Smith, Robert S. Smith, Katherine Swartz, W. Kip Viscusi, Halbert White, and Kenneth Wolpin. Scholars in other fields

---

48. Disclaimer: When I was chief economist of the Department of Labor, I tried to resurrect this program. The idea had considerable support from several agencies, some of which offered to contribute part of their research budgets to the program. But my proposal was put on hold by the Secretary of Labor who (possibly correctly) was concerned that it would look like pork to some members of Congress and be subject to budget cuts.

included Robert Groves, Harry Katz, Craig Olson, and Nancy Tuma. Some grant recipients went on to distinguished careers in public service or academic administration, including Michael Boskin, Kim Clark, Thomas Glynn, Wendy Lee Gramm, and Sharon Smith.

According to DOL records from the late 1970s, about 80 percent of those who received grants were teaching at colleges and universities. Although it is unclear how many grant recipients would have completed graduate school or worked in labor economics and related areas in the absence of such a program, it is likely that the program induced many researchers to work in labor economics who otherwise would not have. Moreover, it is likely that DOL received useful and cost-effective research input from the grant recipients. It is certainly the case that many of the grant recipients produced fundamental research on many topics in labor economics.

Recent Shifts in Job Training Programs

The federal government began several manpower development programs targeted at increasing the employment of women, youth, older workers, minorities, and people with disabilities to alleviate labor shortage problems during World War II. In 1962, the Kennedy administration's Manpower Development and Training Act (MDTA) focused on the same groups, but was designed to create jobs for these individuals or train them for future employment. The CETA program and JTPA programs continued this mission. Other programs and models were also added along the way. For example, the Job Corps program began during the Great Society and continues to provide intensive, multi-pronged training services in a residential setting to over 60,000 economically disadvantaged youth each year.

The effect of job training on participants' employment and earnings has been studied as carefully and thoroughly as any other topic in economics. Although possible general equilibrium effects of training—notably displacement effects and long-term effects on participants (especially youth)—are not well understood, a great deal of progress has been made in this field.[49] There is also more professional agreement on job training's

49. For a review of the literature and overview of job training programs, see Heckman, LaLonde, and Smith (1999).

effects than on most other topics (see table 8-4). As a consequence, I think scholarly research on job training has influenced policy, albeit often with long lags and only partially. After reviewing the literature on job training available through 1994, Robert LaLonde put forward the following list of policy recommendations, which I take to be sensible and widely shared:[50]

> First, these findings suggest that JTPA dollars are misallocated to the extent that sites must deny services to eligible adult women to reserve some of their funds for adult men and especially for youths.

> Second, because Job Corps appears to be the only program that benefits disadvantaged youths, it would make sense to allocate more JTPA funds to this program. . . .

> Third, if public policy makers wish to provide effective services to disadvantaged men and youths and to dislocated workers, they must develop new and probably more intensive long-term training services. . . .

> Finally, the large gains often associated with investments in inexpensive services such as job search assistance suggest that diminishing returns may plague investments in more expensive services such as classroom training and on-the-job training.

The research findings leading to LaLonde's recommendations were echoed in a report released by DOL's Chief Economist's Office in early 1995.[51] In addition, several researchers testified at congressional hearings on job training in 1994 and 1995. As a consequence, many of the relevant findings were known by officials in DOL, members of Congress and their staffs, and the media.

Has actual practice been affected by the research findings? Table 8-5 presents a summary of DOL's actual training budget authority from 1980 to 1999, in constant 1999 dollars. It is difficult to compare the figures by recipient group over time because of the switch from CETA to JTPA, and because separate JTPA figures for youth and adult training are only avail-

---

50. See LaLonde (1995, pp. 165–66).

51. U.S. Department of Labor, Office of the Chief Economist (1995). The report was prepared by Marcus Stanley, under the close direction of the chief economist at the time, Lawrence Katz. I was the chief economist when the report was released.

Table 8-5. *Actual Budget Authority for Department of Labor Job Training Programs, 1980–99*[a]

Millions of 1999 dollars

Program	1980	1981	1982	1983	1984	1985	1986	1987	1988	1989	1990	1991	1992	1993	1994	1995	1996	1997	1998	1999
CETA comprehensive programs	3,926	3,661	1,836	2,764	…	…	…	…	…	…	…	…	…	…	…	…	…	…	…	…
CETA public service employment	2,817	3,361	…	…	…	…	…	…	…	…	…	…	…	…	…	…	…	…	…	…
CETA private sector programs	619	237	377	361	…	…	…	…	…	…	…	…	…	…	…	…	…	…	…	…
CETA youth employment demonstration programs	1,574	1,437	315	302	…	…	…	…	…	…	…	…	…	…	…	…	…	…	…	…
CETA Young Adult Conservative Corps	477	348	…	…	…	…	…	…	…	…	…	…	…	…	…	…	…	…	…	…
Job Corps	792	976	966	977	1,536	903	874	908	956	951	985	1,025	1,077	1,082	1,138	1,165	1,148	1,189	1,271	1,308
Summer Youth	1,159	1,461	1,108	1,296	2,346	1,207	907	1,038	959	909	859	807	1,144	1,148	972	198	656	897	888	871
JTPA youth training grants	…	…	…	…	…	…	…	…	…	…	…	…	…	758	721	82	133	131	133	130
JTPA adult training grants	…	…	…	…	…	…	…	…	…	…	…	…	…	1,137	1,081	1,066	892	922	974	955
JTPA block grant	…	…	…	…	4,998	2,761	2,544	2,547	2,416	2,291	2,142	2,101	2,039	…	…	…	…	…	…	…
JTPA dislocated workers	…	…	…	173	480	326	137	277	384	364	569	623	663	729	1,223	1,314	1,146	1,325	1,372	1,406
School-to-Work	…	…	…	…	…	…	…	…	…	…	…	…	…	…	…	131	178	206	204	125
Youth Opportunity Grants	…	…	…	…	…	…	…	…	…	…	…	…	…	…	…	…	…	…	…	240
National programs	1,007	959	287	430	553	329	300	359	370	334	268	264	263	313	390	222	192	189	245	485
Total	12,371	12,440	4,888	6,302	9,913	5,526	4,761	5,129	5,084	4,848	4,824	4,819	5,186	5,168	5,524	4,177	4,346	4,859	5,088	5,280

Source: Author's calculations based on unpublished data provided by Mark Wichlin of DOL.

a. Youth training programs appear in bold. Data are adjusted to 1999 dollars based on the GDP deflator. An inflation rate of 2 percent is assumed for 1999. Numbers may not add to the total due to rounding. Data are on a fiscal year basis. National programs include several miscellaneous programs, including demonstrations and administration.

able beginning in 1993. The bottom row of the table indicates that total job training expenditures declined sharply at the beginning of the Reagan administration, as was mentioned previously.

The various youth training programs and the Summer Youth Employment Program (which is not really a training program) are high-lighted in bold. Notice first that JTPA Youth Training Grants were eviscer-ated in FY 1995, falling from $721 million to $82 million. The program rebounded a little in subsequent years, but still remains a skeleton of its for-mer self. Expenditures on the Job Corps program do not display a secular trend over the last twenty years, although the Job Corps budget has increased in nine of the last ten years. This shift in the relative allocation of the youth training budget strikes me as consistent with LaLonde's recom-mendations. New youth training initiatives have also begun. For example, the School-to-Work program aims at improving the transition to the job market for non-college-bound students. In 1999 youth training was par-tially restored in the form of a new Youth Opportunity Grants program. This program provides funding for training for long-term employment in empowerment zones and other high poverty areas.

The training budget for disadvantaged adults has declined over the last six years, while the budget for dislocated workers has increased by a greater amount. As a consequence, total spending on adult training increased. Budget figures are not available on adult training by gender. However, data on JTPA-II adult training participants indicate that between 1990 and 1995 the share of program terminees who were women steadily increased from 58 to 67 percent.[52] Perhaps by coincidence, this shift is also in the direction of LaLonde's recommendation.

Because job training is also provided by some federal agencies outside DOL and by many other public and private sources, one should be cau-tious about interpreting the trends shown in table 8-5 as reflecting shifts in the national training budget. Individuals who are denied access to DOL's job training programs may gain access to other programs, and the preva-lence of such training may have changed over time. Substitution of other programs may be particularly important for youth: James Heckman, Robert LaLonde, and Jeffrey Smith, for example, find that 34 percent of male youth and 42 percent of female youth who were randomly denied admission to JTPA nonetheless received some training services.[53]

52. See U.S. House Committee on Ways and Means (1998, table 15-33a, p. 1004).
53. Heckman, LaLonde, and Smith (1999, table 3, p. 1910).

Two other recent changes in the job training system deserve mention. First, on November 24, 1993, the Congress passed legislation requiring the states to implement a Worker Profiling and Reemployment Services (WPRS) program for unemployed workers through their unemployment insurance (UI) systems. This new system has had the effect of channeling many additional UI recipients through inexpensive reemployment services, including job search workshops, counseling, and job clubs. In 1998, nearly one million workers reported for at least one service, and 750,000 completed a service.[54] This would seem to be another policy change in the direction that LaLonde suggested. However, it is unlikely that WPRS has had a noticeable effect on aggregate unemployment because the effect of job search assistance tends to be modest, and because UI claimants account for only a minority of the unemployed.[55]

The second major change is the passage of the Workforce Investment Act (WIA) of 1998, which replaces JTPA. Support for WIA stemmed primarily from a feeling that there were "too many" job training programs and lines of funding; a desire to give participants more flexibility over their type of training and training provider; and a desire to require more accountability of service providers. From my vantage point, it appeared that political discussions of training reform in the mid-1990s all too often disintegrated into complaints about the fragmentation of the system and the "excessive" number of small programs. Indeed, competing reports were released counting the number of programs: 80, 90, 100, more than 100. This debate was certainly unrelated to research and often struck me as misguided. After all, colleges have hundreds of different majors and funding streams, but that does not seem as problematic. The second and third issues are more serious, but unfortunately are also devoid of much empirical research. Indeed, it is unclear whether publicizing information on providers' job placement rates will be very informative to potential participants if social scientists have difficulty inferring causality from such data. There was also a void of information on how program operators selected participants and responded to incentives, although James Heckman, Jeffrey Smith, and Christopher Taber have recently made a start down this road.[56] Nonetheless, on general principles, it is hard to argue with providing more choice and more information.

---

54. These statistics are from Katz and Krueger (1999, p. 46). See Wandner and Messenger (1999, p. 9) for evidence suggesting that most of the job search assistance services provided under WPRS are a net addition to the total amount of government assistance that UI claimants receive.
55. See Katz and Krueger (1999) for an analysis of the effect of WPRS on unemployment.
56. Heckman, Smith, and Taber (1996).

The Workforce Investment Act grew out of training bills that were proposed by DOL under Secretary Robert Reich. There are six major changes introduced by the bill that passed. First, participants will have Individual Training Accounts (ITAs) to use to select training services, instead of being referred to a training provider that contracted with JTPA. Second, states will have the option of developing a unified plan to implement a number of federal programs. Third, each state, or a group of states, will be authorized to establish regional performance measures and coordinate services among local areas. Fourth, the four funding streams under JTPA will be aggregated into three funding streams. Fifth, training providers will be required to meet performance-based eligibility criteria. Sixth, states will be subject to a penalty equal to 5 percent of their federal funding if they fail to meet statewide performance goals.

The states are responsible for phasing in many aspects of the WIA program. I suspect that results of earlier research on JTPA will still be relevant in the new regime because many of the JTPA providers and training services will carry over, and because, at one level, the group undergoing training seems at least as important as the services they receive. Like most legislation, the devil will lie in the details. And an important detail will be the level of funding for the Individual Training Accounts.

Conclusion

The shift in labor policy toward regulation and away from job training documented here cries out for an explanation. Many more features of the labor market—including safety and health, leave time, notification of layoffs, fringe benefits, and discrimination in all aspects of employment—have come under regulation since the beginning of the 1960s. Meanwhile, the Labor Department job training budget has been reduced by two-thirds from its peak in the 1970s. Part of the explanation for these trends probably is related to the recognition that training programs are not a panacea for society's ills. Many training programs have high rates of return and are worth pursuing, but job training in general is unlikely to end poverty as we know it. In addition, the increase in formal education (notably, high school completion) has probably reduced the demand for government job training programs directed at high school dropouts.[57] But these explanations

57. Note, however, that the rise in the payoff to skills in the 1980s would be expected to increase the demand for job training.

leave unexplained the dramatic rise in labor market regulation, and probably can only partly account for the decline in federal job training programs.

The rise of regulation occurred during both Republican and Democratic administrations, so shifts in partisan politics are not a promising explanation. Indeed, President Nixon championed OSHA and other labor market regulatory interventions. Another potential explanation that is unlikely to explain much of the increase in regulation concerns federal budget deficits. It is likely that elected officials' support for regulation rises during periods of budget deficits because it is more difficult to use tax revenue to transfer resources. Regulation can be viewed, in part, as hidden taxes and transfers. Yet labor market regulation increased during periods of both tight budgets and less tight budgets. A final explanation that is unlikely to go very far has to do with the prevailing wisdom among economists. I certainly do not sense a shift in thinking in favor of labor market regulation among economists, although much theoretical work has been done on market failures since the 1960s, and much research has found relatively modest effects (intended and unintended) of certain government interventions.

What *does* explain the secular rise in labor market regulation? I offer three hypotheses that are worth further consideration. First, demographic shifts may be important. The aging of the population may have increased demand for regulation of pensions and health benefits. The increased labor force participation of women may have increased the demand for regulations affecting sex discrimination, pregnancy discrimination, and family and medical leave.[58]

A second hypothesis concerns income growth and the demand for regulation. Dani Rodrik, for example, has identified a positive relationship between income and effort devoted to social protection across countries.[59] And Rodrik and Jonas Agell find that labor market regulations and social protection are positively related to the openness of a country's economy.[60] As the United States has grown richer and more open to international trade since the 1960s, support for regulating features of the labor market may have increased as a consequence.

58. In a similar vein, Ellwood (2000) argues that the rise in employment of women has changed society's definition of the "deserving poor," which in turn has caused "the withdrawal of support for traditional welfare" and *increasing* support for low-income workers."

59. Rodrik (1997).

60. Rodrik (1997); Agell (1999).

A final hypothesis involves the seemingly contradictory role of unions. Unions have traditionally supported many forms of labor market regulation. As unions have declined in membership, their political influence has not declined—and may even have increased. In this regard, unions are like the farm lobby, which seems to have grown in influence as the number of farmers declined. Indeed, the role of unions is even more puzzling than that of farmers because it could be argued that many regulatory policies supported by unions provide benefits to nonunion members that union members already have won at the bargaining table, which in turn diminishes the demand for union representation. Why has labor market regulation expanded during a period of dwindling union membership? One possibility (which may also apply to the farm lobby) is that the decline in union membership has produced a more homogeneous interest group, and union leaders are thus more focused and uniform in their interests. Another possibility is that the demand for regulation among workers has increased because unions are less likely to win the types of protections that workers desire.

Whether any of these three hypotheses explains the rise in labor market regulation remains to be seen. But I would hasten to add that the trend toward increasing regulation could reverse. Indeed, there have been notable examples of deregulation outside of the labor market, and some examples (for instance, trucking) that have affected the labor market. Moreover, there are several examples of innovative developments in the style of regulation outside of the labor market. For example, tradeable permits for sulfur dioxide emissions have been successfully introduced in environmental protection. It is conceivable that in the future there will be a push for labor market deregulation, or for more innovative, efficient, and effective forms of labor market regulation. A shift in emphasis toward research on labor market regulation by economists could help facilitate such changes.

COMMENT BY
James Heckman

I would tell a different story about labor economics, labor policy, and Arthur Okun than Alan Krueger has. It is an odd strategy to use the budget of the Department of Labor as a barometer either for new ideas about the labor market or as a measure of government policy initiatives in the labor market. The Department of Labor has rarely been a source of new thinking about the labor market and arguably has resisted new ideas mightily, supporting descriptive institutional labor economics over analytical labor economics for most of the past third of a century. With the expansion of the welfare state in the mid-1960s, a variety of government agencies have come to enforce policy that directly affects the labor market. The budget of the Department of Labor no longer is a reliable indicator of all of the activities of the federal government in the labor market. The Internal Revenue Service and the Social Security Administration administer regulations that affect labor supply. The Equal Employment Opportunity Commission (EEOC) monitors affirmative action. The Office of Federal Contract Compliance has its authority scattered over numerous cabinet agencies. The War on Poverty was spearheaded by agencies in the Department of Health, Education, and Welfare (HEW) and not in Labor. The Department of Education directs a major component of federal policy toward skill formation.

As an alternative to Alan Krueger's analysis, I would use the published work of Arthur Okun as a gauge to measure progress in both theory and policy. A major revolution in labor economics occurred when price theory was applied to the study of the labor market and responses to wage incentives began to be studied. The pioneers in this endeavor were H. G. Lewis, Jacob Mincer, and Gary Becker, writing in the late 1950s and early 1960s. Early research on labor supply, human capital formation, the value of time, and the economics of discrimination emphasized the responsiveness of workers to incentives. It provided an empirically based neoclassical alternative to an institutional labor economics that remained focused on trade unions and implicitly adopted a Keynesian view of the labor market in which incentives facing workers play virtually no role.

Neoclassical labor economics, and not institutional labor economics, was the analytical framework for the policies of the Great Society. This grand initiative of the mid-1960s emphasized skill formation through on-the-job training and education and antidiscrimination policy as twin pillars of government policy in the labor market. Government agencies, most notably the Office of Economic Opportunity (OEO), sought empirical flesh for the analytical bones of neoclassical labor economics and sponsored social experiments and collection of microdata to measure incentive effects of programs. The main controversies of welfare policy revolved around the disincentive effects of alternative transfer policies.

The developments in labor economics in the 1970s, 1980s, and 1990s provided a more nuanced interpretation of the labor market and modified the spot market view developed at the University of Chicago and

Columbia University in the 1960s to account for various labor market frictions, such as search unemployment, incentive contracts for performance, and specific human capital—although the early papers discussed these possibilities. Until the time of his death, Okun drew on and contributed to this nuanced neoclassical labor economics in an attempt to establish a firm intellectual foundation for unemployment policy. Successive editions of his collections of essays, *The Battle against Unemployment*, show two aspects of Okun's character: his fairness and willingness to listen to and display all sides of an argument; and his growing awareness of the importance of prices and incentives in understanding unemployment and other labor market phenomena.[61] Okun outgrew the crude Keynesian vision of the labor market that characterized macroeconomics and institutional labor economics in the late 1950s and early 1960s. His magnum opus *Prices and Quantities* presents a unique synthesis of an evolving neoclassical labor economics and macroeconomics that anticipated many later developments in both fields.[62] Okun lacked the technical virtuosity to translate deep economic insights into precisely formulated economic models; for this reason his work is often ignored or rediscovered by younger scholars, as Alan Krueger now notes.

Both the shift in Okun's thinking and the increasing reliance of government policymakers on neoclassical and modified neoclassical models of the labor market in framing and evaluating policies belie Alan Krueger's claim that policy and labor economics are moving in different directions. Simple price theory and its extensions became the lingua franca of government policy analysis in the last third of the century, although the Labor Department was slow to adopt this point of view. (Visits to the Department of Labor by Orley Ashenfelter, George Johnson, Frank Stafford, Daniel Hamermesh, and Ernst Stromsdorfer brought it into the modern age of economics. More recent visits by Lawrence Katz, Alan Krueger, and Lisa Lynch revitalized economic analysis in the Department.) As this development has proceeded, the definition of what labor economics is and what labor economists do has radically altered. Many macroeconomists, industrial organization economists, search theorists, incentive theorists, and econometricians also do labor economics in large part because the labor market is now regarded as susceptible to economic

61. Okun (1965, 1972); Okun and Baily (1982).
62. Okun (1981).

analysis—a revolutionary idea from the perspective of mainstream labor economics in the late 1950s.

Turning to specific aspects of Krueger's paper, I question Krueger's use of survey responses to define consensus in the field of labor economics. The definition of the appropriate sample to be polled is far from clear given developments in labor market research in many subfields of economics. The disagreement over "the" labor supply elasticity is undoubtedly a consequence of sophistication on the part of the polled labor economists about the variety of different labor supply elasticities that can be defined for different conceptual choice experiments.[63] The consensus about the magnitude of the union wage differential that Krueger reports is largely a consequence of the pessimism most labor economists have developed about estimating a variety of interesting union–non-union counterfactuals and the agreement to report only least squares (OLS) estimates of the "wage gap." Consensus on this number does not represent understanding of what the world would look like in the absence of unionism, just a convention not to tackle hard problems.

I disagree with Krueger that labor market regulation is understudied. His perception is a consequence of too narrow a definition of labor economics. A broader reading of research by development economists, specialists in law and economics, and macroeconomists reveals a huge body of work dealing with regulation in the labor market, including the consequences of employment severance systems, payroll taxes, unemployment insurance systems, affirmative action policies, and the employment at will doctrine.

In contrasting instrumental variables (IV) methods with selection models, Krueger ignores a substantial body of recent literature that establishes that recent developments in IV estimation—the so-called "Local Average Treatment Effect" of Guido Imbens and Joshua Angrist—make the same assumptions as those used in semi-parametric selection models.[64] There is no real contrast here. Rather, there is congruence.[65]

Krueger chronicles the growth of large-scale consulting firms as advisors to the Department of Labor and their role in producing evidence on labor market policies. He does not discuss the decline in research done within the Department of Labor and the decline in support of basic research by

63. See Browning, Hansen, and Heckman (2000).
64. Imbens and Angrist (1994).
65. See Vytlacil (1999); Heckman and Vytlacil (1999, 2000a, b, c).

the department, except to note that a fellowship program that funded the dissertations of many distinguished economists has now vanished.

I am not convinced that the growth of firms like Manpower Demonstration Research Corporation (MDRC), ABT Associates, SRI, or WESTAT is a healthy development for the formation of a knowledge base about the labor market. These organizations are motivated to produce estimates of "treatment effects" for specific programs. The emphasis in the past twenty years has been on narrow evaluations of specific programs that are not conducted within the framework of modern labor economics. Indeed, the social experiments implemented by those organizations attempt to bypass economics to see if, in any instance, a program "works" in a sense of that term that is not always relevant to policy or economics. By conducting empirical studies of program effectiveness outside the framework of economics, the analyses produced by the large consulting firms do not add to the base of economic knowledge. They do not estimate the structural parameters that can be applied to evaluate a variety of possible programs that emerge in any policy discussion—not merely the one being evaluated by random assignment.

The faith in the power of social experiments to evaluate social programs effectively—implicit in Krueger's paper, in the responses to his questionnaire, and in the Washington policy community—is unwarranted. In work with LaLonde and Smith, I document the severe problems encountered in conducting social experiments.[66] In work with Höhmann and Smith, I document how access to good substitutes for a program being evaluated by a social experiment led to its demise—even though it was an effective program.[67] Both treatment and control groups took essentially the same training program because very good substitutes were available for the training provided by the program under evaluation. Persons randomized out of the "treatment" were able to find excellent government-provided substitutes for the program. An experimental evaluation showing "no treatment effect" emerged because both treatments and controls took essentially the *same* training, which turns out on closer scrutiny to be quite effective, compared to no training at all.

The bigger issue not addressed in Krueger's paper is whether large consulting firms living from hand to mouth off government contracts with short deadlines produce knowledge about the labor market that cumulates in any way. A policy that supports basic research on the labor market and

66. Heckman, LaLonde, and Smith (1999, section 5).
67. Heckman, Höhmann, and Smith (2000).

not short-term "treatment effects" for narrowly defined policies is much more likely to be effective in producing useful knowledge in the long run.[68]

COMMENT BY
Frank Levy

George Perry and James Tobin owe Alan Krueger. They asked Krueger to summarize the last thirty years of labor policy and labor research in a single paper. And Krueger has delivered. He has produced a well-written paper that builds a coherent argument leading to a clear set of conclusions. I learned a lot from the paper, and I commend it to anyone interested in these subjects.

Taken together, labor market policy and labor market research are too broad to be summarized without laying out some boundaries. Krueger draws on his experience as the Department of Labor's chief economist to assess both subjects as they appeared from the Department. This is a sensible choice and yields important insights. I will argue, however, that this window provides a more complete view of labor research than of labor policy.

Krueger's chief conclusion is that labor research has lagged seriously behind the evolution of labor policy originating in the Department of Labor (DOL). As Krueger documents with an informative budget analysis, DOL, driven by legislation and presidential priorities, evolved from an agency heavily concerned with training to an agency heavily concerned with labor market regulation, such as health and safety regulation and parental leave regulation. Labor economists, by contrast, devoted relatively little attention to this kind of regulation. Rather, as Krueger shows, published articles in labor economics tended to concentrate in more traditional areas, such as the effects of unions (despite their declining membership) and unemployment insurance (despite the larger cost of worker's compensation insurance).

There have been some good matches. As Krueger notes, research on labor demand elasticities and, in particular, the minimum wage were important elements in decisions to raise the minimum wage after a period of substantial erosion.[69] The Labor Department's Employment and

---

68. See the discussion in Heckman, LaLonde, and Smith (1999).
69. See, for example, Card and Krueger (1995).

Training Administration was a key player in building support for large-scale controlled experiments to evaluate government training programs. These evaluations, in turn, helped to reduce and reshape DOL support of training programs, many of which were shown to be minimally effective.[70] And as Krueger might have noted, there is now a small but growing literature that does explore increased labor market regulation in ways that Krueger advocates.[71] On the whole, however, Krueger makes his case that DOL policy evolved substantially over this period while labor economics research failed to keep pace.

Krueger concludes by asking what might account for the steady increase in labor market regulation. He offers several possibilities. One centers on demographic changes: the aging of the population, combined with increased women's labor force participation. The second involves the diminished tolerance for risk that is associated with rising income, an association studied intensively and with great humor by the late political scientist Aaron Wildavsky.[72] The third are the findings of Dani Rodrik and others that more open economies are associated with greater demands for governmental social protection.[73]

All three of these ideas are plausible. In particular, an elaboration of the third idea points to the limitation in Krueger's paper, the focus only on those labor policies that have emanated from the U.S. Department of Labor.

Rodrik's original argument—that more open economies lead to greater demands for social protection—is an argument not just about freer trade, but about a shift to freer markets and resulting labor market fluctuations.[74] In practice, the shift to freer markets was a central story line in the U.S. economy over the past thirty years, and the shift was frequently driven by policy.

Krueger rightly catalogs the increased volume of labor market regulation in such areas as health, safety, and parental leave, much of it coming from DOL. But in terms of labor market flexibility and stability, these regulations have been more than offset by other policies, including trade initiatives such as the North American Free Trade Agreement (NAFTA), the

70. Some of these assessments included secondary evaluations of experimental data by academic researchers.
71. See, for example, Autor (1999); Acemoglu and Angrist (1998).
72. See, for example, Douglas and Wildavsky (1983).
73. See, for example, Rodrik (1997).
74. Personal communication with author.

deregulation of many product markets, and the Reagan administration's hostility to unions, signaled by their decision to fire striking air traffic controllers. While job instability has not increased as much as many headlines would have it, the phenomenon is certainly real.[75]

Beyond increased instability, the greater reliance on free markets has also accelerated another of the major labor market developments of the last thirty years: the rising return to education. In this case, an important policy episode was the period of Paul Volcker's semi-shock therapy between 1979 and about 1985. The period began under the Carter administration as Volcker instituted very tight money to break embedded inflation. It continued under the Reagan administration as large budget deficits caused high real interest rates and substantial trade deficits, even as inflation receded. Together these policies put U.S. manufacturing through a very tight wringer, first in the deep recession of 1980–82 and then during the period of the overvalued dollar and the resulting trade deficits of the mid-1980s.

At the beginning of this period, the manufacturing sector employed less than one-quarter of all workers but a far greater share of high-wage, less-educated men. In 1979, durable and nondurable manufacturing combined employed one-third of all prime-age men with high school diplomas or less, and their median earnings averaged about $35,500 (in 1997 dollars).[76] By 1985, this median had declined substantially as perhaps a decade's worth of gradual change had been compressed into a few tumultuous years. This loss of high-wage jobs was one important element in the rising rate of return to education that emerged over this period.[77]

All these events began in the late 1970s or later, so they cannot explain certain prior events, such as the 1970s rise in environmental consciousness. But expanding on Rodrik's argument, it is reasonable to speculate that during the 1980s and 1990s, U.S. attempts to regulate labor markets were an attempt by presidents and Congress to show constituents that the government was aware that these markets were becoming more turbulent—in part due to labor market policy formulated outside of the Department of Labor—and that Congress was "doing" something about it.

75. See Farber (1998).

76. Earnings of similar men in the service sector averaged 8 percent less. For details, see Levy (1998, pp. 61–62).

77. These developments in turn have helped spark a rich literature of "labor" research among macroeconomists interested in the impact of growth and technical change on earnings inequality.

To conclude, I believe that Krueger has done an excellent job summarizing post-1960 labor policy trends, labor research trends, and their somewhat tenuous relationship, all as seen from the Department of Labor. There does not seem to be much to add to Krueger's summary of labor research. But to understand labor policy over this period, one needs a somewhat broader view.

References

Aaron, Henry J. 1989. "Politics and the Professors Revisited." *American Economic Review* 79 (May, Papers and Proceedings): 1–15.

Acemoglu, Daron, and Joshua Angrist. 1998. "Consequences of Employment Protection? The Case of the Americans with Disabilities Act." Working Paper 6670. Cambridge, Mass.: National Bureau of Economic Research (July).

Acemoglu, Daron, and Jörn-Steffen Pischke. 1999. "The Structure of Wages and Investment in General Training," *Journal of Political Economy* 107 (June): 539–72.

Addison, John T., and McKinley L. Blackburn. 1994. "The Worker Adjustment and Retraining Notification Act." *Journal of Economic Perspectives* 8(1): 181–90.

Agell, Jonas. 1999. "On the Benefits from Rigid Labour Markets: Norms, Market Failures, and Social Insurance." *Economic Journal* 109 (February): F143–F164.

Angrist, Joshua D., and Alan B. Krueger. 1999. "Empirical Strategies in Labor Economics." In *Handbook of Labor Economics,* vol. 3A, edited by Orley Ashenfelter and David Card, 1277–1366. Amsterdam: North Holland.

Ashenfelter, Orley. 1970. "Changes in Labor Market Discrimination Over Time." *Journal of Human Resources* 5 (Fall): 403–30.

Ashenfelter, Orley, and Robert S. Smith. 1979. "Compliance with the Minimum Wage Law." *Journal of Political Economy* 87(2): 333–50.

Autor, David H. 1999. "Outsourcing at Will: Unjust Dismissal Doctrine and the Growth of Temporary Help Employment." Massachusetts Institute of Technology, Department of Economics (November).

Bloom, Howard S., L. L. Orr, G. Cave, S. H. Doolittle, and W. Lin. 1997. "The Benefits and Costs of JTPA Title II-A Programs: Key Findings from the National Job Training Partnership Act Study." *The Journal of Human Resources* 32(3): 549–76.

Brecher, Edward M. 1978. "The Manpower Demonstration Research Corporation: Origins and Early Operations." New York: Manpower Demonstration Research Corporation.

Browning, M., L. Hansen, and James J. Heckman. 2000. "Microdata and General Equilibrium Models." In *Handbook of Macroeconomics,* edited by John B. Taylor and Michael Woodford. Amsterdam: North Holland.

Burton, John F., Jr. 1999. "Economics of Safety." In *International Encyclopedia of the Social & Behavioral Sciences* (forthcoming). Elsevier Science.

Card, David E., and Alan B. Krueger. 1995. *Myth and Measurement: The New Economics of the Minimum Wage.* Princeton University Press.

Douglas, Mary, and Aaron Wildavsky. 1983. *Risk and Culture: An Essay on the Selection of Technical and Environmental Dangers.* University of California Press.

Eccles, Mary, and Richard B. Freeman. 1982. "What! Another Minimum Wage Study?" *American Economic Review* 72 (May, *Papers and Proceedings*): 226–32.

Ellwood, David. 2000. "Anti-Poverty Policy for Families in the Next Century: From Welfare to Work—and Worries." *Journal of Economic Perspectives* (Winter): 187–98.

Farber, Henry S. 1998. "Has the Rate of Job Loss Increased in the Nineties?" Paper presented at the Industrial Relations Research Association Fiftieth Annual Proceedings.

Figlio, David. 1994. "Trends in the Publication of Empirical Economics." *Journal of Economic Perspectives* 8(3): 179–87.

Freeman, Richard B. 1973. "Changes in the Labor Market for Black Americans, 1948–72," *Brookings Papers on Economic Activity, 1:1973,* 67–120.

———. 1988. "Does the New Generation of Labor Economists Know More than the Old Generation?" In *How Labor Markets Work,* edited by Bruce E. Kaufman, 205–23. Lexington, Mass.: Lexington Books.

Friedman, Milton, and Simon Kuznets. 1945. *Income from Independent Professional Practice.* New York: National Bureau of Economic Research.

Fuchs, Victor R., Alan B. Krueger, and James M. Poterba. 1998. "Economists' Views about Parameters, Values, and Policies: Survey Results in Labor and Public Economics." *Journal of Economic Literature* 36(September): 1387–1425.

Gilbert, John P., and Frederick Mosteller. 1972. "The Urgent Need for Experimentation." In *On Equality of Educational Opportunity,* edited by Frederick Mosteller and Daniel P. Moynihan, 371–83. Random House.

Goldberg, Joseph P., and William T. Moye. 1985. "The First Hundred Years of the Bureau of Labor Statistics." *Bulletin 2235* (September). U.S. Department of Labor.

Greenberg, David, Mark Shroder, and Matthew Onstott. 1999. "The Social Experiment Market." *Journal of Economic Perspectives* 13(3): 157–72.

Hamermesh, Daniel S. 1993. *Labor Demand.* Princeton University Press.

Harrison, Bennett, and Barry Bluestone. 1988. *The Great U-Turn: Corporate Restructuring and the Polarizing of America.* Basic Books.

Heckman, James J., Neil Höhmann, Michael Khoo, and Jeffrey A. Smith. 2000. "Substitution Bias in Social Experiments: Evidence from the JTPA Study." *Quarterly Journal of Economics* 115 (May).

Heckman, James J., Robert LaLonde, and Jeffrey A. Smith. 1999. "The Economics and Econometrics of Active Labor Market Programs." In *Handbook of Labor Economics,* vol. 3A, edited by Orley Ashenfelter and David Card, 1865–2097. Amsterdam: North Holland.

Heckman, James J., Jeffrey A. Smith, and Christopher Taber. 1996. "What Do Bureaucrats Do? The Effects of Performance Standards and Bureaucratic Preferences on Acceptance into the JTPA Program." Working Paper 5535. Cambridge, Mass.: National Bureau of Economic Research (April).

Heckman, James J., and Edward J. Vytlacil. 1999. "Local Instrumental Variables and Latent Variables Models for Identifying and Bounding Treatment Effects." *Proceedings of the National Academy of Sciences* 96 (April): 4730–34.

———. 2000a. "Econometric Evaluation of Social Programs." In *Handbook of Econometrics,* vol. 5, edited by James Heckman and Edward Leamer. Amsterdam: North Holland.

———. 2000b. "Local Instrumental Variables." In *Nonlinear Statistical Inference: Essays in Honor of Takeshi Amemiya,* edited by C. Hsiao, K. Morimune, and J. Powell. Cambridge University Press.

———. 2000c. "The Relationship between Treatment Parameters within a Latent Variable Framework." *Economics Letters* 66(1): 33–39.

Hirsch, Barry T., and David A. Macpherson. 1999. "Union Membership and Earnings Data Book: Compilations from the Current Population Survey." Bureau of National Affairs.

Imbens, Guido W., and Joshua D. Angrist. 1994. "Identification and Estimation of Local Average Treatment Effects." *Econometrica* 62 (March): 467–76.

Katz, Lawrence F., and Alan B. Krueger. 1999. "The High-Pressure U.S. Labor Market of the 1990s." *Brookings Papers on Economic Activity, 1:1999,* 1–65.

Killingsworth, Mark R. 1983. *Labor Supply.* Cambridge University Press.

Kleiner, Morris M. 1990. "Are There Economic Rents for More Restrictive Occupational Licensing Practices?" *Industrial Relations Research Association, Proceedings:* 177–85. Madison, Wisc.: Industrial Relations Research Association.

Kleiner, Morris M., and Robert T. Kudrle. 1997. "Does Regulation Improve Outputs and Increase Prices? The Case of Dentistry." Working Paper 5869. Cambridge, Mass.: National Bureau of Economic Research (January).

Krueger, Alan B. 1991. "The Evolution of Unjust Dismissal Legislation in the United States." *Industrial and Labor Relations Review* 44(4): 644–60.

Krueger, Alan B., and John F. Burton, Jr. 1990. "The Employers' Costs of Workers' Compensation Insurance: Magnitudes, Determinants, and Public Policy." *The Review of Economics and Statistics* 72(2): 228–40.

LaLonde, Robert J. 1986. "Evaluating the Econometric Evaluations of Training Programs with Experimental Data," *American Economic Review* 76(September): 604–20.

———. 1995. "The Promise of Public Sector-Sponsored Training Programs." *Journal of Economic Perspectives* 9(2): 149–68.

Lazear, Edward P. 1995. *Personnel Economics.* MIT Press.

Levy, Frank. 1987. *Dollars and Dreams: The Changing American Income Distribution.* New York: Russell Sage Foundation.

———. 1998. *The New Dollars and Dreams: American Incomes and Economic Change.* New York: Russell Sage Foundation.

Lewis, H. Gregg. 1963. *Unionism and Relative Wages in the United States: An Empirical Inquiry.* University of Chicago Press.

———. 1986. *Union Relative Wage Effects.* University of Chicago Press.

Manser, Marilyn E. 1998. "Existing Labor Market Data: Current and Potential Research Uses." In *Labor Statistics Measurement Issues,* edited by John Haltiwanger, Marilyn E. Manser, and Robert Topel, 9–46. University of Chicago Press.

Moffitt, Robert A. 1999. "New Developments in Econometric Methods for Labor Market Analysis." In *Handbook of Labor Economics,* vol. 3A, edited by Orley Ashenfelter and David Card, 1,367–98. Amsterdam: North Holland.

Okun, Arthur M. 1965. *The Battle against Unemployment: An Introduction to a Current Issue of Public Policy.* Norton.

————. 1972. *The Battle against Unemployment.* Norton.

————. 1975. *Equality and Efficiency: The Big Tradeoff.* Brookings.

————. 1981. *Prices and Quantities: A Macroeconomic Analysis.* Brookings.

Okun, Arthur M., and Martin N. Baily, eds. 1982. *The Battle against Unemployment and Inflation.* Norton.

Pencavel, John H. 1986. "Labor Supply of Men: A Survey." In *Handbook of Labor Economics,* vol. 1, no. 5, edited by Orley Ashenfelter and Richard Layard, 3–102. Amsterdam: North Holland.

Rees, Albert. 1993. "The Role of Fairness in Wage Determination." *Journal of Labor Economics* 11 (January): 243–52.

Rodrik, Dani. 1997. *Has Globalization Gone Too Far?* Washington: Institute for International Economics.

Stafford, Frank. 1986. "Forestalling the Demise of Empirical Economics: The Role of Microdata in Labor Economics Research." In *Handbook of Labor Economics,* vol. 1, no. 5, edited by Orley Ashenfelter and Richard Layard, 387–423. Amsterdam: North-Holland.

U.S. Bureau of the Census. 1999. *Statistical Abstract of the United States: 1999.* Washington, D.C.

U.S. Department of Labor. Office of the Chief Economist. 1995. *What's Working (and What's Not): A Summary of Research on the Economic Impacts of Employment and Training Programs.*

U.S. House Committee on Ways and Means. 1998. *Green Book.* Government Printing Office.

Vytlacil, Edward J. 1999. "Independence, Monotonicity, and Latent Variable Models: An Equivalence Result." University of Chicago, Department of Economics.

Wandner, Stephen A., and Jon C. Messenger, eds. 1999. "Worker Profiling and Reemployment Services Policy Workgroup: Final Report and Recommendations." U.S. Department of Labor (February).

Contributors

GEORGE AKERLOF
University of California at Berkeley

MARTIN N. BAILY
Council of Economic Advisers

FRANCIS M. BATOR
John F. Kennedy School of Government, Harvard University

WILLIAM BAUMOL
New York University and Princeton University

WILLIAM C. BRAINARD
Yale University

GARY BURTLESS
Brookings Institution

RICHARD N. COOPER
Center for International Affairs, Harvard University

BARRY EICHENGREEN
University of California at Berkeley

ROBERT HAVEMAN
University of Wisconsin

RAY C. FAIR
Yale University

STANLEY FISCHER
International Monetary Fund

BENJAMIN M. FRIEDMAN
Harvard University

ROBERT E. HALL
Hoover Institution, Stanford University

JAMES HECKMAN
University of Chicago

LAWRENCE KATZ
Harvard University

PAUL KRUGMAN
Massachusetts Institute of Technology

ALAN B. KRUEGER
Princeton University

ROBERT Z. LAWRENCE
Council of Economic Advisers

FRANK LEVY
Massachusetts Institute of Technology

MAURICE OBSTFELD
University of California at Berkeley

GEORGE L. PERRRY
Brookings Institution

JEFFREY SACHS
*Center for International
Development, Harvard University*

CHARLES L. SCHULTZE
Brookings Institution

ROBERT M. SOLOW
Massachusetts Institute of Technology

JOHN B. TAYLOR
Stanford University

Index